E21-75 N+

KU-717-088

Handbook for AACR2

Explaining and Illustrating
Anglo-American Cataloguing Rules
Second Edition

WITHDRAWN FROM STOCK

Handbook for AACR2

Explaining and Illustrating
Anglo-American Cataloguing Rules
Second Edition

by Margaret F. Maxwell

American Library Association

Chicago

12971

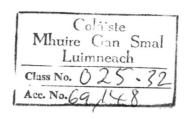

Coláiste
Mhuire Gan Smal
Luimneach

Class No. 025.32

Acc. No. 69148

Library of Congress Cataloging in Publication Data

Maxwell, Margaret F.
    Handbook for AACR2

    Includes bibliographical references and index.
    1. Anglo-American cataloguing rules, 2d ed.
2. Descriptive cataloging—Handbooks, manuals, etc.
I. Title.
Z694.M35 025.3′2   80-17667
ISBN 0-8389-0301-0 (pbk.)

Copyright © 1980 by the American Library Association
    All rights reserved. No part of this publication may be reproduced in any form without permission in writing from the publisher, except by a reviewer who may quote brief passages in a review.

Printed in the United States of America
Second printing, June 1981

Affectionately dedicated to the memory of

ELEANOR M. PUTNEY
1904–1973
Former Head, English Language Section,
Library of Congress
Descriptive Cataloging Division

Mentor, colleague, friend

Contents

Preface

This book is designed to assist library school students and cataloguers in the application of the most commonly used rules for description, choice of access points, and form of heading as set forth in the *Anglo-American Cataloguing Rules,* second edition (*AACR2*). As such, it should be read with *AACR2* in hand.

Although the editors of *AACR2* have included frequent examples to illustrate the rules, these examples are not in full catalogue entry format. Inexperienced cataloguers as well as library school students often find these examples mystifying in their brevity. The present text therefore attempts not only to explain the rules, but also give full catalogue entries to illustrate each rule discussed. Furthermore, it has been the author's experience in many years of teaching cataloguing that one of the most difficult concepts for beginning cataloguers is the translation of the title page (or other chief source) into a catalogue entry. Therefore, in as many instances as possible, a copy of the title page and/or other prescribed source material has been included with each entry.

The user of this text must be aware, however, that although full catalogue entries are given, discussion focuses only on the part of the entry that illustrates a particular rule. For a complete discussion of catalogue entries with citation of all *AACR2* rules governing the cataloguing, the user should turn to the appendix at the end of each chapter.

Many of the readers of this book have worked with the first edition of the *Anglo-American Cataloging Rules* (*AACR1*) and with supplementary *AACR1* chapters 6 and 12. Frequent reference has been made in this text to *AACR1* and its supplements; occasional reference is made to the ALA 1949 rules as well, particularly when *AACR2* differs from previous practice.

Others using this text will be library school students, just beginning their study of cataloguing theory and practice. For this reason, the preponderance of examples selected to illustrate *AACR2* chapter 1 in this text are books. In addition, most of the examples are English-language materials. These choices have been made deliberately, in order to provide a comfortable frame of reference for inexperienced cataloguers, most of whom have more acquaintance with books as library materials than with their nonprint counterparts. Representative examples of nonprint library materials are also included in General Chapter 1; these are covered in detail in the chapters following the General Chapter.

This *Handbook* attempts to follow Library of Congress practice in regard to optional rules and policy revisions, insofar as these LC decisions had been made at the time of writing. Optional rules and LC decisions are discussed as they occur in the text.

AACR2 uses *Webster's Third New International Dictionary of the English Language, Unabridged,* as the authority for spelling. Among the American-British agreements arrived at in the writing of the new code were those pertaining to spelling. If *Webster's* gives a British spelling (*catalogue, honour,* etc.) as an alternative, this spelling will be used in the text of *AACR2.* Otherwise, American usage is followed. Similar compromises were reached in regard to terminology. For example, *AACR2* uses the British term "full stop" instead of the North American "period." This *Handbook* follows the spelling and terminology of *AACR2.*

The reader will notice that chapter numbering in *AACR2* is not entirely consecutive, skipping from chapter 13 to chapter 21 to leave space for possible future additions and also to accommodate the mnemonic structure of the text. Although the chapters in this *Handbook* are numbered consecutively, individual rules are numbered to correspond with *AACR2.* Limitations of space have made it necessary to omit discussion of those rules whose meanings seem self-evident and of certain specialized forms of library materials (such as early printed monographs, manuscripts, and machine-readable data files) not usually acquired by libraries.

This *Handbook* had its inception as long ago as 1967, when the author attended Seymour Lubetzky's seminar on *AACR1* at the University of Illinois. Lubetzky's exposition of cataloguing principles as enunciated at the seminar and on later occasions and his written discussions of rules and theory form the basis for much of the theory presented in this text. The idea of a detailed handbook to *AACR1* developed over the next decade into an unpublished manuscript in much the same format as the present *Handbook.* This original manuscript owed much of its final though still unfinished, form to the good advice of Patricia Glass Schuman, editor extraordinary, formerly of Bowker Company, before it was put aside because of the imminent appearance of *AACR2.* The present work has its roots in this earlier manuscript.

Many individuals have contributed in various ways to the present text. My graduate assistants at the University of Arizona Graduate Library School— Ann Coppin, Sylvia Geiger, Janet Park, Sue Stancu, David Corson, and Midji Stephenson—helped to find cataloguing examples to illustrate the rules, proofread parts of the manuscript, and type finished cataloguing examples. Jo Ann Troutman, Graduate Library School student assistant, typed the index. The librarians at the University of Arizona Library shared their expertise in nonbook cataloguing both in finding examples to illustrate the rules and in reading the chapters on the description of nonbook materials for accuracy and interpretation. I am particularly grateful to Linda Cottrell, Marilyn Craig, Elizabeth

Franklin, Carolyn Kacena, and Elsie Phillips, each of whom generously shared her special knowledge with me. Michael Fitzgerald, Chief, Cataloging and Serials Division, Harvard College Library, read the entire manuscript; his comments and suggestions are greatly appreciated.

As previously mentioned, to aid North American librarians who are likely to follow the lead of the Library of Congress in their own decisions on cataloguing policy and *AACR2*'s optional rules, this *Handbook* follows LC policy, as far as it could be determined at the time of writing. For this reason, I owe a particular debt of gratitude to Ben R. Tucker, chief of LC's Office of Descriptive Cataloging Policy, and to several of the members of the Descriptive Cataloging Division for their help with rule interpretations, clarification of Library of Congress policy, and many other suggestions for improving this handbook.

Helen Cline, managing editor of ALA Publishing Services, took over where the others left off. The final form of this *Handbook* owes much to her persistent prodding and sharp eye for consistency. Any errors of fact or omission which remain in the text are mine; to paraphrase bookseller Henry Stevens of Vermont: If you wish to have the pride of accuracy taken out of you, write a cataloguing handbook!

This is not a self-help manual for beginning cataloguers. Yet it is designed to address itself to problems beginners often find puzzling. It is the author's hope that the following pages may serve as a helpful introduction and a guide to ease the transition from the first to the second Anglo-American cataloguing code.

MARGARET F. MAXWELL
Graduate Library School
University of Arizona

Introduction

When the *Anglo-American Cataloging Rules* appeared in 1967, the code was heralded as a new departure in cataloguing, a unified set of rules based on principle rather than on the enumeration of specific problems. And indeed this was the case. The rules, like the present code, were based on the "Statement of Principles adopted at the International Conference on Cataloguing Principles, Paris, October 1961."[1] This brief statement, usually referred to as the Paris Principles, is of such overriding importance to the full understanding of *AACR2* as well as its predecessor that it is abridged below:

1. SCOPE OF STATEMENT

    The principles here stated apply only to the choice and form of headings and entry words . . . .

2. FUNCTIONS OF THE CATALOGUE

    The catalogue should be an efficient instrument for ascertaining

    2.1 whether the library contains a particular book specified by
    a. its author and title, *or*
    b. if the author is not named in the book, its title alone, *or*
    c. if author and title are inappropriate or insufficient for identification, a suitable substitute for the title; and
    2.2 a. which works by a particular author and
    b. which editions of a particular work are in the library.

3. STRUCTURE OF THE CATALOGUE

    To discharge these functions the catalogue should contain

    3.1 at least one entry for each book catalogued, and
    3.2 more than one entry relating to any book, whenever this is

---

[1] The Paris Principles have been reprinted many times. The definitive text dealing with the Paris Principles is: International Conference on Cataloguing Principles, Paris, 1961. *Statement of Principles*. Annotated edition with commentary and examples by Eva Verona. London: IFLA Committee on Cataloguing, 1971.

necessary in the interests of the user or because of the characteristics of the book . . . .

4. KINDS OF ENTRY

Entries may be of the following kinds: main entries, added entries, and references . . . .

5. USE OF MULTIPLE ENTRIES

The two functions of the catalogue (see 2.1 and 2.2) are most effectively discharged by

5.1 an entry for each book under a heading derived from the author's name or from the title as printed in the book, *and*

5.2 when variant forms of the author's name or of the title occur, an entry for each book under a *uniform heading,* consisting of one particular form of the author's name or one particular title . . . *and*

5.3 appropriate added entries and/or references.

6. FUNCTION OF DIFFERENT KINDS OF ENTRY

6.1 The *main entry* for works entered under authors' names should normally be made under a *uniform heading.* The main entry for works entered under title may be *either* under the title as printed in the book, with an added entry under a uniform title, *or* under a uniform title, with added entries . . . under the other titles . . . .

6.4 *Added entries* . . . should also be made under the names of joint-authors, collaborators, etc., and under the titles of works having their main entry under an author's name, when the title is an important alternative means of identification.

7. CHOICE OF UNIFORM HEADING

The *uniform heading* should normally be the most frequently used name (or form of name) or title appearing in editions of the works catalogued or in references to them by accepted authorities . . . .

8. SINGLE PERSONAL AUTHOR

8.1 The main entry for every edition of a work ascertained to be by a single personal author should be made under the author's name . . . .

9. ENTRY UNDER CORPORATE BODIES

9.1 The main entry for a work should be made under the name of a *corporate body* (i.e. any institution, organized body or assembly of persons known by a corporate or collective name)

9.11 when the work is by its nature necessarily the expression of the collective thought or activity of the corporate body . . . *or*

9.12 when the wording of the title or title-page, taken in conjunction with the nature of the work, clearly implies that the corporate body is collectively responsible for the content of the work . . . .

9.4 The *uniform heading* for works entered under the name of a corporate body should be the name by which the body is most frequently identified in its publications, *except that* . . .

9.44 for states and other territorial authorities the uniform heading should be the currently used form of the name of the territory concerned in the language best adapted to the needs of the users of the catalogue . . . .

9.5 Constitutions, laws and treaties, and certain other works having similar characteristics, should be entered under the name of the appropriate state or other territorial authority, with formal or conventional titles indicating the nature of the material . . . .

9.6 A work of a corporate body which is subordinate to a superior body should be entered under the name of the subordinate body [i.e., as an independent entity] *except that*

9.61 if this name itself implies subordination . . . or is insufficient to identify the subordinate body, the heading should be the name of the superior body with the name of the subordinate body as a subheading . . . .

10. MULTIPLE AUTHORSHIP

When two or more authors have shared in the creation of a work,

10.1 if one author is represented in the book as the *principal author* . . . the *main entry* for the work should be made under [this] name . . . .

10.2 if no author is represented as the principal author, the *main entry* should be made under

10.21 *the author named first on the title-page,* if the number of authors is two or three, *added entries* being made under the name(s) of the other author(s);

10.22 *the title of the work,* if the number of authors is more than three, *added entries* being made under the author named first in the book . . . .

10.3 Collections

The main entry for a collection consisting of independent works or parts of works by different authors should be made

10.31 under the title of the collection, if it has a collective title;

10.32 under the name of the author, or under the title, of

the first work in the collection, if there is no collective title . . . .

11. WORKS ENTERED UNDER TITLE

11.1 Works having their main entry under the title are

11.11 works whose authors have not been ascertained;

11.12 works by more than three authors, none of whom is principal author (see 10.22)

11.13 collections of independent works or parts of works, by different authors, published with a collective title;

11.14 works (including serials and periodicals) known primarily or conventionally by title rather than by the name of the author.

11.2 An added entry . . . should be made under the title for

11.21 anonymous editions of works whose authors have been ascertained

11.22 works having their main entry under the name of the author, when the title is an important alternative means of identification . . . .

11.5 When a serial publication is issued successively under different titles, a main entry should be made under each title for the series of issues bearing that title, with an indication of at least the immediately preceding and succeeding titles . . . .

12. ENTRY WORD FOR PERSONAL NAMES

When the name of a personal author consists of several words, the choice of entry word is determined so far as possible by agreed usage in the . . . language which he generally uses.

AACR1, although it was based on the Paris Principles (PP), suffered from a number of deficiencies which were only partially resolved through a series of revisions in the years between 1967 and the publication of *AACR2*. In the first place, although, as its name suggests, *AACR1* was intended to be a joint British-American code, one which would unify cataloguing practice throughout the English-speaking world, this was never actually achieved. Supported by the Association of Research Libraries, the North American contingent of the *AACR1* code committee decided on two special exceptions to the principle of entry of a corporate body under the name by which it chooses to identify itself (PP 9.4). Local churches and "certain other corporate bodies" (i.e., educational institutions, libraries, galleries, museums, agricultural experiment stations, airports, botanical and zoological gardens, and hospitals) were, under very carefully specified conditions, to be entered under place (*AACR1* 98 and 99). The British representatives on the code committee refused to accept this partial return to ALA 1949 cataloguing rules; they also rejected *AACR1* 23, 24, and 25 (court rules and rules for treaties). *AACR1* was finally issued in two versions, a North American Text and a British Text.

Almost as serious, from the point of view of international unification of cataloguing practice, was the refusal of the Anglo-American code makers to accept the majority position on Paris Principle 10.3, which called for the entry of a collection under title when such a work had a collective title. The Anglo-American preference was for entry under compiler when such a name was openly expressed; *AACR1* 4 and 5 at first reflected this position. A change was made in the rule in 1975 (*Cataloging Service Bulletin* 112, Winter 1975) to bring Anglo-American practice into conformity with Paris Principle 10.3. The lamentable exceptions for entry under place of *AACR1* 98 and 99 were eliminated by *Cataloging Service Bulletin* 109 (May 1974).

A continuing problem since the adoption of *AACR1* has been the Library of Congress's policy of superimposition. Under superimposition, headings established by the Library of Congress before *AACR1* went into effect continued to be used for current cataloguing, even though these headings were not formulated according to provisions of the 1967 code. This led, even for current cataloguing, to a mixture of headings, some catalogued by "old" and some by "new" rules. Librarians who wished to take advantage of Library of Congress cataloguing in their own libraries had to be familiar with ALA 1949 rules, at least to the extent of understanding how ALA 1949 differed from *AACR1*, so that they could interpret Library of Congress headings and assist patrons in their use of the library's catalogue. This problem was partially solved by LC's decision to "de-superimpose" certain headings, as announced in *Cataloging Service Bulletin* 106 (May 1973).

Clearly it was time for an end to ad hoc patchwork, time for a rethinking of the entire structure of the code. The second edition of the *Anglo-American Cataloguing Rules* had its genesis in a meeting of cataloguing experts held in March 1974, at which time it was agreed that a new edition of the cataloguing code was needed. A Joint Steering Committee, composed of representatives from each of the five bodies most directly affected by the code—the American Library Association, the Library of Congress, the (British) Library Association, the British Library, and the Canadian Library Association—was set up at this meeting. Direct implementation of code revision was to be handled by ALA's RTSD Catalog Code Revision Committee in conjunction with the Canadian Committee on Cataloging and the Library Association/British Library Committee on Revision of AACR.

The charge to the Catalog Code Revision Committees was fourfold: (1) The new code was to incorporate all changes authorized since the appearance of *AACR1*; (2) like the first edition, *AACR2* was to conform to the Paris Principles governing choice of access points and form of heading; (3) rules for bibliographic description were to be based on *International Standard Bibliographic Description for Monographs (ISBD(M))*; (4) and finally, committee members were to keep in mind developments in machine processing of catalogue records that might affect cataloguing.[2]

---

[2] For an excellent summary of the immediate background of *AACR2*, see Carol R. Kelm, "The Historical Development of the Second Edition of the Anglo-American Cataloging Rules," *LRTS* 22 (Winter 1978): 22–29.

The Catalog Code Revision Committee (CCRC) set about its assignment almost immediately. In the three years which followed, members spent countless hours in careful study and revision of each part of the 1967 *AACR*. The Paris Principles and *AACR1* were oriented firmly in the concept of the library as a collection of books. Rules for entry and heading did not mention non-print library materials; *AACR1* Part III, rules for descriptive cataloguing of nonbook materials, was a hodgepodge of confusing rules based on format of material rather than type of bibliographic problem. CCRC and the editors of *AACR2* determined that the new rules would be based on principles applicable to *all* types of library materials, both book and nonbook alike. In 1976, the IFLA Working Group on International Standard Bibliographic Description (General) (ISBD(G)) assigned Michael Gorman to work out a framework for the descriptive cataloguing of all types of library materials. This pattern, which was based on the 1974 *ISBD(M)*, served as the basis of Part I, *AACR2:* rules for descriptive cataloguing. For obvious reasons, *AACR2* Part I closely resembles in many respects the revised *AACR Chapter 6* (1974), which was also based on *ISBD(M)*.

Part I begins with a general chapter which sets out rules applying to all types of library materials, both print and nonprint. This general chapter is an effort to approach the ideal enunciated by Eric Hunter in 1975 at the Anglo-Nordic Seminar on the Revision and International Use of AACR held in York, England. "What is really required," said Hunter, "is one International Standard Bibliographic Description which will cover all media and within which the basis of main entry will be title."[3]

While the present code is still based on the concept of main entry under the person or body responsible for the intellectual or artistic content of the item, it is obvious that the shift toward increasing use of title main entry for catalogue records will continue. Under *AACR Chapter 6* (1974), 134D1 alternative rule, the cataloguer could, under certain conditions, omit the author statement in the body of the entry. *AACR2* virtually eliminates this option. Under no circumstances (unless the cataloguer chooses to adopt "first level" descriptive cataloguing; see *AACR2* 1.0D1) will author statement (now called "statement of responsibility") be omitted, as long as it appears "prominently" in the item (*AACR2* 1.1F1). This, in effect, makes the catalogue entry created according to *AACR2* Part I rules a possible title unit entry, to which various access points may be added, with no distinction as to "main" and "added" entries. As a matter of fact, this was an option which *AACR2* Part II, chapter 21, Choice of Access Points, originally allowed. However, this option was dropped in the final version of *AACR2,* chiefly because of the firm grounding of the Paris Principles in the principle of main entry and authorship responsibility, and the charge of the AACR2 Joint Steering Committee to adhere to the Paris Principles.

AACR2 chapter 1, as already mentioned, deals with general principles of bibliographic description applicable to all kinds of library materials. Following

---

[3] "Anglo-Nordic Seminar on the Revision and International Use of AACR, York, 1975," *Catalogue & Index* 37 (Summer 1975): 8.

this general chapter is a series of chapters, each dealing with a special form of library material and special rules to be applied in addition to the general rules. These special chapters refer to applicable rules in the general chapter whenever possible rather than repeating general principles already given. Each special chapter is arranged, like chapter 1, in the following order:

1. Rules for sources of information: the part of the work being catalogued which is to be preferred in transcribing the catalogue entry.
2. Punctuation: prescribed punctuation that must be used between areas and elements of the calalogue entry.
3. Organization of the description: rules governing the transcription of each of the following:
   a. Title and statement of responsibility area
   b. Edition area
   c. Material (or type of publication) specific details (used only when cataloguing cartographic materials and serials)
   d. Publication, distribution, etc., area
   e. Physical description area
   f. Series area
   g. Note area
   h. Standard number and terms of availability area.

As previously stated, all the rules in *AACR2* Part I, are based on *ISBD(G)*. Since *AACR Chapter 6* (1974) was patterned on the first of the International Standard Bibliographic Descriptions (ISBD(M)), the experienced cataloguer will note many similarities both in punctuation and in arrangement between entries for books (monographs) catalogued under *AACR Chapter 6* (1974) and books catalogued according to *AACR2* chapter 2 which concerns itself with special rules applicable to books. The changes in the names of the areas from those given in *AACR Chapter 6* (1974) reflect the editors' effort to expand the terminology of the new code to include all types of library materials: e.g., although the term "author" and "authorship" is appropriate in reference to books, it is often difficult to attribute this same sort of responsibility in the cataloguing of nonprint materials such as films, sound recordings, etc. Therefore, the "title and statement of authorship area" found in *AACR Chapter 6* (1974) has become the "title and statement of responsibility area." Two other terms, "imprint area" and "collation area," which have been part of the cataloguer's professional jargon for many years, are now translated into phrases far more meaningful to the uninitiated. "Imprint" is now called the "publication, distribution, etc. area"; "collation" has become the "physical description area." The experienced cataloguer will also notice the substitution of the term "full stop" for the word "period." And, as a reflection of the fact that this, unlike its predecessor, is truly an "Anglo-American" code, many British preferred spellings are used throughout the text.

The 1967 *AACR* was criticized on the international level for a number of reasons. First, it came under fire for its deviations from the Paris Principles, including too broad a concept of personal authorship, for an unacceptable approach to corporate authorship, and for an unacceptable concept of entry of serials under corporate body.[4] Some cataloguing experts, among them Michael Gorman, have also criticized *AACR1* for its emphasis on the concept of main entry, which Gorman called "a relic of outdated technology" made obsolete by computer-based catalogues with multiple access points for all works contained in the data base.[5] Part II of *AACR2*, rules for access points and headings, addresses itself to these problems, and in some instances makes substantive and worthwhile contributions toward solving them.

Rules for form of name of personal author are fundamentally the same as in *AACR1*, which followed the guidelines of the Paris Principles in most cases. However, *AACR1* rules for both form and choice of entry for corporate bodies were not considered satisfactory. *AACR2* rules for entry under corporate body show the influence of Eva Verona's definitive study of corporate bodies[6] in limiting main entry under corporate heading to works of an administrative nature dealing with the corporate body, its staff, its resources, or official statements recording the collective thought or activity of the body. Entry under government heading is limited to administrative regulations, decrees, laws, court rules, legislative hearings, treaties, charters, and constitutions.

Even before its publication, *AACR2* was criticized by some cataloguing experts as being too traditional in its approach, too firmly rooted in the premachine processing era of bibliographic control. It is possible that it may, indeed, be the last catalogue code based on the concept of main entry; it may indeed be an interim code on the way to a truly revolutionary concept of computer-oriented bibliographical control. However, as it stands, it represents a great step forward toward the ideal of universal bibliographic exchange of cataloguing data.

[4] Ibid., p. 2.
[5] "Rules for Entry and Heading," *Library Trends* 25 (Jan. 1977): 596.
[6] *Corporate Headings* (London: IFLA Committee on Cataloguing, 1975).

1
General Information

Part I of *Anglo-American Cataloguing Rules* deals with descriptive cataloguing: the identification and description of a work in such a fashion that it can be distinguished from all other works, and from other editions of the same work. As Paul Dunkin put it, this is the part of the catalogue entry that tells what the work looks like—rather than who is responsible for it.[1] Rules in *AACR2* Part II tell the cataloguer how to choose the person or corporate body chiefly responsible for the intellectual content of the work described by rules in *AACR2* Part I. They also tell the cataloguer how to construct a heading for the "main entry" thus chosen, as well as correct format for added entries.

```
Dunkin, Paul S.
    Cataloging U.S.A. / by Paul S. Dunkin. --
Chicago : American Library Association, c1969.
    xxii, 159 p. ; 24 cm.

    Bibliography: p. xv-xxii.
    Includes index.
    ISBN 0-8389-0071-2




        I. Title.
```

Figure 1-1. A simple
catalogue entry

[1] Paul S. Dunkin, *Cataloging U.S.A.* (Chicago: ALA, 1969), pp. 48, 23.

In the example shown in figure 1-1, the top line of the entry (Dunkin, Paul S.) is called the main entry. The choice of Dunkin as main entry rather than, for instance, the title is governed by *AACR2* Part II, chapter 21. Chapter 22. Headings for Persons, gives rules for the form in which this entry must appear as main entry. Part I includes rules for everything else in the above entry. Subject headings and classification, which are outside the province of the *Anglo-American Cataloguing Rules,* will not be included in cataloguing samples in this handbook.

Cataloging U.S.A. By Paul S. Dunkin American Library Association Chicago	International Standard Book Number 0-8389-0071-2 (1969) Copyright © 1969 by the American Library Association
Title page	Verso of title page

As mentioned in the Introduction, the descriptive cataloguing rules of Part I are based on *International Standard Bibliographic Description (ISBD).* This is an internationally agreed-upon framework for cataloguing rules for description, which has established essential items of information that must appear in the entry, the order in which these items will be given, and a system of arbitrary punctuation that must be used. The purpose of this standardized format is "to facilitate the international exchange of bibliographic information, whether in written or machine-readable form . . . [and to] permit quick identification of the elements [of a catalog entry] even by the catalog user who is totally unfamiliar with the language of the description."[2]

1.0B. Organization of the description

Elements to be included in the descriptive part of the catalogue entry are divided into areas (an area is a major section of the *ISBD*). If these appear in the item being catalogued, they must be transcribed in the following order:

1. Title and statement of responsibility area. This will be discussed in detail under *AACR2* 1.1.
2. Edition area. To be discussed under *AACR2* 1.2.
3. Material (or type of publication) specific details area. This area is used only with cartographic materials (see discussion under *AACR2* chapter 3) and serials (see discussion under *AACR2* chapter 12).
4. Publication, distribution, etc., area. This area, formerly called the imprint, will be discussed under *AACR2* 1.4.
5. Physical description area. This area, formerly called the collation, will be discussed under *AACR2* 1.5.
6. Series area. To be discussed under *AACR2* 1.6.

[2] Library of Congress, *Cataloging Service Bulletin* 105 (Nov. 1972).

7. Note area. To be discussed under *AACR2* 1.7.

8. Standard number and terms of availability area. As in *AACR Chapter 6* (1974), this is the last area in the catalogue entry. See discussion under *AACR2* 1.8 for details.

1.0C. Punctuation

Except for the first area, each area is preceded by a full stop (period) - space - dash - space (. —). (In typing, a dash consists of two hyphens: --) Elements within each of the areas also have prescribed punctuation. This punctuation will be discussed with the detailed discussion of the areas that follows (1.1 through 1.8).

1.0D. Levels of detail in the description

AACR2 offers a number of options not previously available to cataloguers who wished to follow earlier cataloguing codes carefully. One of these is the option of choice among three levels of detail in cataloguing description.

1.0D1. First-level description. The first level is brief cataloguing. The cataloguer is to include only the title proper, omitting other title information. The statement of responsibility may also be omitted if it is the same as the main entry heading. (See 1.1 for discussion and explanation of the title and statement of responsibility area.) The edition statement is included, but not an accompanying statement of responsibility (see 1.2). Material (or type of publication) specific details statement is included for cartographic materials (see chapter 3) and serials (see chapter 12). Publication data include only the name of the first publisher and the date of publication. Pagination (for books), notes, and standard number, if available, complete the entry. First-level description would probably be sufficient to identify items in a small library collection (see figure 1-2a).

1.0D2. Second-level description. The second level includes all of the information given in level 1 cataloguing. In addition, the cataloguer will include general material designation (1.1C) after the title proper if the library has decided to use it for this type of library material. Parallel titles (1.1D) and other title information (1.1E) will be included. They will be followed by all pertinent statements of responsibility (1.1F). The edition statement together with its first statement of responsibility is included if it is found in the work (1.2). First place, first publisher, and date of publication are given (1.4). The physical description area will include all items specified in applicable rules (1.5) except that accompanying material, if any, will not be given as a part of this area. The series statement is recorded (1.6). Notes and standard number are included as appropriate. This level might appropriately be used in medium-sized libraries (see figure 1-2b).

1.0D3. Third-level description. The third level includes all the rules applicable to the item being catalogued. Third-level description is appropriate to large libraries and research collections (see figure 1-2c). Cataloguing examples in this text are third level.

Kingsley, Charles.
  Madam How & Lady Why. -- Dent, ₁1926₁
  229 p.

    "List of the works of Charles Kingsley": p. x.

Figure 1-2a. First-level description

Kingsley, Charles.
  Madam How & Lady Why : lessons in earth lore for
children / by Charles Kingsley. -- London : Dent,
₁1926₁
    xix, 229 p. : ill. ; 18 cm. -- (Everyman's
library ; no. 777. For young people)

    "List of the works of Charles Kingsley": p. x.

  I. Title.

Figure 1-2b. Second-level description

       I. Title.

Kingsley, Charles.
  Madam How & Lady Why : lessons in earth lore for
children / by Charles Kingsley. -- London : Dent ;
New York : Dutton, ₁1926₁
    xix, 229 p. : ill. ; 18 cm. -- (Everyman's
library ; no. 777. For young people)

    "List of the works of Charles Kingsley": p. x.

Figure 1-2c. Third-level description

    I. Title.

Half title page	Everyman's Library Edited by Ernest Rhys For Young People

Madam How & Lady Why
  Lessons in Earth Lore for Children
  By Charles Kingsley
  London & Toronto   Title page
  Published by J. M. Dent & Sons
  Ltd. & in New York
  By E. P. Dutton & Co.

This is no. 777 of Everyman's Library

Verso of title page

No matter which of the three levels of description the cataloguer decides to use, choice of access points for main entry and form of headings will be the same. (See *AACR2* Part II.) For this reason, it is quite feasible to interfile any or all of the different levels of description into one catalogue. Thus, libraries that use LC cataloguing data can continue to do so, even though they may decide to use one of the simpler levels for original cataloguing done in the home library.

1.1. TITLE AND STATEMENT OF RESPONSIBILITY AREA

As previously mentioned, the first cataloguing area is called the title and statement of responsibility area. General rules for the transcription of this area are included in *AACR2* 1.1, excluding rules for prescribed punctuation, which are covered in section 1.0C.

1.1A2. Transcription of title and statement of responsibility area. In general, the cataloguer transcribes what he or she sees, in the order in which it appears on the title page or other chief source of information (for nonbook materials). However, if the elements of this area are not in prescribed order on the title page, they are transposed to bring them into correct order, which must be: title / statement of responsibility. (See figure 1-3.)

```
Lander, Jeannette.
   Ein Spatz in der Hand-- : Sachgeschichten /
Jeannette Lander. -- 1. Aufl. -- Frankfurt am
Main : Insel, 1973.
   107 p. ; 20 cm.




   I. Title.
```

Figure 1-3. Title and statement of responsibility area—transposition of elements from title page

Jeannette Lander
Ein Spatz in der Hand . . .
Sachgeschichten

Insel

Title page

The title and statement of responsibility area is to be transcribed from the appropriate chief source as given in chapters following chapter 1 exactly as to wording and spelling but not necessarily as to capitalization and punctuation, which follow conventional library rules. For titles in the English language, capitalize the first word of the title and any proper names thereafter. Do not omit any words. Except where specifically authorized, do not add any words. Do not abbreviate any words in the title and statement of responsibility area. *AACR1* authorized certain abbreviations in the transcription of the "author element" (statement of responsibility); by *AACR2* rules this may no longer be done.

As seen in the example in figure 1-4, the title proper is separated from other titles by space - colon - space. The entire title element (title proper and other titles) is separated from the statement of responsibility by space - slash - space. Within the statement of responsibility, if different people perform different functions, each type of authorship responsibility is separated from the others by space - semicolon - space.

```
Up from the pedestal : selected writings in the
   history of American feminism / edited with an
   introduction by Aileen S. Kraditor. -- Chicago :
   Quadrangle Books, c1968.
   372 p. ; 24 cm.

   Bibliography: p. [371]-372.
```

Figure 1-4. Title and statement of responsibility area

```
   I. Kraditor, Aileen S.
```

Title page

Up from the Pedestal
Selected Writings in the History
of American Feminism
Edited with an Introduction by
Aileen S. Kraditor
Chicago
Quadrangle Books

1.1B. Title proper

Transcribe the words of the title proper (main title) exactly as they appear on the work. Except for extremely long titles (see 1.1B4), do not omit any words. Except when correcting an inaccuracy (see 1.0F), do not add any words. Capitalization follows normal usage for the language of the title. Figure 1-3 is capitalized according to German-language practice, which calls for the capitalization of the first word of the title and all nouns thereafter. English-language titles are not capitalized according to usual citation practice, as they would be listed in a bibliography. When transcribing the title of a work in the English language, capitalize the first word and all proper names thereafter. Figures 1-1, 1-2, and 1-4 illustrate standard cataloguing practice for capitalization. See *AACR2* Appendix A for detailed rules.

Punctuation between elements (i.e., title proper, parallel title, other title information, and statement of responsibility) is prescribed (1.0C). Within the title proper, however, punctuation other than the prescribed marks may generally be transcribed from the source or added as necessary to the transcription. For an exception, note that according to 1.1B1 both ellipses (. . .) and half brackets ([ ]) if present within the title proper must be replaced. (See figure 1-3.) Interestingly, one mark of more or less normal punctuation is prescribed in 1.1B9, which requires a full stop (.) to separate the parts of certain titles proper. The full stop, as well as any other mark of normal punctuation retained within the title proper, is given with normal spacing (i.e., no space preceding). The comma represents the most frequent example of this phenomenon, as in the cases of alternative titles or such titles as the following: Herblock, his influence on cartoon art.

An exclamation point (!) or a question mark (?) occurring as part of a title proper will be retained. Sometimes, as in figure 1-5, the title proper consists of two parts separated by such punctuation, which will be transcribed. Note that standard prescribed punctuation separates the title proper from the following element, even though this results in double punctuation.

Under *AACR Chapter 6* (1974) an alternative title (a second title introduced by "or" or the equivalent in another language, e.g. Hans Brinker, or, The silver skates) was regarded as part of the other title element of the first cataloguing area. By 1974 rules, the alternative title was separated from the title proper by space - colon - space. This punctuation is no longer to be used, although the special rule that called for capitalizing the first word of the alternative title still holds. The alternative title is now considered to be part of the title proper. It is punctuated as shown in figure 1-6.

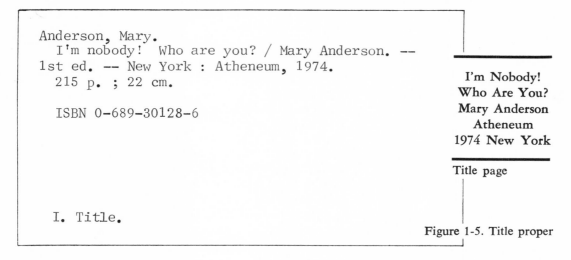

Figure 1-5. Title proper

1.1B2. Transcribe the title proper just as it appears in the chief source of information. If the name of the author, the publisher, etc., appears as an integral part of the title (not simply out of prescribed order, as with figure 1-3), transcribe it as shown in figure 1-7.

In figure 1-7 note capitalization of the first word of the actual title. Contrast this with capitalization used in the example shown in 1.1B2: Marlowe's plays. In this instance the word "plays" is simply a generic term indicative of the content of the work and as such is not separable from its antecedent, "Marlowe's."

Old sleuth.
　　Detective Dale, or, Conflicting testimonies :
a weird detective experience / by Old sleuth. --
New York : J.S. Ogilvie Pub. Co., c1898.
　　84 p. ; 18 cm. -- (Old sleuth's own ; no. 116)

Figure 1-6. Title proper
includes alternative title

　　　　I. Title: Detective Dale.　II. Title: Conflicting testimonies.

Detective Dale:
or
Conflicting Testimonies.
A Weird Detective Experience.
By Old Sleuth.
Copyright, 1898, by Parlor Car Publishing Company.
New York:
J. S. Ogilvie Publishing Company.

Title page

Béhotéguy de Téramond's
Low-Calorie
French Cookbook
with Season-by-Season Diet Menus
Illustrations by Dorothy Ivens
Grosset & Dunlap • Publishers
New York

Title page

Téramond, Béhotéguy de.
　　[300 recettes culinaires pour maigrir (par la
méthode des basses-calories). English]
　　Béhotéguy de Téramond's Low-calorie French
cookbook : with season-by-season diet menus /
illustrations by Dorothy Ivens. -- New York :
Grosset & Dunlap, c1964.
　　224 p. : ill. ; 25 cm.

　　Translation of: 300 recettes culinaires pour
maigrir (par la méthode des basses-calories).
Includes index.

　　　　I. Title: Low-calorie French cookbook.

Copyright © 1964 Editions Pallas
First published in France under the title:
"300 Recettes Culinaires pour Maigrir
(par la Méthode des Basses-Calories),"
Editions de la Pensée Moderne, editeurs, Paris.

Verso of
title page

Figure 1-7. Title proper
includes statement of
responsibility

1.1B3. The title proper is usually different from the name of the person or body responsible for the item, but this is not always the case, as seen in figures 1-8 and 1-9. Transcribe the title information as it appears in the chief source.

```
Three Dog Night.
    Three Dog Night ₁sound recording₁. -- Lombard,
Ill. : ABC Records : ₁Distributed by₁ Sessions
Records, c1977.
    2 sound discs : 33 1/3 rpm, stereo. ; 12 in.

    Contents: Try a little tenderness -- One -- Easy
to be hard -- Eli's coming -- Celebrate -- Mama told
me (not to come) -- Out in the country -- One man
band -- Joy to the world -- Liar -- An old fashioned
love song -- Never been to Spain -- The family of
man -- Black & white -- Pieces of April -- The show
must go on -- Play something sweet (Brickyard
blues) -- Till the world ends -- Let me serenade
                (continued on next card)
```

Figure 1-8. Title proper the same as main entry

```
    Three Dog Night.  Three Dog Night ₁sound recording₁.
    c1977.  (card 2)

you -- Shambala -- I'd be so happy -- Chest fever
-- Nobody -- Heaven is in your mind.
    ARL: 1004.
    G4RS-0065-0068.
```

1.1B4. This rule authorizes the abridgement of a long title proper. Caution: Only in rare instances is it appropriate to abbreviate the title proper. In the nineteenth century and earlier, title pages were often crowded with extraneous information, since they often doubled as an advertisement, which was run off as a broadside and distributed separately. But even in these instances, the title proper was generally concise. "Other title" information is more likely to be overly lengthy and in need of abridgement than is the title proper. See 1.1E3 for discussion and example.

1.1B6. A title proper that includes separate letters or initials, with or without full stops between them, is transcribed as it appears, without any internal spaces. See figure 1-1 for transcription of a title including initials with full stops. See figure 1-10 for a title including initials without full stops between them.

Conference on the Acquisition of Material from
    Africa (1969 : <u>University of Birmingham</u>)
    Conference on the Acquisition of Material from
Africa, University of Birmingham, 25th April 1969 :
reports and papers / compiled by Valerie Bloomfield.
-- Zug, Switzerland : Inter Documentation Co.,
c1969.
    vii, 154 p. ; 21 cm.

    At head of title: Standing Conference on Library
Material on Africa.
    Includes bibliographical references.

    I. Bloomfield, Valerie.   II. Standing Conference
on Library Material on Africa.

**Figure 1-9. Title proper
the same as main entry**

Standing Conference on Library Material on Africa

**Conference
on the Acquisition of Material from Africa
University of Birmingham 25th April 1969
Reports and Papers
compiled by Valerie Bloomfield**

Inter Documentation Company Ag Zug Switzerland

Title page

American Library Association.   <u>Subcommittee on the
    ALA Rules for Filing Catalog Cards.</u>
    ALA rules for filing catalog cards / prepared by
the ALA Editorial Committee's Subcommittee on the
ALA Rules for Filing Catalog Cards ; Pauline A.
Seely, chairman and editor. -- 2nd ed. -- Chicago :
American Library Association, 1968.
    xii, 260 p. ; 25 cm.

    Includes index.

    I. Seely, Pauline A.   II. Title.

**ALA Rules for Filing Catalog Cards
Prepared by the ALA Editorial Committee's
Subcommittee on the ALA Rules for
Filing Catalog Cards
Pauline A. Seely
Chairman and Editor
Second Edition
American Library Association   Chicago 1968**

**Figure 1-10. Title
proper including initials**

Title page

1.1B7. Items lacking a title. If the cataloguer must go beyond the prescribed sources of information to find a title for an item being catalogued, or, if the cataloguer makes up a title for an item (typically something homemade), enclose this title in brackets. (See figure 1-11.)

```
[Stomach of a frog, tangential section] [micro-
   scope slide]. -- [1955]
   1 microscope slide : stained ; 3 x 8 cm.


   Title supplied.
   Made by Robert M. Craig.
   Ten microns; stained with Zenker's stain.



   I. Craig, Robert M.
```

Figure 1-11. A "made up" title in brackets

1.1C. Optional addition. General material designation

The general material designation (GMD) is a generic term used to identify the general category of material to which an item belongs and to distinguish one general category from another in a catalogue containing records for more than one type of material. The area for physical description describes the special nature of the item, whether it be a sound recording, a slide, or a printed text. But cataloguers have long felt that it is helpful to alert library users almost immediately to the fact that some items, such as microfilms or sound recordings, require special equipment for their use, or that other items, such as maps or pictures, are stored and handled in a special manner. For this reason, it has long been customary in many North American libraries to add a medium designator immediately following the title in the catalogue entry for nonbook items.[3]

AACR2 includes two lists of GMDs, one for libraries in the United Kingdom and one for libraries in North America. These two lists are due to the fact that in the United Kingdom there is a strong emphasis on the general character of terms to be used as GMDs, while in North America there is a preference for certain terms even though they tend to the specific rather than the generic in character. Thus, no single list was found to be completely acceptable on both sides of the Atlantic.

[3] In the examples, this text will follow the practice of displaying GMDs for nonbook materials, since this practice is traditional in North America. At the time of writing it was not possible to ascertain Library of Congress practice under *AACR2*. The Library had indicated that GMDs for all types of materials would be present in its machine-readable records, but had not yet made a decision about display.

AACR2 is based on the premise of a fully integrated library collection, with all types of materials being catalogued under the same rules and principles regardless of physical format. Following this premise, *AACR2* allows the cataloguer the option of adding a general material designation not only to nonprint items but also to books. If the cataloguer chooses to add GMD to all types of library materials, figure 1-12 shows how figure 1-4 would be modified.

Some illustrations of GMDs displayed after the titles of other categories of material are shown in figures 1-13 to 1-15.

```
Up from the pedestal [text] : selected writings
   in the history of American feminism / edited
   with an introduction by Aileen S. Kraditor. --
   Chicago : Quadrangle Books, c1968.
   342 p. ; 24 cm.


   Bibliography: p. [371]-372.
```

Figure 1-12. General material designation—books

```
   I. Kraditor, Aileen S.
```

```
         Patterson, A. J.
            Flinch [game] : a game / by A. J. Patterson. --
         Salem, Mass. : Parker, c1938.
            1 game (150 cards) ; in box, 12 x 14 x 3 cm.

            Includes leaflet: Rules for playing.
```

Figure 1-13. General material designation—game

```
            I. Parker Brothers, Inc.   II. Title.
```

```
West Germany [slide] : the land and its people. --
   Chicago : Society for Visual Education, [196-?]
   25 slides : col. + commentary.



   I. Society for Visual Education.
```

Figure 1-14. General material designation—slide

```
Woodland friends ₍filmstrip₎. -- Wilmette, Ill. :
   Encyclopaedia Britannica Films, c1960.
   1 filmstrip (36 fr.) : col. ; 35 mm. -- (Animals
of the forest)
```

Figure 1-15. General
material designation—
filmstrip

```
   I. Encyclopaedia Britannica Films, Inc.
II. Series.
```

1.1D. Parallel titles

Sometimes the chief source of information shows a repetition of the title proper in other languages (the item may or may not contain text matching the languages of the titles). If this is the case, the first title is usually regarded as the title proper of the item. Succeeding repetitions of this title in the other languages are usually regarded as parallel titles.

Parallel titles are separated from the title proper and from one another by space - equals sign - space. (See figure 1-16.)

```
Metropolitan Toronto Central Library.  Languages
   Centre.
   Spanish books = Libros en español : a catalogue
of the holdings of the Languages Centre, Metro-
politan Toronto Central Library. -- ₍Toronto₎ :
Metropolitan Toronto Library Board, 1974.
   299 p. ; 27 cm.

   English and Spanish.
```

Figure 1-16. Parallel
title

```
   I. Title.  II. Title: Libros en español.
```

Spanish Books
Libros en Español
A Catalogue of the Holdings of the
Languages Centre
Metropolitan Toronto Central Library   Title page

Metropolitan Toronto Library Board
1974

1.1D3. Sometimes the chief source of information for a translated work gives the original title as well as the title of the translation. This is regarded as a parallel title (separated from the title proper by space - equals sign - space) if the work includes not only the translated text but also "all or some of the text in the original language." In other words, the work must include text in languages to match the titles as given in the chief source (see figure 1-17).

```
Bhagavadgita.   English & Sanskrit.
  Bhagavad Gita = The song celestial / the
Sanskrit text translated into English verse by
Sir Edwin Arnold ; with an introduction by Sri
Prakasa ; illustrated with paintings by Y.G.
Srimati. -- New York : Heritage Press, c1965.
  xx, 128 p., ₁14₁ leaves of plates : col. ill. ;
26 cm.




  I. Arnold, Edwin, Sir.  II. Srimati, Y. G.
III. Title: The song celestial.
```

Figure 1-17. Translated title as parallel title

Title page

Bhagavad Gita
The Song Celestial
The Sanskrit Text
Translated into English Verse by Sir Edwin Arnold
With an Introduction by Shri Sri Prakasa
Illustrated with Paintings by
Y. G. Srimati

The Heritage Press   New York

Whether or not a translation includes some of the original text, an original title will be recorded as a parallel title if it precedes the title proper in the chief source of information. On the other hand, if the chief source of information for a translated work includes the original title following the title of the translation and the work contains only the translation, the title of the translation will be given as the title proper and the original title will be listed as a note. (See *AACR2* 1.7A4 for form of note.)

Sometimes a work may be reissued under a new title but not translated to another language. If both the new title and the original title are included in the chief source of information, record the original title as "other title" information, separated from the title proper by space - colon - space. (See figure 1-18.)

```
Langton, Jane.
  Her majesty, Grace Jones : formerly The majesty
of Grace / by Jane Langton ; pictures by Emily
Arnold McCully. -- New York : Harper & Row, c1972.
  189 p. : ill. ; 22 cm.
```

Figure 1-18. Original title as other title information

Her Majesty, Grace Jones
formerly The Majesty of Grace
by Jane Langton
Pictures by Emily Arnold McCully
Harper & Row, Publishers
New York, Evanston, San Francisco, London

```
      I. Title.
```

Title page

However, if the chief source of information lists only the new title under which a work is reissued, this is all that will appear in the title element. If the cataloguer knows the original title, this information will appear in a note (1.7A4). Information about earlier titles, original titles, and so on is often found, as in figure 1-19, on the verso of the title page.

```
Roberts, Elisabeth.
  Jumping jackdaws! : Here comes Simon / by Elisa-
beth Roberts ; illustrated by Prudence Seward ;
cover illustrated by Muriel Collins. -- Chicago :
Rand McNally, [1975] c1973.
  192 p. : ill. ; 23 cm.

  Original title: All about Simon and his grand-
mother.
  Summary: Short stories recount the day-to-day
adventures of a little English boy and his grand-
mother.

      I. Title.
```

Figure 1-19. Original title given as a note

Title page

First published 1973 under the title
All About Simon and His Grandmother
Illustrations copyright © 1973
Methuen Children's Books Ltd.

Verso of title page

Jumping Jackdaws!
Here Comes Simon
By Elisabeth Roberts
Illustrated by Prudence Seward
Cover Illustrated by Muriel Collins
Rand McNally & Company
Chicago • New York • San Francisco

1.1E. Other title information

Other title information (see *AACR2* Appendix D, Glossary) is to be transcribed, as is the title proper, exactly as to order, wording, and spelling, but (as with the title proper) not necessarily with the capitalization and punctuation given in the chief source of information. Other title information is separated from the title proper by space - colon - space, as shown in figure 1-20.

```
Monjo, F. N.
  Letters to Horseface : being the story of
Wolfgang Amadeus Mozart's journey to Italy,
1769-1770, when he was a boy of fourteen / by
F.N. Monjo ; illustrated & designed by Don Bolog-
nese & Elaine Raphael. -- 1st ed. -- New York :
Viking, 1975.
  91 p. : ill. ; 25 cm.

  Bibliography: p. 91.




  I. Bolognese, Don.  II. Raphael, Elaine.
III. Title.
```

Figure 1-20. Other title
information

Title page

Letters to Horseface
being the story of
Wolfgang Amadeus Mozart's
journey to Italy 1769–1770
when he was a boy of fourteen
by F. N. Monjo
illustrated & designed by
Don Bolognese & Elaine Raphael
The Viking Press • New York

A catalogue entry may contain more than one segment of other title information. Each segment is preceded by space - colon - space. (See figure 1-21.)

1.1E3. Lengthy "other title" information. If other title information is lengthy, and if it contains no essential information, part of it may be omitted. Indicate omissions by ellipses (. . .), as shown in figure 1-22. Never omit the first five words of other title information.

```
Dickinson, Asa Don.
   The world's best books : Homer to Hemingway :
3000 books of 3000 years, 1050 B.C. to 1950 A.D. /
selected on the basis of a consensus of expert
opinion by Asa Don Dickinson. -- New York :
Wilson, 1953.
   viii, 484 p. ; 24 cm.

   Revision and unification of: The best books of
the decade, 1926-1935; The best books of the
decade, 1936-1945; and One thousand best books.



   I. Title.
```

WITHDRAWN FROM STOCK

Figure 1-21. Other title
information

Title page

The World's Best Books
Homer to Hemingway
3000 Books of 3000 Years
1050 B. C. to 1950 A. D.
Selected on the Basis of a
Consensus of Expert Opinion
By Asa Don Dickinson
The H. W. Wilson Company
New York   1953

```
Frost, John.
   Border wars of the West : comprising the frontier
wars of Pennsylvania, Virginia, Kentucky, Ohio,
Indiana, Illinois, Tennessee, and Wisconsin ... /
by John Frost ; with numerous engravings. -- New
York : Miller, Orton & Mulligan, 1856.
   608 p. : ill., ports. ; 24 cm.
```

Figure 1-22. Other title
abridged

Border Wars of the West: comprising the
Frontier Wars of Pennsylvania, Virginia, Kentucky,
Ohio, Indiana, Illinois, Tennessee, and Wisconsin;
and embracing
Individual Adventures among the Indians,
and exploits of
Boone, Kenton, Clark, Logan, Brady, Poe, Morgan,
the Whetzels, and other border heroes of the west.
By John Frost, LL.D.
With Numerous Engravings.
New York and Auburn:
Miller, Orton & Mulligan.   1856.

```
   I. Title.
```

Title page

Colaiste Mhuire Gan Smal Luimneach 64148

A further example of the abridgement of lengthy "other title" information is shown in figure 1-23.

```
The Treasures of Tutankhamun ₍slide₎ : exhibited
  at National Gallery of Art, Washington, D.C. ...
  -- New York : Metropolitan Museum of Art, ₍1978₎
  41 slides : some col. + 1 sound cassette. --
(Sound/slide library of the Metropolitan Museum
of Art)
  "Narration by Philippe de Montebello."

  I. National Gallery of Art.   II. Metropolitan
Museum of Art.
```

Figure 1-23. Other title abridged

The slide that served as the chief source of information for transcription of the title element read as follows:

The Treasures of Tutankhamun
Exhibited at
National Gallery of Art, Washington, D.C.
Field Museum of Natural History, Chicago
New Orleans Museum of Art
Los Angeles County Museum of Art
Seattle Art Museum
The Metropolitan Museum of Art, New York

The cataloguer may appropriately abridge this information.

Lengthy other title information pertaining to the bibliographic history of the work may more appropriately be included as a note (see figure 1-24). In this case, do not indicate omission by ellipses.

```
Schulz, Charles M.
  How long, Great Pumpkin, how long? / by Charles
M. Schulz. -- New York : Holt, Rinehart and
Winston, 1977.
  ca. 200 p. : all ill. ; 26 cm. -- (Peanuts
parade ; 16)

  Subtitle: Cartoons from You're the guest of honor,
Charlie Brown, and, Win a few, lose a few, Charlie
Brown.

  I. Title.
```

Figure 1-24. Other title information dropped to notes area

How Long, Great Pumpkin, How Long?
Cartoons from You're the Guest of Honor, Charlie
Brown and Win a Few, Lose a Few, Charlie Brown
by Charles M. Schulz
Holt, Rinehart and Winston/New York

Title page

Verso of half title page

Peanuts Parade Paperbacks
1. Who's the Funny-Looking Kid with the Big Nose?
2. It's a Long Way to Tipperary
3. There's a Vulture Outside
4. What's Wrong with Being Crabby?
5. What Makes You Think You're Happy?
6. Fly, You Stupid Kite, Fly!
7. The Mad Punter Strikes Again
8. A Kiss on the Nose Turns Anger Aside
9. Thank Goodness for People
10. What Makes Musicians So Sarcastic?
11. Speak Softly, and Carry a Beagle
12. Don't Hassle Me with Your Sighs, Chuck
13. There Goes the Shutout
14. Always Stick Up for the Underbird
15. It's Hard Work Being Bitter
16. How Long, Great Pumpkin, How Long?

1.1E4. Statement of responsibility included with other title information.
This rule has a parallel in 1.1B2. If a statement of responsibility appears
anywhere in the title element, whether as part of the title proper or as part
of the other title information, and if it is an integral part of the title, transcribe it as it appears (see figure 1-25).

Figure 1-25. Other title
including statement of
responsibility

```
Doré, Gustave.
    A Doré treasury : a collection of the best
engravings of Gustave Doré / edited and with an
introduction by James Stevens. -- [New York] :
Bounty, c1970.
    ix, 246 p. : chiefly ill. ; 32 cm.




    I. Stevens, James.   II. Title.
```

Title page

A Doré Treasury
A Collection of the Best Engravings
of Gustave Doré
edited and with an introduction by
James Stevens
Bounty Books
A Division of Crown Publishers, Inc.

1.1F. Statement of responsibility

The statement of responsibility is separated from the title by space - slash - space. It is transcribed just as it appears in the chief source of information. Do not add words such as "by" or "and" unless these appear in the chief source of information. But if these appear in the source, transcribe them as you see them. That is, "and" must be transcribed as "and"; the ampersand "&" will be transcribed as "&". (See figure 1-26.)

```
Thompson, James Westfall.
  An introduction to medieval Europe, 300-1500 /
James Westfall Thompson & Edgar Nathaniel Johnson.
-- 1st ed. -- New York : Norton, c1937.
  xii, 1092 p., [38] p. of plates : ill., geneal.
tables, maps (some col.), ports. ; 25 cm.

  Bibliography: p. 1053-1067.
  Includes index.



  I. Johnson, Edgar Nathaniel.   II. Title.
```

Figure 1-26. Statement of responsibility

An Introduction To
Medieval Europe
300–1500
James Westfall Thompson
&
Edgar Nathaniel Johnson
W. W . Norton & Company, Inc.
Publishers • New York

Title page

A statement of responsibility appearing in the chief source of information will always be recorded, unless the cataloguer is following the provisions of first-level description (1.0D1) and the statement of responsibility is the same as the main entry heading. In a change from previous practice, no abbreviations may be used in the statement of responsibility unless they appear in the item. The statement of responsibility may include, in addition to or instead of names of authors, names of persons or bodies having other responsibility for the work, such as editors, translators, writers of prefaces, illustrators, etc. Names of persons or bodies performing different functions are separated from one another by space - semicolon - space, unless joined grammatically. In addition to this treatment of punctuation shown in figure 1-27, note the transcription of initials in the statement of responsibility. They are to be recorded with full stops but without spaces between them.

Although in most cases all personal names appearing in the chief source of information will be recorded in the statement of responsibility, the cataloguer should be alert for instances in which an individual's name is included on the source simply because he or she happens to head an agency which is responsible for the production or publication of the work. If this individual has not functioned in the capacity of author or had subsidiary responsibility, or has not worked in some capacity (as, for instance, chairperson) with a corporate body having some sort of authorship responsibility for the work, his or her name will not be included in the catalogue entry. See figure 1-28.

Figure 1-27.
Statement of
responsibility—
subsidiary
author

```
Finberg, A. J.
    Turner's sketches and drawings / A. J. Finberg ;
introduction by Lawrence Gowing. -- 1st Schocken
ed. -- New York : Schocken, 1968.
    xxviii, 163 p., 87 p. of plates : ill. ; 21 cm.

    Includes index.


    I. Turner, Joseph Mallard William.  II. Title.
```

Turner's Sketches and Drawings   Title page
A. J. Finberg
Introduction by Lawrence Gowing
Schocken Books • New York

First Schocken Edition 1968
Copyright © 1968 by Schocken Books Inc.

Verso of title page

```
Myers Demonstration Library Project.
    The Myers Demonstration Library : an ESEA Title
III project. -- Phoenix : Arizona Dept. of Educa-
tion, [1971]
    [14] p. ; 28 cm.


    Cover title.



    I. Arizona.  Dept. of Education.  II. Title.
```

Figure 1-28.
Names not
part of
statement of
responsibility
omitted

The Myers Demonstration Library
An ESEA Title III Project
Arizona
Department of Education
W. P. Shofstall, Ph.D., Superintendent

Title page

1.1F1. Statements of responsibility. A statement of responsibility will be recorded only if it appears "prominently" in the item being catalogued. "Prominently" is defined, according to *AACR2* 0.8, as "a formal statement in one of the prescribed sources . . . for areas 1 and 2" (the title and statement of responsibility area and the edition area). These prescribed sources will be different for each of the various types of library media. They are listed under .0B in the chapters dealing with special kinds of library materials: e.g., 2.0B2 states that for a book, the prescribed source of information for the title and statement of responsibility is the title page or title page substitute; in addition, information appearing "prominently" (i.e., in the prescribed source listed for the edition area) can be transcribed as part of the statement of responsibility. *AACR2* 6.0B2 states that the label on a sound recording disc is the chief source of information, i.e., the prescribed source of information for transcribing the title and statement of responsibility for such an item. In addition, a statement appearing "prominently" (i.e., on accompanying textual material or the container, the prescribed source for the edition area) can be transcribed as part of the statement of responsibility. If such "prominent" information (i.e., information taken from prescribed sources for the edition area) is included as part of the statement of responsibility, it must be enclosed in square brackets.

The cataloguer should exercise judgment about whether to include "prominent" information *not* appearing in the chief source of information as part of the statement of responsibility. Transcribe it only if it is significant; i.e., of such a nature that an added entry will be made based on the information. In figure 1-29 data about illustrators appear on the verso of the title page, which, since it is one of the prescribed sources of information for the edition area, is a "prominent" location. The illustrations, however, are relatively unimportant, and responsibility for these illustrations is diffuse. The information will not be transcribed. On the other hand, see figure 1-32 for an instance where important information appearing on the verso of the title page should be bracketed as part of the statement of responsibility.

```
The Magic of Lewis Carroll / edited by John
    Fisher. -- New York : Simon and Schuster, c1973.
    288 p. : ill. ; 25 cm.

    Bibliography: p. 276-279.
    Includes index.
    ISBN 0-671-21604-X



    I. Fisher, John.
```

Figure 1-29. Statement of responsibility

Copyright © 1973 by John Fisher
SBN 671-21604-X
Line illustrations by Sir John Tenniel, Henry Holiday,
Arthur B. Frost, Harry Furniss and Lewis Carroll;
diagrams by Laura Potter.
The book has been designed by John Lewis

The Magic of Lewis Carroll
Edited by
John Fisher
Simon and Schuster
New York

Verso of title page   Title page

1.1F2. Do *not* construct a statement of responsibility if none appears "prominently" in the item. (See figures 1-28 and 1-30).

```
Population ₍game₎ : a game of man and society. --
   Cambridge, Mass. : Urban Systems, c1971.
   1 game (various pieces) ; in box, 51 x 27 x 5 cm.

   Summary: A simulation game designed to acquaint
players with the problem of population growth and
control.




   I. Urban Systems, Inc.
```

Figure 1-30. No statement of responsibility

1.1F3. If a statement of responsibility precedes the title proper, transpose it to its proper position in the entry. See figure 1-3 for an example. However, if such a name is connected grammatically to the title proper, do not transpose it. See figure 1-7. In such a case, the statement of responsibility following the slash may consist solely of names of persons or bodies performing subsidiary functions. Even though it does not include the name of the author, a statement of responsibility is still to be separated from the title element by space - slash - space. See again figure 1-7.

1.1F5. Rule 1.1F5 is unchanged from *AACR Chapter 6* (1974) 134D7. When more than three persons or bodies performing the same function are named in the source used to record the statement of responsibility, give only the first named, followed by ". . . ₍et al.₎". (See figures 1-31 and 1-32.)

```
Book collecting and scholarship : essays / by
   Theodore C. Blegen ... [et al.]. -- Minneapolis :
   University of Minnesota Press, 1954.
   67 p. ; 20 cm.

   Contents: A glorious court / Theodore C.
Blegen -- Bound fragments of time / James Ford
Bell -- Rare books and the scholar / Stanley
Pargellis -- The specialized collection / Colton
Storm -- American book collectors / Louis B. Wright.


   I. Blegen, Theodore C.
```

Figure 1-31. Statement
of responsibility—
omissions

Book Collecting and Scholarship
Essays by Theodore C. Blegen
James Ford Bell, Stanley Pargellis
Colton Storm, & Louis B. Wright   Title page
1954
University of Minnesota Press • Minneapolis

```
Anglo-American cataloging rules / prepared by
   the American Library Association ...  [et al. ;
   general editor, C. Sumner Spalding]. -- North
   American text. -- Chicago : A.L.A., 1967.
   xxi, 400 p. ; 27 cm.

   Includes index.
```

Figure 1-32. Statement
of responsibility—
omissions

```
   I. American Library Association.  II. Spalding,
C. Sumner.
```

Anglo-American Cataloging Rules
Prepared by the American Library Association
The Library of Congress
The Library Association and
The Canadian Library Association   Title page
North American Text
American Library Association   Chicago 1967

General Editor
C. Sumner Spalding

Verso of title page

1.1F6. More than one statement of responsibility. Often the chief source of information lists more than one type of bibliographic responsibility. For example, in addition to an author's name on the title page of a book, the cataloguer may find names of editors, writers of prefaces or introductions, illustrators, etc. These names are to be recorded in the order in which they appear in the source (see figure 1-33). Separate names of persons or bodies having different kinds of responsibility by space - semicolon - space, unless these names are linked grammatically.

Contrast figure 1-33 with figure 1-31. Names of one to three persons or bodies performing the same function will be transcribed in the entry; if four or more perform the same function, all but the first will be omitted. (This holds true for those performing subsidiary functions such as illustrators, etc., as well as persons or bodies having primary responsibility for the work.)

1.1F7. Titles included with names in the statement of responsibility. Although reworded, this rule is basically the same as 134D8a in *AACR Chapter 6* (1974). Certain titles, *if they appear prominently, in conjunction with the names of persons,* will be transcribed as part of the catalogue entry. Among titles thus to be transcribed are titles of nobility or British titles of honour (Sir, Dame, Lord, Lady). (See figures 1-34 and 1-35.)

```
Perry, James W.
  Machine literature searching / James W. Perry,
Allen Kent, Madeline M. Berry ; with a foreword by
Jesse H. Shera. -- Cleveland : Western Reserve
University Press, 1956.
  xi, 162 p. : ill. ; 27 cm.

  Includes bibliographies and index.




  I. Kent, Allen.  II. Berry, Madeline M.
III. Title.
```

Figure 1-33. More than one statement of responsibility

Title page

Machine Literature Searching
James W. Perry
Allen Kent
Madeline M. Berry
With a Foreword by
Jesse H. Shera, Dean
Western Reserve University Press
Interscience Publishers • New York • London

Sitwell, Osbert, <u>Sir</u>.
  England reclaimed and other poems / Sir Osbert
Sitwell. -- 1st ed. -- Boston : Little, Brown,
1949.
  xv, 122 p. ; 23 cm.

  "An Atlantic Monthly Press book."

  I. Title.

Figure 1-34. British
title of honour included

Title page

England Reclaimed and Other Poems
Sir Osbert Sitwell
An Atlantic Monthly Press Book
Little, Brown and Company • Boston
1949

Philip, <u>Prince, consort of Elizabeth II, Queen</u>
  <u>of Great Britain</u>, 1921-
  The evolution of human organisations / by His
Royal Highness the Prince Philip, Duke of Edinburgh. -- Southampton, [England] : University
of Southampton, 1967.
  27 p. ; 22 cm. -- (Fawley Foundation lecture ;
14)

  At head of title: The Fawley Foundation.
  ISBN 83542-000-8

  I. Title.   II. Series.

Figure 1-35. Title of
nobility included

The Fawley Foundation
The Evolution of Human Organisations
By
His Royal Highness The Prince Philip
Duke of Edinburgh, K.G.
University of Southampton
1967

Title page

Always transcribe a title of address if it is necessary grammatically (see figure 1-36). Include a title of address when its omission would leave only the person's given name, as shown in figure 1-37. Such a title of address is also retained when its omission would leave only the person's surname (see figure 1-38).

```
Florilegio del parnaso americano : selectas
   composiciones poeticas / coleccionadas por
   Michael A. de Vitis ; con un prólogo del Dr.
   Juan Vicente Ramirez. -- Barcelona : Maucci,
   [1927?].
   589 p. ; 21 cm.




   I. Vitis, Michael A. de.
```

Figure 1-36. Title necessary grammatically (following "del")

Florilegio del
Parnaso Americano
Selectas Composiciones Poeticas
coleccionadas por
Michael A. De Vitis
con un prólogo del
Dr. Juan Vicente Ramirez
Casa Editorial Maucci

Title page

```
Gregory, Saint, Bishop of Tours, ca. 540-594.
   History of the Franks / by Gregory, Bishop of
Tours ; selections, translated with notes by
Ernest Brehaut. -- New York : Norton, 1969.
   xxv, 284 p. : geneal. tables, map ; 21 cm. --
(Records of civilization)

   Bibliography: p. 279-280.
   Includes index.
   ISBN 393-09845-1


   I. Brehaut, Ernest.  II. Title.
```

Figure 1-37. Title with given name only

Title page

History of the Franks
By Gregory Bishop of Tours
Selections, Translated with Notes
by
Ernest Brehaut, Ph.D.
W. W. Norton & Company • Inc. • New York

```
Child, Mrs.
  The mother's book / by Mrs. Child. -- 3rd ed. --
Boston : Carter and Hendee, 1832.
  x, 169 p. ; 21 cm.




  I. Title.
```

Figure 1-38. Title with surname only

The Mother's Book.
By Mrs. Child,
Third Edition.
Boston:
Published by Carter and Hendee.
1832.

Title page

For a married woman who writes under her husband's name plus the term of address, it is necessary to include the term of address in order to identify the author correctly. (See figure 1-39.)

```
Dana, William Starr, Mrs.
  How to know the wild flowers : a guide to the
names, haunts, and habits of our common wild
flowers / by Mrs. William Starr Dana ; illustrated
by Marion Satterlee. -- Rev. ed. / by Clarence J.
Hylander. -- New York : Dover, 1963.
  xli, 418 p. : ill. ; 22 cm.




  I. Hylander, Clarence J.  II. Title.
```

Figure 1-39. Title needed for proper identification.

How to Know the Wild Flowers
A Guide
to the Names, Haunts, and Habits of Our
Common Wild Flowers by
Mrs. William Starr Dana
Illustrated by Marion Satterlee
Revised Edition by
Clarence J. Hylander
Dover Publications, Inc.
New York

Title page

Words indicating relationship (junior, filho, etc.) are also included in the statement of responsibility when they appear in the chief source of information. (See figure 1-40.)

```
Henry, Rene A.
  How to profitably buy and sell land / Rene A.
Henry, Jr. -- New York : Wiley, c1977.
  xix, 203 p. : ill. ; 24 cm. -- (Real estate
for professional practitioners)

  "A Wiley-Interscience publication."
  Glossary: p. 166-198.
  ISBN 0-471-37291-9




  I. Title.
```

Figure 1-40. Words indicating relationship included

How to Profitably Buy and Sell Land
Rene A. Henry, Jr.
A Wiley-Interscience Publication
John Wiley & Sons
New York • London • Sydney • Toronto

Title page

Other than exceptions noted above, titles are omitted from names of persons in statements of responsibility. It is particularly necessary to exercise caution when dealing with religious titles. If the person's name includes a surname and forename(s), omit titles, as shown in figure 1-41. Religious

```
Kingsley, Charles.
  The water babies : a fairy tale for a land baby /
by Charles Kingsley ; edited and abridged by J. H.
Stickney. -- Boston : Ginn, 1892.
  vii, 192 p. : ill. ; 18 cm. -- (Classics for
children)
```

Figure 1-41. Religious title omitted

```
  I. Stickney, J.H.  II. Title.
```

The Water Babies
A Fairy Tale for A Land Baby
By
Rev. Charles Kingsley
Edited and Abridged by J. H. Stickney.
Boston:
Published by Ginn & Company
1892.

Title page

titles such as "cardinal," "bishop," "brother," and "father," will be omitted if the person's name includes a surname and forename(s). This practice, shown in figure 1-42, is different from ALA 1949 rules, but was included as part of *AACR1*. Likewise, initials standing for the religious order to which the individual belongs will be omitted when the name includes a surname and forename(s). (See figure 1-43.) Note, by the way, the retention of "Jr." in the transcription of the statement of responsibility in figure 1-43.

```
Newman, John Henry.
  On the scope and nature of university education /
John Henry Newman ; introduction by Wilfrid Ward ;
prefatory note by Herbert Keldany. -- London :
Dent ; New York : Dutton, 1915.
  xli, 237 p. ; 19 cm. -- (Everyman's library ;
no. 273)

    Bibliography: p. xxv-xxvi.
    Includes index.

    I. Title.
```

Figure 1-42. Religious title omitted

Cardinal John Henry Newman
On the Scope and Nature
of University Education
Introduction by Wilfrid Ward
Prefatory Note by Herbert Keldany
of the Newman Association
Dent: London
Everyman's Library
Dutton: New York

Title page

```
Introduction to the great religions / Jean Danielou
    ... [et al.] ; translated by Albert J. La Mothe,
Jr. -- Notre Dame, Ind. : Fides, c1964.
  142 p. ; 21 cm.

Contents: Christianity and the non-Christian
religions / Jean Danielou -- The religions of na-
ture / Andre Retif -- Islam / Joseph Hours --
Buddhism / François Houang -- Hinduism / Maurice
Queguiner -- The religions of Japan / R.P. Dunoyer
-- Judaism / R.P. Demann -- Contemporary atheism /
Gaston ssard -- The transcendence of Christianity /
Jean Danielou.

    I. Danielou, Jean.   II. La Mothe, Albert J.
```

Figure 1-43. Initials of religious order omitted

Introduction to the Great Religions
    Jean Danielou, S.J.   Maurice Queguiner, P.F.M.
    Andre Retif, S.J.   R. P. Dunoyer, P.F.M.
    Joseph Hours, S.J.   R. P. Demann
    Francois Houang   Gaston Fessard, S.J.

Translated by Albert J. La Mothe, Jr.
Fides Publishers, Inc.
Notre Dame, Indiana

Chapter opening

1. Jean Danielou, S.J.
Christianity and the Non-Christian Religions

Omit qualifications, such as scholastic degrees (see figure 1-37) and positions held (see figure 1-36) in all cases. If the name includes both a surname and forenames, omit titles of address (Mr., Mrs., Miss, and foreign equivalents, as shown in figure 1-44) unless necessary for identification (see figure 1-39).

```
Cotarelo y Mori, Emilio.
  Diccionario biográfico y bibliográfico de calí-
grafos españoles / por Emilio Cotarelo y Mori. --
Madrid : Tip. de Revista de Arch., Bibl. y Museos,
1913-1916.
  2 v. : ill., ports. ; 28 cm.

  Includes indices.




  I. Title.
```

Figure 1-44. Title of address omitted

Diccionario Biográfico y Bibliográfico
de Calígrafos Españoles por
Don Emilio Cotarelo y Mori

De la Real Academia Española
Obra Premiada por la Biblioteca Nacional en el
Concurso Público de 1906
É Impresa á Expensas del Estado
Los españoles han sido los mejores
escribanos
del mundo. »
(El Herm. Lorenzo Ortiz, en su Maestro
de escribir, 1696.)
Madrid 1913
Tip. de la « Revista de Arch., Bibl. y Museos »

Title page

1.1F8. Additions to statement of responsibility. As previously mentioned, the cataloguer is not to add words such as "by" or "and" that simply serve to link the statement of responsibility to the title or one collaborating author with another, unless these words are found in the chief source of information. However, if the statement of responsibility as it appears in the source is not clear, or perhaps is misleading, a word or short phrase may be added to clarify it. (See figure 1-45.)

```
Pictures and stories from forgotten children's
   books / ₍selected₎ by Arnold Arnold. -- New York :
Dover, c1969.
   viii, 170 p. : ill. ; 21 x 23 cm. -- (Dover
pictorial archive series)

   ISBN 486-22041-9



I. Arnold, Arnold.
```

Figure 1-45.
Addition
to statement of
responsibility

**Pictures and Stories from
Forgotten Children's Books
By Arnold Arnold**
Title page **Dover Publications, Inc., New York**

1.1F12. This rule is basically the same as 134D1 in *AACR Chapter 6* (1974). It has been reworded and clarified. If a word appearing in the source of information or a word added, according to directions in 1.1F8, to a statement of responsibility is to appear as part of the statement of responsibility, it should be "indicative of the role of the person(s) or body or (bodies) named in the statement of responsibility rather than of the nature of the work." A noun or noun phrase "indicative of the nature of the work" is to be regarded as other title information. Such nouns typically are: an anthology, a report, a collection, a tribute, etc. Note the example shown in figure 1-46.

A word of caution: While it is true that a participle (edited, written, collected, etc.) is generally indicative of the role of the person and a noun is generally indicative of the nature of the work, this is not always the case. Sometimes a noun indicates the role of the person, and when it does, the noun should be included as part of the statement of responsibility. "In case of doubt," include it. See figure 1–17.

1.1F13. This rule is a restatement and clarification of 134D3 in *AACR Chapter 6* (1974). As indicated in 1.1B2, if the author's name is transcribed as part of the title element, it is not necessary for the cataloguer to bracket in a further author statement. The chief source of information is transcribed as it appears. However, if, in addition to the author's name appearing in the title, the name also appears in a separate statement of responsibility in the chief source of information, this is transcribed. (See figure 1-47.)

William Warner Bishop : a tribute, 1941 / edited
  by Harry Miller Lydenberg and Andrew Keogh. --
  New Haven : Yale University Press, 1941.
  vi, 204 p. : port. ; 24 cm.

  Contents: William Warner Bishop / Frederick Paul
Keppel -- Reflections from Ingonish / Herbert Putnam
-- William Warner Bishop / Harry Miller Lydenberg --
Rinaldo Rinaldini (Capo Brigante) and George Wash-
ington / Jens Christian Bay -- The Federation of
Library Associations / A.C. de Breycha-Vauthier --
Some rare Americana / Isak Gustaf Alfred Collijn --
Monsieur William Warner Bishop et la Fédération
internationale des associations de bibliothécaires

         (continued on next card)

William Warner Bishop.   1941.   (card 2)
            Contents--Continued

/ Marcel Godet -- Book divisions in Greek and Latin
literature / Sir Frederic George Kenyon -- The Yale
Library in 1742 / Andrew Keogh -- Palm leaf books /
Otto Kinkeldey -- Sir Henry Ellis in France / Gerhard
Richard Lomer -- Some trends in research libraries /
Keyes DeWitt Metcalf -- De Bibliotheca Neerlandica
Manuscripta de Vreese in Leiden / Tietse Pieter
Sevensma -- The preparation of a main index for the
Vatican Library manuscripts / Eugene, Cardinal
Tisserant -- Optima in library service for the south
by 1950 / Louis Round Wilson.
    I. Lydenberg, Harry Miller.   II. Keogh, Andrew.
III. Bishop, William Warner.

Figure 1-46. "Nature of the work" vs. "role of the persons"

William Warner Bishop
A Tribute
1941
Edited by Harry Miller Lydenberg and
Andrew Keogh
New Haven
Yale University Press
London • Humphrey Milford
Oxford University Press   **1941**

Title page

```
Gilman, Charlotte Perkins.
   The living of Charlotte Perkins Gilman : an
autobiography / by Charlotte Perkins Gilman ;
foreword by Zona Gale. -- New York : Appleton-
Century, 1935.
   xxxviii, 341 p., [7] leaves of plates : ports. ;
22 cm.
```

Figure 1-47. Author
statement repeated

```
I. Title.
```

Title page

The Living of
Charlotte Perkins Gilman
An Autobiography by
Charlotte Perkins Gilman
Foreword by Zona Gale
D. Appleton-Century Company
Incorporated
New York   1935   London

1.1F14. This rule is a rewording of 134D1 in *AACR Chapter 6* (1974), "Statements which would be considered statements of authorship if a person or body were named are transcribed as statements of authorship . . . ." See figure 1-48. See also figure 1-22 for another example of a statement to be transcribed as part of the statement of responsibility even though no engraver's name is included.

```
Orliac, Jehanne d'.
   Francis I, prince of the Renaissance / by
Jehanne d'Orliac ; translated by Elisabeth Abbott ;
with 21 illustrations. -- 1st ed. -- Philadelphia :
Lippincott, 1932.
   253 p. : ports. ; 23 cm.
```

Figure 1-48. Statement
of responsibility
without name of
illustrator

```
I. Title.
```

Title page

Francis I
Prince of the Renaissance
By Jehanne D'Orliac
Translated by Elisabeth Abbott
With 21 Illustrations
Philadelphia & London
J. B. Lippincott Company MCMXXXII

However, such statements are to be included only if they add some information about the work that cannot be brought out in the physical description area. Books, for example, may be described in the physical description area as including a number of specific types of illustration—charts, coats of arms, forms, genealogical tables, maps, music, plans, portraits, samples—as well as the general designation "ill." for illustration (2.5C2). Engravings are not among the types of illustrations that may be specified. The statement "with numerous engravings" therefore adds an important characterization of the book that cannot be brought out in the physical description area. It is included if it is found in the chief source of information even though the engraver's name is not given. The same is true for a statement giving the number of illustrations (figure 1-48). However, the statement "with illustrations" is omitted from the example shown in figure 1-49 because it adds no information to that brought out in the physical description area.

```
Tharp, Louise Hall.
   The Peabody sisters of Salem / by Louise Hall
Tharp. -- Boston : Little, Brown, 1950.
   x, 372 p., [11] leaves of plates : ill., ports. ;
22 cm.



   I. Title.
```

Figure 1-49.
Statement of
responsibility

Title page

The Peabody Sisters of Salem
by Louise Hall Tharp
With Illustrations
Little, Brown and Company • Boston
1950

A statement of responsibility will be transcribed if it includes a phrase referring to a person, even though the person is not named in the statement (figure 1-50).

```
Denison, Carol.
   Passwords to people : a storyboard / by Carol
Denison ; illustrated by the author. -- New York :
Dodd, Mead, 1956.
   135 p. : ill. ; 25 cm.




   I. Title.
```

Figure 1-50. Statement
of responsibility

Title page

Passwords to People
A Storyboard by Carol Denison
Illustrated by the author
Dodd, Mead & Company
New York   1956

The rule also calls for the inclusion of "unnamed bodies" as part of the statement of responsibility, even though according to the cataloguers' definition (21.1B1), corporate bodies cannot be said to function as a unit and will not be given an entry in the catalogue. (See figure 1-51.)

```
General education in school and college : a
   committee report / by members of the faculties
   of Andover ... [et al.] ; the committee, Alan
   R. Blackmer, chairman ... [et al.]. --
   Cambridge, Mass. : Harvard University Press,
   1953, c1952.
   v, 142 p. ; 22 cm.
```

Figure 1-51. Unnamed bodies in statement of responsibility

```
I. Phillips Academy.   II. Blackmer, Alan R.
```

General Education
in School and College
A Committee Report
By Members of the Faculties of
Andover, Exeter, Lawrenceville,
Harvard, Princeton, and Yale
Harvard University Press
Cambridge, Masschusetts
1953

Title page

The Committee
Alan R. Blackmer, chairman
Henry W. Bragdon
McGeorge Bundy
E. Harris Harbison
Charles Seymour, Jr.
Wendell H. Taylor

Verso of half title page

1.1F15. The chief source of information sometimes includes extraneous matter such as mottoes and bits of verse. If these have no connection with the bibliographical information needed to identify the item, they should be ignored. (See figure 1-52.) Do not use ellipses to indicate their omission.

```
Molesworth, Mrs.
   The tapestry room : a child's romance / Mrs.
Molesworth ; illustrated by Walter Crane. -- New
York : Epstein & Carroll ; distributed by Random
House, [196-]
   217 p. : ill. ; 19 cm. -- (Looking glass
library ; 27)




I. Crane, Walter.  II. Title.
```

Figure 1-52. Extraneous material omitted

Title page

The Tapestry Room
A Child's Romance
Mrs. Molesworth
What tale did Iseult to the children say,
Under the hollies, that bright winter's day?
Matthew Arnold
Illustrated by Walter Crane
Looking Glass Library
Distributed by Random House
New York

Figure 1-44 includes two extraneous pieces of information that the cataloguer will properly ignore in transcribing the title and statement of responsibility area. The first one, which follows the author's name, states that this work won a prize in a contest sponsored by the Biblioteca Nacional in 1906 and that it has been printed at the expense of the national government. The second is a quotation from the Spanish author Lorenzo Ortiz claiming that the Spanish people have produced the best writers in the world. Neither statement has any place in the bibliographic framework of the catalogue entry.

But note the inclusion of "words or phrases which are neither names nor linking words" when they are concise and when they provide useful bibliographical information. In the example shown in figure 1-53, "compiled in June 1946" should be retained. As with the example shown in figure 1-28 the names of the heads of the two agencies listed as part of the statement of responsibility are omitted because they had no authorship responsibility for the work.

```
A Survey of the recreational resources of the
   Colorado River basin / compiled in June 1946,
   United States Department of the Interior,
   National Park Service. -- Washington : U.S.G.P.O.,
   1950.
   xxiv, 242 p. : ill., maps (some col.) ; 30 cm.

   Part of illustrative matter in pocket.
   Bibliography: p. 224-232.
   Includes index.


   I. United States.   National Park Service.
```

Figure 1-53. Phrase in statement of responsibility included

Title page

A Survey of the Recreational Resources
of the Colorado River Basin
United States Department of the Interior
Oscar L. Chapman, Secretary
National Park Service
Newton B. Drury, Director
Compiled in June 1946
United States Government Printing Office
Washington • 1950
For sale by the Superintendent of Documents,
Washington, D.C.   Price $3.25

1.1G. Items without a collective title

This rule is an enlargement with minor modifications of 134C6 in *AACR Chapter 6* (1974). Most items that include a number of separate works have a collective title on the chief source of information. Such materials present no problem for the cataloguer. But some items simply list a number of separate titles, with or without their authors, on the chief source of information. *AACR2* 1.1G gives rules for transcription of such materials. It deals with the relatively rare instance in which one of the separate works named in the chief source of an item without a collective title is predominant, as indicated by the typography or the wording of the chief source of information. If this is the case, the predominant title will be transcribed as the title proper. The other titles are omitted from the title statement. Do not use ellipses to show omission. List each title contained in the work in a contents note (see figure 1-54).

```
Wiggin, Kate Douglas.
   The Birds' Christmas Carol / by Kate Douglas Wiggin.
-- Autograph ed. -- Boston : Houghton Mifflin, c1917.
   xv, 330 p., [11] leaves of plates : ill. (some
col.), col. port. ; 22 cm. -- (The writings of Kate
Douglas Wiggin ; v. 1)

   Contents: The Birds' Christmas Carol -- The story
of Patsy -- Timothy's quest -- A child's journey
with Dickens -- Fleur-de-lis.
   Library's copy signed by the author.

   I. Title.  II. Wiggin, Kate Douglas.  The story
of Patsy.  III. Wiggin, Kate Douglas.  Timothy's
quest.  IV. Wiggin, Kate Douglas.  A child's journey
with Dickens.  V. Wiggin, Kate Douglas.  Fleur-de-lis.
```

Figure 1-54. Item without a collective title

The Birds'
Christmas Carol
The Story of Patsy, Timothy's
Quest, and Other Stories
by
Kate Douglas Wiggin
Houghton Mifflin Company
Boston and New York

Title page

The Writings of
Kate Douglas Wiggin
Autograph Edition
Volume I

Half title page

1.1G2. If, on the other hand, no one item predominates on a title page lacking a collective title, record each of the titles in the order in which they are given. Separate the titles by semicolons, even if they are joined by a connecting word or phrase. (This is a change from 134C6 in *AACR Chapter 6, 1974.*) See figure 1-55. If the separate parts are by different authors, give each title with its statement of responsibility. Separate each part by a full stop, as shown in figure 1-56.

```
Martineau, Harriet.
   Feats on the fjord ; and, Merdhin / by Harriet
Martineau. -- London : Dent ; New York : Dutton,
1910.
   xi, 239 p. : ill. ; 18 cm. -- (Everyman's
library ; no. 429. For young people)




   I. Title.  II. Martineau, Harriet.  Merdhin.
```

Figure 1-55. Item without a collective title

Feats on the Fjord and Merdhin by
Harriet Martineau
London & Toronto
Published by J. M. Dent
& Sons Ltd & in New York
by E. P. Dutton & Co.

Title page

1.2. EDITION AREA

An edition may be defined as being "one of the differing forms in which a . . . work . . . is published, e.g. as applied to text, original, revised, enlarged, corrected, etc., . . . ; as applied to format: de luxe, library, paperbound, large-paper, illustrated, etc."[4]

The cataloguer is required to include the edition statement as found, but a statement such as "35th impression" or "9th printing" may be ignored, since it usually simply means that more copies of the work have been made. Such a statement would only be recorded if the cataloguer knew that there was some significant difference, either in content or format, between one printing or impression and another.

Printers and publishers have no regard for the cataloguer's convenience in their use of bibliographical terminology. Not even when the publisher uses the word "edition" or its equivalent in another language can the cataloguer assume that the work in hand is indeed different from other issues of the work. This is especially true in regard to many French publications. The cataloguer is not required to compare copies to verify the validity of an edition statement. Take the word "edition" or its equivalent at face value and record it as it appears (see figure 1-57).

4 *Bookman's Glossary,* 5th ed. (New York: Bowker, 1975), p. 58.

Tauber, Maurice F.
  Cataloging and classification / by Maurice F.
Tauber. Subject headings / by Carlyle J. Frarey.
-- New Brunswick, N.J. : Graduate School of
Library Service, Rutgers, the State University,
1960.
   271, 92 p. ; 23 cm. -- (The State of the library
art ; v. 1, pt. 1-2)

  I. Frarey, Carlyle J. Subject headings.
II. Title. III. Series.

Figure 1-56. Item without a collective title

The State of the Library Art
edited by Ralph R. Shaw
Volume 1, part 1   Cataloging and Classification
by Maurice F. Tauber
Volume 1, part 2   Subject Headings
by Carlyle J. Frarey
Graduate School of Library Service
Rutgers—The State University
New Brunswick, N.J.   1960

Title page

Toon, Ernest R.
  Foundations of chemistry / Ernest R. Toon,
George L. Ellis ; consultant, Russell C. Bovie.
-- 2nd ed. -- New York : Holt, Rinehart and
Winston, c1973.
   xii, 769 p. : ill. (some col.) ; 24 cm. --
(The Holt chemistry program)

  Includes index.
   ISBN 0-03-088484-5

  I. Ellis, George L. II. Title.

Figure 1-57. Edition statement

Title page

Ernest R. Toon   George L. Ellis
Foundations of Chemistry
Consultant Russell C. Bovie,
Science Department Chairman,
Arcadia High School,
Arcadia, California
Holt, Rinehart and Winston, Inc.
New York • Toronto • London • Sydney

The Holt Chemistry Program
Foundations of Chemistry
Toon and Ellis   Second Edition

Half title page

1.2B3. This rule simply reiterates long-standing cataloguing practice: In case of doubt, if a statement appears to be an edition statement (see definition given above under 1.2; see also *AACR2* Glossary, Appendix D), record it in the edition area.

Although in many cases an edition statement will include the word "edition," "version," "issue," or the equivalent in a foreign language, this is not always the case. Note, for example, figure 1-32. The *Anglo-American Cataloging Rules* (1967) were issued in two versions. "North American text" is the edition statement for this version; the statement should be transcribed in the edition area.

However, not all items include an edition statement. Do not add "1st ed." or any other such statement unless you find it in your source (but see 1.2B4, Optional addition). On the other hand, if the item includes an edition statement, transcribe the wording and order just as you find it. Thus, if the item reads:

> Second edition, revised and corrected

transcription will be:

> — 2nd ed., rev. and corr. —

However, if the edition statement reads:
> Revised and corrected second edition

transcription will be:
> — Rev. and corr. 2nd ed. —

Note in the preceding example the use of abbreviations and the transcription of numbers spelled as words to arabic ordinal numerals. You will recall that no abbreviations are allowed in the title and statement of responsibility area. Beginning with the edition area, abbreviations should be used when the word is found in *AACR2* Appendix B (Abbreviations). Numbers written as words or as roman numerals are to be transcribed as arabic numerals, following directions in *AACR2* Appendix C (Numerals).

When transcribing ordinal numerals, note a change from previous practice under which the cataloguer transcribed "second" as "2d" and "third" as "3d." These last vestiges of Melvil Dewey's spelling reform efforts have been abandoned in favor of normal English-language usage. The forms "1st," "2nd," "3rd," "4th," "5th," etc., will now be used in the edition area for statements in the English language, as appropriate. See *AACR2* Appendix C for directions on transcribing numerals in foreign languages.

1.2B4. Optional addition. In a stipulation new to cataloguing rules, the cataloguer is now given the option of adding, in brackets, a made-up edition statement if he or she knows that the work being catalogued includes "significant changes from previous editions." The Library of Congress will not follow this practice, which puts a considerable burden of research and comparison on the cataloguer.[5]

5 "AACR2 Options to Be Followed by the Library of Congress, Chapters 1–2, 12, 21–26," *LC Information Bulletin* 37 (July 21, 1978): 422–28. Hereafter referred to as "AACR2 Options."

1.2C. Statements of responsibility relating to the edition

Occasionally an edition statement is followed by a statement of responsibility pertaining only to the edition in hand: e.g., it may name a revisor, an illustrator, or someone who has performed some other function just for the particular edition. If this is the case, such a statement of responsibility will be transcribed, following space - slash - space, as part of the edition area. In transcribing this statement of responsibility, follow all applicable rules for transcription, punctuation, spacing, etc., as given in 1.1. (See figure 1-58.) No abbreviations may be used.

```
Stebbins, Kathleen B.
  Personnel administration in libraries / by
Kathleen B. Stebbins. -- 2nd ed. / revised and
largely rewritten by Foster E. Mohrhardt. --
New York : Scarecrow Press, 1966.
  373 p. : forms ; 22 cm.

  Includes bibliographical references and index.



  I. Mohrhardt, Foster E.   II. Title.
```

Figure 1-58. Statement of responsibility related to the edition

Personnel Administration
in Libraries
by
Kathleen B. Stebbins
Second Edition
Revised and Largely Rewritten
by
Foster E. Mohrhardt
The Scarecrow Press, Inc.
New York and London   1966

Title page

1.2C2. Many works that lack a formal edition statement are clearly revisions of an earlier work. A cataloguer who chooses to follow the option given in 1.2B4 may create an edition statement and include the statement of revision as a statement of responsibility following the bracketed edition statement, if this statement relates to the edition in hand but not to all editions of the work. (See example given in *AACR2* under 1.2C1.) In case of doubt, however, do not do this. If the item does not include an edition statement, information about revision, etc., of the text will form part of the title and statement of responsibility area. (See figure 1-59.)

```
Bright, James W.
  Bright's Anglo-Saxon reader / revised and
enlarged by James R. Hulbert. -- New York : Holt,
c1935.
  cxxxii, 395 p. ; 20 cm.




  I. Hulbert, James R.   II. Title: Anglo-Saxon
reader.
```

Figure 1-59. Revision with no edition statement

Title page

Bright's
Anglo-Saxon Reader
Revised and Enlarged
by
James R. Hulbert
New York
Henry Holt and Company

1.2D. Subsequent edition statement

This new rule gives guidance not previously included in cataloguing rules about what to do when an item includes more than one edition statement. Both statements are included in the edition area, separated by a comma. (See figure 1-60.)

1.3. MATERIAL (OR TYPE OF PUBLICATION) SPECIFIC DETAILS AREA

This area only appears in catalogue entries for cartographic items and serials. See *AACR2* chapter 3 and chapter 12 for examples and explanation.

1.4. PUBLICATION, DISTRIBUTION, ETC., AREA

Punctuation for this area is unchanged from *AACR Chapter 6* (1974) rules. The basic order of information and punctuation are: — Place (City) : Publisher, date.

1.4B4. This rule is a general restatement of one of the cardinal principles of descriptive cataloguing: Transcribe what you see. Exceptions to this general statement follow in further rules governing the publication element. One of these exceptions is given here. The publication area is condensed as much as it can be and remain clear. Prepositional phrases may be omitted unless case endings would be affected (see figure 1-61).

Lady.
 The child's guide to knowledge : being a collection of useful and familiar questions and answers
on every-day subjects / adapted for young persons
and arranged in the most simple and easy language
by a lady. -- Authorized ed., 57th ed. -- London :
Simpkin, Marshall, 1888.
 v, 480 p. ; 15 cm.

 I. Title.

Figure 1-60. Two
edition statements

Title page

Authorized Edition.
The Child's
Guide to Knowledge;
Being a Collection of
Useful and Familiar Questions and Answers
on Every-day Subjects,
Adapted for Young Persons,
and Arranged in the Most Simple and Easy
Language.
By a Lady.
Fifty-seventh Edition.
London:
Published by Simpkin, Marshall, & Co.,
and Sold by All Booksellers.
MDCCCLXXXVIII.
Price Two Shillings.
The right of Translation and Reproduction is reserved.

Figure 1-61. Phrase
omitted, publisher
statement

English madrigal verse, 1588-1632 / edited from
 the original song books by E.H. Fellowes. --
 2nd ed. -- Oxford : Clarendon Press, 1929.
 xxiv, 644 p. ; 20 cm.

 Includes index.

 I. Fellowes, E. H.

Title page

English Madrigal Verse
1588–1632
Edited from the Original
Song Books by
E. H. Fellowes
Oxford
At the Clarendon Press
M CM XXIX

1.4B8. Two or more places of publication and/or names of publishers.
This rule is identical in its intent to that of 136C in *AACR Chapter 6*
(1974). As a general rule, the publication area includes one place (city) and
one publisher, distributor, etc. Normally, if a work is published in more than
one place (city) or if the chief source of information for the publication area
indicates that it has been published by more than one publisher, transcribe
the first named place and the first named publisher for the publication area.
(See figures 1-62 and 1-63.)

```
Greenaway, Kate.
  The Kate Greenaway treasury : an anthology of
the illustrations and writings of Kate Greenaway /
edited and selected by Edward Ernest, assisted by
Patricia Tracy Lowe ; introduction by Ruth Hill
Viguers. -- Cleveland : World, c1967.
  319 p. : col. ill. ; 27 cm.



     I. Ernest, Edward.   II. Title.
```

Figure 1-62. More than
one place

```
              The Kate Greenaway Treasury
            Introduction by Ruth Hill Viguers
      An Anthology of the Illustrations and Writings
                  of Kate Greenaway,
         Edited and Selected by Edward Ernest,          Title page
            Assisted by Patricia Tracy Lowe
            The World Publishing Company
               Cleveland and New York
```

```
John, Uncle.
  The boy's book of sports and games : containing
rules and directions for the practice of the
principal recreative amusements of youth / by
Uncle John. -- Philadelphia : Appleton, 1851.
  192 p. : ill. ; 15 cm.



     I. Title.
```

Figure 1-63. More than
one place and publisher

The Boy's Book of
Sports and Games,
containing
Rules and Directions
for the practice of the
Principal Recreative Amusements of Youth.
By Uncle John,
Title page   Author of "The Little Boy's Own Book," etc. etc.
With Illustrations
Philadelphia:
George S. Appleton
New York:
D. Appleton & Co.
1851.

There are several instances, however, when the cataloguer will add a second named place and/or publisher. This will be done if the first name is that of a distributor, releasing agent, etc. and the second is that of the publisher. The examples shown in figures 1-64 and 1-65 illustrate a fairly frequent pattern for this type of situation.

```
Forecasting and the social sciences / edited and
   introduced by Michael Young. -- London :
Published for the Social Science Research
Council by Heinemann, 1968.
ix, 166 p. ; 22 cm.

Includes bibliographies.
ISBN 435-82986-7



   I. Young, Michael.   II. Social Science Research
Council (Great Britain).
```

Figure 1-64. Names of
two agents included

Forecasting and the Social Sciences
Edited and introduced by Michael Young
Title page   Published for the
Social Science Research Council by
Heinemann • London

```
Scrabble [game]. -- New York : Manufactured by
  Selchow & Righter Co. for Production & Marketing
  Co., c1953.
  1 game (board, 4 racks, 100 letter tiles) ; in
box, 19 x 37 x 4 cm.

  A word game for 2, 3, or 4 players.
```

Figure 1-65. Names of
two agents included

```
  I. Production & Marketing Company.
```

Motion pictures and videorecordings frequently have more than one distributor, releasing agent, etc., involved with the publication of such a work. In many instances it is appropriate to add a second named place and/or distributor, releasing agent, etc. (See figure 1-66.)

```
Navajo [videorecording] : the fight for survival.
  -- London : BBC-TV ; New York : Released in the
  U.S. by Time-Life Video, [1972?]
  1 videocassette (U standard) (50 min.) : sd.,
col. ; 3/4 in.

  Released in Great Britain under title: Navaho :
the last of the red Indians.
  Summary: Documents the destruction of Indian
civilization since the days of the conquistadores
and chronicles current attempts to preserve Navaho
culture.

  I. BBC-TV.   II. Time-Life Video.
```

Figure 1-66. Names of
two agents included

The cataloguer will add a second place if a city outside the cataloguer's country (for most of the readers of this text, the United States) is named first, followed by a city in the "home" country. (See figure 1-67.)

To reiterate: Always transcribe the first place. If this place is a city outside the country of your cataloguing agency and the item includes the name of a city in your home country, transcribe this also. A cataloguer in the United States will transcribe the publication area of figure 1-67 as given above. A British library would transcribe it: — London : Oxford University Press, 1937. (The first city is in the home country). A Canadian library would transcribe it: — London ; Toronto : Oxford University Press, 1937. (The first place is transcribed, followed by the place in the cataloguer's home country.) A cataloguer in Australia or any other country using *AACR2* other than the three countries specified above would give publication area as: London : Oxford University Press, 1937. (No place in home country; list first place only.)

The same principle holds true when transcribing the name of the publisher. Always name the first publisher (distributor, etc.). If this publisher (etc.) is not located in the country of the cataloguing agency and the source for transcribing the publication area lists a home country publisher (etc.) in secondary position, give this name also. See, for instance, figure 1-42. Publication area will be transcribed as given in example for a cataloguing agency in the United States. However, a British, Canadian, or Australian cataloguing agency would give publication area as: — London : Dent, 1915.

```
The Republics of South America : a report / by a
   study group of members of the Royal Institute of
   International Affairs. -- London ; New York :
   Oxford University Press, 1937.
   x, 374 p., [3] folded leaves of plates : maps
(some col.) ; 25 cm.

   Includes index.




   I. Royal Institute of International Affairs.
```

Figure 1-67. Two places in publication area

Title page

The Republics of
South America
A Report by a
Study Group of Members of the
Royal Institute of International
Affairs
Oxford University Press
London   New York   Toronto
1937

Rule 1.4B covered publication area rules in general. The following rules deal separately with each of the elements in the publication area.

1.4C. Place of publication, distribution, etc.

 1.4C1. Do not translate a place name into an English-language form that might be more familiar to English-speaking users of your library. Transcribe the name as you find it. That is, if the chief source of information gives "Firenze," do not translate it to "Florence." (See figure 1-68.)

```
D'Annunzio, Gabriele.
  La nave : tragedia / di Gabriele d'Annunzio. --
Milano : Treves, 1908.
  249 p. : ill. ; 24 cm.




  I. Title.
```

La Nave
Tragedia Di
Gabriele D'Annunzio
Milano
Fratelli Treves
Editori · MCMVIII

Title page

Figure 1-68. Place of publication in vernacular

 1.4C2. However, if the place as transcribed seems likely to be obscure to your library's users, you may, *at your discretion,* add a more familiar form in brackets. (See figure 1-69.)

```
Birket-Smith, Kaj.
  The Eyak Indians of the Copper River delta,
Alaska / by Kaj Birket-Smith and Frederica De
Laguna. -- København [Copenhagen] : Levin &
Munksgaard, 1938.
  591 p. : ill., geneal. table ; 25 cm.

  At head of title: Det Kgl. Danske videnskabernes
selskab.
  Bibliography: p. 573-591.




  I. De Laguna, Frederica.  II. Det Kgl. Danske
videnskabernes selskab.  III. Title.
```

Figure 1-69. Place of publication with translation added

Det Kgl. Danske Videnskabernes Selskab.
The Eyak Indians of
the Copper River Delta,
Alaska
by

Title page   Kaj Birket-Smith and Frederica De Laguna
København
Levin & Munksgaard
1938

1.4C3. Additions to place names. At the cataloguer's discretion, "if it is considered necessary for identification, or if it is considered necessary to distinguish the place from others of the same name," the name of the state, country, province, etc., may be added to the place in the publication area. Never abbreviate the name of the city. But if the name of the state, province, etc., appears in *AACR2* Appendix B. Abbreviations, use an abbreviation for this distinguishing element. Reiteration: Remember that the abbreviation "N.Y." is used for the state only. Never abbreviate "New York" when you mean the city. (See figure 1-70.)

This rule is basically unchanged from 137B, in *AACR Chapter 6* (1974) and from earlier codes. *ALA Cataloging Rules for Author and Title Entries* (1949) (153C) gave a list of well-known cities in the United States and Canada that are customarily recorded in the imprint without further identification. David Haykin's *Subject Headings, a Practical Guide* has a list of cities outside the United States and Canada for which the designation of country may be omit-

---

Blume, Judy.
  Tales of a fourth grade nothing / by Judy
Blume ; illustrated by Roy Doty. -- 1st ed. --
New York : Dutton, c1972.
  120 p. : ill. ; 22 cm.

  ISBN 0-525-40720-0

I. Title.

Figure 1-70. Well-known city for which place may be omitted in the publication area

Tales of a
Fourth Grade Nothing
by Judy Blume
illustrated by Roy Doty
E. P. Dutton & Co., Inc. New York

Title page

ted. Although these lists were compiled many years ago, they may serve as valid guides to cataloguers who do not wish to add a qualifier to the place of publication for all cities. They are reprinted in Appendix II.

If the place name is not included on these lists, add the larger governmental unit to the name of the place (figure 1-71). If the name of the larger governmental unit is included as part of the main heading and/or the statement of responsibility, it need not be repeated to identify the place of publication. (See figure 1-72.)

```
Laura [filmstrip] : little house, big prairie /
   produced by Media Systems Consultants. --
   Logan, Iowa : Perfection Form Co., 1976.
   1 filmstrip (127 fr.) : col. ; 35 mm. + 1 sound
cassette + 1 script (32 p.). -- (American pageant
sound filmstrip ; 95267)

   Title from container.
   Credits: Script, Wayne De Mouth ; graphics, Perry
Struse ; sound supervision, Robert Dow.
   Based on Laura Ingalls Wilder's Little house
books.
   In container (18 x 14 x 5 cm.)
   Summary: Laura Ingalls Wilder's life in early
twentieth century South Dakota.

   I. Wilder, Laura Ingalls.   II. Media Systems
Consultants.
```

Figure 1-71. Place with larger jurisdiction added in publication area

Cassette label

Laura:
Little House, Big Prairie
American Pageant Sound Filmstrip
   Produced by Media Systems Consultants
   © 1976 The Perfection Form Company,
Logan, Iowa 51546
            DuKane
            Inaudible

Label on container

Laura:
Little House,
Big Prairie
An American Pageant Sound Filmstrip
Produced by
Media Systems Consultants

Label on box

95267
Laura:
Little House, Big Prairie

```
Guidelines for instructional media services
  programs / Pennsylvania Learning Resources
  Association. -- Rev. ed. -- West Chester :
  Service Project and Area Research Center, 1970.
  vii, 90 p. : ill. ; 21 cm.
```

Figure 1-72. Place
without larger
jurisdiction

```
  I. Pennsylvania Learning Resources Association.
```

Title page

Guidelines for instructional media services programs
Revised Edition
Pennsylvania Learning Resources Association
Post Office Box 498
Drexel Hill, Pennsylvania 19026
Service Project and Area Research Center
131 North High Street
West Chester, Pennsylvania 19380
February 1970

1.4C5. This rule is a restatement of the stipulation already given in 1.4B8 and illustrated by figure 1-67.

1.4C6. The place of publication element in the publication area must always contain something. If the name of the place does not appear on the item, it may be taken from appropriate reference sources or other materials.

In the example shown in figure 1-73, the *Directory of Inter-Corporate Ownership* (Simon & Schuster, 1974; v. 1, p. 833) gave information that in 1972 MGM Records was a subsidiary of Metro-Goldwyn-Mayer in Culver City, California. The place is definite. If the cataloguer is not certain of the place, he or she may give a probable city with a question mark. This is the same rule as 137A in *AACR Chapter 6* (1974).

In a new provision the cataloguer may, if a probable city is not known but a probable country or state is, give the country or state alone as the place element. (See figure 1-74.) The rationale for this new rule is plain; the addition of a country or state name is preferable to the third alternative, adding "s.1." (meaning "sine loco," "without place") if the cataloguer has no idea at all of where the item originated. Under no other circumstances is state or country ever given *alone* in the publication area. In all but this instance, "place" means city or town.

```
Osmonds.
    The Osmonds "live" [sound recording]. -- [Culver
City, Calif.] : MGM Records, 1972.
    1 sound cassette : 3 3/4 ips.

    Contents: Intro -- Motown special -- My world is
empty without you -- I'm gonna make you love me --
I can't get next to you, babe -- Double lovin' --
Your song -- Sweet and innocent -- You've lost that
lovin' feelin' -- Proud Mary -- Free -- Go away,
little girl -- Sometimes I feel like a motherless
child -- Where could I go but to the Lord -- Every-
time I feel the spirit -- We gotta live together --

            (continued on next card)
```

```
Osmonds.    The Osmonds "live" [sound recording].
    1972.    (card 2)

Trouble -- I got a woman -- Hey girl -- Down by
the lazy river -- Yo-yo -- One bad apple.
    MGJ: 54826.
```

Figure 1-73. Place
supplied in publication
area

The book used as the basis of figure 1-74 illustrates several cataloguing problems. As can be seen from the facsimile of the title page, no publication information is given in the chief source of information. A careful search of the volume failed to turn up any hint as to place of publication or name of either publisher or printer. The only indication of date of publication is the statement in the Preface that "Mrs. W. J. Crowley of Kingman is now serving (1944)." This is enough evidence for the cataloguer to bracket 1944? as publication date.

As for place of publication, the Arizona Federation of Women's Clubs has never had a permanent headquarters, and so no help can come from this source. Furthermore, nothing in the book suggests that the Federation served as publisher of the book, although this is highly probable. The author's place of residence is not known. However, it is an entirely reasonable supposition that she lived in Arizona when the book was issued, and that the book was printed and published somewhere in Arizona. Therefore, the name of the state should be used alone as place of publication, qualified with a question mark since the information is not certain.

```
Ross, Margaret Wheeler.
  History of the Arizona Federation of Women's
Clubs and its forerunners / written and compiled
by Margaret Wheeler Ross. -- [Arizona? : s.n.,
1944?]
    401 p., [1] leaf of plates : port. ; 24 cm.

  Spine and cover title: The tale is told.
  Subtitle: Forerunners, 1889 to 1901 : Federation
history, November 18, 1901 to April 12, 1944,
inclusive.

  I. Title.  II. Title: The tale is told.
```

Figure 1-74. State used as place alone

Title page

History of the Arizona Federation
of Women's Clubs and Its Forerunners
Written and Compiled by
Margaret Wheeler Ross
Forerunners
1889 to 1901
Federation History
November 18th, 1901 to April 12th, 1944
Inclusive

1.4C7. The cataloguer may, *optionally,* add the full address of a minor publisher to the name of the place. This option, which will be of value to acquisitions librarians, will be exercised by the Library of Congress when the information is readily available for other than major publishers.[6] Generally, full address will *not* be given if the work includes ISBN. In figure 1-72, for example, if the cataloguer chose to add the complete address, the publication area for this work would be:

— West Chester (131 North High Street, West Chester, Pa. 19380) : Service Project and Area Research Center, 1970.

[6] Ibid.

1.4D. Name of publisher, distributor, etc.

The name of the publisher, distributor, etc., is the second element of the publication area.

1.4D2. The publisher's or distributor's name is shortened in the publication area as much as possible, but not so much that it would duplicate the name of another publisher or that it cannot be identified internationally. Previous catalogue codes gave elaborate guidelines for shortening publishers' names. The present rules are not as explicit. The cataloguer must have a knowledge of publishers not only in the United States but also abroad to know that A. S. Barnes & Co. must be distinguished from John W. Barnes, Jr. Publishing, Inc. and therefore that one must be A. S. Barnes in the one publication statement and J. W. Barnes in the other. On the other hand, W. H. Freeman and Co. can be shortened to Freeman, since there is only one Freeman in the publishing business. *Books in Print* and its British counterpart have publisher lists that can be referred to to ascertain whether a publisher's name is unique and therefore susceptible to being truncated to a single word.

A few guidelines can be given.

1. Omit the initial article.

    The Canadian Record   *becomes*   Canadian Record.

2. Omit terms meaning "incorporated" or "limited."

    Caxton Printers, Ltd.   *becomes*   Caxton Printers.

    Artabras, Inc.   *becomes*   Artabras.

3. Omit words or phrases that show the publisher function.

    Bindford & Mort, Publishers   *is shortened to*   Bindford & Mort.

4. Omit words that simply indicate commercial organization.

Dodd, Mead & Co.		Dodd, Mead.
Macmillan Publishing Co., Inc.		Macmillan.
Meredith Corp.		Meredith.
Charles Scribner's Sons		Scribner.
Bramhall House	*is shortened to*	Bramhall.
Fratelli Treves, Editori		Treves.
Penguin Books		Penguin.
Dover Books		Dover.
Avenel Books		Avenel.
The Horn Book, Inc.	*is only shortened to*	Horn Book.

    Use care in shortening names; do not change the meaning of the phrase.

5. Unless two or more publishers have the same surname, forenames of well-known publishers may be omitted entirely.

    Thomas Y. Crowell Co., Inc.   *is shortened to*   Crowell.

    Franklin Watts, Inc.   *is shortened to*   Watts.

Alternately, forenames may be shortened to initials.

Frederick Warne & Co., Ltd.   *is shortened to*   F. Warne.

Now a word of caution. Certain elements of firm names may *not* be shortened.

1. Never omit multiple surnames. Transcribe what appears on the chief source of information with which you are working. These surname combinations may vary from one book to another for we are in a period of publishing house mergers.

   Harper & Brothers, Publishers   *is shortened to*   Harper.
   Harper & Row, Publishers, Inc. *is shortened to*   Harper & Row.
   Coward, McCann & Geoghegan, Inc.   *becomes*   Coward, McCann & Geoghegan.

2. Do not shorten a firm name when the entire name is descriptive of the type of material produced by the firm or of its viewpoint.

   Aviation Book Co.   *is not shortened.*
   Architectural Book Pub. Co. *is not shortened.*
   The Feminist Press   *becomes*   Feminist Press.
   Random House, Inc.   *becomes*   Random House.

   (The name is indicative of the founder's desire to choose titles for publication "at random.")

1.4D3. More phrases that may *not* be omitted from the name of a publisher, distributor, etc.

3. Words or phrases needed to indicate a function other than publishing performed by a body.

   Caxton Printers, Ltd.   *becomes*   Caxton Printers.
   Asia House Gallery   *remains the same.*
   American Camping Association   *remains the same.*
   American Library Association   *remains the same.*
   Boston Public Library   *remains the same.*

The word "press" needs careful consideration. Literally, it indicates a printing function, yet many publishers who do no printing include the word "press" as part of their corporate name. Furthermore, the word "press" sometimes is needed to differentiate between two different corporate bodies; for example:

University of Illinois Press   *remains the same.*
(The University of Illinois may also be a publisher.)

Yet "press" may be omitted from the names of such publishers as

The Viking Press, Inc.   *which becomes*   Viking.
Bradbury Press, Inc.   *which becomes*   Bradbury.

Note in figure 1-75 the inclusion of a phrase indicating that the corporate body named in the publication area has performed a function other than publishing. But do omit phrases or words indicating a publishing function.

```
United States.  President (1963-1969 : L.B. Johnson)
  No retreat from tomorrow : President Lyndon B.
Johnson's 1967 messages to the 90th Congress. --
Garden City, N.Y. : Distributed to the book trade
by Doubleday, [1968?]
  241 p. : ill. (some col.) ; 29 cm.
```

Figure 1-75. Phrase indicating distribution

```
  I. United States.  Congress (90th, 1st session :
1967).  II. Johnson, Lyndon B.  III. Title.
```

No Retreat From Tomorrow
President Lyndon B. Johnson's
1967 Messages to the
90th Congress

Title page

Distributed to the book trade by
Doubleday & Company, Inc. Garden City,
New York

1.4D4. This rule is substantially the same as 138D in *AACR Chapter 6* (1974). Under *AACR1* 140D and earlier cataloguing rules, if the publisher's name was used as the main entry heading, it could be entirely omitted from what was then called the imprint, leaving only the place of publication and the date in this area. *AACR Chapter 6* (1974) rule 138 (rules for publisher) made a number of changes, most of which have been carried over into *AACR2*. One innovation was that something always had to appear in the part of the area reserved for the name of the publisher. But 138D stipulated that if the publisher's name appeared in the title and statement of authorship area, the name of the publisher would appear in abbreviated form in the imprint.

This form will still be used under stipulations of *AACR2* 1.4D4. The intent of the rule is the same as that of the 1974 rule, but certain important clarifications have been made. The name of the publisher in the title and statement of responsibility area simply has to be "in recognizable form." It need not be identical to the form given in the publisher statement on the work. Thus, when a parent body serves as publisher for one of its subordinate units and the name of the subordinate unit, with or without the parent body's name, is given as part of the title and statement of responsibility area, the name of the parent body as publisher may be shortened in the publication area. (See figure 1-76.)

```
Library of Congress.  Processing Dept.
   The cataloging-in-source experiment : a report
to the Librarian of Congress / by the Director
of the Processing Department. -- Washington :
L.C., 1960.
   xxiv, 199 p. : ill. ; 27 cm.




   I. Library of Congress.  II. Title.
```

Figure 1-76. Publisher's name abbreviated

Title page

The
Cataloging-in-Source
Experiment
A Report to the Librarian of Congress
by the
Director of the Processing Department
Library of Congress
Washington : 1960

Initials may be used, as in figure 1-76, to abbreviate the publisher's name if the agency is familiarly known by an initialism. An alternative is to give a generic term standing for the agency. See figure 1-77.

American Philosophical Society.
  A catalogue of portraits and other works of art
in the possession of the American Philosophical
Society. -- Philadelphia : The Society, 1961.
  viii, 173 p., 1 leaf of plates : ill., ports.
(some col.) ; 24 cm. -- (Memoirs of the American
Philosophical Society Held at Philadelphia for
Promoting Useful Knowledge ; v. 54)

  I. Title. II. Series.

Figure 1-77. Publisher's name abbreviated

Memoirs of the
American Philosophical Society
Held at Philadelphia
for Promoting Useful Knowledge
Volume 54

Half title page

Title page

A Catalogue of
Portraits
and
Other Works of Art
in the Possession of the
American Philosophical Society
The American Philosophical Society
Independence Square • Philadelphia
1961

1.4D6. Something must always appear in the publisher, distributor, etc., element of the publication area. If the publisher's name is not known, use the abbreviation "s.n." (meaning "sine nomine," "without a name") in brackets following the place element and before the date. (See figure 1-78.)

1.4D7. It is not always possible to ascertain without research and correspondence whether a corporate body listed in one of the appropriate sources of information has, indeed, functioned as a publisher (i.e., an agency that edits, designs, distributes, sells, etc., books, music, etc.) rather than simply as a printer or manufacturer. Many publishers include the word "press" as a part of their name; some of these "presses" have no facilities for printing; others do. In case of doubt, it is better to record the name of an agency appearing in one of the prescribed sources for the publisher statement rather than use "s.n." in the statement, although in reality the agency may only have functioned as a printer. (See figure 1-79.)

1.4E. Optional addition. Statement of function of publisher, distributor, etc.
  The word(s) "distributor," "publisher," "producer," or "production company" in brackets may be added to the name of a publisher, distributor, etc., at the cataloguer's discretion, when this would clarify the publication statement. The Library of Congress will do this occasionally, when it seems useful.[7] Whenever possible, however, the cataloguer should transcribe information using the wording of the prescribed source. See for example figure 1-75.

[7] Ibid.

```
Reynolds, George.
  Commentary on the Book of Mormon / by George
Reynolds and Janne M. Sjodahl ; edited and arranged
by Philip C. Reynolds. -- 1st ed. -- Salt Lake
City : [s.n.], 1955-
      v. ; 24 cm.


  Contents: v. 1. The small plates of Nephi

  I. Sjodahl, Janne M.   II. Book of Mormon.
III. Title.
```

Figure 1-78. Publisher not known

Title page

Commentary on the Book of Mormon
By George Reynolds and Janne M. Sjodahl
Volume I—The Small Plates of Nephi
Edited and arranged by Philip C. Reynolds
Salt Lake City, Utah   1955

```
Stillwell, Margaret B.
  Rhythm and rhymes : the songs of a bookworm / by
Margaret B. Stillwell. -- Keepsake ed. -- Mount
Vernon, N.Y. : Press of A. Colish, 1977.
    xii, 97 p. : ill. ; 24 cm.


  Limited ed. of 50 copies.
  Library's copy signed by the author.
```

Figure 1-79. Printer or publisher?

```
  I. Title.
```

Title page

Rhythm and Rhymes
The Songs of a Bookworm
By Margaret B. Stillwell
Mount Vernon, New York
MDCCCLXXVII

Copyright © 1977, Margaret B. Stillwell
From The Press of A. Colish,
Mount Vernon, New York

Verso of title page

1.4F. Date of publication, distribution, etc.

The date, the last element in the publication area, is the year of publication, distribution, etc., of "the edition named in the edition area." This means the date of the first impression or printing of an edition. An impression consists of all of the copies of a publication run at one time from a set of photographic plates, type, etc. Frequently, if the publication sells well, the publisher will decide at a later date to run more copies from the same plates or forms of type. Customarily, a second run of a publication will be referred to as a "second impression" or "second printing." This information will usually be printed, possibly along with a date, on the title page or its verso. Generally speaking, succeeding impressions or printings are identical to the first; cataloguers treat them as copies of the first impression of that particular edition. As discussed above under 1.2B, these impression or printing statements are usually ignored in the edition area. They are likewise ignored in the publication area; see figure 1-80.

```
University of Chicago Press.
   A manual of style : containing typographical and
other rules for authors, printers, and publishers /
recommended by the University of Chicago Press ;
together with specimens of type. -- 11th ed. --
Chicago : The Press, 1949.
   x, 533 p. : ill. ; 22 cm.

   Includes index.
```

```
                 I. Title.
```

Figure 1-80. Printing or
impression omitted in
recording date

Title page

A Manual of Style
containing typographical and other
rules for authors, printers, and publishers
recommended by the University of
Chicago Press, together with
Specimens of Type
The University of Chicago Press • Chicago

Copyright 1906, 1910, 1911, 1914, 1917, 1919,
1920, 1925, 1927, 1937, and 1949 by
The University of Chicago
This present edition, the eleventh, was issued in 1949.
Fifth impression 1956

Verso of title page

1.4F2. Sometimes, as shown in figure 1-80, specific statements indicating a date of publication will be found in the item being catalogued. A statement such as "First Schocken edition 1968," which appears as part of the cataloguing data for figure 1-27, is also evidence of publication date for a particular edition.

In actual cataloguing practice, however, few items include a specific statement of publication date. If no such statement appears, the cataloguer simply records whatever information is available in the prescribed source for publication area information. For books at least, a date appearing in the imprint position on the title page may normally be accepted as the publication date. But sometimes the cataloguer knows that the date on the title page or other chief source of information is that of a reissue of a particular edition, i.e., not the actual date of publication. If this is the case, make a correction. (See figure 1-81.)

```
Darton, F.J. Harvey.
  Children's books in England : five centuries of
social life / by F.J. Harvey Darton. -- 2nd ed. --
Cambridge : University Press, 1958 (1970 printing)
  367 p., [8] leaves of plates : ill. ; 23 cm.

  Bibliography: p. 327-334.
  Includes index.
  ISBN 0-521-04774-9


  I. Title.
```

Figure 1-81. Printing
date on title page
included

Title page

Children's Books
in England
Five Centuries of Social Life
by
F. J. Harvey Darton
Cambridge
at the University Press
1970

ISBN 0 521 04774 9
Second Edition 1958
Reprinted   1960
                1966
                1970

Verso of title page

The date in the publication area is limited to the year of publication. Do not transcribe month, day, etc., even if this information is found on the chief source of information. (See figure 1-72.) The date is always transcribed in arabic numerals, even if it is found in the chief source in roman numerals. (See figure 1-60.)

1.4F5. Optional addition. The latest copyright date is not always the same as the actual date of publication. If it differs from the date of publication, it has under previous cataloguing codes been the practice to give both dates: e.g., 1970, c1969. The addition of copyright date to the date of publication is now optional. The Library of Congress will follow this practice.[8] Examples in this text also follow this option, figure 1-82 being one.

```
Pryce-Jones, David.
  Next generation : travels in Israel / David
Pryce-Jones. -- 1st ed. -- New York : Holt,
Rinehart and Winston, 1965, c1964.
  195 p. : map ; 22 cm.

  "Chapter 1 was originally published as 'Israel's
three cities' in Commentary, and a much abbreviated
article on 'The Yossele case' appeared in the New
statesman.  Passages from Chapter 10 were included
in an article for the Spectator"--T.p. verso.

  I. Title.
```

Figure 1-82. Copyright date in addition to publication date when the two differ

Next Generation
Travels in Israel
David Pryce-Jones
Holt, Rinehart and Winston
New York   Chicago   San Francisco

Title page

Copyright © 1964 by David Pryce-Jones
First published in the United States in 1965
Chapter 1 was originally published as "Israel's
Three Cities" in *Commentary,* and a much-abbre-
viated article on "The Yossele Case" appeared in
the *New Statesman.* Passages from Chapter 10
were included in an article for the *Spectator.*
First Edition

Verso of title page

[8] Ibid.

1.4F6. Many works do not specify a date of publication. Give latest copy-right date if this is the case. (See figure 1-83.)

```
A Statement of basic accounting postulates and
   principles / by a study group at the University
   of Illinois. -- ₍Urbana₎ : Center for Interna-
   tional Education and Research in Accounting,
   c1964.
   32 p. ; 23 cm.



   I. University of Illinois.  Center for Interna-
tional Education and Research in Accounting.
```

Figure 1-83. Copyright
date in publication area

Title page

A Statement of Basic
Accounting Postulates
and Principles

by a Study Group at the University of Illinois

Center for International Education and
Research in Accounting

1.4F7. The publication, distribution, etc., area must always include a date, even if it can only be a conjectural interpolation by the cataloguer. All dates taken from other than prescribed sources, whether derived from the item, reference sources, or the cataloguer's conjecture, must be bracketed. (See the various chapters in *AACR2* for specific kinds of library materials. In each chapter, rule 0B prescribes the sources from which data may be taken with-out bracketing.) If no date can be transcribed from any source, then the cataloguer must guess at the date. In such a case the cataloguer's interpola-tion is not only enclosed within half brackets but also displayed as one type of conjecture or another: ₍1971 or 1972₎; ₍1969?₎; ₍ca. 1960₎; ₍197–₎; etc. In the example shown in figure 1-84 the date was taken from the preface.

Most of the time the cataloguer cannot find a dated preface to use for the year of publication. In the example shown in figure 1-75, the title itself is evidence that the book cannot have been published before 1967. Since the book is not copyrighted, there is no copyright statement to refer to. The table of contents lists President Johnson's speeches with the dates of delivery, ranging between January 10 and May 25, 1967. It is possible, though not likely, that this handsomely illustrated book could have appeared toward the end of 1967. But the LC catalog card number is listed as 68-23394 on the verso of the title page. At that time, the first two digits of the LC number stood for the last two digits of the year in which the publisher applied for a preassigned number. It is rather likely that the book appeared in 1968. Therefore the date is recorded in the catalogue entry as [1968?].

```
United States.
  [Constitution]
  The Constitution of the United States of America :
with a summary of the actions by the States in
ratification of the provisions thereof / prepared
and distributed by the Virginia Commission on
Constitutional Government. -- [Richmond] : The
Commission, [1961]
  94 p. ; 22 cm. -- (Historic statements and papers
expounding the role of the States in their relation
to the Central Government ; 8)
  Cover title.

            (continued on next card)
```

```
United States.  [Constitution] [1961].  (card 2)

  Subtitle: To which is appended, for its
historical interest, the Constitution of the
Confederate States of America.


  I. Virginia Commission on Constitutional
Government.  II. Confederate States of America.
Constitution. 1961.  III. Series.
```

Figure 1-84. **Date not from a prescribed source**

Title page

The Constitution of the
United States of America
With a Summary of the Actions by the States
in Ratification of the Provisions Thereof
To which is Appended, for its Historical Interest,
The Constitution of the
Confederate States of America
Prepared and Distributed by the
Virginia Commission on Constitutional
Government

Few books furnish this much internal evidence about probable date of publication. Particularly when dealing with nineteenth-century reprint editions, the cataloguer may fail to find the slightest clue to the date. Under normal circumstances the cataloguer will not search beyond the item itself. But, as with the example shown in figure 1-85a, it is only sensible to do the minimum amount of research necessary to discover that Mayne Reid (1818–1883) was a nineteenth-century American writer of stories for boys and that *The young voyageurs* first appeared in 1853, which gives at least a minimum parameter for the date. Both Dutton and Routledge were well-established nineteenth-century publishers. Reid's novels were widely reprinted until the end of the nineteenth century, but lost popularity after that. Therefore, one can make a safe guess that this edition appeared in the nineteenth century, but without more research than the item warrants, one cannot say more.

```
Reid, Mayne, 1818-1883.
   The young voyageurs, or, The boy hunters in the
north / by Mayne Reid. -- London : G. Routledge ;
New York : Dutton [18--]
   viii, 471 p., [4] leaves of plates : ill. ; 20 cm.




   I. Title: The young voyageurs.  II. Title: The
boy hunters in the north.
```

Figure 1-85a.
Conjectural date

Title page

The Young Voyageurs
or the
Boy Hunters in the North
by Captain Mayne Reid
London
George Routledge and Sons, Limited
New York: E. P. Dutton and Co.

1.4F8. If a work appearing in more than one part does not appear to be complete, the cataloguer gives the earliest date of whatever parts of the item the library has, followed by a hyphen in the date part of the publication area. Figure 1-77 is an example of such a work. When the date is followed by a hyphen in this fashion, the catalogue record is known as an "open entry." When the item is finally completed (this may take a number of years), the cataloguer adds the latest date and closes the entry. See figure 1-44.

A word of caution: Obviously, the cataloguer will not "close" an entry unless he or she has evidence that the work is complete or that no more will be published. In addition, the cataloguer must be aware that not all bibliographical items are issued beginning with part 1. The date in the publication area is the earliest followed by the latest date of publication, whether or not the earliest date is the date of part 1.

1.4G. Place, name, and/or date of manufacture, printing, etc.

The information about manufacture will be given only when the name of the publisher is not known. See also *AACR2* 1.4D7 for guidance in this matter.

1.4G4. The cataloguer may optionally add the place, name, date of manufacture, printing, etc., in addition to the place, name, and date of publication if, in the opinion of the cataloguing agency, this information is considered important. One instance in which this optional rule might be followed would be the addition of a date of printing to the date of publication when significant changes have been made in the particular printing. The Library of Congress will follow this optional rule when it seems appropriate.[9]

1.5. PHYSICAL DESCRIPTION AREA

This area was previously called the collation area, and as such was covered by rule 141 in *AACR Chapter 6* (1974). Previous cataloguing codes have stipulated that this area should begin on a separate line, indented, immediately following the publication area. *AACR2* gives the cataloguer the alternative of continuing this practice or of separating the physical description area from the publication area by full stop - space - dash - space without paragraphing. If the latter practice is followed, the example shown in figure 1-85a would appear as shown in figure 1-85b.

```
Reid, Mayne, 1818-1883.
    The young voyageurs, or, The boy hunters in the
north / by Mayne Reid. -- London : G. Routledge ;
New York : Dutton [18--]. -- vii, 471 p., [4]
leaves of plates : ill. ; 20 cm.




    I. Title: The young voyageurs.   II. Title:
The boy hunters in the north.
```

Figure 1-85b. Alternate format for catalogue entry

Since the Library of Congress is likely to continue to indent the physical description and note areas, most American libraries will follow the indented format. Examples in this text follow Library of Congress practice.

The physical description area includes as applicable, four components:

1. The extent of the item, such as pagination, or number of physical parts
2. Other physical data such as color, presence and type of illustrations, etc.
3. Physical dimensions (size)
4. Accompanying materials.

The physical description area, because it attempts to describe the physical format of the item being catalogued, is unique for each type of library material. For this reason, specific rules have been set forth, following *AACR2* chapter 1, for the physical description area of each type of material. Examples and further discussion of the physical description area are to be found in succeeding chapters of this handbook.

1.6. SERIES AREA

This rule has its counterpart in rule 142 in *AACR Chapter 6* (1974). The series area is separated from size or accompanying materials in the physical description area by full stop - space - dash - space. The series statement is enclosed in parentheses.

As it appears in the work being catalogued, the series statement typically includes several different elements. Primary, of course, is the series title and the volume numbering, if any, of the series. Names of editors may also appear with the series title *in the work*. These are not included as part of the series statement *in the catalogue entry;* see figure 1-86.

1.6B. Title proper of the series

The series title is transcribed exactly as to order, wording, and spelling, following the same rules that govern transcription of the title of the work (1.1B). The series statement is capitalized following the rules for capitalizing a title main entry: that is, if the first word of the title is an article, the word following it is also capitalized. For a reminder of how a title main entry appears in the catalogue record and how it is capitalized if it begins with an article, see figure 1-53. (And for a reminder that titles beginning with an article are *not* capitalized in this fashion if main entry is under a person or corporate body, see, for instance, figure 1-38.) For an example of capitalization of a series title that begins with an article, see figure 1-56.

1.6B2. Sometimes the series title appears in more than one form in the publication. Previous cataloguing rules (for example, 142C in *AACR Chapter 6, 1974*) gave the cataloguer no guidance when this occurred; the cataloguer was told to use "the form that is used for the entry of the series in the catalog" (whatever that meant). The tendency was to choose the most complete form over an abbreviated form of series title when a choice was to be made. *AACR2* has now made a clear statement of the preferred source when series titles vary within the publication. If one of the variant forms appears in the chief source of information (the title page, for a book), use this form. In the example shown in figure 1-87 "The Modern library" appears as the series title on the title page. The half title page reads, "The Modern library of the world's best books." The cataloguer will choose the form found on the title page.

The title page for Schulz's *How Long, Great Pumpkin, How Long?*, shown in figure 1-24, lists the series as "Peanuts parade." Facing the title page is a page headed "Peanuts parade paperbacks." A third variant, "A Peanuts parade book," is to be found on the book cover. The cataloguer will select the title page version to use in the series area.

```
Gilman, Charlotte Perkins, 1860-1935.
  The living of Charlotte Perkins Gilman : an
autobiography / by Charlotte Perkins Gilman. --
Reprint ed. -- New York : Arno Press, 1972.
  xxxviii, 341 p., [7] leaves of plates : ports. ;
23 cm. -- (American women : images and realities)

  Originally published: New York : Appleton-
Century, 1935.



  I. Title.  II. Series.
```

Figure 1-86. Omit names of editors in series statement

| Facing title page | American Women Images and Realities Advisory Editors Annette K. Baxter Leon Stein | The Living of Charlotte Perkins Gilman An Autobiography by Charlotte Perkins Gilman Arno Press New York • 1972 | Title page |

1.6D1. Other title information of series. This rule is basically unchanged from 142A1 in *AACR Chapter 6* (1974). Include only "other title information" that helps identify the series. If other title information is included in the series statement, it is separated from the title proper by space - colon - space. See figure 1-86 for an example of a series statement that includes other title information.

```
Thomas, Aquinas, Saint, 1225-1274.
  Introduction to Saint Thomas Aquinas / edited
with an introduction, by Anton C. Pegis. -- New
York : Random House, c1948.
  xxx, 690 p. ; 19 cm. -- (The Modern library)

  Bibliography: p. 682-690.



  I. Pegis, Anton C.  II. Title.
```

Figure 1-87. Varying form of series title

Copyright, 1948, by Random House, Inc.
Random House is the publisher of
The Modern Library

Verso of title page

The Modern Library
of the world's best books

Half title page

Introduction to
Saint Thomas Aquinas
Edited, with an Introduction, by
Anton C. Pegis
President, Pontifical Institute of
Mediaeval Studies, Toronto
The Modern Library • New York

Title page

1.6E. Statements of responsibility relating to the series

A series is a group of "separate and successive publications on a given subject, having a collective series title and uniform format, and usually all issued by the same publisher."[10] If, as sometimes happens, all of the parts of a series are by the same author, a statement of responsibility will be included as part of the series area. Such a statement is necessary if it appears in conjunction with the title and is considered necessary for the identification of the series. Sometimes, as with a statement of responsibility for a work, the statement of responsibility is joined grammatically to the title proper. If this is the case, transcribe it as it appears. See figures 1-54 and 1-77 for examples.

In the example shown in figure 1-88, the name of the responsible body is part of the series title, although in this case the name has been abbreviated in the prescribed source to an initialism. This initialism is regarded as an integral part of the series title and is so transcribed.

[10] *Bookman's Glossary,* p. 138.

Sometimes the name of the entity responsible for the series has no grammatical connection with the series title, but appears in relatively close proximity to it. If in such a case the name is considered necessary for the identification of the title, the statement of responsibility will be given according to the general rules for transcription of the title and statement of responsibility area (see 1.1F).

```
Symposium on Laboratory Shear Testing of Soils
  (1963 : Ottawa)
  Laboratory shear testing of soils : a symposium /
sponsored by the National Research Council of
Canada and the American Society for Testing and
Materials, Ottawa, Canada, Sept. 9, 1963. --
Philadelphia : A.S.T.M., c1964.
  vii, 505 p. : ill. ; 24 cm. -- (ASTM special
technical publication ; no. 361)

  Includes bibliographies.


  I. National Research Council of Canada.  II.
American Society for Testing and Materials.  III.
Title.
```

Figure 1-88. Responsible body's name part of series

Title page

**Laboratory Shear Testing
of Soils
A symposium sponsored by the
National Research Council of Canada and the
American Society for Testing and Materials
Ottawa, Canada, Sept. 9, 1963
ASTM Special Technical Publication No. 361
Published by the
American Society for Testing and Materials**

The first of the two series in the example given in figure 1-89 includes a formal statement of responsibility. The second series also includes the name of the responsible body, but in this case the statement of responsibility is included as part of the title proper of the series.

1.6F. International Standard Serial Number

A series is closely related to a serial, which may be defined as "a publication issued in successive parts . . . and intended to be continued indefinitely. . . ."[11] Some series are of such a nature that they could be catalogued as

[11] Ibid.

a serial under the series title (see *AACR2* chapter 12 for further discussion and explanation). Some items that show a series statement also show an ISSN, a number often used to identify serials. If an item showing a series statement also shows an ISSN, this information will be recorded immediately after the series title and before the series number, if any. The rule differs from rule 142A1, *AACR Chapter 6* (1974), in that formerly the ISSN was recorded after any series number.

1.6G. Series numbering

If the series includes a number, the number is recorded in the series statement. It is separated from the series title by space - semicolon - space. The cataloguer is to transcribe the number as an arabic numeral no matter how it appears in the source (but see an important exception to this in Appendix C.1D, *AACR2*). Include whatever descriptive term (volume, part, etc.) appears with it, using abbreviations from *AACR2* Appendix B. (See figure 1-90.) If the series number is listed on the item without a descriptive term, do not make one up. (See for example figure 1-89.)

```
In quest of peace and security : selected documents
   on American foreign policy, 1941-1951. --
   ₁Washington₁ : For sale by the Supt. of Docs.,
   U.S.G.P.O., 1951.
   v, 119 p. ; 26 cm. -- (General foreign policy
series / Division of Publications, Office of Public
Affairs ; 53) (Department of State publication ;
4245)

   At head of title: Seal of the U.S. Department of
State.

   I. United States.  Dept. of State.  II. Series.
III. Series: Department of State publication.
```

Figure 1-89. Series includes statement of responsibility

Department of State Publication 4245
General Foreign Policy Series 53
Released October 1951
Division of Publications
Office of Public Affairs
For sale by the Superintendent of Documents
U.S. Government Printing Office

In Quest of
Peace and Security
Selected Documents on
American Foreign Policy
1941–1951

Title page

Verso of title page

Sorry! ₍game₎ : Parker Brothers slide pursuit
   game. -- Salem, Mass. : Parker Bros., c1972.
   1 game (board, cards, 16 playing pieces) ; in
box, 24 x 47 x 4 cm. -- (A Parker game ; no. 390)

   Ages 6 to adult, 2 to 4 players.

Figure 1-90. Series
numbering

   I. Parker Brothers.

1.6H. Subseries

Sometimes a major series may have a number of subordinate parts. If so, the title of the main series is given first, followed by its series numbering, if any. The main series is separated from the subseries by a full stop and two spaces. See figure 1-55 for an example.

1.6J. More than one series statement

This rule is basically the same as 142F in *AACR Chapter 6* (1974). If a work is part of more than one independent series, each of the separate series is enclosed in a separate set of parentheses. If it is possible to make such a distinction, give the more specific series first. Figure 1-89 is an example of such a work.

1.7. NOTE AREA

Information to be recorded in the first five areas of the catalogue entry is, for the most part, standardized in content and presentation. Notes amplify the formal description given in previous areas, providing information that cannot be included there. Some notes are regarded as indispensable; others are given at the discretion of the cataloguer, depending on the intrinsic importance of the work and the needs of a particular library's users.

Among the indispensable notes are those that give information needed to justify an added entry (a secondary entry such as entry for editor, translator, joint author, title, etc., not a subject entry).

One of the basic premises of cataloguing is that each added entry (not subject entry) must be justified by some statement in the catalogue entry. Such information can be included in the body of the entry only if it is found in a prominent position (see *AACR2* 0.8 for definition of "prominent"). If the information does not appear in the body of the entry (the first five areas: title and statement of responsibility area through physical description area), it must be given in the notes area. For example, it is customary to give an added entry to a corporate body that sponsors a conference, a publication, or some other type of intellectual or artistic activity, as long as this relationship is indicative of something more than financial responsibility. Such information can be included in the body of the entry only if it is found in one of the prescribed sources of information. In the example shown in figure 1-91 the sponsorship statement was found in the Publisher's foreword, a source that may not be used for the title and statement of responsibility area. Since the sponsorship statement was needed to justify an added entry, it is given as a note.

```
A Biographical directory of librarians in the
   United States and Canada : (formerly Who's who
   in library service). -- 5th ed. / Lee Ash,
   editor ; B.A. Uhlendorf, associate editor. --
   Chicago : American Library Association, 1970.
   xviii, 1250 p. ; 26 cm.

   Sponsored by: Council of National Library
Associations.


   I. Ash, Lee.   II. Uhlendorf, B. A.   III. Council
of National Library Associations.
```

Figure 1-91. Note needed to justify an added entry

(formerly Who's Who in Library Service)
A Biographical Directory of Librarians
in the United States and Canada
Fifth Edition
Lee Ash, Editor
B. A. Uhlendorf, Associate editor
American Library Association
Chicago 1970

Title page

1.7A1. Punctuation. As with the physical description area, the cataloguer has the option of either starting a new paragraph for each note, as in the example shown in figure 1-91, or simply continuing the entry without paragraphing, as shown in figure 1-85b.

Use of prescribed punctuation (space - colon - space; space - slash - space; space - semicolon - space) in the notes area is limited to actual cataloguing data that includes such punctuation. But space - dash - space (the punctuation prescribed for use between cataloguing areas) is not to be used in notes citing cataloguing data. If more than one area is included in a citation in a note, separate the two areas by a full stop and two spaces. The first note in figure 1-92 shows proper punctuation.

Except when citing cataloguing data that includes prescribed punctuation (as in figure 1-92), conventional punctuation, capitalization, and spacing rules are observed. Words found in *AACR2* Appendix B (Abbreviations) are abbreviated, except in quoted notes. Numbers are transcribed as arabic numerals, except when the number begins the note, in which case it is spelled out as a word. See note 3 in figure 1-11 for an example.

Statements in notes should be as concise and brief as is consistent with clarity. A quotation from the item itself or from another source may be given if it is concise. If a quotation is used, enclose it in quotation marks and cite the source, unless the information is found on the chief source of information. For such a quoted note, with its citation, see figure 1-82. For an example of a note using abbreviation, see figure 1-79.

1.7A4. A note that shows the relationship of the work being catalogued to another work is generally recorded as a formal note. Such a note is prefaced by a brief, standard explanatory word or phrase followed by a colon and the necessary information in standard cataloguing format (except for dash between areas). See figure 1-92.

```
Sheehy, Eugene P.
  Guide to reference books. -- 9th ed. / compiled
by Eugene P. Sheehy, with the assistance of Rita
G. Keckeissen and Eileen McIlvaine. -- Chicago :
American Library Association, 1976.
  xviii, 1015 p. ; 28 cm.

  Revision of: Guide to reference books / Constance
M. Winchell. 8th ed. 1967.
  Includes index.

  I. Winchell, Constance M.  Guide to reference
books.  II. Keckeissen, Rita G.  III. McIlvaine,
Eileen.  IV. Title.
```

Figure 1-92.
Punctuation of
a note citing
cataloguing data

Guide to Reference Books
Ninth Edition
Compiled by Eugene P. Sheehy
with the assistance of
Rita G. Keckeissen
and Eileen McIlvaine
American Library Association
Chicago 1976

Title page

1.7B. Kinds of notes and order in which they should be given

This rule gives guidance about various types of notes that may be included in the notes area. When more than one type of note is needed, give them in the order in which *AACR2* lists them.

1.7B1. Nature, scope, or form of item. If the nature, scope, or literary or artistic form of the item is not apparent from the information in the formal part of the catalogue entry, and if the cataloguer feels that such information would be useful, a note may be given. Figures 1-93 and 1-94 show typical notes dealing with nature, scope, and form.

```
Eliot, T.S. (Thomas Stearns)
   Four quartets / T.S. Eliot. -- New York :
Harcourt, Brace & World, c1943.
   39 p. ; 23 cm.


   Poems.
   Contents: Burnt Norton -- East Coker -- The
Dry Salvages -- Little Gidding.



   I. Title.
```

Figure 1-93. Literary form note

Title page

Four Quartets
T. S. Eliot
New York
Harcourt, Brace & World, Inc.

```
Quinnam, Barbara.
   Fables : from incunabula to modern motion
picture books : a selective bibliography / compiled
by Barbara Quinnam. -- Washington : General
Reference and Bibliography Division, Reference
Dept., Library of Congress, 1966.
   viii, 85 p. : ill.
   ; 24 cm.


   Annotated.



   I. Title.
```

Figure 1-94. Scope note

Fables
from Incunabula
to Modern Picture Books
A Selective Bibliography Compiled by
Barbara Quinnam

General Reference and Bibliography Division
Reference Department
The Library of Congress
Washington : 1966

Title page

1.7B2. Language of item. Give a note about the language if the information is not evident from the catalogue entry. (See figure 1-95.)

```
Baudelaire, Charles.
  ₍Les fleurs du mal.  English & French₎
  The flowers of evil and other poems of Charles
Baudelaire / translated by Francis Duke. --
₍Charlottesville₎ : University of Virginia Press,
1961.
  294 p.  ; 24 cm.

  Translation, with original French text, of: Les
fleurs du mal.
  Bibliography: p. 294.
  Errata slip tipped in.


  I. Duke, Francis.   II. Title: The flowers of evil.
```

Figure 1-95. Language note

The Flowers of Evil
and other poems
of
Charles Baudelaire
Translated
by Francis Duke
University of Virginia Press : 1961

Title page

1.7B3. Source of title proper. Give this note if the title proper is not taken from the chief source of description for the item. For a book, this means that if the item lacks a title page, the source used as a substitute will be specified (see figure 1-96). See also figures 1-11 and 1-84 for additional examples of items not catalogued from the prescribed chief source of description and thus in need of a note to explain the source of the data.

1.7B4. Variations in title. The title must be taken from the chief source of information; in a book, for instance, this is the title page. A variant title will sometimes appear elsewhere in the item, on the spine or cover of the book, for example. Since library users are likely to think of the item by its variant title, a note should be made of the variant, if it is different enough from the formal title that it would file in a different place in the library catalogue. In the example shown in figure 1-74 the title *The Tale Is Told,* a much more memorable and distinctive title than the title page title, is both on the spine and the cover of the book. A note is made, and an added entry for the variant title will be added to the catalogue record.

```
Tucson (Ariz.).  Mayor.
   A city in action, 1951 to 1955 : four years of
progress / City of Tucson, Office of the Mayor. --
[Tucson] : Office of the Mayor, [1955]
   7 leaves ; 28 cm.


   Caption title.
   Text signed: "Fred Emery, Mayor, April 29, 1955."



   I. Emery, Fred.  II. Title.
```

Figure 1-96. Source of title proper

Caption title

City of Tucson
Office of the Mayor
A City in Action—1951 to 1955
Four Years of Progress

An original title is also given as a note if it cannot be transcribed according to 1.1D3 as part of the title and statement of responsibility area. (See figure 1-19.) See *AACR2* 1.1D3 also for the rare instance in which an original title of a translated work will appear as part of the title proper and thus *not* appear in the notes area. Almost always, if the cataloguer can discover the original title of a translated work, a note is given. See figure 1-95 for an example of a "translation of" note.

1.7B5. Parallel titles and other title information. *AACR2* 1.1D4 directs the cataloguer to record parallel titles in a note if they are found outside the chief source of information; likewise, 1.1E3 indicates that lengthy other title information pertaining to the bibliographic history of the work may more appropriately be included in the notes area. See figures 1-23 and 1-74 for examples.

1.7B6. Statements of responsibility. If an added entry is to be made for persons or bodies having responsibility for the item being catalogued and if this information cannot, according to rules for the title and statement of responsibility area, be included in that area, a note will be made giving the necessary information. See for examples, figures 1-89 and 1-91.

In the example shown in figure 1-97 information about the author of the music is found in the preface, which is not prominent. The information would not be transcribed in the title and statement of responsibility area. Since the statement is concise, it is quoted.

1.7B7. Edition and history. These notes serve to show bibliographical relationship of one item to another when it is not evident from the formal part of the catalogue entry. Such notes are of various types. For instance, when a revision is entered under a different author, or when a revision has a changed title, give sufficient information about the earlier edition so that it may be identified. (See figure 1-92.)

A literary work that is continued by another work is given a sequel note (see figure 1-98). A literary work that continues another story is given a slightly different note, an example of which is shown in figure 1-99.

```
Stein, Gertrude.
   Four saints in three acts : an opera to be sung /
Gertrude Stein ; introduction by Carl Van Vechten.
-- New York : Random House, 1934.
   57 p. ; 22 cm.


   "Orchestrated by Virgil Thomson"--Pref.
Without music.



   I. Thomson, Virgil.  Four saints in three acts.
II. Title.
```

Figure 1-97. Statement of responsibility note

Title page

Gertrude Stein
Four Saints in Three Acts
An Opera to be Sung
Introduction by Carl Van Vechten
New York • Random House
1934

```
Johnston, Norma.
   Of time and of seasons / Norma Johnston. -- 1st
ed. -- New York : Atheneum, 1975.
   282 p. ; 24 cm.


   Sequel: A striving after wind.
   Summary: The newly begun Civil War is only one
more complication in the lives of Bridget's family
in which everyone seems talented--except Bridget.
   ISBN 0-689-30479-X



   I. Title.
```

Figure 1-98. Sequel note

Title page

Of Time and of Seasons
Norma Johnston
Atheneum   1975   New York

```
Johnston, Norma.
  A striving after wind / Norma Johnston. -- 1st
ed. -- New York : Atheneum, 1976.
  250 p. ; 24 cm.


  Sequel to: Of time and of seasons.
  Summary: As Bridget continues her search for her
own identity in her talented family, she learns to
deal with an officious woman and her daughter, a
near-romance with an aging actor, and her confused
feelings about a male friend.
  ISBN 0-689-30540-0


  I. Title.
```

Figure 1-99. Sequel note

Title page

A Striving After Wind
Norma Johnston
Atheneum • 1976 • New York

For works other than works of the imagination, use "continues" or "continued by" as appropriate. This wording is a much used note with serials particularly. See discussion of notes in *AACR2* chapter 12 for examples.

1.7B8. Material specific details. This note is appropriate only with cartographic or serial materials. See *AACR2* chapters 3 and 12.

1.7B9. Publication, distribution, etc. Important information regarding publication, etc., that is not included in the publication, etc., area may be given as a note. (See figure 1-100.) Caution: Compare this note with 1.7B7, which covers previous publication, revisions, etc.

```
Milne, A.A.
  Winnie-the-Pooh / A.A. Milne ; with decorations
by Ernest H. Shepard. -- New York : Dutton, c1926.
  x, 161 p. : ill. ; 21 cm.


  Published simultaneously in Great Britain by
Methuen.




  I. Shepard, Ernest H.  II. Title.
```

Figure 1-100. Publication note

A. A. Milne
Winnie-the-Pooh
with decorations by
Ernest H. Shepard
E. P. Dutton & Co., Inc.
Title page Publishers : New York

1.7B10. Physical description. Important information not brought out in the title and statement of responsibility area that is of a type which, according to rule, cannot be included in the physical description area should be given in a note. A note may also be given to amplify information that is transcribed in any of the preceding areas. Give a note, for instance, to record the presence of a map on the endpapers of a book, since such a map could be removed from a copy of the book when it is rebound. If the map is duplicated on front and back endpapers, as in the example shown in figure 1-101, say "Map on lining papers." If the maps are different, say "Maps on lining papers."

```
Fairchild, David.
  Garden islands of the great East : collecting
seeds from the Philippines and Netherlands India
in the junk "Chêng Ho" / by David Fairchild. --
New York : Scribner, 1943.
   xiv, 239 p. : ill., map ; 24 cm.


Map on lining papers.
```

Figure 1-101. Note that amplifies physical description

Garden Islands of the Great East
Collecting Seeds from the Philippines
and Netherlands India in the Junk "Chêng Ho"
by
David Fairchild
New York
Charles Scribner's Sons
1943

I. Title.

Title page

A note is often appropriate to amplify the physical description area for a nonbook item. See the following chapters and the example shown in figure 1-102.

1.7B11. Accompanying materials and supplements. Material accompanying the work that cannot be described with a simple word or phrase should be listed in a note rather than included at the end of the physical description area (1.5E). The second note in figure 1-103 is of this type. For other methods of recording supplements and accompanying materials, see *AACR2* 1.5E, 1.9, and 13.6.

1.7B12. Series. A series statement of such complexity that it requires explanation may be given as a note rather than in the series area. This will be done only rarely. A note about the series may be given when cataloguing a reprint if the original work was part of a series.

Faces and feelings ₍slide₎ / author, George A.
   Lane ; produced by Society for Visual Education,
   Inc., in cooperation with Loyola University Press.
   -- Chicago : Singer Education & Training Products,
   c1971.
   20 slides : col. + 1 teacher's guide. -- Slodeas
₍Slideas₎ for creative expression ; SD-10)

   Slides in flat plastic holder (28 x 23 cm.)
punched for insertion in 3 ring binder.
   "Intended to evoke ideas and provide a starting
point for student discussions and a variety of
creative expressions."
   I. Lane, George A.   II. Society for Visual
Education.   III. Series: Slideas for creative expression ; SD-10.

Figure 1-102.
Note that
amplifies physical
description

Teachers guide

Faces and Feelings
Slodeas for creative expression
Author: George A. Lane, S.J., Associate Director,
Loyola University Press
Singer Education & Training Products
Produced by Society for Visual Education, Inc.
in cooperation with Loyola University Press
Chicago, Ill. 60657

1.7B13. Dissertations. Use the word "thesis" to designate all types of
academic theses, dissertations, etc. Qualify this term with the degree (M.A.
or Ph.D.), as shown in figure 1-104. New to *AACR2* is the stipulation that
if these qualifications do not apply, the cataloguer is to add "Thesis (doctoral)" or "Thesis (master's)," as appropriate. This designation will most
commonly be used when cataloguing European dissertations. A somewhat
different note is used for a thesis revised for publication (see figure 1-105).

1.7B14. Audience. Officially, at least, previous cataloguing rules allowed
no indication of the intellectual level of an item except for the use of the
dash-subdivision (—*Juvenile works*), which might appear after subject headings for material below the level of high school. Now, if the information
is stated in the item, a note about the intended audience may be given. In
the example shown in figure 1-106 information regarding the earlier edition
and the intended audience was taken from the foreword.

1.7B15. References to published descriptions. These notes are used ordinarily in connection with the cataloguing of early printed books. A reference

to one of the detailed descriptions in one of the standard bibliographies of such materials makes exact identification for these often complex bibliographical entities possible in a manner not possible for the cataloguer following *AACR2*. (See *AACR2* 2.12–2.18.)

```
Jones, Patricia.
  Rumpelstiltskin : an adaptation from Grimms'
Fairy tales / by Patricia Jones ; pictures by Jan
B. Balet. -- ₍Chicago₎ : Container Corp. of
America, c1954.
  31 p. : col. ill. ; 25 cm. -- (Slottie library
books)

  "A Concora book."
Cardboard punch-out figures tipped into back
cover.

  I. Grimm, Jakob. Rumpelstiltskin. II. Title.
```

Figure 1-103.
Accompanying material

An Adaptation from Grimms' Fairy Tales
by Patricia Jones
R u m p e l s t i l t s k i n
Pictures by Jan B. Balet
A Concora Book
Published by Container Corporation of America

Title page

```
Maxwell, Margaret F.
  Anatomy of a book collector : William L. Clements
and the Clements Library / by Margaret Nadine
Finlayson Maxwell. -- 1971.
  viii, 420 leaves, ₍1₎ leaf of plates : col. ill.,
port. ; 28 cm.

  Typescript (photocopy).
  Published as: Shaping a library : William L.
Clements as collector. Amsterdam : N. Israel, 1973.
  Abstract (3 leaves) bound with copy.
  Thesis (Ph.D.)--University of Michigan, 1971.
  Bibliography: leaves 412-419.

  I. Title.
```

Figure 1-104. Thesis note

Title page

Anatomy of a Book Collector: William L. Clements
and the Clements Library
by
Margaret Nadine Finlayson Maxwell
A dissertation submitted in partial fulfillment
of the requirements for the degree of
Doctor of Philosophy
(Library Science)
in The University of Michigan
1971

Doctoral Committee:
    Professor Russell E. Bidlack, Chairman
    Professor Wallace J. Bonk
    Professor Edmon Low
    Professor Howard H. Peckham

Maxwell, Margaret F.
   Shaping a library : William L. Clements as
collector / by Margaret Maxwell. -- Amsterdam :
N. Israel, 1973.
   364 p., [17] p. of plates : ill., ports. ; 21 cm.

   Originally presented as the author's thesis
(Ph.D.--University of Michigan) under the title:
Anatomy of a book collector.
   Bibliography: p. 348-356.
   Includes index.
   ISBN 90-6072-631-6

   I. Title.

Figure 1-105. Thesis note

Title page

Shaping a Library:
William L. Clements as Collector
by
Margaret Maxwell
Nico Israel/Amsterdam
1973

1.7B17. Summary. A brief, one-sentence summary may be included if it amplifies and clarifies the catalogue record. Summaries are particularly useful for entries for nonbook materials as they are generally not easy to browse through. (See for examples figures 1-30 and 1-66.) Summaries are also frequently included as part of the cataloguing data for stories for adolescents and children. For examples see figures 1-98 and 1-99.

1.7B18. Contents. Give a list of the titles of individual works contained in an item. Add to the titles statements of responsibility not included in the title and statement of responsibility area. For examples of contents note, see figures 1-43, 1-46, 1-54 and 1-73.

The Record of mankind / A. Wesley Roehm ... ₎et
    al.₎ . -- Boston : Heath, c1956.
    vi, 754 p., ₎2₎ leaves of plates : ill., maps
(some col.), ports. ; 24 cm.

    Revision of: World civilization / by Hutton
Webster and Edgar Bruce Wesley.
    High school text.
    Includes bibliographies and index.

Figure 1-106. Audience note

    I. Roehm, A. Wesley.   II. Webster, Hutton.
World civilization.

The Record of Mankind
A. Wesley Roehm • Morris R. Buske
        Hutton Webster
        Edgar B. Wesley   Title page
D. C. Heath and Company • Boston

1.7B19. Numbers borne by the item. Numbers such as the Superintendent of Documents number on United States Government publications serve as important means of identifying the item; in some libraries, government documents are arranged by SUDOC number. Always list this number if it is available. Other items, such as technical reports, also show important numbers that must be transcribed. Other miscellaneous numbers sometimes included by commercial publishers are of no particular significance and can safely be ignored.

1.7B20. Copy being described and library's holdings. A note may record matters unique to the library's copy. The fact that the library's copy is autographed is usually noted. (See figures 1-54 and 1-79.) The presence of a tipped-in errata slip should also be noted, as such a slip may not be in all copies of the book. (See figure 1-95.)

1.7B21. "With" notes. The presence of an item that is physically inseparable from the item being described is noted unless this has been brought out in the formal description for the work. This statement is made whether (as with books) the items were separately published and later bound together or they were originally issued together as a unit. A note of this type is used when the description is of a separately titled part of an item lacking a collective title.

1.8. STANDARD NUMBER AND TERMS OF AVAILABILITY AREA

The last area of the catalogue entry is standard number and terms of availability. Publishers began using International Standard Book Numbers (ISBN) about 1968; International Standard Serials Numbers (ISSN) followed a year or so later. Therefore, materials that appeared before 1968 will not have such numbers. Because publishers include these numbers on a voluntary basis, not all materials with publication dates after 1968 will have them. If a book has a standard number, in most instances the number will be found on the verso of the title page. Record this number as the last item, following the notes area. (See figure 1-105.)

1.8D. Optional addition. Terms of availability

Price may be added following the standard number if it seems useful. The Library of Congress will generally add price for current items.[12] Examples in this text will not follow this option.

1.9. SUPPLEMENTARY ITEMS

In contrast to the confusing and sometimes contradictory provisions of *AACR1*, *AACR2* rules are clear for the description of such materials as separately issued continuations, supplements, indexes, or other materials so closely related to another work as to be more or less dependent on it. In no case will a "dash" entry (*AACR Chapter 6*, 1974, rule 155) be used. By *AACR2* rules, if in the cataloguer's judgment the supplementary material is important in its own right, the item may be catalogued as a separate work (see 21.28). Supplementary material of lesser importance may be catalogued as part of the entry for the larger work. Two methods of describing accompanying material have been discussed and illustrated already.

1. The supplementary item may be added as accompanying material at the end of the physical description area. See *AACR2* 1.5E and figure 1-102.
2. If supplementary material is of minor importance but of such nature that it cannot be listed succinctly in the physical description area, it may be added as a note. See *AACR2* 1.7B11 and figure 1-103.

A third method of describing supplementary items dependently is by using multilevel description (13.6). By this method one or more parts of a multipart work that has been catalogued as a unit may be brought out, i.e., "analyzed." This technique was developed originally for national bibliographies, for which some kind of separate entry must be prepared for each part of an ongoing work. It is anticipated that most libraries will prefer alternatives 1 or 2 for the description of dependent material.

---

[12] "AACR2 options."

1.10. ITEMS MADE UP OF SEVERAL TYPES OF MATERIAL

Many library items are made up of several parts: e.g., an encyclopedia in twenty-four volumes, a set of filmstrips, or four sound recordings that form a unit. For cataloguing, the items are described as a unit; description of the parts is basically a simple enumeration of their physical extent.

But in many instances library items clearly designed to function as a unit are made up of components that belong to different types of material: e.g., a book with an accompanying sound recording, a plastic model of a cuneiform tablet with a printed pamphlet of explanation.

1.10B. If such a multimedia item has one predominant part, the cataloguer will make the catalogue record from this part. Subsidiary parts will be added as accompanying materials, either at the end of the physical description area or as a note (1.5E and 1.7B11). (See figure 1-107; see also figures 1-12 and 1-13 for other examples of multimedia items with one clearly dominant part.)

```
Learning "look-it-up" skills with an encyclopedia
  [transparency] / prepared by the Department of
Educational Services in cooperation with Audio-
Visual Services, Field Enterprises Educational
Corporation. -- Chicago : The Corporation, c1966.
8 transparencies : col. ; 26 x 26 cm.

"Directions for teachers" included on folder.
```

Figure 1-107. Multimedia item with one predominant component

```
   I. Field Enterprises Educational Corporation.
Dept. of Educational Services.   II. Field Enter-
prises Educational Corporation.   Audio-Visual
Services.
```

1.10C. Sometimes a package of different kinds of media, all of the components of which are related and intended to be used together, has no predominant component. Such a package is called a "kit," using North American terminology, or "multimedia," by British GMD. A kit is commonly issued in a container with a title on it that will serve as a collective title for the entire item. When this is the case, catalogue the item under provisions of 1.1C4. Only very rarely does a package of components designed to be used together lack a collective title. But if this should be the case, follow the example of 1.10C1. Physical description for a kit may be done in one of two ways; see the examples shown in figures 1-108a and 1-108b (the latter a more detailed physical description of the different components).

```
How steel is made [kit] / prepared by United States
   Steel. -- New ed. -- New York : Distributed by
   Public Relations Dept., U.S. Steel, c1962.
   1 filmstrip, 5 samples, teacher's guide and
filmstrip text, in container ; 26 x 22 x 6 cm.

   Samples (iron ore, coke, limestone, pig iron,
and steel rod) in plastic bottles.




   I. United States Steel.
```

Figure 108a. Physical description of a kit

```
How steel is made [kit] / prepared by United States
   Steel. -- New ed. -- New York : Distributed by
   Public Relations Dept., U.S. Steel, c1962.
   1 filmstrip (55 fr.) : col. ; 35 mm.
   5 samples : irone ore, coke, limestone, pig
iron, steel rod ; in bottles, 8 cm. high.
   Teacher's guide and filmstrip text (61 p. :
ill. ; 22 cm.)




   I. United States Steel.
```

Figure 108b. Physical description of a kit (alternate)

1.11. FACSIMILES, PHOTOCOPIES, AND OTHER REPRODUCTIONS

This rule is an enlargement and clarification of 136D in *AACR Chapter 6* (1974). It is important that cataloguers understand this rule. Most libraries own many reprint editions of books, and libraries will increasingly acquire them as reprint publishers and reprint editions proliferate.

Basically, the rule stipulates that the catalogue entry must describe the reprint. Any information pertaining to the original edition, even if it appears in the chief source of information, will be omitted from the body of the entry. Do not indicate such omission by ellipses. All necessary information about the original edition will be given in a single note in the notes area.

Sometimes the original title page is reproduced for the reprint edition, with the reprint publisher's imprint added. Such is the case with the example shown in figure 1-109. Note that the data pertinent to the *reprint publisher* has been transcribed in the publication area; information about the original publisher is given in a formalized note. For form of note, see 1.7A3.

Some reprints include a separate title page for the reprint edition. Omit any information about the facsimile given in this source; such information will appear in a formal note as stipulated in 1.7A3. In figure 1-110, note omission of information about the original work in the transcription of the title page and the inclusion of this information in the first note.

```
Haebler, Konrad.
  The study of incunabula / by Konrad Haebler ;
translated from the German by Lucy Eugenia Osborne ;
with a foreword by Alfred W. Pollard. -- New
York : Kraus Reprint, 1967.
  xvi, 241 p. ; 23 cm.

  Reprint of: New York : Grolier Club, 1933.
  Includes index.



  I. Title.
```

Figure 1-109. Reprint

The Study of Incunabula
by Konrad Haebler
Translated from the German
by Lucy Eugenia Osborne
With a Foreword
by Alfred W. Pollard
New York
The Grolier Club
1933
Kraus Reprint Corporation
New York
1967

Title page

Caution: Give information in the note that corresponds to data found in the original work in the format appropriate to the original work. The work catalogued in figure 1-110 is a facsimile of an early printed monograph (book published before 1821). Cataloguing data for the original would be transcribed according to 2.12–2.18. Publication area data as given in figure 1-110 follows 2.16F.

1.11B. The example shown in figure 1-111 has a title different from the original title. Both the reprint title and the original title, as well as more data about the original, are found on the reprint title page. The catalogue record represents the reprint. All information on the title page about the original, except the original title, is omitted from the body of the entry but is given in a note (described in 1.7A3). Observe the format of the note. *AACR2* 1.7A3 stipulates that prescribed punctuation should be used in notes citing cataloguing data, except that the dash is not to be used between areas.

```
Fielding, Sarah.
   The governess, or, Little female academy /
Sarah Fielding ; with an introduction and biblio-
graphy by Jill E. Grey. -- London : Oxford Univer-
sity Press, 1968.
   vii, 375 p. : ill. ; 20 cm. -- (The Juvenile
library)

   Reprint of: London : Printed for the author and
sold by A. Millar, 1749.
   Bibliography: p. 349-369.
   Includes index.

   I. Title: The governess.   II. Title: Little
female academy.
```

Figure 1-110. Reprint

Sarah Fielding
The Governess
or, Little Female Academy
A facsimile reproduction of the first edition of 1749,
with an introduction and bibliography by
Jill E. Grey
London
Oxford University Press
1968

Title page

Verso of reprint
title page

The Juvenile Library
General Editor
Brian W. Alderson

Title page

The Governess;
or, Little Female Academy.
being
The History of Mrs. Teachum,
and Her Nine Girls.
with
Their Nine Days Amusement.
calculated
For the Entertainment and Instruction of
Young Ladies in Their Education.
By the Author of David Simple.
London:
Printed for the Author;
and Sold by A. Millar, M.DCC.XLIX

```
Moore, Clement C.
   The night before Christmas : (A visit from St.
Nicholas) / Clement C. Moore ; with a life of
Moore by Arthur N. Hosking. -- New York : Dover,
1971.
   [16], 36 p. : ill., ports. ; 16 cm. -- (Dover
books for children)

   Reprint of: New York : H.M. Onderdonk, 1848.
   "Bibliography of the works of Clement Clarke
Moore": p. 34-36.
   ISBN 0-486-22797-9 (pbk)

   I. Hosking, Arthur N.   II. Title.
```

Figure 1-111. Reprint

Facsimile title page

**The Night Before Christmas
(A Visit from St. Nicholas)
Clement C. Moore
Facsimile of the Original 1848 Edition
With a Life of Moore by
Arthur N. Hosking
Dover Publications, Inc.
New York**

Facsimile title page

A Visit from St. Nicholas.
by Clement C. Moore, LL.D.
With Original Cuts,
designed and engraved by Boyd.
New-York:
Henry M. Onderdonk,
1848.

2
Books, Pamphlets, and Printed Sheets

A book, by definition, is a printed "non-periodical literary publication containing forty-nine or more pages, not counting covers."[1] A pamphlet has less than forty-nine pages; a printed sheet (otherwise called a broadside or broadsheet) is "a sheet of paper printed on one side only, usually intended to be posted, publicly distributed or sold."[2] Librarians call the type of material included in *AACR2* chapter 2 monographic. As opposed to a serial, a monograph is a printed work which either is complete as it is issued, or one which has a projected termination point, e.g., an encyclopedia issued in parts.

For the description of a printed work issued in microform reproduction, see *AACR2* chapter 11. For printed material issued serially, see *AACR2* chapter 12 in addition to rules in *AACR2* chapter 2.

The cataloguing of books will be governed by all appropriate rules in *AACR2* chapter 1, General Rules for Description. Additional special rules that apply only to books, pamphlets, and printed sheets, and not to other types of library materials, are contained in *AACR2* chapter 2.

2.0B. Sources of information

These rules are basically the same as those given in *AACR Chapter 6* (1974) rule 132. The title page is the chief source of information. If a book has no title page, the cover, half title page, caption, colophon, or running title may be used as a substitute; preference should be given to the source with the most complete information. Make a note if you have used a substitute for a title page. See figure 1-96.

If title page information is spread over two facing pages without repetition, it is transcribed as if it were found on one page. See figure 1-51.

2.0H. Items with several title pages

Sometimes a book has more than one title page. Follow guidelines under

[1] *Bookman's Glossary*, 5th ed. (New York: Bowker, 1975), p. 21.
[2] *Ibid.*, p. 28.

AACR2 1.0H. Prefer a title page giving a later publication date or, as with the example shown in figure 2-1, prefer the title page with the publication date rather than an engraved title page without a publication date (1.0H2).

```
The Gift : a Christmas and New Year's present
   for 1840 / edited by Miss Leslie. -- Philadel-
   phia : Carey & Hart, 1839.
   viii, p. 18-328, [9] leaves of plates : ill. ;
19 cm.
```

Figure 2-1. More than one title page

```
Added title page, engraved.
"Fourth volume of the Gift"--Advertisement.
```

```
I. Leslie, Miss.
```

Title page

The Gift:
A Christmas and New Year's
Present for 1840.
Edited by Miss Leslie.
Philadelphia:
Carey & Hart.

A bilingual dictionary often has separate facing title pages in two languages. Following guidelines under 1.0H4c, choose the title page in order of languages listed in the rule. If one of the title pages is in English, use that title page. See figure 2-2.

```
Larousse's French-English, English-French dic-
   tionary / by Marguerite-Marie Dubois, Denis J.
   Keen, Barbara Shuey, with the assistance of
   Jean-Claude Corbeil, Lester G. Crocker. -- Rev.
   and enl. -- New York : Pocket Books, 1971.
   565 p. ; 16 cm.
```

Figure 2-2. More than one title page

```
Added t.p. in French.
ISBN 671-77401-8
```

```
   I. Dubois, Marguerite-Marie.   II. Keen, Denis J.
III. Shuey, Barbara.
```

Dictionnaire
Français-Anglais Anglais-Français
Larousse
par
Marguerite-Marie Dubois
Denis J. Keen   Barbara Shuey
avec la collaboration de
Jean-Claude Corbeil   Lester G. Crocker
Édition revue et augmentée
Published by Pocket Books New York

Larousse's
French-English English-French
Dictionary
by
Marguerite-Marie Dubois
Denis J. Keen   Barbara Shuey
with the assistance of
Jean-Claude Corbeil   Lester G. Crocker
Revised and enlarged
Published by Pocket Books New York

Facing title page

Title page

Revised and enlarged
Pocket Book edition published May, 1971
12th printing . . . . December, 1973
Revised and enlarged edition copyright, ©, 1971, by
Librairie Larousse, Paris, France.

Verso of title page

2.1. TITLE AND STATEMENT OF RESPONSIBILITY AREA

See general discussions in this text under 1.1B and 1.1F1. The prescribed source of information for transcription of the title and statement of responsibility area is the title page, or if the book lacks a title page, the title page substitute (cf. 2.0B1). In addition, statements of responsibility appearing "prominently" (i.e. in the preliminaries and the colophon as well as the title page, all prescribed sources for the edition area) may be recorded as part of the statement of responsibility.

2.1B. Title proper

Refer to *AACR2* 1.1B and to supporting examples and discussion in this text for general comments and rules covering the recording of the title proper.

The example shown in figure 2-3a is a straightforward monograph that in itself offers no problems to the cataloguer.

The publisher has also issued a "Teacher's resource book" to supplement the main volume. Refer to *AACR2* 1.5E1 and 1.7B11 and to examples and discussion in this text for two ways of handling supplementary material; a supplement may be added at the end of the physical description area (1.5E1) or it may be mentioned in a note (1.7B11). If, however, the supplement has a different title and/or different author from the main volume, 21.28B stipulates that it should be given a separate catalogue entry. This is a change from *AACR1* 19A, which called for entry of many such works under the same author and title as the work to which they were related, usually as a "dashed-on" entry on the same catalogue card.

Current, Richard N.
  United States history / Richard N. Current,
Alexander DeConde, Harris L. Dante. -- Glenview,
Ill. : Scott, Foresman, c1967.
  832 p. : ill. (some col.), col. maps, ports. ;
24 cm.

  Bibliography: p. 777-781.

  I. DeConde, Alexander.   II. Dante, Harris L.
III. Title.

Figure 2-3a.
Monograph

Title page

United States History
Richard N. Current
Alexander DeConde
Harris L. Dante
Scott, Foresman and Company

If the supplement title is entirely different from that of the main work, the description of the supplement presents no problem. But if the title proper of the supplement consists of the title of the main volume and title of the supplement, or if the two titles are grammatically independent of each other, the cataloguer follows a special procedure. Record the title and statement of responsibility of the main volume first. Close this part of the entry with a full stop. Do not separate title and statement of responsibility of the main volume with space - slash - space, since this is not a catalogue entry for the main volume. The supplement's title is transcribed following main volume information.

The cataloguer must disregard the order in which the foregoing elements are presented in the chief source of information (the title page of the supplement). The order must be: Main volume information. Supplement title.

All of this information constitutes the title proper of the supplement. Note figure 2-3b. The title proper consists of everything before the space - slash - space.

2.1B2. In almost all cases, transcribe the title page information as it appears. But if the title page for a work that contains several separate parts includes a collective title as well as the titles of the individual works, transcribe only the collective title in the title–statement of responsibility area. Do not use ellipses to indicate omission. Give the titles of the individual works in a contents note; see figure 2-4. This rule is identical to rule 134C5, *AACR Chapter 6* (1974).

2.1C. Optional addition. General material designation
See discussion of general material designation under 1.1C. If a library chooses to add GMD to materials covered by chapter 2, GMD "text" will be added

immediately after the title proper. As previously mentioned, examples in this text will follow traditional North American library practice of displaying GMD for nonbook materials but not for materials covered by rules in chapter 2.

```
Dante, Harris L.
  United States history [by] Richard N. Current,
Alexander DeConde, Harris L. Dante.  Teacher's
resource book / Harris L. Dante, Robert F. Harris.
-- Glenview, Ill. : Scott, Foresman, c1967.
  159 p. ; 23 cm.



  I. Harris, Robert F.  II. Current, Richard N.
United States history.  III. Title.
```

Figure 2-3b. Title proper—supplement

Title page

United States History
Richard N. Current
Alexander DeConde
Harris L. Dante
Teacher's Resource Book
Harris L. Dante
Robert F. Harris
Scott, Foresman and Company

2.1D. Parallel titles
See 1.1D for general instructions, discussion, and examples.

2.1E. Other title information
See 1.1E for discussion and examples.

2.1F. Statements of responsibility
See 1.1F for general instructions, discussion, and examples.

As discussed in this text under 1.1F7, the name of an author or subsidiary author is to be transcribed just as it appears on the title page or its substitute, except that titles of address, honor, and distinction will be omitted in most instances (see 1.1F7). Figure 2-5 is an interesting example of the inclusion of a title of address and some other information. The title "Mrs." is retained because its omission would leave only the author's surname. "Ennis Graham" is a pseudonym occasionally used by the author. Since it appears with the author's name on the title page, it is included as a part of the statement of responsibility.

Three classic Spanish plays / edited and with
  introductions by Hymen Alpern. -- New York :
  Washington Square Press, 1963.
  x, 229 p. ; 17 cm. -- (The ANTA series of
distinguished plays)

  Contents: The sheep well / by Lope de Vega --
Life is a dream / by Calderón de la Barca -- None
beneath the king / Rojas Zorrilla.

  I. Alpern, Hymen. II. Vega Carpio, Lope de.
Fuente ovejuna. English. III. Calderón de la
Barca, Pedro. La vida es sueño. English. IV.
Rojas Zorrilla, Francisco de. Del Rey abajo
ninguno. English. V. Series.

Figure 2-4. Title proper —collective and individual titles

The ANTA Series of Distinguished Plays
Three Classic Spanish Plays:
The Sheep Well
by Lope de Vega
Life Is a Dream   Title page
by Calderón de la Barca
None beneath the King
by Rojas Zorrilla
Edited and with Introductions by
Hymen Alpern, Ph.D.
Washington Square Press, Inc. • New York

Verso of title page

Three Classic Spanish Plays
1963
Published by
Washington Square Press, Inc.: Executive Offices, 630
Fifth Avenue; University Press Division, 32 Washing-
ton Place, New York, N.Y.
Introduction copyright, ©, 1963, by
Washington Square Press, Inc.

```
Molesworth, Mrs.
   Carrots : just a little boy / by Mrs. Molesworth
(Ennis Graham) ; illustrated by Walter Crane. --
1st ed. -- London ; New York : Macmillan, 1876
(1910 printing)
   241 p., [7] leaves of plates : ill. ; 19 cm.
```

Figure 2-5. Statement
of responsibility

I. Title.

Title page

"Carrots:"
Just a Little Boy
by
Mrs. Molesworth
(Ennis Graham)
Author of "Tell Me a Story" "Cuckoo Clock"
"Grandmother Dear" etc.
Illustrated by Walter Crane
Macmillan and Co., Limited
St. Martin's Street, London
1910

Macmillan and Co., Limited
London • Bombay • Calcutta
Melbourne
The Macmillan Company
New York • Boston • Chicago
Atlanta • San Francisco
The Macmillan Co. of Canada, Ltd.
Toronto
First Edition Printed October, 1876
Reprinted 1906, 1908, 1910

Verso of title page

2.1F3. Additions in statement of responsibility. This rule is almost identical to
1.1F8, which see. See also discussion and figure 1-45. Generally speaking, the
cataloguer is to transcribe the statement of responsibility as it appears on the
title page. Nothing will be omitted; nothing will be added. However, if the
addition of a word or short phrase will clarify an otherwise misleading author
statement, this may be done (see figure 2-6).

```
From age to age : life and literature in Anglo-
  Saxon England / [compiled by] Bernice Grohskopf.
  -- 1st ed. -- New York : Atheneum, 1968.
  xxiv, 231 p. : ill., maps ; 24 cm.

  Bibliography: p. 214-216.
  Includes index.
```

Figure 2-6. Addition in statement of responsibility

```
  I. Grohskopf, Bernice.
```

Title page

Bernice Grohskopf
From Age to Age
Life and Literature in Anglo-Saxon England
                            Atheneum   1968   New York

2.1G. Items without a collective title

See *AACR2* 1.1G for examples and discussion of the general rule. Note the difference in punctuation between present instructions, which call for separating individual titles by one author with space - semicolon - space whether or not they are joined with linking words, and former instructions as given in rule 134C6, *AACR Chapter 6* (1974). The same illustration is included in both the 1974 and 1978 codes. Check them carefully to note the different punctuation.

2.2. EDITION AREA

See *AACR2* 1.2B for discussion and examples of the transcription of the edition statement.

2.2B3. Optional addition. The cataloguer may, if desired, create a brief edition statement, which may be added to the catalogue entry for a work known to contain significant changes. Since the Library of Congress does not intend to follow this practice, it is doubtful that many American libraries will do this.

2.2C. Statement of responsibility relating to the edition

See discussion and examples under 1.2C. For additional examples, see figures 1-39, 1-91, etc.

2.2D. Subsequent edition statement

See 1.2D for discussion and examples. In most cases a reissue is identical to the first printing of a particular edition. Note information about a reissue as a subsequent edition statement only if the reissue contains significant changes. This will not often be the case.

2.4. PUBLICATION, DISTRIBUTION, ETC., AREA

For general discussion and examples of the publication area, see 1.4. The prescribed sources of information for publication area are the title page, preliminaries (half title, verso of title page, cover), and colophon. If information is taken from a source other than these, it must be enclosed in brackets.

Prescribed order and basic punctuation for information included in the publication area are: Place : Publisher, Date. All three elements must be given. See discussion and examples under 1.4C, 1.4D, and 1.4F for procedure when one or more of these elements does not appear at all. Abbreviations are used in the publication area if they are found in *AACR2* Appendix B.

2.4C. Place of publication

See 1.4C for general discussion. Reminder: The cataloguer will *always* list the first place appearing in the prescribed source of information. If this place is in the country of the cataloguing agency (for cataloguers in the United States, a city in the U.S.A.), all subsequent places are ignored. If a city in another country is given first, it will be recorded. But if a city in the country of the cataloguing agency is named, it will be given in addition to the first city.

This practice holds true even if the name of the "home" city appears in a different place in the book than the source being used to transcribe the publication data. Prescribed sources should be used in the order in which they are listed in 2.0B2; that is, for the publication area, use title page information first, supplementing it with information from the other preliminaries and finally the colophon, if appropriate.

The catalogue entry for Mrs. Molesworth's *Carrots* (figure 2-5) illustrates this point. The title page gives only London, which will be recorded as the first place in the publication area. The verso of the title page lists not only a place in the United States but also one in Canada. A cataloguer in the United States will list New York as the second place of publication in the publication area, as was done in cataloguing for figure 2-5. However, if this book had been catalogued for a Canadian library, publication area would read:

— London ; Toronto : Macmillan, 1876 (1910 printing)

For a less unusual example of this practice see figure 1-67.

2.4D. Name of publisher

See discussion and examples under 1.4D.

The publisher's name is separated from the place by space - colon - space. It is given in the shortest form in which it can be understood and identified internationally.

As with the recording of place of publication, the cataloguer will in all cases record the first place and first publisher appearing on the title page of the book being catalogued (1.4B8). If this place and publisher are in the country of the cataloguing agency, all other names will be ignored. See figure 2-7 for an example of cataloguing done by a cataloguer in the United States.

```
Parish, Peggy.
   Hermit Dan / Peggy Parish ; illustrated by Paul
Frame. -- New York : Macmillan, c1977.
   177 p. : ill. ; 23 cm.

   Sequel to: Pirate Island adventure.
   Summary: Liza, Bill, and Jed stir up excitement
when they try to discover the secret of Hermit
Dan's buried box.
   ISBN 0-02-769840-8


   I. Frame, Paul.   II. Title.
```

Figure 2-7. Publication area

Title page

Peggy Parish
Hermit Dan
Illustrated by Paul Frame
Macmillan Publishing Co., Inc.
New York
Collier Macmillan Publishers,
London

Copyright © 1977 Margaret Parish
Copyright © 1977 Macmillan Publishing Co., Inc.

Verso of title page

A cataloguer in Great Britain would give the publication area for figure 2-7 as:

New York : Macmillan ; London : Collier Macmillan, c1977.

This would be done according to rule 1.4B8, which stipulates that if a publisher in the country of the cataloguing agency is listed in a secondary position, both the first and second will be given. However, a cataloguer in Canada (or, for that matter, Australia, Germany, or any other place in the world except Great Britain) would catalogue figure 2-7 as shown in the example.

2.4E. Optional addition

See 1.4E for discussion of the statement of function of distributor.

2.4F. Date of publication

See 1.4F for discussion and examples.

2.5. PHYSICAL DESCRIPTION AREA

Chapter 2 gives special rules for describing books, pamphlets, and printed sheets.

2.5B. Number of volumes or items and/or pagination

Single volumes or items

2.5B1. Extent of the item. The extent is always the first element of the physical description area. A single book is described in terms of its pages or leaves (see 2.5B2, etc.). Although books are the most numerous class of materials covered by *AACR2* chapter 2, the chapter also covers other printed materials. A poster if it shows predominantly written material may be catalogued by *AACR2* chapter 2 rules. Posters, handbills, and other separately published sheets defined in *AACR2* Appendix D as broadsides are also included in *AACR2* chapter 2. (See figure 2-8.)

```
Poesia = Poetry : Friday, March 17, 7:30 p.m.,
   El Pueblo Community Center, 6th and Irvington :
   mecha dance following poetry, 9:00 p.m. / Fer-
   nando Tápia ... [et al.] ; a Campo-El Pueblo/Gon-
   zalez Co-production. -- [Tucson, Ariz.] : The
   Producers, [1978]
   1 broadside : ill. ; 44 x 28 cm.

I. Tápia, Fernando.
```

Figure 2-8. Broadside

Broadside

Poesia/Poetry
fernando tápia
chocolate brown
marta bermudez
miguel mendez
elena parra
aristeo brito

Friday, March 17, 7:30 p.m.
El Pueblo Community Center
6th and Irvington
Mecha dance following poetry, 9:00 p.m.
A Campo-El Pueblo/Gonzalez Co-Production

A portfolio (two covers joined at the back holding loose sheets of paper) is described as such. The number of pieces included in the portfolio (bracketed unless numbered on the pieces) and the type of material are designated. See figure 2-9.

```
Nelson, Stan.
   Typefounding by hand : a suite of prints / by
Stan Nelson. -- Kalamazoo, Mich. : Private Press
& Typefoundry of P.H. Duensing, 1977.
   1 portfolio (5 sheets) : ill. ; 42 cm.

   Previously published in: Typefounding / by
Stanley Nelson. 1972.
   Limited ed. of 25 signed and numbered copies.
This is no. 15.

   I. Nelson, Stan. Typefounding. II. Title.
```

Figure 2-9. Portfolio

Typefounding by Hand
A Suite of Prints by
Stan Nelson
Privately Printed
1977

Title page

Colophon

This suite of five prints first appeared in *Typefounding* by Stanley Nelson, printed in a limited edition for the 1972 meeting of the Typocrafters. With the artist's permission, the original blocks have been reprinted on handmade Kome paper, in an edition of 25 copies at The Private Press & Typefoundry of Paul Hayden Duensing, Kalamazoo, Michigan in September, 1977, of which this is No. 15

A broadside, a portfolio, or one or more loose sheets are described as such in the physical description area. A single volume book is described in terms of pages or leaves. Record the last *numbered* page or leaf of each section. A leaf is a single sheet in a book. It consists of two pages, one on each side. If the leaf is printed on both sides, the book is described in terms of pages (e.g., ix, 67 p.). Most modern trade books are printed and the pages numbered in this fashion. The cataloguer must be alert, however, for works printed and numbered only on one side of the leaf. These are described in terms of leaves; that is, if we may speak of ordinary books as being "paged," these books are "foliated." See, for example, figure 1-96.

2.5B6. Sometimes a publication may be an extract from a larger work. Inclusive paging is given for such a publication.

2.5B7. If a work is neither paged nor foliated, count the pages or leaves and record the number in brackets. (See figure 2-10.)

Cole, William.
  That pest Jonathan / by William Cole ; pictures
by Tomi Ungerer. -- New York : Harper & Row, c1970.
  [32] p. : col. ill. ; 20 cm.

Figure 2-10. Unpaged
work

I. Ungerer, Tomi. II. Title.

Title on two
facing pages

That Pest Jonathan
by William Cole
Pictures by Tomi Ungerer
Harper & Row, Publishers
New York, Evanston, and London
Text copyright © 1970 by William Cole
Pictures copyright © 1970 by Tomi Ungerer

2.5B8. A volume with complicated paging. If there are various numbered
sections in a single volume monograph, count the total number of pages or
leaves and record the total followed by the words "in various pagings." (See
figure 2-11.) If the item is foliated rather than paged, record the total number
followed by the words "in various foliations."

Tacitus, Cornelius.
  Cornelii Taciti Historiarvm libri / recognovit
breviqve adnotatione critica instrvxit C.D. Fisher.
-- Oxonii [Oxford] : E Typographeo Clarendoniano,
1911.
  270 p. in various pagings ; 19 cm. --
(Scriptorum classicorum bibliotheca Oxoniensis)

Figure 2-11.
Complicated pagination

I. Fisher, C. D.

Title page

Cornelii Taciti
Historiarvm Libri
Recognovit
Breviqve Adnotatione Critica Instrvxit
C. D. Fisher
Oxonii
E. Typographeo Clarendoniano

If there are not more than three main numbered sections, record pagination as shown in figure 2-12.

```
Catholic Church.
   The Liber usualis : with introduction and rubrics
in English / edited by the Benedictines of Soles-
mes. -- Tournai, Belgium ; New York : Society of
St. John the Evangelist : Desclée, c1956.
   xlix, 1880, 100, 80 p. : music ; 19 cm.




                                              Figure 2-12.
                                              Complicated pagination

   I. Benedictines of Solesmes.   II. Title.
```

Title page

The Liber Usualis
With Introduction and Rubrics
in English
Edited by the
Benedictines of Solesmes
Society of St. John the Evangelist
Desclée & Cie
Tournai (Belgium)
New York, N.Y.

2.5B10. Leaves or pages of plates. See *AACR2* Appendix D, Glossary, for a definition of what constitutes a plate. Before the 1974 revision of *AACR Chapter 6*, plates were specified as a type of illustration; they were not counted as part of the physical extent of the volume. Since in many cases plates bulk large as a part of the total makeup of a book, they are now included at the end of the sequences of pagination, whether they are found together or are scattered through the work.

The type of paper used for printing has nothing to do with whether a leaf is a plate or not. The important thing to watch for is that "plate" material must be outside the regular numbering of the book. In the example described by figure 2-13, a large section of illustrations printed on coated paper and labeled "Plates" follows immediately after the text. The "plates" section has been included in the total numbering of the volume and receives no special mention in the physical description area. However, scattered through the first part of the volume are three leaves, one printed on one side, the other two printed with illustrations on both sides. These leaves are not paged with the rest of the text. These will be recorded as plates; the larger section of "plates" are simply included as part of the main paging.

```
Taylor, Basil.
   Stubbs / Basil Taylor. -- 1st U.S. ed. -- New
York : Harper & Row, c1971.
   220 p. [5] p. of plates : 156 ill. (some col.),
port. ; 29 cm. -- (Icon editions)

   Includes index.                          Figure 2-13. Plates
   ISBN 06-438613-9


   I. Stubbs, George.        Basil Taylor
                             Stubbs
                             Icon Editions
                             Harper & Row Publishers
                             New York, Evanston, San Francisco, London
              Title page
```

Note, by the way, that in a change from *AACR Chapter 6* (1974) 141B1d, plates will be recorded either as "leaves of plates" or "pages of plates," depending on whether they are printed on both sides of the leaf or only on one. If the enumeration by the printer does not accurately reflect the number of pages or leaves of plates, or if the plates are not numbered, the cataloguer should count them and record the number in brackets.

Figure 2-13 is an example of a work which contains both leaves and pages of plates. Of the plates that are to be enumerated, one is a leaf printed on one side. Two other leaves are printed on both sides, constituting four pages. Thus, the entire count is as given in the physical description area.

2.5B11. Folded leaves. For an example, see figure 1-67.

2.5B17. Publications in more than one volume. Generally speaking, if a monograph consists of more than one physical volume, record the number of volumes; e.g., 3 v.

2.5B18. See the definition of "volume" in *AACR2* Appendix D, Glossary. If the term "volume" is not appropriate for a multipart monograph, one of the terms listed under 2.5B18 may be used. This is an inclusive list. Do not use terms other than these in describing multipart monographs.

2.5B19 and **2.5B20.** The item on which figure 2-14 is based is paged continuously, beginning with volume 1 and ending with the last page of volume 6. The set is in six bibliographical volumes, bound in three physical volumes.

Arabian nights. English.
   The book of the thousand nights and a night : a
plain and literal translation of the Arabian
nights entertainments / made and annotated by
Richard F. Burton ; decorated with illustrations
by Valenti Angelo. -- New York : Heritage Press,
c1934.
   6 v. in 3 (3975 p.) : ill. ; 22 cm.

   I. Burton, Richard F.   II. Angelo, Valenti.
III. Title.

Figure 2-14. More than
one volume

Title page

The Book Of
The Thousand Nights and a Night
A Plain and Literal Translation of the
Arabian Nights Entertainments
Made and Annotated by
Richard F. Burton
Decorated with Illustrations by
Valenti Angelo
The Heritage Press, New York

2.5C. Illustrative matter

The abbreviation "ill.," separated from the pages or volume numbering of
the text by space - colon - space, is used to describe all types of illustrations
unless one or more of the special types listed in *AACR2* 2.5C2 are considered
to be important. The list given in 2.5C2 is inclusive; do not use any term not
found here. If the work includes a type of illustration not on the list (for example,
photographs), simply call it "ill." When the book consists of a mixture of
general illustrations together with other specific types of illustrations, the word
"ill." is listed first, followed in alphabetical order by the other types. See, for
example, figure 1-106.

Caution: If all of the illustrations in the book are of a type that can be
specifically designated, simply give the designation(s) as appropriate. It is not
always necessary to include "ill." as part of the illustration statement. See, for
example, figures 1-82, 1-86, etc.

2.5D. Size

Except for items measuring less than ten centimetres, size is measured in
centimetres. For a book, measure the height of the cover. Fractions of a centimetre are counted to the next centimetre.

2.5D2. Give height followed by width if width is less than half the height or greater than the height. See figure 1-45.

2.5D4. A single sheet or broadside is measured height by width. (See figure 2-8.) Note under rule 2.5D4 instructions for designating folded sheets.

2.5E. Accompanying material

See 1.5E for general discussion of accompanying material. Certain kinds of materials intended to be used with the work being catalogued are added as a fourth element of the physical description area (see figure 2-15). If desired, and if the description is not complex, physical description of the material may be added following the designation of the accompanying material.

```
Green, Nancy.
   The bigger giant : an Irish legend / retold by
Nancy Green ; pictures by Betty Fraser. -- New
York : Scholastic Book Services, c1963.
   ₍32₎ p. : ill. ; 23 cm. + 1 sound disc (13 min.
: 33 1/3 rpm, mono. ; 7 in.)



   I. Fraser, Betty.  II. Title.
```

Figure 2-15.
Accompanying material

	The Bigger Giant
	An Irish Legend
Title page	Retold by Nancy Green
	Pictures by Betty Fraser
	Scholastic Book Services
	New York • Toronto • London • Auckland • Sydney

2.6. SERIES AREA

See discussion and examples under 1.6.

2.7. NOTE AREA

Follow instructions on format and order of notes as given in 1.7A. In addition, use categories of notes stipulated under 2.7B.

2.7B1. Nature, scope, or artistic form. See discussion under 1.7B1; see also figures 1-93 and 1-94.

2.7B2. Language and/or translation or adaptation. See discussion under 1.7B2; see figure 1-95 for example.

If it is not evident from the formal part of the description, make a note to indicate that the work is an adaptation from another work. An author-title added entry is made for the earlier work (see figure 2-16).

```
Green, Norma.
   The hole in the dike / retold by Norma Green ;
pictures by Eric Carle. -- New York : Crowell,
c1974.
   [32] p. : col. ill. ; 28 cm.

   Adapted from a story in: Hans Brinker, or, The
silver skates / by Mary Mapes Dodge.
   Summary: A little boy's courage saves Holland
from destruction by the sea.

   I. Carle, Eric.  II. Dodge, Mary Mapes,
1831-1905.  Hans Brinker, or, The silver skates.
III. Title.
```

Figure 2-16.
Adaptation note

Title page

The Hole in the Dike
Retold by Norma Green
Pictures by Eric Carle
Thomas Y. Crowell Company • New York
Copyright © 1974 by Norma B. Green.
Illustrations copyright © 1974 by Eric Carle.

2.7B3. Source of title proper. See discussion under 1.7B3; see also figure 1-96.

2.7B4. Variations in title. See discussion under 1.7B4; see also figures 1-74, 2-2, etc., for examples of this type of note.

2.7B6. Statements of responsibility. See discussion under 1.7B6. An "At head of title" note is given for a name not transcribed in the statement of responsibility that appears at the top of the title page. The most frequent "At head of title" information is the name of a corporate body appearing in this position whose relationship to the work is not certain, but for whom an added entry should be given because of its prominent position on the title page (21.30E). See figure 2-17.

2.7B7. Edition and history. For discussion and examples of this kind of note, see 1.7B7 and figures 1-92, 1-98 and 1-99.

Notice the absence in *AACR2* chapter 2 of a rule 2.7B8. The omission of this number was not accidental. As previously pointed out, the rules in *AACR2* chapters 2–12 are correlated with the general rules in *AACR2* chapter 1; e.g.,

2.7B7 is a particular application for monographs of general principles governing edition and history notes set forth in 1.7B7. Rule 1.7B8 has to do with notes pertaining to the "material specific details" area, a special area found only in entries for cartographic materials and serials. Since a monograph entry does not include the material specific details area, this sort of note is not pertinent to monographs. Therefore the number is skipped in *AACR2* chapter 2.

2.7B9. Publication, distribution, etc. See discussion under 1.7B9.

```
International Conference on Cataloguing Principles
  (1961 : Paris)
  Statement of principles adopted at the Interna-
tional Conference on Cataloguing Principles, Paris,
October 1961. -- Annotated ed. / with commentary
and examples by Eva Verona ; assisted by Franz
George Kaltwasser, P.R. Lewis, Roger Pierrot. --
London : IFLA Committee on Cataloguing, 1971.
  xviii, 119 p. ; 25 cm.

  At head of title: International Federation of
Library Associations.
  Bibliography: p. x-xii.
  ISBN 0-903043-00-9

  I. Verona, Eve.  II. International Federation of
Library Associations.  III. Title.
```

Figure 2-17. "At head of title" note

International Federation of Library Associations
Statement of Principles
Adopted at the International Conference on
Cataloguing Principles
Paris, October, 1961
Annotated Edition
with Commentary and Examples
by
Eva Verona
assisted by
Franz Georg Kaltwasser
P. R. Lewis, Roger Pierrot
London
IFLA Committee on Cataloguing
1971

Title page

2.7B10. Physical description. See figure 2-9; also see figures 1-79 and 1-101.
2.7B11. Accompanying material. See figure 1-103 and discussion under 1.7B11.

2.7B13. Dissertations. Unless a thesis or dissertation has been published (i.e., issued for public sale or distribution), such a work will be catalogued following the rules for manuscripts (*AACR2* chapter 4). See discussion of the matter of dissertations in *LC Cataloging Service Bulletin* 118: 8 (Summer 1976).

For an example of an unpublished dissertation in typical format, see figure 1-104. For an example of the note appropriate to a revised, published version of a dissertation, see figure 1-105.

2.7B14. Audience. See figure 1-106 for an example of such a note.

2.7B17. Summary. See figure 2-16, etc., for an example of such a note. This note is particularly useful with juvenile works.

2.7B18. Contents. Format for the contents note is somewhat different from that called for under rule 148, *AACR Chapter 6* (1974). Contents are no longer to be recorded as they appear on the title page or in the table of contents. The cataloguer is to transcribe each item in title and statement of responsibility area format as it appears at the head of the part referred to. Forenames of authors are no longer to be abbreviated to initials; the name is transcribed as it appears in the source. Figure 1-43 shows how this should be done. See also figures 1-46 and 1-54.

Certain parts of an item are also specified when such materials are considered important and would not be brought out otherwise. Bibliographies, discographies, and filmographies are noted if they are important, with inclusive pages if the bibliography is in one, two, or three places in the item.

Bibliography: p. 123-124.
Bibliography: v. 1, p. 345; v. 2, p. 123; v. 3, p. 401-404.

If the item has more than three bibliographies, use the note

Includes bibliographies.

If bibliographical references are important and take the place of a formal bibliography, use the note

Includes bibliographical references.

The presence of an index is noted. Do not give pages; simply give this note:

Includes index.

If the bibliography note would appropriately read "Includes bibliographies" or "Includes bibliographical references" and the item has an index, combine these notes.

Includes bibliographies and index
Includes bibliographical references and index.

The bibliography and index notes are the most common notes in the catalogue entry.

2.7B20. Copy being described. See discussion under 1.7B20; also see last note for figure 2-9.

2.7B21. "With" notes. See figure 1-92.

2.8. STANDARD NUMBER AREA

See discussion under 1.8.

3

Cartographic Materials

AACR2 chapter 3 covers all sorts of cartographic materials. The most common variety of cartographic material is a map, which may be defined as any kind of graphic representation of any place in the universe, on the earth, or in the heavens, real or imaginary. Relief maps, globes, atlases, and the photographs and surveys that are the raw materials from which conventional maps are made are all regarded as cartographic materials and are also covered by rules in *AACR2* chapter 3.

Once again, it must be emphasized that none of the chapters in *AACR2* Part I, including chapter 3, say anything about main or added entries. These rules are to be found in *AACR2* Part II, chapter 21. Specific mention of maps is made only once in chapter 21: "cartographers are the authors of their maps" (21.1A1). A rule follows this definition, stating that a work (any kind of library material) should be entered "under the heading for the personal author." If a map lacks a personal author (cartographer), it is rather likely (though not certain) to be entered under title main entry because of the rigid limitations of corporate authorship responsibility. See discussion of this matter in *AACR2* under 21.1B.

Official Anglo-American cataloguing preference for entry under person or body primarily responsible for the intellectual, etc., content of a work is of long standing, going back at least as far as Charles Ammi Cutter's *Rules for a Dictionary Catalogue*, which states, "The designer or painter copied is the author of engravings; the cartographer is the author of maps. . . ."[1]

Entry under cartographer may have fit in nicely with the principle of authorship responsibility, but it does not seem to have been a very helpful method of arrangement for most library users. The average library user generally comes to the library with a request for a map of Boston, or a literary map of Great Britain, or a map showing Arizona's weather patterns—a topographic or topo-

[1] Washington: GPO, 1876, p. 19, rule 6 1/2.

graphic-subject approach rather than an author approach. As early as 1921, Sir Herbert Fordham summarized the difficulty in his statement, "A map lies in character between a book and a picture, and combines the features of both. The classification and the bibliographical description of maps are thus difficult, and require a good deal of attention."[2]

Fordham presented the difficulty but offered no real suggestion other than that title main entry for maps should be preferred, a position adopted by the Royal Geographical Society in the next decade.[3] As for librarians in the United States, in most cases, unless they were map specialists, they controlled maps in a number of different homemade, informal fashions, usually keeping them apart from the rest of the library's collection.

It was not until 1945 when Samuel W. Boggs and Dorothy C. Lewis presented their monumental *The Classification and Cataloging of Maps and Atlases* that anyone gave concentrated attention to the solution of the problem of proper identification and collocation of maps in a general library catalogue. Boggs and Lewis discarded the concept of author entry for maps in favor of an entry that was "to present that information which the experienced map user is entitled to find, taking into account the essential characteristics of maps (e.g. scale and map projection); and . . . to make the map catalog cards conform to present library practice. . . . This should make it possible to consolidate the map catalog with the book catalog. . . ."[4] Boggs and Lewis suggested that cataloguing should be based on title unit entry consisting of title followed by author, edition (if any), place, publisher, and date. Added entries to bring out geographic area and date, or area, subject, and date would be added as needed.

Boggs and Lewis's work had a great impact on practical library cataloguing of maps; it had little impact on official catalogue-code makers. The *ALA Cataloging Rules*, which were published four years later, still prescribed entry for maps under "the name of the person or corporate body responsible for the content of the map, as, cartographer, editor, publisher, government bureau, society or institution."[5] But an almost apologetic footnote following the rule recognized at least that such author entry presented problems for both cataloguer and library user. It stated, "Small libraries may . . . find that an entry under subject (i.e., area mapped) is all that is necessary . . . and special collections may prefer a main entry under area, a scheme for which is worked out in the Boggs and Lewis Manual."[6]

Map librarians remained unhappy with the official cataloguing rules. Among the articles written during the period between the appearance of the 1949 ALA rules and the formulation of *AACR1* was one by Bill M. Woods, entitled "Map Cataloging: Inventory and Prospect."[7] Woods summarized some of the

---

[2] *Maps: Their History, Characteristics, and Uses* (Cambridge: University Press, 1921), pp. 4–5.

[3] R. G. Crone, "The Cataloguing and Arrangement of Maps," *Library Association Record*, ser. 4, 3 (March 1936): 98–104.

[4] *The Classification and Cataloging of Maps and Atlases* (New York: Special Libraries Association), p. 3.

[5] *ALA Cataloging Rules for Author and Title Entries* (Chicago: ALA, 1949), rule 10, p. 26.

[6] Ibid.

[7] *LRTS*, 3 (Fall 1959): 257–73.

differences between maps and books that should be reflected in their bibliographical control. Among these differences was "the primary identification of maps with area rather than with authority or author." Also different from books and of impotance for identification of a map, said Woods, were subject information, date, scale, size of the map, projection, and color. Not only was entry under author illogical for maps, but also, since most map titles tend to be vague, title entry was of little value, stated Woods. Woods's conclusion agreed with that of the final report of the Special Libraries Association's Geography and Map Division Committee on Map Cataloging, which he summarized. Maps, said Woods and the committee, require their own cataloguing rules, which should be based on area-subject-date rather than the principle of authorship.[8]

Presumably SLA's suggestion was considered by the editors of the 1967 *Anglo-American Cataloging Rules.* As it turned out, though, the editors were under pressure to get the 1967 *AACR* into print, and so the rules for nonbook materials, which made up Part III, are, for the most part, a reprint of the Library of Congress's own rules for handling these materials. *AACR1* chapter 11, "Maps, Atlases, etc.," is firmly based in ALA 1949 rule 10. *AACR1* rule 210 states, "A map, a series or set of maps, an atlas, a relief model, or a globe is entered under the person or corporate body that is primarily responsible for its informational content" if this responsibility is explicit (211A). If it is not explicit, main entry might be, in order of preference, under "the individual whose survey provided the basis for the cartography . . . the cartographer . . . the engraver . . . the corporate body . . . that prepared the maps," or, as a last choice, the title of the map (21.1B).

Map cataloguers in the period following the appearance of *AACR1* continued to be unhappy with the official rules for entry. The Library of Congress, of course, followed the official rules. However, their coverage of maps as reflected in the *National Union Catalog* was not adequate to assure libraries of LC copy for maps in local libraries. Many map librarians disregarded *AACR1* rules and adopted Boggs and Lewis's manual, the American Geographical Society's *Cataloging and Filing Rules for Maps and Atlases in the Society's Collections* (New York: American Geographical Society, 1969), or the simpler rules advocated by the Canadian Library Association[9] or the Association for Educational Communications and Technology.[10]

Now that *AACR2* has appeared, it is to be hoped that some of the problems have been solved. Map librarians will find fewer maps entered under corporate author and more entered under title as main entry than was the case with *AACR1.* The addition of a new area preceding the publication area, the mathematical data area, gives emphasis to scale and projection by including this important information as a part of the formal catalogue entry rather than as a note. But the overriding concern of *AACR2* with the principle of authorship responsibility governing main entry for all types of library materials will con-

[8] Ibid., 268–69.
[9] Canadian Library Association, *Nonbook Materials* (Ottawa: CLA, 1973).
[10] Association for Educational Communications and Technology, *Standards for Cataloging Nonprint Materials*, 4th ed. (Washington: AECT, 1976).

tinue to mean main entry under cartographer or other responsible author when this information is available. In a fully integrated catalogue, one that includes entries for all types of library materials, such entry would seem necessary.

3.0B. Sources of information

Bibliographical information for map catalogue entries has not been standardized on the face of maps in the same fashion as it has been for most books, where most of the information usually may be found on the title page. Cataloguing information may be taken from *any* part of the map; no longer, as was true with *AACR1* rule 212A1, is preference given to information contained within the border of a map. Punctuation and arrangement of data follows the general pattern set forth in *AACR2* chapter 1; rules given there should be followed as applicable.

3.0J. Description of whole or part

Many maps are issued as a set, sometimes over a long period of time in many parts, sometimes at one time. A library may decide to catalogue each of the individual maps that make up the set, or it may decide to catalogue the set as a unit, possibly making a separate entry for one or more individual parts of the set if this seems useful. The Geological Survey of Great Britain issues several sets of this kind, of considerable complexity. Another example of a map set is that catalogued as an illustration for 3.1G4 and 3.1G5, figures 3-7a and 3-7b.

3.1B. Title proper

Record the title proper for a map as instructed in 1.1B, following wording and order exactly, but following conventional library capitalization and punctuation rules.

3.1B2 and **3.1B3.** A map may bear more than one title. If this is the case, follow instructions under 1.1B8.

The title sometimes includes information about the scale of the map. Although the scale statement is given formally as part of the mathematical data area, it will still be transcribed as part of the title proper if appropriate (see figure 3-1).

```
Bartholomew one inch map of the Lake District. --
   Rev. -- Scale 1:63,360. -- Edinburgh : Bartholo-
   mew, 1971.
   1 map : col. ; 71 x 82 cm. folded to 21 x 12 cm.

   ISBN 85152-362-5 (paper). -- ISBN 85152-363-3
(cloth)



   I. John Bartholomew & Son.
```

Figure 3-1. Scale as part of title transcription

Bartholomew One Inch Map of the Lake District
Revised 1971   Scale 1:63360—1 inch to the mile
© John Bartholomew & Son Ltd, Edinburgh
SBN   85152 362 5 paper   85152 363 3 cloth

Information from map

3.1C. Optional addition. General material designation

The general material designation "map" or "globe" in brackets as appropriate will be added elsewhere immediately following the title proper, if the library uses GMD. Following Library of Congress practice, examples in this text do not show GMD for cartographic materials.

3.1D. Parallel titles

A parallel title will be recorded as instructed in 1.1D (see figure 3-2). The order of the titles is governed by the layout of the map; record titles from top to bottom, or left to right, as given on the chief source.

```
Suidelike Afrika / Driehoeksmeting = Southern
   Africa / Trigonometrical Survey. -- 3. uitgawe.
   -- Scale 1:2,500,000 ; Albers' equal-area proj.,
   S 18°, S 32°. -- Pretoria : Staatsdrukker, 1972
   (1977 printing)
   1 map : col. ; 93 x 68 cm. -- (T.S.O. misc. ;
4793)

   Glossary in Afrikaans, English, and Portuguese.
```

Figure 3-2. Parallel title

```
   I. South Africa.  Trigonometrical Survey.   II.
Title: Southern Africa.
```

Southern Africa
Third Edition 1972
1:2 500 000
Albers's equal-area projection,
standard parallels
18° South and 32° South.
Reprinted and Published by the
Government Printer,
Private Bag X85, Pretoria 1977.

Information from map face

Suidelike Afrika
Derde Uitgawe 1972
1:2 500 000
Albers se vlaktroue projeksie,
standaard parallele 18° Suid en 32° Suid.
Herdruk En Uitgegee Deur Die Staatsdrukker,
Privaatsak X85, Pretoria, 1977.
Driehoeksmeting
Trigonometrical Surey
T.S.O. Misc. 4793

Information from map face

3.1E. Other title information

Other title information will be recorded following general rules 1.1E (see figure 3-3).

```
Wintle, William.
   The Golden Chain Council highway map of the
northern & southern mines : the Mother Lode /
delineation & cartography by William Wintle. --
Scale ca. 1:700,000. -- Murphys, Calif. : Golden
Chain Council of the Mother Lode, [1971?]
   1 map : col. ; 57 x 43 cm. folded to 22 x 10 cm.

   Panel title: California'a golden chain : the
Mother Lode highway.
   Includes 16 insets, ill. of early mining opera-
tions + mileage charts.  On verso: Text and photos.
of area by county.
   I. Golden Chain Council of the Mother Lode.   II.
Title.   III. Title: The Mother Lode highway.   IV.
Title: California's golden chain.
```

Figure 3-3. Other title information

Information from map

**The Golden Chain Council Highway Map of
The Northern & Southern Mines
The Mother Lode
Delineation & Cartography
by
William Wintle**

Verso of map

**California's
Golden
Chain
The
Mother
Lode
Highway
published by
The Golden Chain Council©
of the Mother Lode, Inc.,
Murphys, California
© The Golden Chain Council of the Mother Lode**

3.1E2. Since the most prominent unit of the catalogue record for many, if not most, maps will be the title, add the geographic area covered by the map as bracketed other title information, if the title gives no indication of the geographic area (see figure 3-4).

```
Tulsa Metropolitan Area Planning Commission.
  Existing land use, 1964 : ₍in Tulsa, Oklahoma₎ /
Tulsa Metropolitan Area Planning Commission. --
Scale ca. 1:140,000. -- ₍Tulsa₎ : The Commission,
1965.
  1 map : col. ; on sheet 48 x 40 cm.
```

Figure 3-4. Area added
as other title
information

```
I. Title.
```

Information from map

October, 1965   Scale in Miles
Tulsa Metropolitan Area Planning Commission
Existing Land Use–1964

3.1F. Statements of responsibility

The statement of responsibility, as indicated in 1.1F, includes names of all persons or corporate bodies that have some responsibility other than for simple publication or distribution of the item, as long as these names appear "prominently" (i.e., in the chief source of information or accompanying printed material, the prescribed sources for areas 1 and 2 of cartographic materials), see figure 3-5. See also discussion in this text under 1.1F1.

Refer to discussion of figures 1-28 and 1-53 for the omission of names of Doyle and Grosvenor from the catalogue entry.

```
British Columbia, Alberta, and the Yukon Territory
  / produced by the Cartographic Division, National
  Geographic Society ; William T. Peele, chief
  cartographer, Richard K. Rogers, assistant chief
  cartographer. -- Scale 1:3,500,000. 1 cm. to
  35 km. 1 in. to 55.2 miles ; Lambert conformal
  conic proj. -- Washington : The Society, 1978.
  1 map : col. ; 89 x 58 cm. folded to 23 x 15 cm.
-- (Close-up : Canada)

  Suppl. to: National geographic magazine, v. 153,
no. 4, April 1978, p. 548A.

            (Continued on next card)
```

Figure 3-5. Statement
of responsibility

British Columbia, Alberta, and the Yukon Territory. 1978. (card 2)

On verso: Canada's Rocky Mountain parks. Scale 1:2,375,000 -- Yukon Territory. Scale 1:4,900,000 -- Victoria and Vancouver. Scale 1:1,750,000 -- Beauty to flaunt and bounty to grow on [text].

I. Peele, William T. II. National Geographic Society. Cartographic Division. III. National geographic magazine. IV. Series.

Close-up: Canada
British Columbia
Alberta
and the Yukon Territory
Produced by the Cartographic Division
National Geographic Society
Robert E. Doyle, President
National Geographic Magazine
Gilbert M. Grosvenor, Editor
William T. Peele, chief cartographer
Richard K. Rogers, assistant chief cartographer
Washington   April 1978

Victoria and Vancouver
British Columbia
Scale 1:1,750,000

Verso of map

Information from map face

Supplement to the National Geographic,
April 1978, Page 548 A, Vol. 153 No. 4
Close-up: Canada
Lambert Conformal Conic Projection,
Standard Parallels 62° 20′ and 51° 40′
Scale 1:3,500,000
1 centimeter = 35.0 kilometers or 1 inch = 55.2 miles
Copyright © 1978 National Geographic Society,
Washington, D.C.

Beauty to flaunt
and bounty to grow on
[Text follows]

Verso of map

Information from map face

Verso of map

Yukon Territory
Scale 1:4,900,000

3.1G. Items without a collective title

An item lacking a collective title may be described in several different fashions.

3.1G2. Such an item may be described as a unit, following directions in 1.G1. The example shown in figure 3-6a–c has been catalogued in this fashion.

This item has two maps, one on each side of a sheet. The folded title of the item is "Western United States." On one side of the sheet is a map of the western United States; on the other side is a map of the central United States. The folded title information in conjunction with the position of the map of the western United States makes that side of the map the predominant part of the item. Thus, the entry begins with this map.

3.1G4. Each of the separately titled parts of the map, the cataloguing for which is shown in figures 3-6a–c, may, if the cataloguer desires, be catalogued as a separate unit. If it is, the other map will be named in a note.

```
Western United States ; Central United States /
   Rand McNally & Co. -- Scale ca. 1:3,104,640. --
   Chicago : American Oil Co., c1969.
   1 map : col. ; 92 x 65 cm. folded to 23 x 10 cm.

   Includes 15 insets.



   I. Rand McNally & Co.  II. American Oil Company.
III. Title: Central United States.
```

Figure 3-6a. Item without a collective title catalogued as a unit

```
Western United States / Rand McNally & Co. --
   Scale ca. 1:3,104,640. -- Chicago : American
   Oil Co., c1969.
   on side 1 of 1 map : col. ; 92 x 65 cm. folded
to 23 x 10 cm.

   Includes 7 insets.
   With (on verso): Central United States.
```

Figure 3-6b. Item without a collective title—titles catalogued separately

American Oil Company
Western United States
One inch equals approximately 49 miles
Copyright © 1969

```
   I. Rand McNally & Co.  II. American Oil Company.
```

Information from map

Central United States / Rand McNally & Co. --
    Scale ca. 1:3,104,640. -- Chicago : American
    Oil Co., c1969.
    on side 2 of 1 map : col. ; 92 x 65 cm. folded
to 23 x 10 cm.

    Includes 8 insets.
    With (on recto): Western United States.

**Figure 3-6c. Item
without a collective
title—titles catalogued
separately**

        I. Rand McNally & Co.   II. American Oil Company.

**American Oil Company
Central United States
One inch equals approximately 49 miles
Copyright © 1969**

Information from map

A collection of separate maps lacking a collective title may be catalogued
separately, following stipulations of 3.1G4. The examples shown in figure 3-7a
are based on five climatology maps issued as a set by the Arizona Resources
Information System, described in figure 3-7b.

National Weather Service stations as of March
    1975 : Arizona / prepared under the direction
    of the State Climatologist, the Laboratory of
    Climatology, Arizona State University. -- Scale
    1:1,000,000 ; Lambert conformal conic proj. --
    [Phoenix] : Available from ARIS, 1975.
    1 map : col. ; 81 x 64 cm. -- ([Climatology maps
of Arizona ; 1]) (Arizona Resources Information
System cooperative publication ; no. 5)

    "Satellite image base, 1972-1973, prepared and
published by the U.S. Geological Survey in cooperation with the National Aeronautics and Space Administration (ERTS-1, Proposal SR 211) ... 1927 North

    (Continued on next card)

**Figure 3-7a.
Map from a
set catalogued
separately**

National Weather Service stations as of March 1975.
  1975. (card 2)

American datum ... Highway and name base by Arizona
Department of Transportation, 1974."

  I. Arizona State University. State Climatologist.
II. Arizona Resources Information System. III.
Series. IV. Series: Arizona Resources Information
System cooperative publication ; no. 5.

Climatology Maps of Arizona

Mimeographed cover letter

Scale 1:1,000,000
Lambert conformal
conic projection
Arizona Resources
Information System
Cooperative
Publication No. 5
Available at a nominal cost
from ARIS or the
Laboratory of Climatology.

National Weather Service Stations as of March 1975
Satellite Image Base   1972–1973
Prepared and published by the U.S. Geological Survey
in cooperation with the National Aeronautics and
Space Administration (ERTS—1, Proposal SR 211)
Imagery from NASA Earth Resources Technology
Satellite (ERTS—1)
Controlled to photoidentified ground positions
1927 North American Datum
Highway and name base by Arizona Department of
Transportation   1974
Prepared under the Direction of the State Climatologist
The Laboratory of Climatology
Arizona State University, Tempe AZ 85281 May 1975

Information from map face

[Climatology maps of Arizona] / prepared under
  the direction of the State Climatologist, the
  Laboratory of Climatology, Arizona State University. -- Scale 1:1,000,000 and ca. 1:3,000,000 ;
  Lambert conformal conic proj. -- [Phoenix] :
  Available from ARIS, 1975.
  16 maps on 5 sheets : col. ; 81 x 64 cm. and
23 x 20 cm. -- (Arizona Resources Information
System cooperative publication ; no. 5)

  Parts: [1] National weather service stations as
of March 1975 -- [2] Evaporation and evapotranspi-
ration -- [3] Arizona precipitation -- [4] Solar
energy -- [5] Arizona temperatures.

      (Continued on next card)

**Figure 3-7b. Supplied
title for a collected set**

[Climatology maps of Arizona]. 1975. (card 2)

I. Arizona State University. State Climatologist.
II. Arizona Resources Information System. III.
Series.

3.1G5. If a set lacking a collective title is to be kept together and catalogued as a unit, and if it consists of a large number of items (this might be interpreted to be more than three items), the cataloguer may supply a collective title descriptive of the entire set. According to instructions in 3.1B4, the title must include the name of the area covered. (See figure 3-6a–c for a set without a collective title that includes two items).

The example shown in 3-7b illustrates cataloguing for the set from which figures 3-7a was taken. The collective title was taken from descriptive information about the set from the issuing body. Since it was not found on the chief source, it is enclosed in brackets. Each of the five maps in the set has an identical statement of responsibility and series statement (including series number). Each map is titled separately.

3.2. EDITION AREA

If a cartographic item includes an edition statement, it will be transcribed according to general directions given in 1.2.

3.2B4. If an item contains an edition statement in more than one language, give the statement that matches the language of the title proper. Figure 3-2 includes such a statement. The title proper on this map is in Afrikaans; therefore the Afrikaans-language edition statement is recorded rather than the English-language statement.

3.2C. Statements of responsibility relating to an edition

Record a statement of responsibility that relates to a particular edition, but not to all editions, according to 1.2C. Note in regard to this, however, figure 1-59 and the discussion of it. If the chief source of information does not include an edition statement, such a revision statement forms a part of the title and statement of responsibility area for the entire work. The example shown in figure 3-8 illustrates this.

3.2D1. Subsequent edition statement. A map may be reissued with partial revisions pertaining to a particular edition. The edition statement should be transcribed, following provisions of 1.2D.

Earthquake fault map of a portion of Salt Lake
   County, Utah / revised in 1976 by Bruce N.
   Kaliser. -- Scale ca. 1:160,000. -- Salt Lake
   City : Distributed by Utah Geological and
   Mineral Survey, 1976.
   1 map ; 26 x 20 cm. -- (Map / State of Utah,
Department of Natural Resources, Utah Geological
and Mineral Survey ; 42)

   "Originally issued in 1968 as Map 18."

   1. Utah. Geological and Mineral Survey. II.
Kaliser, Bruce N. III. Series.

Figure 3-8. Revision
statement

Map 42 State of Utah Department of Natural Resources Utah Geological and Mineral Survey Originally issued in 1968 as Map 18 Revised in 1976 by Bruce N. Kaliser	Earthquake Fault Map of a Portion of Salt Lake County, Utah Distributed by Utah Geological and Mineral Survey Donald T. McMillan, Director 606 Black Hawk Way Salt Lake City, Utah 84108

Information from map

3.3. MATHEMATICAL DATA AREA

The mathemetical data area is used only with cartographic materials. Such essentials as scale, projection, grid, and direction, all formerly included in the note area, are to be included in the mathematical data area.[11]

3.3B. Statement of scale

The first element of the mathematical data area is the statement of scale.

3.3B1. No matter how the statement may be given in the item, scale is expressed in the mathematical data area as a fraction with a ratio 1: (e.g. 1:250 would mean that one inch on the map represented 250 inches of area). Note that even if the scale has been recorded as part of the title proper, it will be repeated—translated into the proper fraction if necessary—in the mathematical data area. See figure 3-1.

---

[11] Cataloguers who find the technicalities of map interpretation intimidating may find aid and comfort in John V. Bergen's "Map Reading and Map Appreciation," *Illinois Libraries* 56 (May 1974): 349–59. Another good general discussion for nonspecialists of map librarianship is the *Drexel Library Quarterly* 9 (October 1973). The entire issue is devoted to various aspects of the subject.

If only a verbal scale is given, translate this into a representative fraction preceded by "ca." Do not enclose the figure in brackets. See figures 3-6a and 3-6b. Whenever an approximate scale is given, the fraction should be preceded by "ca."

Sometimes, as in the basis for figure 3-4, a map includes a bar graph rather than a scale statement. Scale can be arrived at by using a scale indicator (a device for measuring bar graphs and grids to convert them into a representative fraction).

If no grid, bar graph, or verbal statement is found on a map, compare the map to another of known scale and give an approximate scale.

3.3B2. Optional addition. If it seems appropriate, the fractional scale statement may be followed by additional scale information. If the cataloguer chooses to do this, each element is separated by a full stop. For an example see figure 3-5.

3.3B3. Sometimes the scale used on a single item varies. If this is the case, give the largest fraction followed by the smaller fraction, connecting the two by a hyphen.

Note, by the way, that English-language terms are always used in the mathematical data area (see figure 3-9).

```
Frankfurt a.M. Offenbach. -- 31. Aufl. -- Scale
   1:16,500-1:27,500 ; hyperboloid proj. -- Hamburg ;
   New York : Falk, [1970?]
   1 map : col. ; 73 x 103 cm. folded to 21 x 11 cm.
-- (Falk-Plan ; 118)

   Legend in German, English, and French.
   Imprint on label pasted on cover: New York :
French and European Publications.
   Contains: Index map of Frankfurt and Strassen-
verzeichnis. Nordweststadt.  Scale 1:8,000--Hanau.
Scale 1:28,000 inserted in Strassenverzeichnis.

   I. Falk-Verlag.
```

Figure 3-9. Scale
statement

Falk Plan
Frankfurt a.M. Offenbach
In Hyperboloid - Projektion mit Kilometernetz
Maßstab 1:16 500 - 1:27 500
Falk-Verlag
Hamburg • Den Haag • Paris

Information from map

Berlin • London • New York

3.3B4. If an item with more than one part is collected under one title, the scale statement must fit all of the parts of the item. If the scales vary and there are not more than two scales for all the parts of the item, show the scale statement as stipulated in the rule. Figure 3-7b is an example with added complications. (The scale for the first map was stated on the map; scale for the other maps, which were all the same size, was approximated following 3.3B1).

3.3B5. If maps in a collected set are drawn to more than two scales, use the statement "Scales vary."

3.3B7. For some cartographic items, scale would be inappropriate. Such items include imaginary maps. Often a pictorial "bird's eye view" of an area is not drawn to an accurate scale. If no scale is stated on such an item, do not try to approximate one. Use the statement "Not drawn to scale" (see figure 3-10).

```
Dyer, C. J.
   Bird's eye view of Phoenix, Maricopa Co.,
Arizona : view looking North-East / sketched by
C.J. Dyer ; W. Byrnes, litho. -- Not drawn to
scale. -- [Phoenix] : Phoenix Historical Society,
1976.
   1 map view : col. ; 33 x 51 cm.

   Reprint of: Phoenix : Daily Phoenix Herald, 1876.


   I. Title.
```

Figure 3-10. "Bird's eye view"

Information from map

Bird's Eye View of
Phoenix   Maricopa Co.   Arizona
View Looking North-east
Sketched by C. J. Dyer
Phoenix, Arizona
W. Byrnes, Litho.
Reissued 1976 by the Phoenix Historical Society

Some maps, particularly those designed for tourists, are deliberately not drawn to scale, in order that certain areas or features may be highlighted. The same statement: "Not drawn to scale" is appropriate for such items (see figure 3-11).

Tour map, metro Saint John, New Brunswick, Canada /
    produced by the Saint John Department of
    Promotion. -- Not drawn to scale. -- Saint John,
    N.B. : The Dept., 1973.
1 map : col. ; 41 x 46 cm. folded to 23 x 11 cm.

Cover title: Saint John, New Brunswick, tour map
: Canada's loyalist city.
    Includes 3 insets. On verso: Points of interest in
Saint John.

    I. Saint John (N.B.). Dept. of Promotion.

Figure 3-11. Not drawn to scale

Information from map

Tour Map – Metro Saint John
New Brunswick, Canada
Produced by the Saint John Department
of Promotion
This map is not to scale

3.3C. Statement of projection

If a map includes a statement of projection, mention of it follows the statement of scale, being separated from it by space - semicolon - space. See, for example, figure 3-5.

3.4. PUBLICATION, DISTRIBUTION, ETC., AREA

Data to be included in this area are recorded according to the general rules given in 1.4.

3.5. PHYSICAL DESCRIPTION AREA

The physical description area consists of the number of items (qualified by one of the terms included in the list under 3.5B1), colour (if any), material (if other than paper), mounting (if any), and size.

3.5B3. Atlases. An atlas shares the characteristics of both book and cartographic material. The source of information for an atlas is, as for a book, the title page (3.0B1). In most cases, scale statement will be given according to 3.3B3 (see figure 3-12).

3.5B4. Note the physical description area in figures 3-6b and 3-6c. Each is based on a separately titled map of a single item that lacks a collective title.

Oxford economic atlas of the world / prepared by
the Economist Intelligence Unit and the Cartographic Department of the Clarendon Press. -- 3rd
ed. -- Scale varies ; Oxford equal-area proj. --
London ; New York : Oxford University Press,
1965.
1 atlas (viii, 286 p.) : col. ; 27 cm.

Includes statistical index.

Figure 3-12. Atlas

I. Economist Intelligence Unit, Ltd.   II.
Clarendon Press. Cartographic Dept.

Oxford Economic Atlas
of the World
prepared by
The Economist Intelligence Unit   Title page
and the
Cartographic Department of
the Clarendon Press
Third Edition
Oxford University Press

3.5C. Other physical details

As with other library materials, the presence of colour in a cartographic
item is noted with the abbreviation "col." as part of the second element of the
physical description area. Some special features of maps may be noted: If a
map is printed on material other than paper, this is indicated; if the item has
been mounted, this is noted. For atlases (3.5C2) the number of maps will be
specified if the maps are numbered or if they are listed in such a fashion that
the number can easily be ascertained. If this is not the case, describe the maps
that make up the atlas as otherwise stipulated under 3.5C.

3.5D. Dimensions

For maps, give height by width, measuring between the neat lines (the inner-
most of a series of lines that frame the map). If a map lacks such lines, or if it is
extremely irregularly shaped, give dimensions of the sheet (see figure 3-4).
(Note: 3.5D1 stipulates that the map itself should be measured in such a case,
if this is feasible.)

3.5D2. Atlases. Measure atlases according to the rules for books: i.e., give
the height of the cover in centimetres. (See figure 3-12.) For a map designed to

be folded, include the dimensions of the folded map as well as the dimensions of the sheet (see figure 3-1, etc.).

3.5E. Accompanying material

See 1.5E for methods of handling various types of materials issued with a map and intended to be used with it.

3.6. SERIES AREA

Maps are frequently issued as part of a series. Series statements will be recorded following instructions in 1.6. For examples of map series, see the following:

Figure 3-5, a series with other title information.

Figure 3-7b, the series as an important unifying element for the 5 maps of the set. Each of them bears the statement: Arizona Resources Information System cooperative publication no. 5.

Figure 3-8, a series that includes a statement of responsibility (1.6E1).

Figure 3-10, a numbered publisher series.

3.7. NOTE AREA

Notes follow the general pattern stipulated in 1.7. In addition to directions on the order of notes given in 1.7B, follow the order of notes indicated in 3.7B.

```
Shope, Irvin.
   The Santa Fé Trail / Irvin Shope. -- Not drawn
to scale. -- Manchester, N.H. : Issued by American
Pioneer Trail Association, 1946.
   1 map : col. ; 38 x 57 cm.

   Pictorial map; shows other early trails.
   "Issued ... as part of 1946 national commemoration
honoring pioneers of trade in America.



   I. American Pioneer Trail Association.    II. Title.
```

Figure 3-13. Scope note

The Santa Fé Trail

Irvin Shope '46

Issued by American Pioneer Trail Association
as part of 1946 National Commemoration
Honoring Pioneers of Trade in America

Information from map face   **The Clarke Press, 68 Depot St., Manchester, N.H.**

3.7B1. Nature and scope. If the map contains any features not evident from the rest of the description, which one would not expect to find in such an item, make a note. (See figure 3-13.)

3.7B11. Accompanying material. If material issued with a map and intended to be used with it is too complex in its nature to be added at the end of the physical description area (see discussion in this text under 1.5E for criteria), in many cases it may appropriately be added in the note area. (See figure 3-14.)

```
Lemmon, Robert E.
   Geologic map of the Fruitland quadrangle, North
Carolina / prepared in cooperation with Tennessee
Valley Authority by Robert E. Lemmon and David E.
Dunn. -- Scale 1:24,000. -- [Raleigh] : State of
North Carolina, Dept. of Natural and Economic
Resources, Office of Earth Resources, 1973.
   1 map : col. ; 58 x 48 cm.

   In envelope bearing title: Geologic map and
mineral resources summary of the Fruitland quad-
rangle, North Carolina.
   Accompanied by pamphlet: Mineral resources sum-
mary of the Fruitland quadrangle, North Carolina

         (Continued on next card)
```

Figure 3-14.
Accompanying material

```
Lemmon, Robert E.  Geological map of the Fruitland
   quadrangle, North Carolina.  1973.  (card 2)

/ by Robert E. Lemmon.
   Includes insets listing mineral resources and
linear features of the quadrangle.
   Publisher's no.: GM 202-NW (map). -- MRS 202-NW
(pamphlet)

   I. Dunn, David E.   II. Tennessee Valley Author-
ity.  III. North Carolina.  Office of Earth Re-
sources.  IV. Title.  V. Title: Geological map and
mineral resources summary of the Fruitland quad-
rangle, North Carolina.  VI. Title: Mineral re-
sources summary of the Fruitland quadrangle, North
Carolina.
```

Scale 1:24000
Geologic Map of the Fruitland Quadrangle,
North Carolina
by Robert E. Lemmon and David E. Dunn 1973
State of North Carolina
Department of Natural and Economic Resources
Office of Earth Resources
Prepared in cooperation with
Information from map face   Tennessee Valley Authority

Geologic Map
and
Mineral Resources Summary
of the
Fruitland Quadrangle
North Carolina
Raleigh
1973

Information from
envelope

Pamphlet

Mineral Resources Summary
of the
Fruitland Quadrangle
North Carolina
by
Robert E. Lemmon

4

Music

(*AACR2* Chapter 5 and rules 21.18–21.22)

AACR2 chapter 5 covers the description of published music. Rules in chapter 5 do not deal with choice and form of main and added entries. These are covered in *AACR2* chapters 21 through 24. Nor does chapter 5 concern itself with rules for uniform titles that are often needed to organize entries for musical works. These rules are contained in chapter 25, particularly rules 25.25 through 25.36.

The cataloguing of music, because of the special nature of the material, presents unique problems. Indicative of these problems is the fact that a fairly substantial section of *AACR2* chapter 21 (rules 21.18–21.22) is given over to specific rules for choice of entry for musical works. All of these special rules are based on general rule 21.9, "Works that are modifications of other works." If a musical work has been modified in such a way that "the modification has substantially changed the nature and content of the original," entry will be under the heading appropriate to the new work. Otherwise, entry is under the heading for the original work. The special rules in chapter 21 for music help the cataloguer to make the proper decision in this regard.

It must be emphasized that the general principles governing choice of main entry for other types of library materials apply equally to musical works. In fact, 21.1A1 specifically states that "composers of music are the authors of the works they create." Entry for original musical works is under the name of the composer (see figure 4-1).

21.18. MUSICAL WORKS: GENERAL RULE

This rule concerns itself with choice of entry for musical arrangements, free transcriptions, and other arrangements that in some way are different from the composer's original work.

21.18B. Arrangements, transcriptions, etc.

This rule is basically the same as 231A in *AACR1*. A simple arrangement (not a paraphrase or free transcription) will be entered under the name of the original composer (see figure 4-2). The rule is analogous to 21.12, revisions of texts.

Bach, Johann Sebastian, 1685-1750.
⌐Orgelbüchlein┐
The liturgical year : forty-five organ chorals = (Orgelbüchlein) / by Johann Sebastian Bach ; edited by Albert Riemenschneider. -- Philadelphia : Ditson : T. Presser Co., distributers, c1933.
xvi, 138 p. of music ; 30 cm.

Words in English and German.
Based on the Bach Gesellschaft ed.

I. Riemenschneider, Albert. II. Title. III. Title: Orgelbüchlein.

Figure 4-1. Entry under name of composer

Title page

The Liturgical Year (Orgelbüchlein)
by Johann Sebastian Bach
Forty-five Organ Chorals
edited by Albert Riemenschneider
Oliver Ditson Company
Theodore Presser Co., Distributors
1712 Chestnut Street
Philadelphia

Wagner, Richard.
⌐Tannhäuser. Selections; arr.┐
Piano selection from Tannhäuser / by Richard Wagner ; arranged by Otto Hackh. -- New York : G. Schirmer, c1897.
45 p. of music ; 31 cm. -- (Schirmer's library of musical classics ; v. 1193)

I. Hackh, Otto. II. Title.

Figure 4-2. Transcription for another instrument under original composer

Title page

Schirmer's Library of Musical Classics
Vol. 1193
Piano Selection from
Tannhäuser
by Richard Wagner
arranged by Otto Hackh
New York : G. Schirmer
Boston : The Boston Music Co.
Copyright, 1897, by G. Schirmer

21.18C. Adaptations

This rule is analogous to 21.10, Adaptations of texts. If the nature and content of a musical work has been modified so much that it is substantially changed, main entry will be under the heading for the adapter. Name-title added entry will be made under the name of the original (see figure 4-3).

```
Liszt, Franz, 1811-1886.
   ₍Grandes études de Paganini. 3.  La cam-
panella₎
   La campanella / Paganini-Liszt ; newly edited
by Ferruccio Busoni. -- Wiesbaden : Breitkopf &
Härtel, c1944.
   19 p. of music ; 31 cm. -- (Sechs Etüden nach
Paganini-Liszt / Ferruccio Busoni ; nr. 3)

   Includes original version by Liszt and new ver-
sion by Busoni.
   Pl. no.: 27885.

   I. Paganini, Nicolò, 1782-1840.  La campanella.
II. Busoni, Ferruccio.  III. Title.  IV. Series:
Busoni, Ferruccio.  Sechs Etüden nach Paganini-
Liszt.
```

Figure 4-3. Entry under name of adapter

	La Campanella
	Paganini-Liszt
First page of score	Newly edited by
	Ferruccio Busoni
Copyright 1916/1944 by Breitkopf & Härtel	27885

21.19. MUSICAL WORKS THAT INCLUDE WORDS

This rule is somewhat analogous to rule 21.11, illustrated texts. A vocal work that includes music and words will have main entry under the name of the composer (as appropriate under 21.1–21.6). If the words are "fully represented," give their author an added entry (see figure 4-4). This is a change from *AACR1* 230A, which applied the same criterion but exceptionally did not allow an added entry for the author of the words of a single song.

For a musical work with words based on a different text, give name-title added entry for the original text. (See figure 4-5.)

Schubert, Franz, 1797–1828.
    [Die schöne Mullerin. English & German]
    The lovely milleress : for voice and piano — (Die
schöne Müllerin) / by Franz Schubert ; English
words by Richard Dyer-Bennet. -- New York : G.
Schirmer, c1967.
    76 p. of music ; 28 cm.

    German words by Wilhelm Müller.
    Publisher's no.: 46127.

    I. Müller, Wilhelm.   II. Dyer-Bennet, Richard.
III. Title.   IV. Title: Die schöne Müllerin.

Figure 4-4. Musical
work with words

Title page

**The Lovely Milleress
(Die Schöne Müllerin)
For Voice and Piano by
Franz Schubert
English Words by
Richard Dyer-Bennet
G. Schirmer, Inc./New York**

Vaughan Williams, Ralph, 1872–1958.
    [Serenade to music. Vocal score]
    Serenade to music / words by Shakespeare, The
merchant of Venice ; music by R. Vaughan Williams.
-- London : Oxford University Press, c1938.
    1 vocal score (20 p.) ; 26 cm.

Figure 4-5. Text based
on previously published
text

    I. Shakespeare, William.   The merchant of Venice.
II. Title.

Title page

**Serenade to Music
Words by Shakespeare
The Merchant of Venice
Music by
R. Vaughan Williams
Oxford University Press**

21.19C. Writer's works set by several composers

This rule, which calls for entry of a collection of musical settings of songs, etc., with text by one writer and music by more than one composer as a collection, is the same as *AACR1* rule 230C. Based on *AACR2* 21.7, entry will be under title if such a musical collection has a collective title. See figure 4-6.

```
Songs from Shakespeare's plays and popular songs
   of Shakespeare's time / compiled and edited by
   Tom Kines. -- New York : Oak Publications, c1964.
   104 p. of music : ill., ports. ; 26 cm.

   Principally unacc.  Includes guitar symbols.
   Bibliography: p. 104.
   ISBN 0-8256-0068-5

   I. Kines, Tom.  II. Shakespeare, William.
```

Figure 4-6. Collection of musical settings, text by one author

Title page

Songs from Shakepeare's Plays
and Popular Songs of Shakepeare's Time
Compiled and edited by Tom Kines
Oak Publications   New York, N.Y.
Music Sales Limited   London

21.20. MUSICAL SETTINGS FOR BALLETS, ETC.

This rule is the same as *AACR1* rule 230A. Main entry will be under the name of the composer of the music; an added entry will be given to a choreographer, etc., whose name appears in the chief source of information. Martha Graham is the choreographer for the work on which figure 4-7 is based.

AACR2 rules 21.18–21.22 are concerned with special problems of entry of musical works. The rules in *AACR2* chapter 5 deal with the description of such works.

5.0B1. Chief source of information. As with printed books (*AACR2* chapter 2), the chief source of information for a musical work is the title page. One type of title page, a "list" title page, is simply a list of the composer's works issued by the publisher or lists of related music from the publisher. Included in the list will be the title of the work being catalogued. When dealing with this type title page, the cataloguer is directed to use either the "list" title page, a caption title page (title on first page of musical text), or a cover title page, whichever provides the fullest information. The list title page furnished the information for the example shown in figure 4-8. Note the omission from the catalogue entry of the other titles listed on the page.

```
Copland, Aaron, 1900-
  ₁Appalachian spring, orchestra₁
  Appalachian spring : (ballet for Martha) / Aaron
Copland. -- New York : Boosey & Hawkes, c1945.
  1 score (82 p.) ; 26 cm. -- (Hawkes pocket
scores ; no. 82)

  Condensed version of the ballet, arr. for sym-
phony orchestra.
  Duration: about 20 min.
  Pl. no.: B. & H. 9054.


  I. Graham, Martha.  II. Title.
```

Figure 4-7. Music for ballet

Title page

Aaron Copland
Appalachian Spring
(Ballet for Martha)
Boosey & Hawkes

```
Willan, Healey.
  Fair in face : (B.V.M.). -- New York : C. Fischer,
sole agents for the publishers : Oxford University
Press, Music Dept., c1928.
  1 score (4 p.) ; 26 cm. -- (Liturgical motets /
by Healey Willan ; L.M. 4) (Oxford music)

  For chorus (SATB), includes keyboard acc. for
rehearsal only.
  Based on responsaries from an office of our
Lady (8th century).
  Publisher's no.: O.X. 996.

  I. Title.  II. Series: Willan, Healey.  Motets.
Selections ; L.M. 4.
```

Figure 4-8. "List" title page

L.M. 4   Oxford Music   Liturgical Motets
By Healey Willan
1.   Preserve us, O Lord (Evening)
2.   O King, all Glorious (Saints' Days)
3.   I beheld her Beautiful as a Dove (B.V.M.)
4.   Fair in Face (B.V.M.)
5.   Rise up, my Love, my Fair One (Easter)
6.   O King of Glory (Ascensiontide)
7.   Lo, In the Time Appointed (Advent)
8.   O King, to Whom all Things do Live (Funerals)
Carl Fischer, Inc., Sole Agents for the Publishers
Oxford University Press Music Department
O. X. 996, Cooper Square, New York

List title page

5.1. TITLE AND STATEMENT OF RESPONSIBILITY AREA

5.1B. Title proper
The chief source of information must be used in transcribing the title proper. General rule 1.1B governs the transcription of titles of musical works. In addition, because musical works are frequently issued in different editions with varying titles, and because in many cases the titles of published works are not adequate for a proper organization of a composer's file, the cataloguer often interposes a uniform title between the main entry heading and the title proper as it appears on a single work. See 25.25–25.36 for rules for uniform titles for musical works.

5.1B2. Sometimes the title consists of a generic term followed by medium of performance, key, opus numbering, etc. All of this information is included as part of the title proper (see figure 4-9).

Willan, Healey.
    ₁Sonatas, violin, piano, no. 1, E minor₁
    Sonata no. 1, in E minor, for violin and piano /
Healey Willan. -- Toronto : BMI Canada ; New York :
Associated Music Publishers, c1955.
    1 score (24 p.) + 1 part ; 31 cm.

I. Title.

Figure 4-9. Generic term title

Healey Willan
Sonata No. 1 in E Minor
For Violin and Piano
BMI Canada Limited
Toronto   Montreal
Associated Music Publishers, Inc.
1 W 47th St., New York

Title page

If a title that includes medium of performance, key, etc., does not begin with a generic term, treat medium of performance, key, etc., as other title information. (See figure 4-10.)

```
Bach, Johann Sebastian, 1685-1750.
  ₁Preludes and fugues, harpsichord₁
  Short preludes and fugues : for the pianoforte /
Johann Sebastian Bach ; edited and fingered by Wm.
Mason. -- New York : G. Schirmer, c1895.
  35 p. of music ; 31 cm. -- (Schirmer's library
of musical classics ; v. 15)




  I. Mason, William.   II. Title.
```

Figure 4-10.
Nongeneric title

Title page

Schirmer's Library of Musical Classics
Vol. 15
Johann Sebastian Bach
Short Preludes and Fugues
for the
Pianoforte
Edited and Fingered by
Dr. Wm. Mason
G. Schirmer, Inc. New York
Copyright, 1895, by G. Schirmer, Inc.

5.1C. Optional addition
The cataloguer may optionally add the general material designation "music" in brackets immediately following the title proper. Following probable Library of Congress practice, examples of music in this text do not include GMD.

5.1D. Parallel titles
Parallel titles are recorded according to stipulations of general rule 1.1D. See figures 4-1 and 4-4 for examples.

5.1E. Other title information
This information is recorded following general rule 1.1E. See figure 4-7, etc.

5.1F. Statements of responsibility
These statements follow general instructions given under 1.1F.

5.4. PUBLICATION, DISTRIBUTION, ETC., AREA

General rule 1.4 is to be followed in transcribing this area. *AACR1* rule 245D1 stipulated that publishers' numbers or plate numbers were to be added as the final element in this area for music that did not include a date of publication, printing, or copyright, since these numbers may serve as a clue to approximate printing date for libraries with access to publishers' catalogues. (A plate number is a number that appears at the bottom of each page of music when the music is reproduced by engraving. The publisher's number is a number that usually appears on the title page, if at all.) *AACR2* rule 5.4D2 specifies that these numbers will be recorded in the note area (dealt with in detail in 5.7B19). See, for instance, figures 4-3, 4-4, etc.

5.5. PHYSICAL DESCRIPTION AREA

The physical description area follows the general pattern for other types of library materials.

5.5B. Extent of item and specific material designation

The number of physical units is stated together with the specific format of music, e.g.: 1 score (32 p.) ; 4 parts. See *AACR2* Appendix D, Glossary, for definition of terms listed under 5.5B1. If none of the listed terms is appropriate, use, as appropriate, *v. of music*, *p. of music*, or *leaves of music*.

5.5B2. If the item consists of a score and parts, these are recorded separately, the score being listed first. See figure 4-9.

5.5C. Illustrations

Illustrations are recorded following stipulations of 2.5C.

5.5D. Dimensions

The height of the musical work is measured, following stipulations of 2.5D.

5.6. SERIES AREA

Rules for the series statement follow general rule 1.6.

5.7. NOTE AREA

Notes follow the general order and are of the same type as those listed under 1.7.

5.7B19. Plate numbers and publishers' numbers. See 5.4D2.

5

Sound Recordings

(*AACR2* Chapter 6)

AACR2 chapter 6 includes rules for the description of all types of sound recordings. Once again it must be emphasized that the rules in chapter 6 have nothing to say about choice of main and/or added entries. For guidance on these matters the cataloguer must turn to *AACR2* chapter 21, "Choice of Access Points." Main entry for sound recordings is based on the same principles of authorship governing other types of library materials; entry will be under "the person chiefly responsible for the creation of the intellectual or artistic content of a work." This means, for the most part, that main entry will be under the composer of a musical work that has been recorded, or the writer of a book or other material that is being narrated, applying rules 21.1 through 21.22 as appropriate. In some instances, an individual performer or performing group is regarded as the author of a sound recording and will be given main entry (21.23C). Indicative of the fact that entry for sound recordings presents special difficulties is that a separate section in *AACR2* chapter 21 is devoted to rules governing this type of material. These may be briefly summarized.

21.23A. Sound recording of one work

Enter a sound recording of one work under the person or body chiefly responsible for the intellectual or musical content of the work, following general rules as indicated above.

A sound recording of a single work of a composer will be entered under the name of the composer. Form for entry of the composer's name is governed by *AACR2* chapter 22, "Headings for Persons." Transcription of the title is governed by chapter 5, "Music." Much classical music entered under composer has been issued many times under varying titles. If this is the case, a uniform title is interposed between the author heading and the title proper. Such a title brings all the editions, translations, etc., of a musical composition together in the same place in the catalogue. See *AACR2* chapter 25, "Uniform Titles," for specific rules and guidance in this matter. Note that the Library of Congress will probably apply option 25.5E, which means that GMD will appear twice: at the end of the uniform title and after the title proper in catalogue entries that show uniform title. Examples in this text follow this option. See for example, figure 5-1.

```
Victoria, Tomás Luis de, 1548-1611.
   [Missa pro defunctis (1583).  Latin.  Sound
recording]
   Requiem mass [sound recording] / Victoria. --
Camden, N.J. : RCA Victor, c1958.
   1 sound disc (ca. 22 min.) : 33 1/3 rpm, stereo. ;
12 in.
   Choir of the abbey of Mount Angel, David Nichol-
son, director ; Portland Symphonic Choir, C. Robert
Zimmerman, director.
   Programme notes and English translation of the
text on container.
   RCA Victor: LM 2254.
   I. Mount Angel Abbey.  Choir.  II. Portland
Symphonic Choir.
```

Figure 5-1. A recorded musical work

Disc label

LM 2254
Side 1
Red Seal
RCA Victor
New Orthophonic high fidelity
In Latin
Victoria
Requiem Mass
1-Introitus   2-Kyrie
3-Graduale   4-Offertorium
Choir of the Abbey of Mount Angel
Dom David Nicholson, O. S. B., Director
and the Portland Symphonic Choir
C. Robert Zimmerman
Director
Long 33 1/3 play
Trade mark registered
Radio Corporation of America, Camden, N.J.

A sound recording made from a book will be entered under the heading appropriate to the book, as long as the narrator retains the original words of the book. (See figure 5-2.)

Carroll, Lewis.
    Alice's adventures in Wonderland ₍sound recording₎
: the Lewis Carroll classic, complete / music
composed by Alec Wilder ; produced by Modern
Voices. -- New York : Released by Bill Grauer
Productions, ₍1957?₎
    4 sound discs (ca. 176 min.) : 33 1/3 rpm, mono. ;
12 in.
    Read and sung by Cyril Ritchard; music played by
the New York Woodwind Quintet.
    Recorded in New York City, spring and summer 1957.
    Text (facsim. of 1865 ed., 192 p.) laid in
container; notes on container.
                    (continued on next card)

Carroll, Lewis.   Alice's adventures in Wonderland
    ₍sound recording₎.   ₍1957?₎   (card 2)

    Summary: Alice goes down a rabbit hole to a
strange world of fantasy.
    Riverside: SDP 22.

**Figure 5-2. A recorded
literary work**

    I. Ritchard, Cyril.   II. New York Woodwind
Quintet.   III. Wilder, Alec.   IV. Title.

**Riverside
Alice's Adventures in
Wonderland
The Lewis Carroll classic—complete
read and sung by Cyril Ritchard**   Disc label
**Long Playing SDP 22   Side 1 Microgroove
Music composed by Alec Wilder; played by
the New York Woodwind Quintet
Bill Grauer Productions
New York City**

And, of course, a recording may be an original work never intended for any other medium. (See figure 5-3.) What more effective way could there be for a master storyteller to reveal some of her secrets than orally, using cassette?

```
Tooze, Ruth.
   Storytelling [sound recording] / Ruth Tooze. --
Los Angeles : Listener Corp., [197-?]
   4 sound cassettes (ca. 216 min.) : 1 7/8 ips, 2
track, mono. -- (Listener in-service cassette
library ; album 6)

   In container (24 cm.)
   Synopsis and biographical note on container.
   Contents: 1. Why we tell stories. What makes
a story good to tell -- 2. How to tell a story --
3. Selected stories -- 4. Poetry for today's
child.

   I. Title. II. Series.
```

Figure 5-3. Single work

Container

Listener
In-Service Cassette Library
Album 6
Storytelling
Ruth Tooze
Listener Corporation
6777 Hollywood Boulevard, Hollywood,
California 90028

21.23B. This rule is analogous to 21.4A. It states that a sound recording of two or more works by one individual or body will be entered under the name of that individual or group. (See figure 5-4.)

21.23C. The general definition of authorship states in certain cases "performers are the authors of sound recordings . . ." (21.1A1). Following this definition, 21.23C stipulates that main entry for recordings containing works by different persons will be under the principal performer of those works.

Rule 21.23C is analogous to 21.9, which states that a modification of another work will be entered under the heading appropriate to the new work. As the old adage puts it, "The singer, not the song." Figure 5-5 is a clear example of entry under the name of the performer.

A sound recording containing works by different persons (a collection) will be entered under the name of the first performer or first performing group listed if two or three individuals or groups are responsible for the collection and if no one of these can be called the principal performer. Make added entries for the other performer(s) or group(s). (See figure 5-6.)

```
Bizet, Georges.
   [L'Arlésienne.  Suite, 1.  Sound recording]
   L'Arlésienne, Suiten 1 & 2 ; Carmen, Suite 1
  sound recording  / Georges Bizet. -- [New York] :
Deutsche Grammophon, [1971?]
   1 sound cartridge (ca. 46 min.) : 3 3/4 ips,
stereo.
   Berliner Philharmoniker, Herbert von Karajan,
conductor.
   Available as disc.
   Deutsche Grammophon: 89 433.

   I. Bizet, Georges.  L'Arlésienne.  Suite, 2.
Sound recording.  II. Bizet, Georges.  Carmen.
Suite 1.  Sound recording.  III. Karajan, Herbert
von.  IV. Berliner Philharmonisches Orchester.
V. Title.
```

Figure 5-4. Entry under composer—two or more works by one person

Cartridge label

Deutsche
Grammophon
Gesellschaft
Georges Bizet
L'Arlésienne-Suiten 1 & 2 - Carmen-Suite 1
Berliner Philharmoniker   Herbert von Karajan
Stereo
Program One: Carmen Suite No. 1 - Prelude
Entr'acte III - Entr'acte IV - Entr'acte II -
L'Arlésienne Suit No. 1 - Prelude (Part 1)

Program Two: L'Arlésienne Suite No. 1
Prelude (Part 2) - Minuetto - Adagietto

Program Three: L'Arlésienne Suite No. 1
Carillon - L'Arlésienne Suite No. 2 - Pastorale
Intermezzo (Part 1)

Program Four: L'Arlésienne Suite No. 2
Intermezzo (Part 2) - Menuet - Farandole

Berlin Philharmonic
Herbert von Karajan, Conductor
Bizet
Carmen Suite No. 1
L'Arlésienne Suites Nos. 1 & 2
DG 8-track stereo

89 433
Deutsche
Grammophon

Denver, John.
   Rocky Mountain high [sound recording] / John
Denver. -- New York : RCA Victor, c1972.
   1 sound disc (32 min.) : 33 1/3 rpm, stereo. ;
12 in.

   Songs; John Denver accompanying himself on the
6 or 12 string guitar, instrumental and vocal
ensemble.
   Texts on album.
   Contents: Rocky Mountain high / John Denver with
Mike Taylor (4 min., 41 sec.) -- Mother Nature's
son / John Lennon & Paul McCartney (2 min., 26 sec.)

        (continued on next card)

Denver, John. Rocky Mountain high [sound recor-
   ding]. c1972. (card 2)

              Contents continued
-- Paradise / John Prine (2 min., 20 sec.) -- For
Baby (for Bobbie) / John Denver (2 min., 58 sec.)
-- Darcy Farrow / Steve Gillette and Tom Campbell
(4 min., 22 sec.) -- Prisoners / John Denver (3 min.,
38 sec.) -- Goodbye again / John Denver (3 min.,
36 sec.) -- Season suite / John Denver, with Mike
Taylor and Dick Kniss (10 min.)
   RCA Victor: LSP 4731.

   I. Title.

Figure 5-5. Entry under
performer—collection
of songs by different
persons

Disc label

Side 1 Stereo
LSP-4731 (BPRS-5155)

Rocky Mountain High
John Denver

1 Rocky Mountain High (Denver-Taylor)
RCA   **Victor**
2 Mother Nature's Son (Lennon-McCartney)
3 Paradise (Prine)
4 For Baby (For Bobbie) (Denver)
5 Darcy Farrow (Gillette-Campbell)
6 Prisoners (Denver)
dynaflex
TM(s)   RCA Corp. Made in U.S.A.
P 1972 RCA Records

N.C.R.V. Vocaal Ensemble.
   Renaissance choral music for Christmas ₍sound
recording₎. -- New York : Nonesuch Records, ₍1965₎
   1 sound disc (33 min.) : 33 1/3 rpm, stereo. ;
12 in. -- (A Camerata recording)

   Sung in Latin or German.
   N.C.R.V. Vocaal Ensemble, Marinus Voorberg, con-
ductor ; Kaufbeurer Martinsfinken, Ludwig Hahn,
conductor ; Niedersächsischer Singkreis, Willi
Träder, conductor.
   Texts, with English translations, on container.
   Contents: Praeter rerum seriem / Josquin Desprez
(6 min., 54 sec.) -- Egredietur virga-Radix Jesse /

(continued on next card)

Figure 5-6. A collection recorded by three groups

N.C.R.V. Vocaal Ensemble. Renaissance choral
   music for Christmas ₍sound recording₎. ₍1965₎
   (card 2)
         Contents continued
Jacobus Gallus (Handl) (2 min., 28 sec.) -- Quem
vidistis pastores / Andrea Gabrieli (2 min., 55
sec.) -- Der Engel sprach zu den Hirten / Heinrich
Schutz (3 min., 5 sec.) -- Hodie Christus natus est
/ Giovanni Gabrieli (2 min., 33 sec.) -- O Jesu mi
dulcissime / Giovanni Gabrieli (6 min., 14 sec.) --
Joseph, lieber Joseph mein / Johann Walter (1 min.,
45 sec.) -- Ein Kind geborn zu Bethlehem / Bartholo-
maus Gesius, Michael Praetorius, Melchior Vulpius

      (Continued on next card)

N.C.R.V. Vocaal Ensemble. Renaissance choral
   music for Christmas ₍sound recording₎. ₍1965₎
   (card 3)
            Contents continued.
(1 min., 23 sec.) -- Es ist ein Ros entsprungen /
Michael Praetorius (2 min., 42 sec.) -- In dulci
jubilo / Samuel Scheidt (3 min., 5 sec.)
   Nonesuch: H-71095.

   I. Kaufbeurer Martinsfinken. II. Niedersächsicher
Singkreis. III. Title.

Nonesuch Records
Renaissance Choral Music
for Christmas

Stereo

H-71095-A

Side One

1. Josquin Desprez: Praeter rerum seriem   6:54
N.C.R.V. Vocaal Ensemble, Hilversum,
Marinus Voorberg, conductor

2. Jacobus Gallus (Handl): Egredietur virga-Radix
Disc label   Jesse   2:28

3. Andrea Gabrieli: Quem vidistis pastores   2:55
Kaufbeurer Martinsfinken, Ludwig Hahn, conductor

4. Heinrich Schutz: Der Engel sprach zu den
Hirten, SWV 395   3:05
Niedersächsischer Singkreis, Hannover, Willi Träder,
conductor

5. Giovanni Gabrieli: Hodie Christus natus est   2.33
Kaufbeurer Martinsfinken, Ludwig Hahn, conductor
a Camerata recording,
Nonesuch Records, 15 Columbus Circle,
New York, N.Y.

21.23D. Collection by more than one person or body, performed by more than three performers or groups

This rule is analogous to 21.6C2, which states that if a work has more than three authors, it will be given title main entry. Likewise, a sound recording collection with four or more performing individuals or groups will be entered under title. The example shown in figure 5-7 includes a solid gold hit from each of twenty different performing groups and individuals, from Love Unlimited Orchestra and Hog Heaven to Aretha Franklin. Mercifully, since such a number of items is contained in the item, the cataloguer may be spared listing the total splendour of the offering in a contents note.

The cataloguer should be reminded that a sound recording may be issued as a serial. In most instances, a serial sound recording will include works by more than one person or group, performed by more than three performers or groups, since a serial by definition is a publication intended to be continued indefinitely. (See *AACR2* chapter 12.) Such a serial will be entered under title, following stipulations of 21.23D. For an example of a serial sound recording, see figure 10-1.

Rule 21.23 addresses itself to special problems of main entry for sound recordings. Rules in *AACR2* chapter 6 deal with the description of such works.

```
20 solid gold hits [sound recording] : original
   hits / by original artists. -- [s.l.] : Adam
   VIII Ltd., c1975.
1 sound cartridge : 3 3/4 ips, quad.

Adam VIII Ltd.: 8016.



   I. Adam VIII Ltd.
```

Figure 5-7. More than three artists or groups —title main entry

6.0B1. Chief source of information. Although chapter 6 includes rules for diverse types of sound recordings, the chief source of information is the same in all cases: The label affixed to the recording is the preferred source. If the item includes more than one label (as, for instance, a phonograph disc), both labels are regarded as one source. For tape, a reel, cassette, or cartridge is also considered part of the chief source. For film, the container as well as the label is the chief source. For any type of sound recording, accompanying textual material or a container may be used as the chief source of information whenever it furnishes a collective title not found on the parts or their labels. In this case, make a note to indicate the source.

6.1B. Title proper

The chief source of information must be used in transcribing the title proper. See 1.1B for general rules governing such transcription.

In addition, when transcribing the title of a musical work, refer to 5.1B. In the example shown in figure 5-8, the title proper consists of the generic term "Concerto," the key, and the opus number (5.1B2). As previously mentioned, a uniform title is often interposed between the main entry heading and the title proper in music cataloguing. See 25.25–25.36 for rules on uniform titles for music.

6.1C. Optional addition. General material designation

Following Library of Congress practice, most cataloguers will use GMD "sound recording" for all types of sound recordings. It is added immediately following the title proper.

6.1E. Other title information

Other title information follows the GMD (see figure 5-9). See general rules under 1.1E for punctuation and transcription.

6.1F. Statements of responsibility

The statement of responsibility is to be transcribed according to general instructions found in 1.1F. However, a special exception to the general rules is made for the transcription of statements of responsibility for sound recordings.

Names of narrators or performers are in most cases omitted and given in the note area (see 6.7B6). The statement of responsibility is limited to writers, composers, and collectors of field material if these names appear prominently. See, for instance, figure 5-1 and 5-2.

6.1F3. A short phrase may be added to clarify an ambiguous statement of responsibility as shown in figure 5-10.

```
Mozart, Wolfgang Amadeus, 1756-1791.
  [Concerto, flute, harp, orchestra, K. 299, C
major. Sound recording]
  Concerto in C major, K 299 [sound recording] /
Mozart. -- [London] : Angel, c1964.
  on side 1 of 1 sound disc (31 min.) : 33 1/3 rpm,
stereo. ; 12 in.

  Elaine Shaffer, flute ; Marilyn Costello, harp ;
Philharmonia Orchestra, Yehudi Menuhin, conductor.
  Programme notes on container.
  Angel: S 36189.
  With: Suite in A minor / Telemann.

  I. Shaffer, Elaine.  II. Costello, Marilyn.  III.
Menuhin, Yehudi.  IV. Philharmonia Orchestra.
```

Figure 5-8. Title proper

	Angel			Angel
Side 1	Stereo		Side 2	Stereo
	S. 36189			S. 36189
	(2YEA-X-834) 33 1/3			(2YEA-X-835) 33-1/3
Mozart—Concerto in C major, K. 299			Telemann—Suite in A minor	
(1) - 1st Movement: Allegro - Cadenza			Ouverture	
(by Flothuis)			Les Plaisirs	
(2) - 2nd Movement: Andantino - Cadenza			Air à l'Italien	
(by Flothuis)		Disc	Menuet 1 & 2	
(3) - 3rd Movement: Rondo (Allegro) -		label	Réjouissance	
Cadenza (by Flothuis)			Passepied 1 & 2	
Elaine Shaffer (Flute) &			Polonaise	
Marilyn Costello (Harp)			Elaine Shaffer (Flute)	
and The Philharmonia Orchestra			and The Philharmonia Orchestra	
conducted by Yehudi Menuhin			conducted by Yehudi Menuhin	
Recorded in England			Recorded in England	
Mfd. in U.S.A.			Mfd. in U.S.A.	
Mfd. by Capitol Records, Inc.,			Mfd. by Capitol Records, Inc.,	
a subsidiary of			a subsidiary of	
Capitol Industries, Inc., U.S.A.			Capitol Industries, Inc., U.S.A.	

Genesis of a novel ₍sound recording₎ : a documentary
  on the writing regimen of Georges Simenon. --
  Tucson, Ariz. : Motivational Programming Corp.,
  c1969.
  1 sound cassette (24 min.) : 1 7/8 ips, 2 track,
mono. -- (20th century European authors)

  Summary: An account of the development of
Georges Simenon's book, The premier.
  Bibliography on container.

  I. Motivational Programming Corporation.
II. Series.

Figure 5-9. Other title information

Cassette label

010 12201   **Genesis of a novel**
            A documentary on the writing
            regimen of Georges Simenon.
Motivational Programming Corporation
512 Transamerica Building, Tucson, Arizona 85701

Arlen, Harold.
  The wizard of Oz ₍sound recording₎ : musical and
dramatic selections recorded directly from the
sound track of M-G-M's technicolor film / ₍lyrics
by₎ Harburg ; ₍music by₎ Arlen. -- ₍New York₎ :
MGM Records, ₍1939?₎
  1 sound disc (ca. 42 min.) : 33 1/3 rpm, mono. ;
12 in.

  Starring Judy Garland and others ; M-G-M Studio
Orchestra and Chorus, Herbert Stothart and George
Stoll, conductors.
  Selections from the motion picture adaptation of:
The wizard of Oz / by L. Frank Baum.
  Programme notes on container.
        (continued on next card)

Figure 5-10. Statement of responsibility

Arlen, Harold. The wizard of Oz ₍sound recording₎.
  ₍1939?₎ (card 2)

  Contents: Over the rainbow -- If I only had a
brain -- If I only had a heart -- If I only had the
nerve -- Ding, dong! The witch is dead -- We're
off to see the wizard -- If I were king of the
forest.
  MGM: E 3464 St.

  I. Garland, Judy. II. Harburg, E. Y. III. Baum,
L. Frank. The wizard of Oz. IV. Metro-Goldwyn-
Mayer, Inc. Studio Orchestra. V. Title.

M-G-M
"The Wizard of Oz"

Disc label

E3464 St.   (Harburg-Arlen)   Side 1
Starring
Judy Garland, Ray Bolger, Bert Lahr,
Jack Haley and Frank Morgan
with Billie Burke, Margaret Hamilton
Over the Rainbow — Judy Garland
If I only had a Brain — Ray Bolger
If I only had a Heart — Jack Haley
If I only had the Nerve — Bert Lahr
Ding-Dong! The witch is dead
We're off to see the Wizard
M-G-M Studio Orchestra and Chorus
Conducted by Herbert Stothart
and George Stoll
Musical and dramatic selections
Recorded directly from the sound track of
M-G-M's Technicolor Film
MGM Records—A Division of LOEW'S Incorporated—
Made in U.S.A.

6.1G. Items without a collective title

Items without a collective title may be handled in either of two ways. According to 6.1G2, such an item may be described as a unit (see figure 5-11). See 1.1G for general instructions on procedures and for prescribed punctuation. If all of the selections are by a single composer, the titles are separated by space - semicolon - space.

Vivaldi, Antonio.
  [Concertos. Selections. Sound recording]
  Concerto per flautino C-dur, PV 79 ; Concerto per violoncello c-moll, PV 434 ; Concerto con violino principale, et altro violino per eco in lontana A-dur, PV 222 ; Concerto con viola d'amor e leuto e con tutti gl'istromenti sordini d-moll, PV 266 [sound recording] / Antonio Vivaldi. -- Hannover : Archiv Produktion, [1962?]
  1 sound disc (50 min.) : 33 1/3 rpm, stereo. ; 12 in. -- (Archiv Produktion. 8, Forschungsbereich : das italienische Settecento. Serie A, Das Konzert)
  Hans Martin Linde, sopranino-recorder (P. 79) ;
          (continued on next card)

Vivaldi, Antonio. [Concertos. Selections. Sound recording] [1962?] (card 2)

Klaus Storck, violoncello (P. 434) ; Susanne Lautenbacher, Ernesto Mampaey, violins (P. 222) ; Emil Seiler, viola d'amore, Karl Scheit, lute (P. 266) ; Emil Seiler Chamber Orchestra, Wolfgang Hofmann, conductor.
  Recorded in 1962.
  Programme notes in German, English, and French on container.
  Archiv Produktion: 198 318.

  I. Linde, Hans Martin.   II. Emil Seiler Chamber Orchestra.   III. Series.

Figure 5-11. Item without a collective title

Archiv
Produktion
Antonio Vivaldi
1. Concerto per Flautino C-dur, PV 79
2. Concerto per Violoncello c-moll, PV 434
Stereo
198 318   33
Hans-Martin Linde, Piccoloblockflöte
Klaus Storck, Violoncello
Kammerorchester Emil Seiler
Dirigent: Wolfgang Hofmann

Cover of container

VIII. Forschungsbereich
Das italienische Settecento
Serie A: Das Konzert
Archiv
Produktion
Antonio Vivaldi
Concerto per Flautino C-dur, PV 79
Concerto per Violoncello c-moll, PV 434

Disc label

If, on the other hand, selections on a sound recording lacking a collective title are by more than one composer, and if the item is to be described as a unit, make entry as shown in figure 5-12 (see 1.1G2).

```
Mozart, Wolfgang Amadeus, 1756-1791.
  [Concerto, flute, harp, orchestra, K. 299, C
major.  Sound recording]
  Concerto in C major, K. 299 / Mozart.  Suite in
A minor / Telemann [sound recording]. -- [London] :
Angel, c1964.
  1 sound disc (59 min.) : 33 1/3 rpm, stereo. ;
12 in.

  Elaine Shaffer, flute ; Marilyn Costello, harp ;
Philharmonia Orchestra, Yehudi Menuhin, conductor.
  Durations: 31 min. ; 28 min.
  Programme notes on container.
  Angel: S 36189.
  I. Telemann, Georg Philipp, 1681-1767.  Suite,
flute, string orchestra, A minor.  II. Shaffer,
Elaine.  III. Costello, Marilyn.  IV. Menuhin,
Yehudi.  V. Philharmonia Orchestra.
```

Figure 5-12. Item without a collective title—two composers

6.1G4. Optionally, the cataloguer may make a separate catalogue entry for each item without a collective title. One side of the sound recording catalogued as a unit in figure 5-12 above appears in figure 5-8. The other side of the recording would be catalogued as shown in figure 5-13 if the cataloguer chooses to follow this optional practice.

```
Telemann, Georg Philipp, 1681-1767.
  [Suite, flute, string orchestra, A minor.  Sound
recording]
  Suite in A minor [sound recording] / Telemann. --
[London] : Angel, c1964.
  on side 2 of 1 sound disc (28 min.) : 33 1/3 rpm,
stereo. ; 12 in.

  Elaine Shaffer, flute ; Philharmonia Orchestra,
Yehudi Menuhin, conductor.
  Programme notes on container.
  Angel: S 36189.
  With: Concerto in C major, K. 299 / Mozart.

  I. Shaffer, Elaine.  II. Menuhin, Yehudi.
III. Philharmonia Orchestra.
```

Figure 5-13. Separate entry for a single item from recording without a collective title

6.2B. Edition statement

The edition statement for a sound recording must be enclosed within square brackets if transcribed from a source other than one of those prescribed: chief source of information (see 6.0B1), accompanying textual matter, and the container (cf. 6.0B2). In addition, follow general directions under 1.2.

6.4. PUBLICATION, DISTRIBUTION, ETC., AREA

6.4C. Place of publication, distribution, etc.

General rules under 1.4C are to be followed. In contrast to *AACR1* rule 252C1, publication area will in all cases include place. The prescribed sources of information for the entire publication area include the chief source of information, any accompanying textual material, or the container, in that order of preference. If place or other elements of this area are taken from sources other than these, they must be enclosed in brackets.

The cataloguer must often search to find the place of publication, distribution, etc., since this information is often omitted from the recording and its accompanying material. The following reference sources should prove helpful:

Billboard International Buyer's Guide (annual). Los Angeles: Billboard Publications. Popular recording companies.

The Music Yearbook, edited by Arthur Jacobs. New York: St. Martin's Press, 1973. British classical recording companies.

Pavlakis, Christopher. *The American Music Handbook*. New York: Free Press, 1974. Chiefly classical music, American sources.

Sandberg, Larry and Dick Weissman. *The Folk Music Sourcebook*. New York: Knopf, 1976. Recording companies specializing in folk music.

6.4D2. Name of publisher, distributor, etc. Prefer a trade name or brand name rather than the name of the publisher if both appear on the label. Prefer label information rather than information appearing in accompanying material or container. See, for instance, figure 5-12. The brand name "Angel" will be preferred to the name of the manufacturer, Capitol Records, inc. In figure 5-10, MGM Records is listed as "A division of Loew's Incorporated." Prefer the name of the division to that of the parent body. In figure 5-11, the record sleeve gives: Archiv Produktion, Musikhistorisches Studio der Deutschen Grammophon Gesellschaft. Prefer the smaller unit over the parent organization.

6.4D3. Trade name as series. The example shown in figure 5-14 includes a trade name that appears to be a series. It should be recorded as such, rather than using it as the name of the publisher.

6.4F. Date of publication

Follow general instructions under 1.4F.

6.4F2. If no date of publication is available, the date of recording may be used as the basis for a conjectural publication date. Make a note of the recording date, however, when known, whether this date has been used as a conjectural publication date or not. See figures 5-2 and 5-11.

Shakespeare, William, 1564-1616.
  [Selections. Sound recording]
  John Barrymore reads Shakespeare [sound record-
ing]. -- [New York] : Audio Fidelity, [19--]-
    sound discs : 33 1/3 rpm, mono. ; 12 in. --
(Audio rarities)

  Programme notes on container.
  Contents: v. 1. Scenes from Hamlet -- Scenes from
Twelfth night -- Scenes from Richard III -- Scenes
from Macbeth

  Audio Fidelity: 2280.

  I. Barrymore, John. II. Title. III. Series.

Figure 5-14. Trade
name as series title

Audio Rarities
John Barrymore Reads Shakespeare
Audio Fidelity   2280-1
Audio Fidelity Enterprises, inc.   Side 1
33 1/3 rpm
Long Play

Disc label

1. Scenes from "Hamlet"
2. Scenes from "Twelfth Night"
(Mr. Barrymore reads both
Sir Toby Belch and Malvolio)

6.5. PHYSICAL DESCRIPTION AREA

6.5B1. Extent of item (including specific material designation). State the number
of physical units, together with the specific type of sound recording, using terms
listed under 6.5B1. Libraries that do not choose to include the general material
designation "sound recording" as part of the catalogue entry should include the
word "sound" as part of the specific designation. If "sound recording" has been
included as GMD in the entry, the word "sound" may be dropped as being
redundant from the specific material designation. Following Library of Congress decision, this will not be done in cataloguing examples in this text.

In many cases, playing time is included on the item as part of the information
on the label, container, or accompanying material. If this is the case, such
information should be included in the physical description area. If no such
indication is given, and the cataloguer has the time and inclination to listen to
the recording, an approximate time may be given, preceded by "ca." The
cataloguer is under no obligation to do this, however. The time may be omitted
from the physical description area if it is not known.

6.5B3. If a separately titled part of a sound recording has been catalogued as an independent work, give the physical extent as shown in figures 5-8 and 5-13.

6.5C. Other physical details

Whereas for visual material, such as a book, it is appropriate to give details such as the type of illustration or the presence of colour as part of this element, for a sound recording the analogous items are playing speed, number of tracks, number of sound channels, etc. These details are separated from the physical extent by space - colon - space.

6.5D. Dimensions

The size of the item is always the last element in the physical description area (unless, of course, accompanying material is present). Unlike most other library items, sound recording discs are measured in inches, since this is the standard measurement used in the recording industry. Dimensions are omitted for rolls, cartridges, and cassettes if they are standard size.

6.5E. Accompanying material

As explained under 1.5E, accompanying material may be added as the last element of the physical description area if its description is simple. Figure 5-15 shows an example of a recording issued as a serial. Each disc is accompanied by a booklet containing the text of the disc so that the child listener can read along with the recording. Since the booklets were issued regularly with the recordings, they may be added as the last element of the physical description area (12.5E1).

```
Miranda.
   Reading records ₍sound recording₎. -- Vol. 1-
= RR 1001-    . -- Memphis, Tenn. : Reading
Records, c1963-
   sound discs : 33 1/3 rpm, mono. ; 12 in. +
booklets.

   "(ASCAP-Muhoberac-Huddleston) with Mary Shelton."
   Intended audience: Preschool children.
   Summary: Stories and poems, told by Miranda, with
booklet for the child to read along with the
recording.
   Series: RR 1000.  Each vol. numbered separately
in addition to general number.

   I. Shelton, Mary.  II. Title.
```

Figure 5-15.
Accompanying material

Reading Records   R R 1 0 0 1
Monaural   33 1/3 RPM
Vol. 1   Side 1
(ASCAP-Muhoberac-Huddleston)
with Mary Shelton
Copyright 1963 by Reading Records, Inc.
Memphis, Tenn.

Disc label

However, if authorship or publication details are different from those on the main item being catalogued, either give the accompanying material a separate entry (1.5E1; see figure 2-3) or list the accompanying material in a note (6.7B11; see figure 6-2).

6.6. SERIES AREA

See 1.6 for general directions and examples; see also figures 5-3, 5-6, and 5-14.

6.7. NOTE AREA

Notes follow the general order and are of the same type as notes listed under 1.7, which see.

6.7B1. Nature or artistic form and medium of performance. If the medium of performance for a musical work is not evident from the title or the uniform title, a note should be given. See figure 5-5.

6.7B2. Language. Such a note is appropriate either for spoken or sung recordings unless the language is evident from the rest of the description. No note is necessary to indicate the language of a sung mass (figure 5-1) unless the mass is not in Latin. See figure 5-6 for an instance in which a note about the language is appropriate.

6.7B3. Source of title proper. See discussion under 6.0B1 for circumstances in which the cataloguer should give a note indicating the source of the title proper.

6.7B4. Variations in title. Rather frequently, title information on the record sleeve or other container will differ, sometimes markedly, from title information on the label of the item. If the difference is enough to affect filing, make a note of the variant title and give it a separate title added entry. (See figure 5-16.)

```
Fox, Virgil.
   Virgil Fox playing the organ at the Riverside
Church [sound recording]. -- [New York] : RCA
Victor, c1959.
   1 sound disc (ca. 48 min.) : 33 1/3 rpm, mono. ;
12 in.

   Title on container: Virgil Fox encores.
   Programme notes on container.
   Contents: Fugue in G minor (The little) / J.S.
Bach -- Canon in B minor / Schumann -- Jesu, joy of
man's desiring / J.S. Bach -- Concerto no. 4 in F.
Allegro / Handel -- Ye sweet retreat / Boyce --
Thou art the rock / Mulet -- Trumpet tune and air /
Purcell -- Trio sonata no. 6 in G / J.S. Bach --

              (continued on next card)
```

Figure 5-16. Variant title

Fox, Virgil.   Virgil Fox playing the organ at the
    Riverside Church [sound recording].   c1959.
    (card 2)

Tenth concerto for string. Aria / Handel -- Now
    thank we all our God / J.S. Bach -- Air on the G
    string / J.S. Bach -- Symphony no. 5 in F minor,
    op. 42, no. 1. Toccata / Widor.
    RCA Victor: LM 2268.

I. Title.   II. Title: Virgil Fox encores.

RCA Victor
"New Orthophonic" High Fidelity

LM-2268   Side 1
(J2RP-8490)   Red Seal
    Band 1—J. S. Bach   Fugue in G minor (The Little)
    Band 2—Schumann   Canon in B minor
    Band 3—J. S. Bach   Jesu, Joy of Man's Desiring
    Band 4—Handel   Concerto No. 4 in F
              First Movement: Allegro
    Band 5—Boyce   Ye Sweet Retreat   Disc label
              (Arr.: Harold Bauer)
    Band 6—Mulet   Thou Art the Rock
              Virgil Fox
          Playing the organ
      at The Riverside Church
              Monaural
    Tmk(s) Registered—Marca(s) Registrada(s)—
      Radio Corporation of America
          Made in U.S.A.

6.7B5. A long subtitle may be omitted from the body of the card and given
as a note. See 1.7B5 and 1.1E3 for guidance.

6.7B6. Statements of responsibility. As already noted, names of performers
ordinarily are not transcribed as part of the formal statement of responsibility
in the body of the entry. If, in the cataloguer's opinion, names of singers,
readers, orchestra, etc., are important, these names should be given in a note.
The note may be quoted from the prescribed source if it is concise; otherwise,
the cataloguer should make up a brief descriptive note. See figures 5-1, 5-2, etc.

6.7B10. Physical description. In addition to other important physical details, duration times may be given for a multipart item without a collective title that has been described as a unit. See figure 5-12.

6.7B11. Accompanying material. See figures 5-1, 5-2, etc., for appropriate notes.

6.7B16. Other formats available. If other formats (disc, cartridge, cassette, etc.) are known, this information is given in a note. (See figure 5-4.) Schwann catalog is one of the sources for this kind of information.

6.7B17. Summary. A brief summary may be given for the contents of a spoken sound recording. See figure 5-9 and 5-15.

6.7B18. Contents. List titles of individual works catalogued under a collective title if these are considered important. Follow title and statement of responsibility pattern as directed in 1.7B18. If time is given for individual works, include this information. See, for example, figure 5-5, etc.

6.7B19. Notes on publishers' numbers. According to *AACR1* rule 252C1, serial album and record numbers were recorded as part of the imprint (publication area). These numbers have been removed from this area and will be listed as a note. The number is to be preceded by the label name and a colon.

6.7B21. "With" notes. See figures 5-8 and 5-13 for examples.

6
Motion Pictures and Video Recordings

(*AACR2* Chapter 7)

AACR2 chapter 7 includes rules for the descriptive cataloguing of all types of media involving a sequence of images projected in rapid succession so that they create the illusion of movement. These include videorecordings with all of their manifestations such as videotapes, videocassettes, videodiscs, videocartridges, etc. (see *AACR2* Appendix D, Glossary). Also included are motion pictures, which come in many packages such as film cartridges and film cassettes as well as film reels. Filmstrips are not included in this chapter. For rules governing filmstrips, see *AACR2* chapter 8, "Graphic Materials."

The problem of main entry for motion pictures has troubled cataloguers for many years. British cataloguing authority Anthony Croghan feels that a film "is a collaborative work, and there are essentially three authors: the director, the cameraman, and the script writer. The director is the principal author, and the cameraman and scriptwriter are secondary authors."[1] Following Croghan's line of reasoning, main entry for films would be the name of the director. But Croghan's idea has had little support among cataloguers, either at the present or in the past. Previous cataloguing codes, CLA and AECT as well as *AACR1* (Chapter 12, "Motion Pictures and Filmstrips"), were in agreement in stipulating title main entry for all motion pictures.

The present rules for choice of access points (*AACR2* chapter 21) make no specific mention of motion pictures as such; the same rules of authorship responsibility which govern other types of library materials are to be applied to motion pictures and videorecordings. In most instances, numerous people and many different groups contribute in various ways to the creation of the intellectual or artistic content of a motion picture or videorecording. (See figure 6-1.) Because of this diffusion of responsibility, main entry for most motion pictures will continue to be under title according to *AACR2* practice as it was under previous rules.

[1] "A Feasibility Study of a Multimedia Catalog," in Pierce Grove, ed., *Bibliographical Control of Nonprint Media* (Chicago: ALA, 1972), p. 134.

A film may be sponsored by a society, corporation, institution, or other corporate body.[2] If the content of the film is "of an administrative nature dealing with the corporate body," its procedures, and/or its operations, main entry will be under the name of the sponsoring body (21.B2a). Figure 6-7 is of this type. The example shown in figure 6-2 is not; entry is under title.

```
Japanese tea ceremony [motion picture] / Walt
   Disney Productions. -- Santa Ana, Calif. :
   Doubleday Multimedia, 1971.
   1 film cartridge (4 min.) : si., col. ; super 8
mm. + 1 study guide. -- (Japan series)

   From the 1961 motion picture entitled: Japan
harvests the sea.
   Released by International Communications Films
in 1968.
   Summary: Shows the teahouse and the complete
ritual, including trained young ladies as hostesses,
the preparation of tea, and proper etiquette.

   I. Walt Disney Productions.  II. Japan harvests
the sea [motion picture].  III. Series.
```

Figure 6-1. Motion picture—entry under title

```
Boeing 737 [motion picture]. -- Seattle : Cameron
   Film Productions Co., 1967.
   1 film reel (ca. 6 min.) : sd., col. ; 16 mm.

   Sponsored by the Boeing Company.
   Summary: Describes the flight testing program
of the twin engine, short range Boeing 737 jet
liner.


   I. Boeing Company.  II. Cameron Film Productions
Co.
```

Figure 6-2. A sponsored motion picture

Motion picture versions are frequently based on books. Entry for such works normally is covered by 21.9, since in virtually every instance such versions involve substantial changes in the nature and content of the original, to say nothing of the fact that the medium of expression is different. *AACR2* rule 21.9

[2] A sponsor is "the company, institution, organization, or individual other than the producer who finances the production of the material. Sponsorship often involves the promotion, either directly or indirectly, of a product or point of view." (Alma M. Tillin and William J. Quinly, *Standards for Cataloging Nonprint Materials*, 4th ed. [Washington: AECT, 1976], p. 16).

stipulates that main entry will be under the heading "appropriate to the new work." Since many individuals normally are involved in the production of films, entry under the name of an adapter is usually not possible. Title main entry should be made, with an author-title added entry for the original work (see figure 6-3).

```
Alice in Wonderland [motion picture] / Walt Disney
   Productions ; producer, Ben Sharpsteen ; director,
   Clyde Geronimi ; animation, Milt Kahl. -- Santa
   Monica, Calif. : RKO Radio Pictures, 1951.
   3 film reels (ca. 75 min.) : sd., col. ; 35 mm.

   Credits: Story, Winston Hibler ; music, Oliver
Wallace ; film editor, Lloyd Richardson.
   Based on: Alice's adventures in Wonderland / by
Lewis Carroll.

   I. Carroll, Lewis.  Alice's adventures in Wonder-
land.  II. Sharpsteen, Ben.  III. Geronimi, Clyde.
IV. Walt Disney Productions.
```

Figure 6-3. Motion picture adaptation of a book

The example shown in figure 6-4 is an unusual twist on the standard pattern of a motion picture adaptation of a previously published book. In this case, the motion picture was produced first, followed in two years by a faithful reproduction in book format under the same title, *Arrow to the Sun*. The film and the book, which won the Caldecott Award, are both by Gerald McDermott. He wrote the script of the motion picture, designed and drew the animated cartoons, and directed and produced the entire film. His responsibility for the intellectual and artistic content of the film is clear. Entry is under his name.

McDermott's book is a faithful reproduction of the film. A note is made to indicate publication in the earlier version (see figure 6-5).

Examples given above illustrate several ways of entering a motion picture in the library catalogue. The rules for main entry for motion pictures may be summarized by stating once again that general principles governing authorship apply to motion pictures as well as to other types of library media. If authorship responsibility can be attributed by definitions and rules of 21.1, entry will be under personal or corporate author. However, the difficulties involved in ascribing authorship or creator responsibility for most motion pictures mean that, as a general rule, they will be entered under title.

7.0B. Sources of information
The chief source of information for films, as it is for other types of library

materials, is the work itself. When a book is catalogued, the title page is the chief source of information. For maps, the map itself is the chief source. For sound recordings, the label affixed to the disc, cassette, cartridge, etc., is the chief source. By analogy the chief source of information for a film is printed information appearing on the film itself. If the film is permanently encased in a cassette or cartridge, a label appearing on this container is also regarded as a chief source.

McDermott, Gerald.
   Arrow to the Sun [motion picture] : a Pueblo Indian tale / designed and directed by Gerald McDermott ; produced by Gerald McDermott & Texture Films, Inc. -- [New York] : Texture Films, c1973.
   1 film reel (ca. 15 min.) : sd., col. ; 16 mm.

   Credits: Music, Thomas Wagner ; camera, Frank Koenig ; voice of the boy, Joquin Brant ; story and research consultant, Charles Hofmann.
   Summary: The son of the Sun god is shot on an arrow to the Sun. He successfully passes four trials and returns to Earth, bringing the magic of the Sun with him.

   I. Texture Films, Inc. II. Title.

Figure 6-4. Motion picture entered under creator

Figure 6-5. Book version of a film

McDermott, Gerald.
   Arrow to the Sun : a Pueblo Indian tale / adapted and illustrated by Gerald McDermott. -- New York : Viking, c1974.
   [42] p. : col. ill. ; 25 x 29 cm.

   Book version of the 1973 film produced by Gerald McDermott and Texture Films, Inc.

   I. Arrow to the Sun [motion picture]. II. Title.

Some films lack title frames. If no printed information appears on the film, accompanying material may furnish information or a title presented orally on the film may be used.

Texture Films, inc., presents
Arrow to the Sun
A Pueblo Indian Tale

Title frame

Designed and directed by
Gerald McDermott
Music
Thomas Wagner
Camera
Frank Koenig
Voice of the boy
Joquin Brant
Story and research consultant
Charles Hofmann
Produced by Gerald McDermott
and Texture Films, inc.
Arrow to the Sun, c1973, Texture Films, inc.

End frame

7.1. TITLE AND STATEMENT OF RESPONSIBILITY AREA

The title must be transcribed from the chief source, in most cases, the film itself. The statement of responsibility may also include information from accompanying material; such information should be enclosed in brackets (1.1F1). Title frames at the beginning of the film and frames at the end may include pertinent information to be recorded in the title and statement of responsibility area. Some information on the title or end frames may be given about individuals whose contribution to the film is best included in the note area (7.1F1). Other information may be ignored if it is not important to the cataloguing agency (7.7B6). If material is omitted from transcription of title and end frames, do not indicate such omission by ellipses.

7.1B. Title proper

Transcribe the title exactly as it appears on the title frames, following the general rules under 1.1B. If the title on the title frame includes a statement of responsibility, transcribe it as it appears. (See figure 6-4.)

7.1C. Optional addition. General material designation

Add in brackets "motion picture" or "videorecording" as appropriate, immediately following the title proper.

7.1E. Other title information

Other title information is transcribed, following general rule 1.1E, as it appears in the chief source of information. (See figure 6-6.)

7.1F. Statements of responsibility

Ordinarily, three types of activity enter into the creation of a motion picture. The sponsor, if the film has one, has a primary role that often includes promoting the initial idea of the film, financing the production, and arranging for production. Boeing Company is the sponsor of the film illustrated by figure 6-2. The producer or production company is responsible for the mechanics of making the motion picture. In figure 6-1, Walt Disney Productions is a production company. A releasing agent issues the completed motion picture to the public. In figure 6-3, RKO Radio Pictures is a releasing agent.

```
Governance in the academic library [videorecording]
 : a program / presented under the auspices of the
Committee on Academic Status of the Association
of College and Research Libraries. -- Chicago :
Distributed by ACRL, 1974.
 1 videocassette (Sony U-Matic, UC-60) (ca. 40 min.)
 : sd., b&w ; 3/4 in.

    Participants: David Laird, Jane Flener, Ellsworth
Mason, Stuart Forth, and Frederick Duda ; moderator,
Eldred Smith.
    Summary: Patterns of administration in academic
libraries, a panel discussion.

    I. Association of College and Research Libraries.
Committee on Academic Status.
```

Figure 6-6. Other title information—a videorecording

Title frame

Governance in the Academic Library: A Program Presented under the Auspices of the Committee on Academic Status of the Association of College and Research Libraries 1974

Under *AACR1* rule 223, statements about sponsorship, production, and release were transcribed following the title and the GMD. Place of publication, distribution, etc., was not ordinarily included as part of the catalogue entry for a motion picture; the entry did not include a formal imprint (publication area) such as was given for entries for monographs (*AACR Chapter 6* [1974], rule 136).

When the rules for cataloguing motion pictures were revised, it seemed evident that the sponsoring body and the producer had a type of author-creator responsibility, and that the name of the releasing agent or distributor definitely belonged in the publication area. Therefore, rule 7.1F1 limits information included in the statement of responsibility to persons or bodies actually involved in the production of the film—if these are named prominently. If they are not so named, and their relationship to the film should be brought out, give this information in a note. (See figure 6-2; title frame on this film gives title only. Sponsorship information was taken from *Educator's Guide to Free Films*, 1973.) The name of the releasing agent or distributor is given as part of the publication area; names of other persons or groups such as principal performers, etc., are given in a note, even if they appear as part of the information in the chief source of information (7.7B6).

7.1F3. If the names of both the sponsor and the producer are given in a single statement of responsibility, the information will be so transcribed. Whether the sponsor's name is given as the main entry depends, obviously, on the nature of the material. See 21.1B2 for guidance. In the example shown in figure 6-7, main entry is under the name of the sponsor (agency for which the film was produced) because the film concerns itself with the activities of the sponsor (21.1B2a).

```
TRW Electronics Group.
   Beats reading the annual report [motion picture] /
[sponsored by] TRW Electronics Group ; produced for
TRW Electronics Group by TRW Systems Group, Motion
Picture Department. -- [Redondo Beach, Calif. :
Distributed by TRW Systems Group, 1970]
   1 film reel (ca. 15 min.) : sd., col. ; 16 mm.

   Summary: Shows electronic products manufactured
by TRW Electronics Group; summarizes TRW Electronics
Group operations for the previous year.


   I. TRW Systems Group.   Motion Picture Dept.
II. Title.
```

Figure 6-7. Sponsor and producer in statement of responsibility

Title frame

**Beats Reading
The Annual Report
TRW Electronics Group**

End frame

**Produced for TRW Electronics Group
Los Angeles, California
by
TRW Systems Group, Motion Picture Department.**

7.4. PUBLICATION, DISTRIBUTION, ETC., AREA

7.4C. Place of publication, distribution, etc.

As previously mentioned, under *AACRl* rule 223B place was given as part of the catalogue entry only if a foreign producing company was responsible for the film. The cataloguing rules for motion pictures now conform to the general pattern for other types of library materials in that they stipulate that place will always be included as the first element of the publication, distribution, etc., area. Place is not always given on the film, nor is this information always included with the material that may accompany the film. Good sources of general information about films that will be helpful in giving the location of distributors, releasing agents, etc. are:

> *The Film Daily Year Book.* New York: J. W. Alicoate, 1927– .
> *International Television Almanac.* New York: Quigley Publishing Co.,
> *International Television Almanac.* New York: Quigley Publishing Co.,
>   1956– .
> *Variety.* New York: Variety Publishing Co., 1905– .

7.4D. Name of publisher, distributor, etc.

As previously mentioned, note that the name of the releasing agent is among the types of bodies that should be included as the second element of this area. (See figure 6-3.)

7.4F. Date of publication, distribution, release, etc.

The date is recorded as the last element of the area. A date of original production that is different from the distribution date may be given in the note area. (See figure 6-1, note 2.)

7.5. PHYSICAL DESCRIPTION AREA

The physical description area for motion pictures and videorecordings, like the physical description area for other types of library materials, is divided into the three major elements described in 7.5B–7.5D.

7.5B. Extent of item

The number of physical units followed by one of the specific material designators listed under 7.5B1 is the first element in the physical description area. If the GMD is used following the title proper, the words "film" and "video" may be omitted from the specific material designators. Following Library of Congress decision, "film" and "video" have not been omitted from specific material designation in this text.

    7.5B2. If the exact playing time is stated on the item, on the container, or elsewhere, it is listed following the extent of the item. If exact time is not given and the cataloguer times the item, precede this statement by "ca."

7.5C. Other physical details

For all types of motion pictures and videorecordings, indicate whether the film is sound or silent, and whether it is in color or black and white. In addition, give special characteristics as stipulated in the rules.

7.5D. Dimensions

The critical dimension for a motion picture or a videorecording, since it affects hardware used for playback, is the width of the film. A motion picture film is measured in millimetres, a videotape in inches.

7.5E. Accompanying material

Follow directions in 1.5E for recording accompanying material at the end of the physical description area. For example, see figure 6-1.

7.6B. Series statements

Record series statements according to general directions given in 1.6.

7.7. NOTE AREA

Notes follow the general order and are based on types given under 1.7, which see for guidance.

7.7B6. Statements of responsibility. This note lists performers and other individuals not directly involved with the production of the film or with its sponsorship, and thus, according to 7.1F1, not to be given in the title and statement of responsibility area in the formal part of the description. This note is flexible; list names considered by the cataloguing agency to be of importance. See, for example, figures 6-3, 6-4, 6-6. Sometimes the statement of responsibility note should be combined with the summary note; see figure 6-8 for an example.

7.7B7. Edition and history. For examples of this type of note, see figures 6-1, 6-3, etc.

7.7B17. Summary. Because film and videorecord collections are not easy to browse through, a brief summary note is important unless the content of the item is evident from other parts of the catalogue entry. See previous examples. Sometimes such a note may combine information about the content of the film and persons responsible for it, as in the example shown in figure 6-8.

```
Apollo 11 [motion picture] : man on the Moon :
   official NASA footage. -- [Burbank, Calif.] :
   Columbia Pictures, [197-]
   1 film reel (ca. 10 min.) : si., b&w ; super 8 mm.

   Summary: Motion pictures taken by Neil Armstrong
and Michael Collins during the first Moon landing,
July 1969.



   I. Armstrong, Neil.   II. Collins, Michael.
III. United States.   National Aeronautics and
Space Administration.
```

Figure 6-8. Summary note

Title frame

Apollo II
Man on the Moon
Official NASA footage

End frame

The End
Columbia Pictures

7

Graphic Materials

(*AACR2* Chapter 8)

AACR2 chapter 7 dealt with rules for the description of pictures that give the illusion of movement when projected. In contrast, chapter 8 covers all kinds of still pictures, both opaque and transparent. Rules for filmstrips, which were formerly coordinated with rules for motion pictures (*AACR1* chapter 12, "Motion Pictures and Filmstrips"), are now included with other two-dimensional (flat) media, such as art originals, charts, flash cards, slides, technical drawings, and transparencies.

The full rules given in chapter 8, as in other sections of *AACR2* Part I, are appropriate only for the description and identification of materials felt to be of significance and of some permanent importance to the library's collection. Some of the kinds of graphic materials included in chapter 8 may be ephemeral in nature; these may be more appropriately catalogued according to minimum levels of description (see 1.0D) or possibly kept in a vertical file without cataloguing. Examples and discussion in this text assume full cataloguing.

The general rules for main and added entries as given in *AACR2* chapter 21 apply to graphics as they do to other types of library materials. For example, in cataloguing an original art work, the artist is regarded as the "author" of the work. Entry will be under the name of the artist (21.1A1) as shown in figure 7-1.

```
Mosley, Shelley.
  ₁Black cat with yellow flower₁ ₁art original₁ /
SM. -- ₁1977₁
  1 art original : acrylic on poster board ; 16 x
27 cm.

  Unmounted.
```

Figure 7-1. Entry under artist—art original

Likewise, a photographic or other photomechanical reproduction of an art work will be entered under the name of the original artist (21.16B); see figure 7-2.

```
Manet, Édouard, 1832-1883.
   The fifer [picture] / Manet. -- [New York] :
Shorewood Press, [19--]
   1 art reproduction : photogravure, col. ; 57 x
70 cm.


   Original in Louvre Museum, Paris.
   Unmounted.


   I. Shorewood Press.   II. Title.
```

Figure 7-2. Entry under artist—art reproduction

The rationale behind entry of a photographic or other photomechanical reproduction of an art work under the original artist's name is the same as that governing other facsimile reproductions also entered under the heading for the original work. However, art librarians felt strongly that other forms of reproduction involved another artist's intervention, e.g. the person who executes the engraving, the lithograph, etc. These constitute adaptations in the same sense that a literary work rewritten in a different literary form (e.g. a novel adapted as a play) is an adaptation. If literary adaptations are to be entered under the heading for the adapter (21.10), artistic adaptations should also be entered under adapter. Thus, as in *AACR1* rule 261B, if an art work is adapted from one medium to another (e.g. an engraving is made from an oil painting), such a work will be entered under the heading for the adapter. See the examples under *AACR2* 21.16A, Adaptations of Art Works. Among them Turner will be given main entry for his etching of Joshua Reynolds's painting *Children Crying Forfeits*.

In the examples shown in figures 7-3 and 7-4, Phillipe Galle made an engraving

```
Brueghel, Pieter, 1520?-1569.
   Death of the Virgin [art original]. -- [1564]
   1 art original : tempera on wood ; 26 x 55 cm.




   I. Title.
```

Figure 7-3. Entry under artist—art original

from Pieter Brueghel's tempera painting *Death of the Virgin*. Although placement of the figures is the same, it is evident that Galle's work is an adaptation of the original, not a reproduction.

```
Galle, Phillipe.
  The death of the Virgin [picture]. -- [1574]
1 art print : b&w engraving ; 31 x 42 cm.

  Based on the tempera painting by Pieter Brueghel
the elder.



  I. Brueghel, Pieter, 1520?-1569.  Death of the
Virgin.  II. Title.
```

Figure 7-4. Entry under adapter—engraving based on art original

---

Except for 21.16 chapter 21 does not refer specifically to graphic materials. The basic assumption of the Paris Principles, which calls for entry under author or creator responsible for the intellectual or artistic content of a work when this can be determined, holds true equally for graphic materials as it does for books. And, as with other materials, if authorship responsibility is diffuse or indeterminate, main entry will be under title.

8.0B1. Chief source of information. As with other types of library materials, the chief source of information for a graphic item is the item itself. Only if the item does not include information will cataloguing data be taken from the container, accompanying textual material, or other sources. However, if an item consists of a number of physical parts with individual titles in a container that furnishes a collective title for the set, the container is to be preferred as the chief source of information. The container furnished the cataloguing data for the example shown in figure 7-5.

```
Subtraction [flash card]. -- Racine, Wis. :
  Western Pub. Co., c1962.
  43 flash cards : col. ; 9 x 6 cm. -- (Whitman
help yourself flash cards for home and school ;
no. 4571:39)

  Summary: Prepares the child for abstract think-
ing in arithmetic.



  I. Series.
```

Figure 7-5. Container as chief source of information

8.1 TITLE AND STATEMENT OF RESPONSIBILITY AREA

The prescribed source of information for transcription of this area is the chief source of information, in most cases, the item itself.

8.1B. Title proper

Follow general guidelines given in 1.1B for transcribing the title proper. Transcribe the title as it appears in the chief source of information. The title for the example shown in figure 7-6 was transcribed from the chart itself.

```
The Great ages of man [chart]. -- [New York :
   Time Inc., 1967]
   1 chart : col. ; 53 x 63 cm. folded to 27 x 21
cm.

   Summary: Shows, in tabular form, principal
events in western, central, and eastern civiliza-
tions from 4500 B.C. to the 20th century.



   I. Time Inc.
```

Figure 7-6. Title proper from chief source

8.1C. General material designation

The GMD is to be added immediately following the title proper. British cataloguers will use the GMD "graphic" for all graphic materials. North American cataloguers should select one of the following terms, as appropriate: art original, chart, filmstrip, flash card, picture, slide, technical drawing, or transparency (see list given under 1.1C1). Use the GMD "kit" (North American) or "multimedia" (British) in brackets when cataloguing a set of two or more different types of media, designed to be used together, none of which is the dominant type. See figure 7-7.

See 1.10 for special rules governing the cataloguing of kits. See figure 1-108a for a further example of a kit.

8.1D. Parallel titles

Follow general directions under 1.1D for the transcription of parallel titles. Figure 7-8 shows an item in which the parallel title also includes "other title" information. See 1.1E5 for general directions.

8.1F. Statements of responsibility

Follow general guidelines in 1.1F in transcribing the statements of responsibility. The title frame in the filmstrip of the example shown in figure 7-9 furnished all of the information in the title and statement of responsibility area.

Bishop, Dorothy Sword.
   Leonardo y Ramon [kit] : the story of the lion
and the mouse / told in Spanish and English. --
Skokie, Ill. : National Textbook Co., c1972.
   1 booklet, 1 filmstrip, 1 sound cassette, 1
teacher's guide, in container ; 24 x 38 x 4 cm. --
(Fábulas bilingües = Bilingual fables) (The Bilingual series)

   Adaptation by Dorothy Sword Bishop of the Aesopic
fable, The lion and the mouse.
   Designed for children who are in a language
development program.

          (Continued on next card)

Bishop, Dorothy Sword.   Leonardo y Ramon [kit].
  c1972.   (card 2)

  Summary: A tiny mouse saves the mighty lion
when he becomes entangled in a net.

  I. Aesop.   The lion and the mouse.   II. Title.

Figure 7-7. Kit as GMD

Box cover

**Leonardo
y Ramon
The Story of
The Lion and the Mouse
Told in Spanish and English**

© **National Textbook Company, Skokie, Illinois 60076**   Box cover

---

Box cover

**Bilingual Fables
A Series of Fables in Spanish and English**

**Fábulas bilingües
Una serie de fábulas en español e inglés**

5 children [kit] : a cultural awareness sound
  filmstrip program for early childhood = 5
  niños : un programa bilingüe para la primera
  enseñanza. -- New York : Scholastic, c1974.
  5 filmstrips, 5 sound cassettes, 2 teacher's
guides, 1 wallchart, in container ; 21 x 22 x 5 cm.

Sound recordings in Spanish ; text on filmstrips
in Spanish ; teacher's guides in English.
For children ages 3-8.
Also available with sound discs.
Summary: Teaches children to appreciate cultural
differences.

    (Continued on next card)

5 children [kit]. c1974. (card 2)

    Titles of filmstrips and cassettes: Feliz
cumpleanos, Howard -- Hijo del pescador -- Vaquero
-- La carta de Sara -- Mira Mira Marisol.

Figure 7-8. Parallel title

    I. Scholastic Magazines, Inc. II. Title: 5
niños.

5 Children
A Cultural Awareness Sound Filmstrip Program
for Early Childhood
5 Niños
Un Programa Bilingüe para la Primera Enseñanza
Vaquero
Mira Mira Marisol
Feliz Cumpleaños Howard
Hijo del Pescador
La Carta de Sara

Box cover

Box cover

Produced by
Scholastic
50 West 44th Street, New York, N.Y. 10036

Media programs for individual schools [filmstrip] /
    produced by the American Library Association and
    the National Education Association. -- Washing-
    ton : NEA, c1969.
    1 filmstrip (75 fr.) : col. ; 35 mm. + 1 sound
    tape reel (10 min. : 3 3/4 ips, 1 track, mono. ;
    5 in.) + 1 guide + 1 script.
        Based on the book: Standards for school media
    programs / by American Library Association and
    National Education Association.
        Summary: Stresses the usefulness and importance
    of school media programs. Suggests standards.

        I. American Library Association. Standards for
    school media programs.   II. American Library Asso-
    ciation.   III. National Education Association of
    the United States.

Figure 7-9.
Statement of
responsibility

8.1F2. Additions to statement of responsibility. A word or phrase may be added if needed to clarify the relationship to the work of a person or corporate body included in the statement of responsibility. In the example shown in figure 7-10, each of the sixty posters in the set has a picture and some explanatory text. John M. Carroll wrote the text and selected the pictures. A brief phrase is added to clarify his responsibility. Since the posters have no common title, the *Contents and Teacher's Guide* has been used as the chief source (8.0B1).

Carroll, John M.
    American Indian posters [picture] / [text by]
John M. Carroll. -- [United States?] : Class
National Pub., c1971.
    60 posters : b&w ; 28 x 43 cm. + 1 guide.

Figure 7-10. Phrase
added to statement of
responsibility

        I. Title.

Title page
of guide

American Indian Posters
John M. Carroll
Copyright, 1971, by Class National Publishing, Inc.

8.2. EDITION AREA

The edition statement may be transcribed from the chief source of information, the container, or any accompanying material (8.0B2). Record the edition statement following general directions given in 1.2.

In the example shown in figure 7-11, each of the thirty-five presidential portraits includes a series statement, an edition statement, and the name of the publisher. Since the pictures do not have a collective title, this information has been transcribed from the booklet accompanying the pictures.

```
The Perry pictures of our thirty-five Presidents
   [picture] / biographies by Olive M. Spring. --
Boston ed. -- Malden, Mass. : Perry Pictures,
[196-]
   35 pictures : b&w ; 21 x 15 cm. + 1 booklet. --
(The Perry pictures)

   Portraits of U.S. Presidents, George Washington
through Lyndon B. Johnson.


   I. Spring, Olive M.  II. Perry Pictures, Inc.
```

Figure 7-11. Edition area

Title page
of booklet
accompanying pictures

**The Perry Pictures of
Our Thirty-Five Presidents**
Biographies by
Olive M. Spring
Perry Pictures, Inc.
Malden, Mass.

8.4. PUBLICATION, DISTRIBUTION, ETC., AREA

The three standard elements of the publication area: place, publisher (etc.), and date will be transcribed following the general rules under 1.4.

8.4A2. Art originals, unpublished photographs, etc. The conventional elements (place, publisher, date) of the publication area are inappropriate for the catalogue entry for certain types of materials that are, in most instances, unique items. These include manuscripts (*AACR2* chapter 4), some types of realia (*AACR2* chapter 10), original art works, and unpublished photographs. For such items the publication area includes only the date of production. See 8.4F2 and 8.4F3; see also figures 7-1, 7-3, and 7-4 in this text.

8.5. PHYSICAL DESCRIPTION AREA

Following the general pattern of 1.5, the physical description area includes three elements, with a possible fourth, if the item has accompanying material with it.

8.5B. Extent of item and specific material designation

As with other types of library materials, the first element is the extent of item and specific material designation element. The GMD following the title proper is a fairly general generic term. A list of nineteen generic terms, some of which are more specific than the GMDs listed under 1.1C1, is given under 8.5B1. These terms are designed to describe the type of material more specifically than the GMD allows. Preceded by the number of items, one of these terms appears as the first element of the physical description area. Note: This list is inclusive. Do not use terms other than those included under 8.5B1 to describe graphic materials unless optional rule is adopted (8.5B1 option).

The following terms, defined and discussed below, are among those permitted according to 8.5B1.

Art original: Generally speaking, an art original is a unique item. See *AACR2* Appendix D, Glossary, for definition. GMD is "art original." The following rules specifically mention art originals: 8.5B1, 8.5C1, 8.5D4. See figures 7-1 and 7-3 for examples of art originals.

Art print: An art print is a work reproduced from a plate, a woodblock, etc., which has been prepared by an artist. Lithographs, etchings, engravings, wood-cuts, linoleum block prints, etc., are subsumed under this term. The GMD is likely to be "picture"; it will not be "art original," according to the definition of the term given in Appendix D, unless the cataloguer is cataloguing the actual woodblock, etching plate, etc.

Sometimes an art print is a copy of an art original in another medium (see figure 7-4). In other cases, the original artist and the etcher, engraver, etc., are one and the same. In either case, main entry is under the name of the etcher, engraver, lithographer, etc.

If an art print is not commercially published, publication area data will appear as given in figure 7-4, even though the engraving may exist in a number of copies. On the other hand, some art prints are issued by commercial publishers. Conventional publication area data is appropriate for such an item. See the example shown in figure 7-12. Other rules that may apply are 8.5B1, 8.5C2, 8.5D4, and 8.7B8.

Art reproduction: Any sort of photomechanical reproduction of an original art work or art print is called an art reproduction. Obviously, the quality of an art reproduction may vary according to the quality of the equipment used for the reproduction, but the end product is still regarded as being a representation of the original, without any intervening redrawing or adapting as occurred in figure 7-4. The GMD "picture" is most likely to be used for an art reproduction. See figure 7-2 for an example of an art reproduction. Most art reproductions are commercially produced, as is this one; publication area will include all three of the conventional elements.

```
Josset, Lawrence.
   The George Inn, Southwark ˌ[picture] / drawn and
etched by Lawrence Josset. -- Godalming, ˌEnglandˌ :
Stevens & Brown, 1978.
   1 art print : b&w etching ; 17 x 24 cm.

   Extracted from: Calendarivm Londinense, or The
London almanack for the year 1978.




                                           Figure 7-12. Art print


   I. Stevens & Brown.   II. Title.
```

Calendarivm Londinense
or the London Almanack for the Year 1978
The George Inn
Southwark

Calendar

drawn and etched by
Lawrence Josset, A.R.C.A. (Lond.), R. E.
published by Stevens & Brown, Ltd., Ardon House,
Mill Lane, Godalming, Surrey.

Some of the rules that may apply to art reproductions are 8.5B1, 8.5C3, 8.5D4, and 8.7B8.

Chart: See *AACR2* Glossary, Appendix D, for definition. If a chart is designed with large print and illustrations in such a way that it can successfully be interpreted at a distance, and if it is meant to be displayed on a wall, use the specific material designation "wall chart" rather than "chart." The GMD "chart" will appear following the title proper for both charts and wall charts. See, for example, figure 7-6. Some of the rules for charts are 8.5B1 and 8.5D6.

Filmslip: As might be guessed, a filmslip is a short filmstrip, sometimes mounted so as to lie flat instead of being rolled as a filmstrip generally is. The GMD "filmstrip" is used for both filmslips and filmstrips. All rules for filmstrips apply also to filmslips, e.g., 8.5B1, 8.5B2, 8.5B5, 8.5C4, and 8.5D2.

The chief source of information for a filmslip, as it is for a filmstrip, is the film itself. Generally a title frame at the beginning and possibly a frame at the end will furnish information. Title and statement of responsibility information should come from either of these sources if possible. The container and/or accompanying material may be used for data for other parts of the catalogue entry. In the example shown in figure 7-13, all of the cataloguing information except for the location of Encyclopaedia Britannica Films appears on the title frame of the filmslip.

Different kinds of plants [filmstrip] / collaborator, Illa Podendorf ; produced by Encyclopaedia
  Britannica Films. -- [Wilmette, Ill.] : Encyclopaedia Britannica Films, c1963.
  1 filmslip (14 fr.) : col. ; 35 mm. + 1 student
guide. -- (Plants around us)
  Filmslip and student guide in plastic envelope
28 x 13 cm.
  Summary: Describes differences among plants,
including size, age, and color.
  I. Podendorf, Illa.   II. Encyclopaedia Britannica
Films. III. Series.

Figure 7-13. Filmslip

Plants around us
Different Kinds of Plants
Collaborator: Illa Podendorf
The University of Chicago Laboratory School

Title frame

Produced by Encyclopaedia Britannica Films

© 1963 by Encyclopaedia Britannica Films
Copyright and all rights of reproduction,
including by television, reserved.

Filmstrip: See *AACR2* Glossary, Appendix D, for definition. The GMD
"filmstrip" is used following the title proper. The number of frames is to be
added to the designation "filmstrip" in the physical description area (see figure
7-14). If the frames are not numbered, count them, beginning with the first

Walt Disney's Kidnapped [filmstrip] / adapted from
  the Walt Disney motion picture version of the
  novel by Robert Louis Stevenson ; produced by
  Encyclopaedia Britannica Films in cooperation
  with Walt Disney Productions and in collaboration
  with Paul A. Witty ; Oscar E. Sams, producer. --
  [Wilmette, Ill.] : Encyclopaedia Britannica Films,
  c1960.
  1 filmstrip (54 fr.) : col. ; 35 mm. -- (Walt
Disney famous stories retold)

Figure 7-14. Filmstrip

  Summary: David Balfour's perilous venture to
claim his inheritance from a villainous and miserly
Scottish uncle.
  I. Stevenson, Robert Louis. Kidnapped. II. Walt
Disney Productions. III. Encyclopaedia Britannica
Films. IV. Title: Kidnapped. V. Series.

title frame and ending with credits, etc., frame at the end (8.5B2). Other special rules for filmstrips include 8.5B1, 8.5B2, 8.5B5, 8.5C4, and 8.5D2.

Frame 1

Encyclopaedia Britannica Films
presents

Frame 2

Walt Disney
Famous Stories Retold
a series of filmstrips

Frame 3

Walt Disney's
Kidnapped
Adapted from the Walt Disney motion
picture version of the novel by
Robert Louis Stevenson
© MCMLX by Walt Disney Productions.
Copyright and all rights of Reproduction,
Including by Television, Reserved.

s

Frame 4

Produced by
Encyclopaedia Britannica Films
in cooperation with
Walt Disney Productions
and in collaboration with
Paul A. Witty, Ph.D.
Northwestern University
Oscar E. Sams, Producer

Flash card: See *AACR2* Glossary, Appendix D, for definition. The GMD "flash card" is used following the title proper. The cards themselves are the chief source of information if they include a collective title. If not, use information on a container or with accompanying material. The container served as the chief source for the flash cards catalogued as figure 7-5. In the example shown in figure 7-15, title information is found on the back of each card; this source was used for transcription of the title proper. The container furnished publication area information, the series, and a publisher's number. Information about the creator and designer of the cards was taken from the *Guide*.

Flipchart: A flipchart is a set of charts hinged at the top so that information may be presented in a logical sequence. The GMD "chart" follows the title proper (see figure 7-16). The entire flipchart is used as the chief source of information. Special rules for flipcharts are 8.5B1, 8.5B3, 8.5C6, and 8.5D1.

```
Brown, Esther.
    Parts and wholes ₍flash card₎ / ₍by Esther
Brown₎. -- Boston : Teaching Resources Corp.,
c1973.
    69 flash cards : col. ; 10 x 8 cm. - 1 guide. --
(Language skills)

    Summary: Designed to develop an understanding of
the relationship of parts to wholes.
    Catalog no. 84-310.
```

Figure 7-15. Flash card

```
    I. Teaching Resources Corporation.   II. Title.
III. Series.
```

Guide
Language Skills Development
Parts and Wholes
Picture Cards   Guide title page
by Esther Brown
Teaching Resources Corporation
100 Boylston Street, Boston, Massachusetts 02116

Language Skills   Container   **Parts and Wholes**
Parts and Wholes
Catalog No. 84-310
                                            Back of card—chief source of information

```
Bergwall, Charles.
    Vicalog ₍chart₎ : Eye Gate visual card catalog /
conceived and designed by Charles Bergwall and
Sherwin S. Glassner. -- Jamaica, N.Y. : Eye Gate
House, ₍196-₎
    1 flipchart (6 sheets) : b&w ; 22 x 36 cm.

    2 heavy cardboard sheets with 4 transparencies
hinged at the top.
    Shows the parts of a catalog card.


    I. Glassner, Sherwin S.   II. Eye Gate House.
III. Title.
```

Figure 7-16. Flipchart

Vicalog
Eye Gate Visual Card Catalog
Another Eye Gate Audio Visual Product
Eye Gate House, Inc.
146-01 Archer Ave., Jamaica 35, N.Y.

Coversheet

Instructions for using "Vicalog"
[text follows]
Conceived and designed by Charles Bergwall
and Sherwin S. Glassner

Photograph: As with other unpublished graphic items, a complete publication area is inappropriate to a photograph. Unless the photograph has been reproduced commercially for public sale or distribution, give only the date of creation in the publication area (8.4F2). In most cases, the GMD for a photograph will be "picture." The photograph itself is the chief source of information. Unless a title is given on the item, the cataloguer will make up a brief descriptive title, bracketing it in the title and statement of responsibility area. Special rules for photographs are 8.5B1, 8.5C7, and 8.5D1.

Picture: This term is used as the specific material designation in the physical description area when the item cannot appropriately be called by another of the more specific pictorial terms under 8.5B1. In addition, "picture" may be used to describe a collection that is a mixture of different types of reproduction. For example, the thirty-five Presidential pictures of figure 7-11 include photographs of more recent Presidents and black-and-white reproductions of oil paintings and drawings of earlier Presidents. The term "picture" embraces all of these variations and should be used. Special rules for pictures are 8.5B1, 8.5C8, and 8.5D1.

Postcard: Like "picture," the term "postcard" may be used as the specific material designation in the physical description area when one is cataloguing an item as a postcard. Although this case is not explicitly mentioned in *AACR2* chapter 8, "postcard" would be particularly appropriate as the designation for a collection of items all of which are postcards but of varying content, e.g. art reproductions, photographs, technical drawings. For particular items 8.5B1 lists the various specific designations and includes an option allowing the cataloguer to substitute one designation for another or to use a term of his or her own formulation if a very specific statement is appropriate. This means that, optionally, one may use "art reproduction," "organization chart," etc., in place of "postcard" as the specific material designation.

In the example shown in figure 7-17, "postcard" is the most appropriate designation for the group of postcards, each of which is a photomechanical reproduction of sculpture. Each postcard bears the same statement on the verso: "Fernand Hazen, éditeur, Paris. Printed in France. Distributed in USA by Artext Prints Inc. Westport Conn." The postcards have no common title; a brief descriptive title appropriate to the collection has been supplied by the cataloguer (8.1B2).

```
₁Sculpture₁ ₁picture₁. -- Paris : F. Hazen ;
  Westport, Conn. : Distributed in USA by Artext
  Prints, ₁19--₁
  4 postcards : b&w ; 11 x 15 cm.

  Contents: Sculpture grecque : Victoire de
Samothrace -- Sculpture égyptienne : groupe de
Sennefer et de sa femme -- L'homme-cactus / Julio
González -- La danseuse de quatorze ans / Degas.
```

Figure 7-17. Postcard

Poster: A poster is a large sheet intended for display. A poster that contains only printed text, or one in which text is the dominant element, is called a broadside. A broadside is catalogued according to *AACR2* chapter 2, Monographs. For an example of broadside cataloguing, see figure 2-8 and discussion.

However, if the emphasis of the poster is pictorial or otherwise graphic, use the rules in chapter 8 for cataloguing. A chart, an art print, an art reproduction, etc., may be a poster, i.e., a large sheet intended for display. Use these more specific materials designations in preference to "poster" if they are applicable.

Figure 7-10 is a set of graphic materials, each of which is about half pictorial and half text. However, the chief intent of the set seems to be illustrative; therefore, it should be catalogued as graphic material rather than as a set of broadsides (*AACR2* chapter 2). The pictures are of different media: one photograph of an Indian woman; several reproductions of paintings of Indians, which would be called "art reproductions"; and engravings, which are adaptations of paintings (21.16A). Taking all factors into consideration, it seems appropriate to use the generic term "poster" for the specific material designation for the set.

Aside from 8.5B1, specific rules for posters are 8.5C10 and 8.5D1.

Radiograph: The most familiar type of material subsumed under the term "radiograph" is an x-ray negative. The only specific rule for such material is 8.5C11, which stipulates that the second element of the physical description area is to be omitted. See the illustration of physical description for a radiograph under 8.5D1.

Slide: A slide is a small transparent image made of film or glass and mounted for projection. A microscope slide is not considered to be a graphic item. Since it usually is made up of a bit of "realia" sandwiched between two pieces of glass, such a slide is categorized as realia. (See *AACR2* chapter 10.)

The chief source of information for a slide is the slide itself. In the example shown in figure 7-18, the slides are obviously designed to be used as a unit, in sequence, almost as one would utilize a filmstrip. Each of the four sets included in the collection begins with a slide that gives title information; for example:

GERMAN PAINTING
OF THE
TWENTIETH CENTURY
Set 1

In each set, the last slide has the following information:

THE END
Copyright 1962, by
Herbert E. Budek Company inc.

If individual slides in a slide set do not provide a collective title for the entire set, the container or material accompanying the slides may be used as the chief source. In the slide set entitled "West Germany" (figure 1-14), each slide bears the name and address of the producer and a title descriptive of the subject matter of the particular slide. The commentary with the slide set furnished the collective title for the set.

```
German painting of the twentieth century [slide].
  -- East Providence, R.I. : H.E. Budek Co., c1962.
122 slides : col. + commentary.

  In flat plastic holders (28 x 23 cm.) punched for
insertion in 3 ring binder.
  Summary: Chronological development of German
painting from the beginning of the century to the
post war period of the 1950's.  The works of Kubin,
Kokoschka, Kandinsky, Klee, etc.
```

Figure 7-18. Slide

For a further example of slide cataloguing, see figure 1-102.

Stereograph: By definition a stereograph is "a picture composed of two superimposed stereoscopic images that gives a three dimensional effect when viewed with a stereoscope or special spectacles."[1] One type of stereograph is the postcard-size opaque double-image photograph of the late nineteenth and early twentieth century that was designed to be viewed through Grandpa's stereoscope, and which delighted many of us in our childhood. The modern version of the old stereoscope and its double-image photographs is the View-master viewer with its double-frame stereoscopic slides. The chief source of information for this and other types of stereographic material is the item itself, which in the case of View-master reels usually includes a label. (See figure 7-19.)

Special rules for stereographs include 8.5B1, 8.5B2, 8.5C13, and 8.5D3.

[1] *Webster's New Collegiate Dictionary* (Springfield, Mass.: Merriam, 1973), p. 1140.

Cairo, Egypt ₁slide₁. -- Portland, Or. : Sawyer,
  c1950.
  1 stereograph reel (View-master) (7 double fr.) :
col. + commentary. -- (View-master travelogue ;
reel no. 3301)

I. Sawyer's Inc.   II. Series.

3301
Cairo
View-Master
Reel
Egypt
Copyright 1950
Sawyer's Inc.
Portland 7, Oregon

**Figure 7-19.
Stereographic reel**

Cairo, Egypt Reel No. 3301
View-Master Travelogue

Container

Reel label

Study print: A study print is a graphic item that has been prepared specifically for teaching purposes. It is generally pictorial; it may or may not include text. The specific material designation "study print" rather than one of the other terms listed under 8.5B1 should be assigned to an item or a collection of items if the term reflects the intent of the author or creator of the material. (See figure 7-20.)

Transparency: A transparency is a transparent image, either mounted or unmounted, designed for use on an overhead projector. The chief source of information is the transparency itself. It should be used as the source for transcribing the title and statement of responsibility. In addition, information appearing "prominently" (i.e., on the container or accompanying material) may

Fegely, Tom.
  How does your organic garden grow? ₁picture₁ /
photos by Tom Fegely, Tom Gettings ; text by Bud
Souders, Tom Fegely ; edited by Rita Reemer. --
Emmaus, Pa. : Rodale Press, Educational Services
Division, c1973.
  14 study prints : col. ; 34 x 46 cm. + 1 booklet
(35 p.). -- (Organic classroom series)
  Intended audience: Elementary school students.
  Summary: Discusses and illustrates organic gar-
dening, from soil composition through harvesting.

  I. Gettings, Tom. II. Souders, Bud. III. Reemer, Rita. IV. Series.

**Figure 7-20. Study
print**

Organic Classroom Series
How Does Your Organic Garden Grow?
Rodale Press
Guide title page   Educational Services Division
Photos by Tom Fegely, Tom Gettings
Text by Bud Souders, Tom Fegely
Edited by Rita Reemer

be given in brackets as part of the statement of responsibility (1.1F1). Each of the transparencies in the set shown in figure 7-21 bears the title "Africa." The statement of responsibility is found on the accompanying material.

Africa ₁transparency₁ / ₁collaborators, Nadine I.
   Clark, Herbert S. Lewis ; producers, Weking
   Schroeder, Penelope Wilmot ; produced by Encyclopaedia Britannica Films in cooperation with Compton's pictured encyclopedia₁. -- Chicago : Encyclopaedia Britannica Educational Corp., c1963.
   16 transparencies : some col. ; 22 x 22 cm.

   Teacher's guide on envelope.
   With plastic frame, 27 x 26 cm.   Figure 7-21.
   For junior and senior high schools.   Transparency
   Contents: unit 1. The land (8 transparencies) --
unit 2. The people (3 transparencies) -- unit 3.
Africa, past and present (5 transparencies)
   Series 30040.
   I. Clark, Nadine. II. Lewis, Herbert S. III.
Encyclopaedia Britannica Films. IV. Compton's
pictured encyclopedia.

Series: Africa   Unit I: The Land
Encyclopaedia Britannica Educational Corporation
Transparency   425 North Michigan Avenue • Chicago, Illinois 60611
© 1963 by Encyclopaedia Britannica
Educational Corporation

Series 30040 Africa
Unit I, 8 transparencies
The Land
Produced by Encyclopaedia Britannica Films
   in cooperation with Compton's Pictured   Envelope
   Encyclopedia
Collaborators: Nadine I. Clark, Herbert S. Lewis
Producers: Weking Schroeder, Penelope Wilmot

If individual transparencies in the set do not have a common title, the container or material accompanying the transparencies may be used as the chief source for the entire title and statement of responsibility.

Special rules for transparencies include 8.5B1, 8.5B4, 8.5B5, 8.5C16, and 8.5D4. For another example of cataloguing of a transparency, see figure 1-107.

Wall chart: See under *chart* for discussion.

8.7. NOTE AREA

Follow general instructions under 1.7. Notes are to be listed in the order in which they appear in 8.7B.

8.7B2. Language. Give a note on the language of the item unless it is evident from the rest of the description. See, for example, figure 7-8, note 1.

8.7B7. Edition and history. As with other notes, make this note only if the information is not evident elsewhere in the entry. The note connects the work being catalogued with other versions, editions, etc. See, for example, figures 7-4, 7-7, and 7-9. Because information about the adaptation appears in the statement of responsibility, such a note is not necessary in figure 7-14.

8.7B8. Characteristics of original. See figure 7-2 for such a note.

8.7B10. Physical description. See figure 7-1, 1-102, etc.

8.7B11. Accompanying material. See discussion under 1.7B11 for guidance about when this note is needed.

8.7B14. Audience. Give this note only if the information is stated on the item, the container, or accompanying material. See figure 7-7, 7-8, etc.

8.7B17. Summary. Since graphic materials are often stored so that they are not easy to browse, a summary of the content of the item is particularly useful unless content is obvious from the rest of the entry. See, for instance, figures 7-5, 7-8, etc.

8.7B18. Contents. See 1.7B18 for guidance on format for contents note. See, for instance, figures 7-8, 7-17, etc.

8.7B19. Numbers. Give important numbers that may serve to identify the item (but not series numbers, ISBNs, or ISSNs). See, for example, figure 7-21.

8.10. ITEMS MADE UP OF SEVERAL TYPES OF MATERIAL

Items consisting of various types of material, if they lack a predominant component, take the GMD "kit" (North American) or "multimedia" (British). See 1.10 for instructions; see also figures 7-7 and 7-8 for examples of kits.

8
Three-Dimensional Artefacts and Realia

(*AACR2* Chapter 10)

AACR2 chapter 10 gives rules for the description of all kinds of three dimensional items—handmade, manufactured, and natural—with the exception of those covered in other chapters. Globes and relief maps, for example, are considered cartographic materials and are covered in *AACR2* chapter 3.

AACR2 chapter 21 has no specific rules for main and added entries for three dimensional objects, other than the stipulation that "artists [and, by extension, sculptors, weavers, and other creators] . . . are the authors of the works they create" (21.1A1). Thus, a sculptor will be given main entry for his or her work (figure 8-1).

```
Maxwell, Robert.
   Pig 10 [art original] / Robert Maxwell. --
[196-?]
   1 sculpture : unglazed clay, brown ; 8 x 9 cm.

   Stylized wide-mouth pig designed as a container
for small objects.




   I. Title.
```

Figure 8-1. Main entry under creator

In addition, *AACR2* 21.16B states that a reproduction of an art original (e.g. a painting, drawing, or sculpture; see *AACR2* Glossary, Appendix D) will be entered under the heading for the original work. Thus, replicas of sculpture that are intended to simulate the appearance of the original piece are entered under

199

the heading for the original work, whether they are the same size as the original or not.

10.0B1. Chief source of information. Descriptive cataloguing rules that govern other types of library materials will be applied to the cataloguing of three-dimensional objects. The object itself or a label permanently attached to it serves as the chief source of information, along with any accompanying textual material and a container issued by the "publisher" or manufacturer (figure 8-2).

```
Tok-bak [realia]. -- [Niles, Ill.] : Developmental
    Learning Materials, [197-]
    1 sound intensifier : plastic, blue ; 20 x 12 cm.

    Device which fits over the ears and mouth so as
to intensify the sound of the wearer's voice.




    I. Developmental Learning Materials (Firm).
```

Figure 8-2. Object as chief source

10.0H. Many of the three-dimensional artefacts covered by *AACR2* chapter 10 have more than one part. If the individual items in the set do not bear a common title, take cataloguing information from the container. The container furnished all the information for the example shown in figure 8-3.

```
Ploutz, Paul F.
    Evolution [game] : geologic time chart : the
historical record of life on earth ... / by Paul
F. Ploutz. -- Athens, Ohio : Union Print. Co.,
c1972.
    1 game (board, cards, 4 tokens, 1 die, chips,
glossary) ; in box, 37 x 39 x 4 cm.

    Ages 10 to adult.
    Summary: Game traces the development of life from
algae to modern man; for 2-6 players.


    I. Title.   II. Title: Geologic time chart.
```

Figure 8-3. Container as chief source

	Geologic Time Chart The historical record of life on earth becomes a simplified playing board for a fun educational game for science entitled Evolution
Chart	

by Paul F. Ploutz, Ed.D.

© Copyright 1972

10.1. TITLE AND STATEMENT OF RESPONSIBILITY AREA

Record the information according to general guidelines in 1.1. In figure 8-1 the title of the sculpture and the name of the sculptor were incised on the base of the object. The information was transcribed accordingly. But many, if not most, noncommercially produced three-dimensional artefacts will not be labeled in this fashion. If no title appears on the object, a container, or accompanying textual material, the cataloguer makes up a brief descriptive title, which is transcribed within brackets as the first part of the title and statement of responsibility area (1.1B7). No statement of responsibility will be given unless the item was signed or the information appeared on one of the locations considered part of the chief source. This information, if taken from another source, appears in a note.

10.4. PUBLICATION AREA

For commercially produced three-dimensional artefacts the three elements (place, publisher, etc., and date) prescribed by 1.4 will be included and general guidelines under it will be followed. However, place and name of publisher or manufacturer, obviously, is inappropriate for a noncommercial item. Give the year of creation as the sole element in the publication area for such objects (10.4F2). See figure 8-4.

```
Fingal, Ingrid.
   [Hand weaving] [realia]. -- [1978]
   1 sampler : cotton, col. ; 125 x 30 cm.


   Woven by Ingrid Fingal.
   Pattern: Crackle weave.
```

Figure 8-4.
Noncommercial
artefact

10.4F2. Date. The date will also be omitted when describing a naturally occurring object (figure 8-5).

```
₁Scorpion₁ ₁realia₁.
  1 scorpion : tan ; in dome, 4 cm. high x 10 cm.
diameter.

  Obtained in Arizona desert, August 1972.
```

Figure 8-5. Natural object—no publication area

10.5. PHYSICAL DESCRIPTION AREA

For the cataloguing of three-dimensional artefacts, this area includes the same general elements used to describe other library materials: extent of item, other details, dimensions, and, when appropriate, accompanying material.

10.5B1. Extent of the item. Give the number of units followed by a specific material designation. The six terms listed under 10.5B1 are not the only terms that may be used as specific material designators in the physical description area. As already demonstrated, everything from samplers to scorpions may be catalogued by rules given in *AACR2* chapter 10. If one of the six terms listed under 10.5B1 is appropriate to the three-dimensional object being described, use it. Otherwise, give the name of the object as the specific material designator.

Caution: Although the specific material designator list may be enlarged at the cataloguer's discretion, this is not the case with the GMD given following the title proper. The cataloguer is limited to the terms listed in 1.1C1 for the GMD.

Diorama: See *AACR2* Glossary, Appendix D, for definition of a diorama. The diorama itself is the preferred source for cataloguing data. If appropriate information is not found on the object, data may be transcribed from the container or from accompanying material. In the example shown in figure 8-6, the title was transcribed from the envelope in which the folded diorama was stored; publication area information is from the diorama itself.

Exhibit: An exhibit is "a collection of objects and materials arranged in a setting to convey a unified idea."[1] An exhibit may be made up of a number of

[1] Alma M. Tillin and William J. Quinly, *Standards for Cataloging Nonprint Materials*, 4th ed. (Washington: AECT, 1976), p. 215.

different types of materials; if so, the GMD will be "kit" (North American) or "multimedia" (British). If the materials are unified, use an appropriate GMD from the list under 1.1C1 (see figure 8-7). An exhibit is to be studied and observed; it is not meant for user interaction.

```
Christmas scene [diorama]. -- Providence, R.I. :
   Providence Lithograph Co., 1959.
   1 diorama (various pieces) : cardboard, col. ;
37 x 56 x 26 cm. folded to 26 x 38 x 2 cm.

   Includes 3 groups of figures: Mary, Joseph, the
baby Jesus, and 2 groups of shepherds and sheep
with stable background; in envelope.
   Stock DF 211.
```

Figure 8-6. Diorama

```
   I. Providence Lithograph Company.
```

```
Coal [realia] : plant life to plastics. -- Washing-
   ton : Bituminous Coal Institute, Education Dept.,
   [196-?]
   1 exhibit (12 pieces) : col. ; in folder, 25 x
17 x 2 cm.

   Samples of coal and coal products.
```

Figure 8-7. Exhibit

```
   I. Bituminous Coal Institute.  Education Dept.
```

Game: See *AACR2* Glossary, Appendix D, for definition. Unless individual pieces in the game bear a common title, the container will be the chief source of information. Supplement this as needed with information from accompanying material. (See figure 8-8.)

Alice in Wonderland card game set ₁game₁ : with the
   original illustrations in full color. -- New
York : Merrimack Pub. Corp., ₁196-?₁
1 game (48 cards) : col. ; 10 x 7 x 2 cm.

Reproduced from the antique original set ;
featuring John Tenniel illustrations.
   No. 1974S.

   I. Carroll, Lewis. Alice in Wonderland.
II. Tenniel, John.

Figure 8-8. Game

48 Piece Antique Replica
Alice in Wonderland
Card Game Set
Container   with the original illustrations
in full color

Microscope slide: A microscope slide is a special slide produced for use with
a microscope. It is generally made of two pieces of glass put together sandwich
fashion, with some realia between the layers. Cataloguing information will be
taken from the slide itself, a container, or accompanying material. If none of
these sources furnishes cataloguing data, the cataloguer constructs an entry as
has been done with figure 1-16. Special rules governing microscope slides are
10.5C1, 10.5C2, and 10.5D1.

Mock-up: See *AACR2* Glossary, Appendix D, for definition. A mock-up is a
teaching device that should involve interaction with the user. Thus, a dummy
steering wheel and dashboard used to teach automobile driving is a mock-up;
a plastic piano keyboard sometimes used in teaching class piano is a mock-up
(figure 8-9).

₁Piano keyboard₁ ₁model₁. -- ₁s.l. : s.n., 196-?₁
   1 mock-up : plastic ; 16 x 36 cm.

   Silent keyboard, two octaves, for use in teaching
piano.

Figure 8-9. Mock-up

Model: See *AACR2* Glossary, Appendix D, for definition. A mock-up (q.v.) is one kind of a model, generally one with moving parts. A model may have moving parts, but it differs from a mock-up in that it is basically noninteractive; it is simply an artefact to be examined, not a training tool.

The chief source of information for a model, as for other three-dimensional objects, is the object itself, together with the container and accompanying textual material. (See figure 8-10.)

```
Pictograph—cuneiform unit ₍model₎ / prepared by
   the Educational Division of Alva Museum Replicas ;
   educational consultant, Hyman Kavett. —— Long
   Island City, N.Y. : Alva Museum Replicas, c1968.
   6 tablets : plastic, brown ; in box, 30 x 32 x
6 cm. + 1 teacher's guide (8 p.) + 1 student
activity program (8 p.). —— (Alva class research
kit ; 1/2)
   Replicas colored to simulate an early Sumerian
pictograph (ca. 3000 B.C.) and a cuneiform tablet
with its 2 part envelope (ca. 1800 B.C.); includes
4 pictographs and 2 cuneiform tablets.
   Bibliography: p. 8 of the teacher's guide.
   I. Alva Museum Replicas.  Educational Division.
II. Series.
```

Figure 8-10. Model

10.6. SERIES AREA

Follow general instructions under 1.6 for transcription of series. See, for instance, figure 8-10.

10.7. NOTE AREA

Notes are of the same type and are listed in the same order as that indicated in 1.7. See this rule for general guidance. See Appendix I, chapter 8, for examples of notes used in the cataloguing of three-dimensional items.

9

Microforms

(*AACR2* Chapter 11)

A microform may be defined as "a miniature reproduction of printed or other graphic matter which cannot be utilized without magnification."[1] Since a microform requires special equipment for its use, under *AACR2* rules it is regarded as a special type of library material rather than as a variant type of book, as was the case under *AACR1* rules.

Under *AACR1* rule 191, a microform was to be described in terms of the original work; that is, a microform that reproduced a monograph would be catalogued according to monographic cataloguing rules, including a physical description area, which gave the number of pages, illustration statement, and size of the original book, if this could be determined. Microform publication details were relegated to a note.

AACR Chapter 6 (1974) suggested that a microform edition of an eye-readable work should be added to the card for the original work as a dashed-on entry (rule 152C). This was to be done if the library owned both the original, hard-copy edition and the microform version. If the library had only the microform, *AACR Chapter 6* (1974) rule 156A stipulated treatment in the same fashion as *AACR1* rule 191. For an original edition in microform, the instructions in *AACR1* 191C and *AACR Chapter 6* (1974) 156C were identical. In this instance only, the physical description area (collation line) gave information about the microform itself.

In contrast to previous rules, *AACR2* chapter 11 rules for the description of microforms are analogous to rules for the cataloguing of facsimiles (1.11). In all cases, the cataloguer is to describe the microform item. Any data about the original work (except for mathematical data of a cartographic item, 11.3A, or numeric and/or chronological or other designation, 11.3B) will be ignored in transcribing information in the body of the card. Data about the original work are to be given in a note.

[1] Jean Riddle Weihs, *Nonbook Materials*, 1st ed. (Ottawa: Canadian Library Assn., 1973), p. 53.

11.0B. Sources of information

As with other types of library materials, the chief source is the item itself.

Microfilm: The title frame (or a succession of frames) at the beginning of the microfilm, which gives data about the microfilm publication of the item, is the chief source of cataloguing data for a microfilm. Information for the example shown in figure 9-1 was transcribed from four successive microfilm frames at the beginning of the item.

```
MacLeod, Anne Scott, 1930-
   A moral tale [microform] : children's fiction and
American culture, 1820-1860 / by Anne Scott MacLeod.
-- Ann Arbor, Mich. : University Microfilms, c1973.
   1 microfilm reel ; 35 mm.
```

Figure 9-1. Microfilm

```
   Thesis (Ph. D. )--University of Maryland, 1973;
includes bibliography.
```

```
I. Title.
```
73
28868
Microfilmed   1973

Frame 1

Information to users
   (about quality of microfilming)
Xerox University Microfilms, 300 N. Zeeb Road,
   Ann Arbor, Mich. 48106

Frame 2

73-28,868
MacLeod, Anne Scott, 1930–
   A moral tale: children's fiction and American
      culture, 1820–1860.
University of Maryland, Ph.D., 1973
History, modern.
University Microfilms, a Xerox Company
   Ann Arbor, Michigan.
   Copyright by Anne Scott MacLeod   1973

Frame 3

A moral tale: children's fiction and American
   culture, 1820–1860
            by Anne Scott MacLeod

Frame 4

Aperture card: This card, usually 9 × 19 cm., includes an opening for a micro-film insert. Aperture cards are usually punched for machine manipulation and retrieval. The chief source of information is the card.

Microfiche: See *AACR2* Glossary, Appendix D, for definition of microfiche. The title frame at the beginning of the microfiche serves as the chief source. Eye-readable data at the top of the fiche is also to be used as needed. (See figure 9-2.)

```
Library History Seminar (4th : 1971 : Florida
   State University)
   Library History Seminar, no. 4 [microform] :
proceedings, 1971 / edited by Harold Goldstein,
John M. Goudeau. -- Tallahassee : Journal of
library history, c1972.
   4 microfiches : negative ; 11 x 15 cm.
```

Figure 9-2. Microfiche

```
   I. Goldstein, Harold.   II. Goudeau, John M.
III. Journal of library history.
```

Library History Seminar
  No. 4, Proceedings, 1971
  Edited by
  Harold Goldstein
  John M. Goudeau
            The Journal of Library History
            School of Library Science
            Florida State University
            Tallahassee, Florida

Frame 1

(Blank)

Frame 2

Library History Seminar
No. 4, Proceedings, 1971
Copyright 1972 by the Journal of Library History

Frame 3

Microopaque: See *AACR2* Glossary, Appendix D, for definition of micro-opaque. The title frame at the beginning of the microopaque is the chief source; eye-readable data at the top of the card may also be utilized. In the example shown in figure 9-3, the title frame furnished only the title and statement of responsibility information and a publisher number. The rest of the data—publication area and series—appeared at the top of the card in eye-readable type.

```
Georgi, Charlotte, 1920-
   Twenty-five years of Pulitzer Prize novels,
1918-1943 ₁microform₁ : a content analysis / by
Charlotte Georgi. -- Rochester, N.Y. : University
of Rochester Press for Association of College and
Research Libraries, 1958.
   4 microopaques ; 8 x 13 cm. -- (ACRL microcard
series ; no. 96 )

   Thesis (M.S.L.S.)--University of North Carolina,
1956; includes bibliography.
   Microcard: UR-58 RL 22.

   I. Title.  II. Series.
```

Figure 9-3.
Microopaque

UR-58
RL 22   Frame 1
Micro Card

Twenty-five years of Pulitzer Prize novels, 1918–1943:
A content analysis by
Charlotte Georgi
A thesis submitted to the Faculty of
the University of North Carolina in
partial fulfillment of the requirements
for the degree of Master of Science in
the School of Library Science
Chapel Hill 1956

Frame 2

11.1. TITLE AND STATEMENT OF RESPONSIBILITY AREA

Follow guidelines given in 1.1 for transcribing this area. If the title of the microform is different from that of the original, give the microform title in the title and statement of responsibility area.

11.2. EDITION AREA

The edition statement may be transcribed from the chief source of information, the rest of the item, and the container. The edition statement given in the edition area must be that of the microform. The item may also include an edition statement pertinent to the original work. Such information will be given in a note.

11.3. SPECIAL DATA FOR CARTOGRAPHIC MATERIALS AND SERIALS

This information may be transcribed from the chief source of information, the rest of the item, or the container. Data about the *original item* are to be given in this area; aside from the note area, this is the only place where information about the original work appears in the entry.

11.3A. Cartographic material

Record mathematical data for a map reproduced in microformat as instructed in 3.3. See discussion and examples in this text for mathematical data area.

11.3B. Serials

Record numeric and/or other designation area as instructed in 12.3 for a serial in microformat, either an original or a reproduction. See this text for discussion and examples of numeric and/or other designation area.

Cataloguing information for the example shown in figure 9-4 was taken from four consecutive title frames at the beginning of the microfilm reproduction of the periodical.

```
Frank Leslie's boys' and girls' weekly [microform].
   -- Vol. 1, no. 1 (Oct. 13, 1866)-v. 36, no. 905
   (Feb. 9, 1884). -- [Washington] : Library of
   Congress Photoduplication Service, 1969.
   11 microfilm reels : ill. ; 35 mm.

   Original published: New York : F. Leslie, 1866-
   1884.



   I. Leslie, Frank.
```

Figure 9-4. Periodical on microfilm

Start   Frame 1

Frank Leslie's boys' and girls' weekly.
     New York   Frame 2
Shelf no. 20365 (AP 200.F65)

(photocopy of LC card)

Frank Leslie's boys' and girls' weekly, an illustrated
   record of outdoor and home amusements.   36-
                                               -Feb. 9, 1884.

Frame 3   New York, F. Leslie,   -84.
               Subtitle varies.
               No more published.

Microfilmed 1969, Library of Congress Photoduplica-
tion Service.

Frame 4   October 13, 1866 thru April 25, 1868
          (Reel 1)

11.4. PUBLICATION, DISTRIBUTION, ETC., AREA

Publication details are those of the microform, not the original, if the microform is a reproduction of another publication.

11.5. PHYSICAL DESCRIPTION AREA

As with other types of library materials, the physical description area includes
four elements:

11.5B. Extent of item and specific material designation

11.5C. Other physical details

11.5D. Dimensions

11.5E. Accompanying material (if any)

See preceding examples for illustrations of the application of rules for the
physical description area.

11.6. SERIES AREA

A series statement pertaining to the microform will be included in the series
area. See figure 9-3 for an example of an extensive microform series. A series
statement pertaining to the original publication will be given in a note (11.7B12).

11.7. NOTE AREA

Notes pertaining to the microform come first. Then, as stipulated in 11.7B,
give notes relating to the original, combined in a single note. Notes describing
the original should be given in the order in which they appear under 11.7B.

11.8. STANDARD NUMBER AREA

Although it seems a contradiction in terms, a microform publication sometimes includes an International Standard Book Number. If one appears somewhere on the item, or if the ISBN (or other standard number) pertaining to the item is given in any other source, it is to be transcribed as part of the entry. (See figure 9-5.)

```
Allen, Sue.
   Victorian bookbindings [microform] : a pictorial
survey / Sue Allen. -- Chicago : University of
Chicago Press, 1972.
   4 microfiches : col. ill. ; 11 x 15 cm.

   ISBN 0-226-01418-5




   I. Title.
```

Figure 9-5. Standard book number

Key to contents   Frame 1
   (Fiche number and frame show location of items)

Victorian bookbindings: a pictorial survey   Sue Allen
The University of Chicago Press, Chicago 60637
The University of Chicago Press, Ltd. London
©1972 by the University of Chicago   Frame 2
All rights reserved. Published 1972
Library of Congress Catalog card number 72-94380
International Standard Book Number 0-226-01-418-5

As library collections increase in size and as the cost of hard-copy editions increases, microform publications will continue to proliferate. Their importance in the library world is acknowledged by the fact that no longer is a microform reproduction of an eye-readable work to be treated as a stepchild, relegated to a modest note on the card. In all cases, a microform edition, whether original or a reproduction of another work, will be described independently.

10

Serials

(*AACR2* Chapter 12)

A serial, by definition, is "a publication in any medium issued in successive parts bearing numerical or chronological designations and intended to be continued indefinitely."[1] Serials include everything from annual reports and yearbooks of learned societies through *Mad Magazine*, *The Perils of Pauline*, and the local newspaper; "serial" is a state of issue, not a kind of material. Anything, print or nonprint, may be a serial, as long as it is issued in parts, numbered or dated in some fashion, and as long as it has no planned termination point.

The basic rules and principles governing main entry and added entries for serials are the same as for monographs. These rules are covered in *AACR2* Part II, chapter 21. *AACR2* chapter 12, as well as other chapters in Part I, deals only with rules for descriptive cataloguing.

Since, as Michael Gorman has correctly pointed out, "serials constitute a type of publication rather than a condition of authorship,"[2] there is little specific mention of serials as such in *AACR2* chapter 21. The only specific directives are in regard to a change in the title proper of a serial (21.2C) and to a change in the name of the person or corporate body responsible for a serial (21.3B). However, in view of the problems that serial publications often pose for cataloguers, it seems appropriate to give some attention to the evolution of rules for serials cataloguing that has resulted in the present rules.

The *ALA Cataloging Rules for Author and Title Entries* (1949) included a number of separate rules for treatment of various kinds of serials: periodicals and newspapers were covered by 5C; almanacs, yearbooks, and similar materials by 5D; directories by 5E; and series by 5F. As already stated, the International Conference of 1961, which resulted in the Paris Principles, was an attempt to arrive at a set of principles governing entry that would eliminate such multipli-

---

[1] *Anglo-American Cataloguing Rules*, 2nd ed. (Chicago: ALA, 1978), p. 570.
[2] Michael Gorman, "The Current State of Standardization in the Cataloging of Serials," *LRTS* 19 (Fall 1975): 302.

cation of rules. It is possibly significant that almost nothing was said about serial publications as such, at the conference, since the fact that a publication may be issued serially has nothing necessarily to do with the question of authorship responsibility. Paris Principle 11.14 says that "works (including serials and periodicals) known primarily or conventionally by title rather than by the name of the author" should be entered under title. Paris Principle 11.5 states: "When a serial publication is issued successively under different titles, a main entry should be made under each title. . . ."

Following the International Conference of 1961, the editors of *AACR1* proceeded to draw up a code based on the Paris Principles. The problem of formulating a rule for the entry of serials following the directive of Paris Principle 11.14 was a thorny one that troubled the editors greatly. The result of their efforts, *AACR1* rule 6, was, as Sumner Spalding admitted, rather arbitrary.[3] Briefly, rule 6 divided serials into three groups:

1. Those issued by commercial corporate bodies and not of personal authorship (to be entered under title)
2. Those issued by a corporate body—be it professional, civic, or political—that is in some way more than commercially interested in the publication (chiefly, but not entirely to be entered under title)
3. Those by a personal author (to be entered under author)

All serials in the first group (rule 6A) were to be given title main entry. But those serials in the second group (rule 6B) proved difficult to categorize. This enormous category of serials issued by a corporate body was subdivided into two parts. The first group (6B1) was limited to periodicals, monographic series, serially published bibliographies, indexes, directories, biographical dictionaries, almanacs, and yearbooks not covered by 6A and 6C. Most of the serials in this group would also be entered under title, with added entry for the sponsoring or issuing corporate body. However, the committee felt that the wording of the serial title had to be taken into consideration, in accordance with Paris Principle 9.12, which directed entry under corporate body "when the wording of the title or title page, taken in conjunction with the nature of the work, clearly implies that the corporate body is collectively responsible for the content of the work . . . e.g. serials whose titles consist of a generic term (Bulletin, Transactions, etc.) preceded or followed by the name of a corporate body, and which include some account of the activities of the body."

It seemed too much to expect the cataloguer to decide in each case whether such serials did indeed "include some account of the activities of the body," and so a rather complex set of exceptions to 6B1's general premise of entry under title evolved. Entry would be under the name of the corporate body if the title included the name of the corporate body (*Library of Congress Information Bulletin, Journal of the Optical Society of America*); or if the title included an abbreviation of the name of the corporate body (*NEA Handbook*); or if the title consisted "solely of a generic term [such as journal, newsletter, annals, etc.]

[3] Colloquium on the Anglo-American Cataloging Rules, University of Toronto, 1967, *The Code and the Cataloguer* (Toronto: Univ. of Toronto Pr., 1969), p. 25.

that requires the name of the body for adequate identification of the serial" (the American Theological Library Association's publication titled *Newsletter*).

As previously mentioned, serials covered by 6B1 were limited to periodicals, monographic series, serially published directories, indexes, bibliographies, biographical dictionaries, almanacs, and yearbooks. Entry for any other type of serial "issued by or under the authority of a corporate body" was to be under the name of the body (6B2), without exception.

In accordance with Paris Principle 11.5, and in a change from ALA 1949 rule 5, *AACR1* rule 6D stipulated that serials that changed their names would be entered separately under each title. The rationale behind this rule, which is still in effect under *AACR2* 21.2C and 21.3B, was the fact that a change in the name of a serial, even though it might not be accompanied by a change in the sponsoring organization, generally meant a shift in emphasis, a change of direction for the serial. Such a shift often meant that the serial was in effect a new entity. Thus, under the general principles that governed both the Paris Principles and *AACR1*, the serial should be given a new entry, even though the volume numbering might be continuous.

In the years following publication of *AACR1*, serials cataloguers, particularly those concerned with machine-readable records, were increasingly unhappy with the complexities of *AACR1* rule 6. By 1975 many serials experts had rejected the concept of entry under personal or corporate author entirely. Opposing viewpoints were aired at a meeting held at ALA Midwinter Meeting, January 19, 1975.[4] Those advocating title main entry for all serials won out at the ALA Conference of summer 1975; for several months it seemed that type of format rather than authorship responsibility would be the deciding factor for serials entry rules in the coming revision of *AACR*.

In the midst of the turmoil over choice of main entry, a new international code for the bibliographical description of serials: *International Standard Bibliographic Description for Serials (ISBD(S))* was formulated.[5] *ISBD(S)* was the result of the efforts of a joint working group set up by the IFLA Committee on Cataloguing, which was responsible for *ISBD(M)*, together with the IFLA Committee on Serials Publication. *ISBD(S)* was in many respects a close parallel to *ISBD(M)* and its American counterpart, *AACR Chapter 6* (1974).

Although the present rules for descriptive cataloguing of serials as set forth in *AACR2* chapter 12 bear much resemblance to *ISBD(S)*, the charge of the editors to adhere to the Paris Principles of authorship responsibility means that serials rules will not satisfy those who prefer title main entry for all serials. However, as Sumner Spalding so ably put it:

> If those who process incoming serial issues and those who store them can do their work better by using the title as the means of organizing

[4] Two of the papers presented at the January 19, 1975, meeting were printed in *LRTS* 19 (Fall 1975): "No Special Rules for Entry of Serials" (Michael Carpenter) and "AACR, ISBDS, and ISSN: a Comment" (Paul Fasana). Almost the entire issue is devoted to the serials question.

[5] *ISBD(S): International Standard Bibliographic Description for Serials*, 1st standard ed. (London: IFLA International Office for UBC, 1977).

the records and the stock of serial issues, they should do so. The present cataloging rule does not prevent this . . . . So this is all the issue seems to hang on: must we undermine a fundamental principle in our existing cataloging system because a certain class of change in serial publications could thereby be handled somewhat more simply? I think not.[6]

12.0B1. Sources of information for printed serials. For nonprint serials, the chief source of information is the same as for nonprint monographic publications. For the instructions for cataloguing the cassette serial illustrated by figure 10-1, see *AACR2* chapter 6, rules 6.0B, etc.

```
Black box [sound recording]. -- 1-      . -- Wash-
   ington : New Classroom, 1972-
      sound cassettes (90 min. each) : 1 7/8 ips,
stereo., Dolby processed + pamphlets.

   Bimonthly.
   Poetry and music.
   Program notes with each issue.
   Each issue contains 2 C-90 sound cassettes.
```

Figure 10-1. Nonprint serial

Program notes

Black Box is published bi-monthly in Washington, D.C. as a service of The New Classroom, a nonprofit educational cooperative.

Cassette label

Black Box
Copyright: © 1972 • The New Classroom

For a printed serial, as with a monograph (*AACR2* chapter 2), the title page is the chief source of information. This instruction is unchanged from *AACR1* rule 161B, with one very important difference. Under 161B, the cataloguer was to catalogue from the title page or title page substitute of the latest volume. In contrast, *AACR2* 12.0B1 stipulates that the *first available issue* must be used. This change was made so that the serial may be catalogued as it actually *is*, rather than on the basis of a particular library's holdings.

In the case of serials such as a yearbook, an annual report, a serially published biographical dictionary, directory, almanac, index, etc., locating a title page poses no problem. The piece in hand usually includes a fairly conventional looking title page that will serve as the chief source of information (see figure 10-2).

6 "ISBDS and Title Main Entry for Serials," *LC Information Bulletin* 33 (Nov. 22, 1974): A-232.

Who's who of American women : a biographical
    dictionary of notable living American women. --
    1st ed. (1958-1959)-   . -- Chicago : Marquis
    -Who's Who, 1958-
        v. ; 28 cm.

    Biennial.
    Subtitle varies.
    First and 2nd eds. called also v. 1-2.
    ISSN 0083-9841

Figure 10-2.
Biographical dictionary

Title page

Who's Who of American Women
A Biographical Dictionary of Notable
Living American Women
Volume I
(1958-1959)
First Edition
Marquis-Who's Who
Chicago 11, Illinois

When cataloguing periodicals, however, locating a title page may be a problem.[7] Generally speaking, the first issue of a periodical does not include a formal title page. The title page is generally issued separately with the last number of the periodical in the volume, if the publisher is library minded enough to furnish a formal title page, that is. Consequently, if the cataloguer uses the title page of the first volume as the chief source of information, according to 12.0B1, he or she must usually wait until the completion of that volume of the periodical before doing the cataloguing.

Even after the cataloguer has waited for the completion of the first volume, the publisher of the periodical may not issue a formal title page. Furthermore, library policy may call for cataloguing to be done from the first issue of a periodical, rather than waiting a year or so for the completion of the first volume. If the periodical has no title page, the cataloguer will take cataloguing information from a title page substitute, in this order of preference:

1. The cover of the first issue of the serial
2. The caption page of the first issue (The caption is the title and other information that appears at the head of the first page of text.)

[7] Cataloguers define a periodical as "a serial appearing or intended to appear indefinitely at regular or stated intervals, generally more frequently than annually, each issue of which normally contains separate articles, stories, or other writings" (*AACR1*, p. 345).

3. The masthead of the first issue (This section, near the front of the serial usually, gives details of ownership, advertising, subscription rates, etc.)

Even aside from the lack of uniformity in such matters as title pages, serials pose unique problems simply because they continue over a long period of time. Editors change; the sponsoring body or publisher may change; even the title of the serial itself may change. The catalogue entry for a serial publication must show not only the original status of the serial but also changes that have taken place. In order to provide this information, some modifications of the conventional patterns for monographic cataloguing are necessary. A special area—the area for numeric, chronological, etc., designations—comes just before the publication area for serials. This numeric area describes volume numbering and dates for the entire serial, beginning with its first issue and ending finally with its indeterminate demise. The serial is catalogued from the first issue; notes show later variations such as a change in the name of the publisher or a changed subtitle. The date in the publication area is left open, as stipulated in 1.4F7, since a serial is a multipart item that is not yet complete.

The Journal of Library History is a fairly straightforward, uncomplicated (relatively speaking) serial. Its catalogue entry is shown in figure 10-3.

```
The Journal of library history : philosophy and
   comparative librarianship. -- Vol. 1, no. 1
   (Jan. 1966)-    . -- Tallahassee, Fla. : Library
   School, Florida State University, 1966-
      v. ; 23 cm.
```

Figure 10-3. Serial

```
   Quarterly.
   Published: Tallahassee : School of Library Science,
Florida State University, Apr. 1968-fall 1976;
Austin : Graduate School of Library Science, the
University of Texas at Austin, winter 1977-

   I. Florida State University. Library School. II.
Florida State University. School of Library Science.
III. University of Texas at Austin. Graduate
School of Library Science.
```

Title page

> The Journal of Library History
> Philosophy and Comparative Librarianship
> Louis Shores, Editor
> 1966   Volume I
> Library School
> Florida State University
> Tallahassee, Florida

The formal title page for *The Journal of Library History* was used as the chief source of information. The title of the serial was transcribed from this source. Notice, however, that the editor's name was not transcribed as part of the entry. *AACR2* 12.1F3 states that the editor's name is not to be recorded as part of the statement of responsibility. This is because most serials have a series of editors; if each editor's name were included as part of the entry, the catalogue record would need to be constantly updated. However, if library users are likely to identify the serial by the name of the editor, an added entry for editor may be made. If this is done, the cataloguer will give the editor's name in a note, following 12.7B6. See figure 10-11 for an instance when this would be appropriate.

Because a serial is to be catalogued from the first issue, the volume number and date (as appropriate) are included just as they appear on the first issue as the first part of the "numeric and/or alphabetic, chronological, or other designation area." The cover of *The Journal of Library History* furnished the necessary information for this area, which always precedes the publication area.

Following the general pattern for cataloguing, the last area of the formal description is the publication area. *AACR1* rule 164 in most cases limited the information given here to place of publication and name of publisher. Date was omitted if it appeared in the "holdings statement" (numeric area). Under *AACR2*, in order that cataloguing information for serial publications should follow as closely as possible the general pattern for descriptive cataloguing as outlined in *AACR2* chapter 1, publication date will be included as the last element in this area. This will be done even if it repeats information already given in the numeric area. The date will be left open until the serial ceases publication.

The physical description area describes the entire serial, not just the first issue. The number of volumes will be indicated when a printed serial ceases publication. Until then, the cataloguer transcribes "v." as the first part of the area, leaving three spaces to fill in the volume numbers when the serial is complete. Illustrations and dimensions are given as appropriate (12.5).

Notes are given as appropriate for each serial. All serials include as the first note a statement about frequency of publication, unless it is obvious from the title (e.g. *Library Quarterly*). (See 12.7B1.) Figure 10-3 has an additional note about a change of publisher (10.7B9).

12.1B. Title proper

Record the title proper of a serial according to general rules under 1.1B. The title proper of a serial may be long or it may simply be a generic term.[8] Look carefully at the content of a serial with this kind of title. Many such serials are official publications of a society, institution, or other corporate body. If such a serial emanates from a corporate body and deals with its policies, procedures, operations, etc., main entry will be under the name of the corporate body (21.1B2).

[8] ISDS definition of a generic term is "one which indicates the kind and/or periodicity of a publication." Some examples of generic terms are: transactions, journal, circular, official report, research paper, annual report, bulletin, etc. Information from Library of Congress, *Cataloging Service Bulletin* 112 (Winter 1975).

Under ALA 1949 rules, if the volume numbering was continuous, a serial was considered a single serial despite a change in its title or the name of the corporate body under which it was entered. Thus the entire serial was recatalogued under a new title or different name of corporate body, with the earlier title or corporate name given in a note. This practice was called "latest entry cataloguing." This treatment was changed by *AACR1* 6D, which directed that a new entry be made for a serial that changes its title or that is entered under a corporate body that changes its name during the course of publication. The old entry was closed off. This treatment is known as "successive entry cataloguing."

AACR2 21.3B is the same as *AACR1* 6D. The reason for this rule is sound. A change in the name of a corporate body most generally is accompanied by a shift in direction, emphasis, or makeup of the entire body. Therefore, even if the name of the periodical remains the same and the volume numbering continues, a periodical entered under such a corporate body will be given a new entry for issues under the changed name.

The *Newsletter* of the Midwest Inter-library Center is such a periodical. In 1966, the Midwest Inter-library Center changed its name to the Center for Research Libraries. The entry for the *Newsletter* published by the center under its earlier name was closed (see figure 10-4) and a new entry was started for issues of the *Newsletter* published after the center changed its name (see figure 10-5).

```
Midwest Inter-library Center.
   Newsletter : a monthly report to members / issued
by the Midwest Inter-library Center. -- No. 1
(Oct. 1949)-no. 102 (Feb. 1966). -- Chicago : The
Center, 1949-1966.
   102 v. ; 28 cm.

   Subtitle varies: A periodic report to members /
issued by the Midwest Interlibrary Center, May 1963
-Feb. 1966.
   Continued by: Newsletter : a quarterly report to
members / issued by the Center for Research
Libraries.

   I. Title.
```

Figure 10-4. Title proper

Caption title page

Newsletter
A Monthly Report to Members Issued by the
Midwest Inter-library Center
at Room E51 • 1116 East Fifty-ninth Street
Chicago 37, Illinois   No. 1   October 31, 1949
[text follows]

Center for Research Libraries.
   Newsletter : a quarterly report to members /
issued by the Center for Research Libraries. --
No. 103 (Mar. 1966)-   . -- Chicago : The Center,
1966-
   v. ; 28 cm.

   Continues: Newsletter : a monthly report to
members / issued by the Midwest Inter-library
Center.

   I. Title.

Figure 10-5. Title proper—serial name change

Heading

Newsletter
A Quarterly Report to Members Issued by the
Center for Research Libraries
5721 Cottage Grove Avenue • Chicago • Illinois 60637
Teletype CG 1516
No. 103   March 30, 1966
[text follows]

The cataloguer should read rule 21.3B carefully. A new entry will be made for a serial only if main entry is under the name of the changed corporate body. In the example shown in figure 10-3, *The Journal of Library History*, two changes have occurred in the publisher, one of them being a change in the name of the publisher, the other being a shift to an entirely different publisher. Such changes are handled by notes.

Sometimes the title proper of a serial changes. When this happens, 21.2C stipulates that a new entry will be made for issues under the changed title. The two serials are connected with notes in a similar fashion to those used in figures 10-4, 10-5, 10-6, and 10-7.

The title proper may include an initialism standing for the name of a sponsoring corporate body. Record such a title according to directions in 1.1B6. *AACR1* rule 6B1 exception called for entry of a serial with a title that included an abbreviation of the name of a corporate body under the corporate body, regardless of the content of the serial. Under *AACR2* rules, wording of the title is not a consideration in choice of main entry. Only serials falling into one of the categories of 21.1B2 will be given main entry under the name of the body from which they emanate.

The *GARC Newsletter* includes material on general developments in the graphic arts as well as announcements of Graphic Arts Research Center activities. According to 21.1B2, entry under the name of the Center is inappropriate, and so main entry will be under title with added entry under the name of the Center (see figure 10-8).

The Journal of typographic research. -- Vol. 1,
    no. 1 (Jan. 1967)-v. 4, no. 4 (autumn 1970). --
    Cleveland : For M.E. Wrolstad by the Press of
    Western Reserve University, 1967-1970.
    4 v. : ill. ; 23 cm.

    Quarterly.
    Continued by: Visible language.

Figure 10-6. Title
proper—changed title

The Journal of Typographic Research
January 1967

Title page

Masthead

**The Journal of Typographic Research, Volume 1,
Number 1, January 1967. Published four times a year
(January, April, July, and October) for Dr. Merald
E. Wrolstad by The Press of Western Reserve
University, 2029 Adelbert Road, Cleveland, Ohio
44106. Copyright © 1967 by The Press of
Western Reserve University.**

Visible language : the journal for research on the
    visual media of language expression. -- Vol. 5,
    no. 1 (winter 1971)-   . -- Cleveland : M.E.
    Wrolstad, 1971-
        v. : ill. ; 23 cm.

    Quarterly.
    Continues: The Journal of typographic research.

Figure 10-7. Title
proper—changed title

Dr. Merald E. Wrolstad,
Editor and Publisher
c/o The Cleveland
Museum of Art,
Cleveland, Ohio,
USA 44106.

Masthead

Visible Language
The Journal for Research on the Visual Media
of Language Expression
Volume V, Number 1, Winter 1971

Cover

```
GARC newsletter. -- Vol. 1, no. 1 (Jan. 1973)-   .
  -- Rochester, N.Y. : Graphic Arts Research Center,
  Rochester Institute of Technology, 1973-
     v. : ill. ; 30 cm.

  Monthly.
  Continues in part: Graphic arts progress.
  Vols. 2-3: 24 cm.
  Vol. 2, no. 8 (Sept. 1974) is special issue:
Graphic arts experience '74.


  I. Rochester Institute of Technology.  Graphic
Arts Research Center.
```

Figure 10-8. Title proper with initialism

January 1973   Volume 1   Number 1
                 GARC Newsletter
Caption title   Published by Graphic Arts Research Center,
                      Rochester Institute of Technology
                      [text follows]

The **GARC Newsletter** is published monthly by the Graphic Arts Research Center, College of Graphic Arts and Photography, Rochester Institute of Technology. Subscriptions are free upon request. Contents consist of announcements and activities at GARC and comments on the events in graphic arts and graphic communication.
Address all correspondence to:
Editor, GARC Newsletter, Graphic Arts Research Center, Rochester Institute of Technology, One Lomb Memorial Drive, Rochester, New York 14623

Masthead

12.1B6. Title with variable date or number. The title will be recorded exactly as it is found in the chief source unless it includes a variable number or a date. Omit the number or date from the title statement. If it occurs anywhere but at the beginning of the title, indicate omission by ellipses (see figure 10-9). However, if the number or date occurs at the beginning of the title, do not show omission by ellipses (see figure 10-10).

The ALA yearbook : a review of library events ...
   -- 1975-   . -- Chicago : American Library
   Association, 1976-
      v. : ill. ; 29 cm.

Vol. for 1976: Centennial ed.

I. American Library Association.

Figure 10-9.
Title with
variable date

Title page

1976 Centennial Edition
The ALA Yearbook
A Review of Library Events 1975
American Library Association
Chicago, Illinois

Henry E. Huntington Library and Art Gallery.
   Annual report / Henry E. Huntington Library and
Art Gallery. -- 1st (July 1, 1927-June 30, 1928)
   -    . -- San Marino, Calif. : The Library, 1929-
      v. ; 24 cm.

I. Title.

Figure 10-10.
Title with
variable
number

Henry E. Huntington
Library and Art Gallery
First Annual Report
July 1, 1927—June 30, 1928
San Marino, California
1929

Title page

12.1E. Other title information

AACR1 162A specified that subtitles were to be omitted in the transcription of the serials entry. The reason for this was that serials subtitles often change; the editors felt that recataloguing could be avoided if this element was not recorded. *AACR2* 12.1E calls for following the general rules for transcription; if the title page for a printed serial includes a subtitle, it will be recorded. A note is made if other title information changes (12.7B5); see figure 10-11.

The Unabashed librarian : a letter for innovators.
   -- No. 1 (Nov. 1971)-   . -- New York : M.H.
   Scilken, 1971-
      v. : ill. ; 28 cm.

Quarterly.
Subtitle varies.
Founded, edited, and published by Marvin H.
Scilken.

I. Scilken, Marvin H.

Figure 10-11. Other
title information

Cover

The
U*n*a*b*a*s*h*e*d
Librarian
A Letter for Innovators
Number 1   November 1971
© U.L. 1971 G.P.O. Box 2631, New York, N.Y. 10001

12.1E1. If the title proper of a serial consists of an acronym or initialism, the full form is treated as other title information when it appears in the chief source.

This rule must not be taken as a direction always to choose the initials over the full form as the title proper. One must first decide what is the title proper without any help from the rules. If one decides that the initials are the title proper, only then does the rule come into play. (See figure 10-12.)

```
RSR : reference services review. -- Vol. 1, no. 1
   (Jan./Mar. 1973)-    . -- Ann Arbor, Mich. :
   Pierian Press, 1973-
      v. ; 28 cm.
                                       Figure 10-12. Initialism
                                       in title
   Quarterly.
   Title from caption.
   Pilot issue, unnumbered, Nov./Dec. 1972.
```

RSR
Reference Services Review
January/March 1973   Volume 1, Number 1

Cover

Masthead

Pierian Press
Editorial Offices: 931 S. State,
Ann Arbor, Michigan 48104,
Mailing Address: Box 1808,
Ann Arbor, Michigan 48106,
Cable Address: Pierianpress,
Ann Arbor, Michigan, U.S.A.
313/662-1777

12.1F. Statements of responsibility

Together with 12.1E, rule 12.1F represents one of the most significant breaks with the past in serials cataloguing. *AACR1* 160D prohibited the transcription of the author statement. In a rule that is exactly the opposite *AACR2* (12.1F) states that a statement of responsibility appearing in the chief source of information for a serial will be recorded as directed in 1.1F. (Exception: Editor's name will not be recorded; see 12.1F3.)

Figure 10-13 shows a serial entered under the name of a personal author. In order for main entry to be under the name of a person, 21.1A1 states that this person must be "chiefly responsible for the creation of the intellectual or artistic content of a work." If four or more authors are involved with the creation of a work, main entry will be under title (21.6C2). Only rarely does a serial publication meet the criteria for entry under personal author. *The Forerunner*, one of the rare examples, is a magnificent tour de force, a substantial monthly publication containing poetry, articles, short stories, and even advertisements, every word written by Charlotte Perkins Gilman. But even the indefatigable Gilman ran out of steam (and funds) after seven years of heroic effort, and *The Forerunner* breathed its last.

```
Gilman, Charlotte Perkins.
  The forerunner / by Charlotte Perkins Gilman.
-- Vol. 1, no. 1 (Nov. 1909)-v. 7, no. 12 (Dec.
1916). -- New York : Charlton Co., 1909-1916.
  7 v. ; 25 cm.

  Monthly.




  I. Title.
```

Figure 10-13.
Statement of
responsibility

Volume 1. No. 1.   November 1909
                    The Forerunner
              by Charlotte Perkins Gilman.
                  The Charlton Company
                  67 Wall St.   New York

Cover

12.1F2. Statement of responsibility as part of title. As instructed under 1.1F, transcribe the title as it appears; if it includes a statement of responsibility or the name of a sponsoring body, etc., transcribe it. (See figure 10-14.)

```
The Yale University Library gazette. -- Vol. 1,
  no. 1 (June 1926)-     . -- [New Haven] : The
  Library, 1926-
     v. : ill. ; 27 cm.

  Quarterly.




  I. Yale University.  Library.
```

Figure 10-14.
Sponsoring body's
name in title

Cover

                  The Yale University Library
                            Gazette
              Volume 1   June 1926   Number 1

The title of the serial may include part of the name of the responsible corporate body (figure 10-15). Notice once again that main entry is no longer dependent (as it was under *AACR1* 6B1 exception) on the wording of the title. Entry is governed by 21.1B2 and other general rules of authorship responsibility in *AACR2* chapter 21. *The Harvard Librarian* is devoted to Harvard University Library matters; the *Yale University Library Gazette* is not.

```
Harvard University.  Library.
  The Harvard librarian / issued from the office
of the director, Harvard University Library. --
Vol. 1, no. 1 (Dec. 1957)-    . -- Cambridge,
Mass. : The Library, 1957-
    v. : ill. ; 28 cm.


  Frequency varies.
  Suspended June 1966-Sept. 1968.




  I. Title.
```

Figure 10-15.
Sponsoring body's
name in title

Caption title

The Harvard Librarian
issued from the
Office of the Director
Harvard University Library
Cambridge 38, Massachusetts

Vol. 1, No. 1   December, 1957

The statement of responsibility may appear as part of other title information. Record it as it appears. If a name in the statement of responsibility appears in abbreviated form, give expansion, when necessary, in a note (12.7B6); see figure 10-16.

12.1F3. Omission of editor's name in statement of responsibility. As noted in discussion of figure 10-3, a person named as the author of a serial publication will be named in the statement of responsibility (see figure 10-13), but an individual listed as editor will not be so recorded. If the editor's contribution has been such that the periodical is likely to be known by that individual's name, a note will be made, following 12.7B6. In the example shown in figure 10-17, Ada P. McCormick served as editor, and indeed did a substantial part of the writing, for *Letter* during the six years of its existence.

12.2B2. Edition statement. If the edition statement on a serial publication changes with each issue, it is to be regarded as numeric information and included in the numeric area. For an example of such an edition statement, see figure 10-2.

International cataloguing : quarterly bulletin of
    the IFLA Committee on Cataloguing. -- Vol. 1,
    no. 1 (Jan./Mar. 1972)-   . -- London : The
    Committee, 1972-
        v. ; 30 cm.

    Issued by: International Federation of Library
Associations, Committee on Cataloguing.

Figure 10-16.
Statement of
responsibility in other
title information

    I. International Federation of Library Associa-
tions. Committee on Cataloguing.

International Cataloguing
Caption title Quarterly Bulletin of the IFLA Committee
on Cataloguing
        Volume 1 Number 1 January/March 1972

Masthead   International Cataloguing is published quarterly by the
IFLA Committee on Cataloguing, c/o The Department
of Printed Books, The British Museum, London, WC1B
3DG, Great Britain.

Letter. -- Vol. 1, no. 1 (Jan. 1943)-v. 5, no. 9
    (1949). -- Tucson, Ariz. : A.P. McCormick,
    1943-1949.
    5 v. : ill. ; 20 cm.

    Irregular.
    Editor: Ada P. McCormick.

Figure 10-17. Name of
editor in note

    I. McCormick, Ada P.

Cover   Vol. 1

Letter

January, 1943   No. 1

Published monthly, 111 Olive Road, Tucson, Arizona

Editor—Ada P. McCormick

12.3. NUMERIC AND/OR ALPHABETIC, CHRONOLOGICAL, OR OTHER DESIGNATION AREA

The numeric area, formerly called the "holdings statement," is found only in entries for serials. Under *AACR1* rule 163 and previous rules, the holdings statement was just that, a statement of the volumes of a serial that a particular library had in its collection. If the library had the first issue of *The Journal of Library History* (figure 10-3), the holdings statement read

> v. 1–   Jan. 1966–

with space left to close the entry when the periodical finally ceased publication. *AACR1* 163A2 stipulated, "If the library does not have the first issue, the holdings statement is omitted and a note is added, if the information is available, to provide the date when publication began. . . ."

As can be seen, *AACR1* and other previous serials cataloguing rules were based on the concept that the catalogue entry for a particular serial should reflect the actual holdings of the particular library doing the cataloguing. With the increasing interest in international exchange of cataloguing data not only for monographs but also for serials, it is not surprising that *AACR2* rules for serials stipulate that the serial should be described in its entirety, starting with the first issue, even if the library does not have that issue. (Check *New Serial Titles* or *Union List of Serials* to find the starting date for the periodical.)

As stated in the *ISBD(S)* standards for description of serials, "Numbers and dates . . . are identifying elements of a serial. They are not to be confused . . . with the numbers and dates by which the local holdings of a specific collection are recorded and which can vary from one collection to another."[9] If the library does not have a complete run of a serial, this information can be given in a note (12.7B20).

12.3B3. Continuous volume numbering for a serial with a changed title. For an example of continuous numbering, see figure 10-7.

12.4. PUBLICATION, DISTRIBUTION, ETC., AREA

In contrast to *AACR1* 164, *AACR2* provides that the general rules (under 1.4) applicable to all types of library materials will be followed for the publication area for serials.

[9] *ISBD(S)*, p. 25.

12.4F. Date of publication will be given, even if it duplicates dates in the numeric area. This is a change from *AACR1* rule 164A1.

12.5. PHYSICAL DESCRIPTION AREA

12.5B. Extent of the item
Because the extent, like the rest of the physical description area, describes the entire serial, the number in the specific material designation is omitted; this part of the entry is left open until the serial ceases publication.

12.5C. Other physical details
If illustrations are a feature of the serial, a general term, "ill.," is sufficient unless particular types of illustrations, colour, etc., are important. This element reflects the entire run of the serial; it should not take into account single illustrations of a particular type (e.g. a map, a portrait, etc.).

12.5D. Dimensions
See chapter on particular type of material (e.g. for printed serials, see *AACR2* 2.5D) for directions on recording dimensions.

12.5E. Accompanying material
Record accompanying material only if it is issued regularly with the serial. See figure 10-1; a pamphlet is included with each issue. Frequency of accompanying material is indicated in a note (12.7B11).

12.7. NOTE AREA

Follow general instructions given in 1.7A concerning format and the order of notes. Also, include any necessary notes pertinent to the specific type of library material being catalogued. For instance, for a cassette serial (see figure 10-1), refer to *AACR2* chapter 6, rule 6.7.

12.7B1. Frequency. This note must be given unless frequency is obvious from the title: e.g. *The ALA Yearbook; The Library Quarterly*.

12.7B5. Other title information. For example of practice, see figures 10-2 and 10-11.

12.7B6. Statements of responsibility. If a statement of responsibility such as the fact that a serial is the official organ of a society or other corporate body, is not transcribed in the title and statement of responsibility area, give it as a note. (See figure 10-18.) Use the terminology found in the publication itself if possible.

For examples of the expansion of a name appearing in abbreviated form as part of the title, see figures 10-16 and 10-19.

A note is made to give the name of an editor of a serial when an added entry is to be made for this individual. See figures 10-11 and 10-17.

12.7B7. Relationship with other serials. When a serial changes its identity in any fashion, a note is made. A variety of these notes have appeared in preceding examples.

12.7B7b. Continuation: See figures 10-5 and 10-7.
12.7B7c. Continued by: See figures 10-4 and 10-6.

12.7B7d. Merger: See figure 10-18.
12.7B7e. Split: See figure 10-8.

Library resources & technical services. -- Vol. 1,
   no. 1 (winter 1957)-   . -- ₍Richmond₎ : ALA
   Resources and Technical Services Division,
   1957-
      v. ; 24 cm.
   Quarterly.
   Official publication of: the Resources and Tech-
nical Services Division of the American Library
Association.
   Merger of: Serial slants; and, Journal of
cataloging and classification.
   ISSN 0024-2527
   I. American Library Association. Resources and
Technical Services Division.

Figure 10-18.
Statements of
responsibility as notes

Cover

Library Resources & Technical Services
                                Vol. 1 No. 1

Library Resources & Technical Services
Vol. 1, No. 1   Winter, 1957   Contents page
   ALA Resources and Technical Services Division

Masthead

Library Resources and Technical Services, the quarterly official publication of the Resources and Technical Services Division of the American Library Association is published at 1407 Sherwood Ave., Richmond 5,
Va.

12.7B7k. *Supplements.* Unless the title of the serial clearly indicates that a
serial is a supplement to another publication, a note explaining the relationship
is given. A similar note on the main serial entry records the titles of its supplements. In the examples shown in figures 10-19 and 10-20, a note is not needed
on *ACRL News* or its changed title *College & Research Libraries News* to indicate
its supplemental status since in each case the title makes this clear. A note is
needed on the entry for the parent serial, *College and Research Libraries* (figure
10-21).

ACRL news : a supplement to College & research
  libraries. -- No. 1 (Mar. 1966)-no. 9 (Dec. 1966).
  -- Chicago : American Library Association, 1966.
  9 v. : ports. ; 24 cm.

  Monthly.
  Subtitle varies.
  Issued by: Association of College and Research
Libraries.
  Continued by: College & research libraries news.

  I. College and research libraries.   II. Association of College and Research Libraries.

Figure 10-19.
Supplement

Caption title

ACRL News
No. 1, March 1966
A Supplement to College & Research Libraries,
Vol. 27, No. 2

College & research libraries news : ACRL news issue
  (A) of College & research libraries. -- No. 1
  (Jan. 1967)-   . -- Chicago : American Library
  Association, 1967-
      v. : ports. ; 24 cm.

  Monthly.
  Issued by: Association of College and Research
Libraries.
  Continues: ACRL news.

  I. College and research libraries.   II. Association of College and Research Libraries.

Figure 10-20.
Supplement with
changed title

Caption title

College & Research Libraries News
No. 1, January, 1967
ACRL News Issue (A) of College & Research Libraries,
Vol. 28, No. 1

College and research libraries. -- Vol. 1 (Dec. 1939)- . -- Chicago : American Library Association, 1939-
  v. ; 25 cm.

Quarterly (1939-1955), six issues yearly (1956-)
Official organ of: the Association of College and Reference Libraries, 1939-1957; Association of College and Research Libraries, 1958-
  Supplement: ACRL news (Mar. 1966-Dec. 1966); College & research libraries news (Jan. 1967-)
  ISSN 0010-0870

I. Association of College and Reference Libraries. II. Association of College and Research Libraries.

Figure 10-21. Supplement note

Title page

College and Research Libraries
Title Page and Index to Vol. 1, 1939–40
Association of College and Reference Libraries

College and Research Libraries is the official organ of the Association of College and Reference Libraries. It is published by the American Library Association.

Masthead

12.7B8. Numbering and chronological designation. Notes on irregularities in numbering, etc., are given in a note.

Sometimes an introductory number of a periodical will be issued to sound out the market before the new venture is officially launched. Information about such an introductory issue is given in a note. Cataloguing will not be done from this issue; 12.0B1 stipulates the use of the "first" issue, i.e., first regular issue. (See figure 10-12.)

11

Choice of Access Points

(AACR2 Chapter 21)

AACR2 chapter 21 gives rules for determining the main entry (the principal heading under which a work will be entered in the library's catalogue) and added entries. The rules in chapter 21 are based on the following general principles:

1. Main entry will be under the personal author chiefly responsible for the artistic creation of the work or its intellectual content (21.1A).
2. For a work emanating from a corporate body, main entry will be under the heading for the body if the content of the work is of the five types listed under 21.1B2.
3. If personal authorship is diffuse (four or more authors), indeterminate (doubtful), or unknown (anonymous), main entry will be under title (21.1C1) or a uniform heading (*AACR2* chapter 25).
4. For a work not of personal authorship emanating from a corporate body that is not subsumed under the five categories listed under 21.1B2, main entry will be under title (21.1C3).

Many libraries today are looking toward on-line or computer-output micro-film catalogues if they are not already using them. Other libraries, reluctant to abandon the traditional card catalogue, use printed unit cards, one of which functions as the main entry and other duplicate cards are overprinted with added points of access to the work. In view of this, many cataloguers question the continued emphasis of the *Anglo-American Cataloguing Rules* on rules for choice of main entry. There are several reasons. Despite the general library custom of multiple entries for most library items, many bibliographical sources, such as union catalogues, booktrade directories, etc., cite works by a single entry. Also, a single entry is needed to identify a work about which something has been written: e.g. a commentary on Milton's *Paradise Lost*.

Some people argue with considerable logic that the title of the work should always serve as main entry, with all other points of access as added entries. Certainly there is something to be said for that, despite the counter argument that many titles are indistinct, such as those beginning with the word "journal" or "proceedings," etc. Early bibliographies in the Western world were customarily arranged by title; Oriental practice calls generally for title main entry. However, the Paris Principles are based on the concept of author responsibility. As mentioned previously,[1] the Joint Steering Committee of *AACR2* charged the Catalog Code Revision Committee and other organizations involved in shaping the new code to adhere to the Paris Principles, as *AACR1*, had done. The Joint Steering Committee and the editors of *AACR2* in this regard follow traditional Western library practice, and it may be said that *AACR2* is basically a conservative code.

21.0B. Sources for determining access points

The most important source for determining access points—in fact, the most important source for the transcription of the bibliographic description—is the part of the item that may be termed "prominent." For a determination of "prominence" it is necessary to consult *AACR2* 0.8, where prominence is limited to the sources prescribed for the first two areas of description (the title and statement of responsibility area and the edition area). The prescribed sources for these two areas vary somewhat from category to category of material (see rule designated .0B2 in each chapter; e.g. for microforms, 11.0B2). In some cases these prescribed sources may amount to the whole item. Thus, data that are prominent within an item should furnish the necessary information to determine the main entry and added entries. Only rarely does the cataloguer need to read a book, listen to a sound recording, or watch a motion picture to determine appropriate access points.

21.0D. In view of the fact that the Library of Congress will not apply the option of adding a designator for function to added entry headings,[2] it is unlikely that designators will be used by many North American libraries. Designators will not be used in examples in this text. If a library chooses to apply this option, designations should be limited to those listed under 21.0D.

21.1. BASIC RULE

21.1A1. Personal authorship. The definition of personal authorship given under 21.1A1 is basically the same as that in *AACR1*[3]; A work will be entered under personal author when appropriate according to the rules that follow (21.4, 21.5, 21.6, etc.).

21.1B. Entry under corporate body

The definition of a corporate body given under 21.1B is a modification, clarification, and enlargement of the definition given in *AACR1*.[4] The important thing to remember is that, for cataloguing purposes, a corporate body must be an organization or group of persons that has a formal name. Rule 21.1B1 gives

[1] See p. 5.
[2] *LC Information Bulletin* 37 (July 21, 1978): 425.
[3] Page 9, footnote 2.
[4] Page 11, footnote 4.

several criteria for deciding whether a group does indeed have a name. The idea is not new, but the careful delineation and explication probably has its roots in Eva Verona's monumental study of corporate headings, a document that had much influence on this section of the code.[5]

21.1B2. General rule. The general rule governing entry under corporate body is much more restrictive than *AACR1* rule 1A, which simply stated that a work should be entered "under the person or corporate body that is the author." Thus, under *AACR1*, many works issued by a corporate body were entered under the body simply because the work lacked a personal author. As Verona phrased it, "AACR [1] avoids, as far as possible, entry under title proper."[6] Verona suggests a definition of corporate authorship that, although not explicitly stated in the stipulations of 21.1B2, obviously enunciates the principle underlying the rule:

> A work should be considered to be of corporate authorship if it may be concluded by its character or nature that it is necessarily the result of the creative and/or organizational activity of a corporate body as a whole, and not the result of an independent creative activity of the individual(s) who drafted it.[7]

Following Verona's lead, 21.1B2 totally abandons the principle of corporate authorship in favor of a very restrictive set of guidelines for corporate responsibility under which entry will be made under the heading for the body. A work emanating from a corporate body will have main entry under the heading for the body *only* if its content is as follows:

21.1B2a. *Work of administrative character.* Official reports, rules and regulations, and catalogues of an institution's resources clearly represent the "creative and/or organizational activity of a corporate body as a whole." These are to be entered under the name of the corporate body. A newsletter reporting activities of the corporate body will be entered under the body; see figure 10-4. An annual report will be entered under corporate body; see figure 10-10. A manual of procedure reflecting rules and regulations of a corporate body will be entered under the name of the body; see figures 1-80 and 11-1.

A catalogue of the resources of an institution will be entered under the name of the institution; see figure 1-77. A report of an official of a corporation, institution, or other corporate body dealing with administrative affairs, procedures, etc., of the corporate body will be entered under the body; see figure 1-76.

21.1B2b. Also to be entered under the corporate body responsible for them is a group of works that Verona calls "Primary legal acts." Included are laws (21.31), treaties (21.35), and constitutions and charters (21.33); these will be considered further in this chapter. Also entered under corporate heading are decrees of the chief executive (21.31) and administrative regulations (21.32).

---

[5] *Corporate Headings* (London: IFLA Committee on Cataloguing, 1975), pp. 3–7.
[6] Ibid., p. 9.
[7] Ibid., p. 13.

Library of Congress. Descriptive Cataloging
   Division.
   Cooperative cataloging manual for the use of
contributing libraries / the Library of Congress,
Descriptive Cataloging Division. -- Washington :
U.S.G.P.O., 1944.
   104 p. : forms ; 24 cm.

Figure 11-1. Policies
and procedures

I. Title.

Title page

Cooperative Cataloging Manual
for the use of contributing libraries
The Library of Congress
Descriptive Cataloging Division
United States Government Printing Office
Washington, D.C., 1944

A legislative hearing is to be entered under the name of the legislative body
that has called the hearing; see figure 11-2.

21.1B2c A work that records "the collective thought of the body" will be
entered under the name of the body; see figure 11-3.

21.1B2d. A work that reports "the collective activity of a [named] conference"
will be entered under the name of the conference; see figure 11-4. For discussion
of conferences and criteria for determining whether a conference is a named
conference, see 24.7. (For example, see figure 11.5.)

21.1B2e. A performing group is also regarded as a corporate body. In certain
cases, the performing group will be given the main entry. See 21.23C and
figure 5-6.

21.1B3. If a work issued by a corporate body does not fit in one of the five
categories listed under 21.1B2, it will not be entered under the corporate body.
If no personal author is given, the work will, in many cases, be entered as a
work of unknown authorship—under title. Give added entry to the corporate
body; see figures 11-6 and 11-7.

A work issued by a corporate body that is not of a type included in the five
categories of 21.1B2 may have a personal author or authors. If so, entry will be
governed by the number of persons involved in the intellectual content of the
work. The example shown in figure 11-8 is entered under personal author by
stipulations of 21.4A. Added entry is made for the issuing corporate body.

Figure 11-9 shows a work issued by a corporate body but which is not one
of the five categories of 21.1B2. It has four personal authors who are responsible
for the content of the work. Entry is under title by provisions of 21.6C2.

United States. <u>Congress</u>. <u>House</u>. <u>Committee on
Education and Labor</u>. <u>Special Subcommittee on
Education</u>.
Discrimination against women : Congressional
hearings on equal rights in education and employment / edited by Catharine R. Stimpson in conjunction with the Congressional Information Service.
-- New York : Bowker, 1973.
  xvii, 558 p. ; 24 cm. -- (Bowker/CIS congressional
document series)

  I. Stimpson, Catharine R. II. Congressional
Information Service. III. Title. IV. Series.

Figure 11-2. Legislative
hearing

Title page

Discrimination against Women
Congressional Hearings on Equal Rights
in Education and Employment
Edited by Dr. Catharine R. Stimpson, Barnard College,
in conjunction with
the Congressional Information Service,
Washington, D.C.
R.R. Bowker Company
New York & London, 1973
A Xerox Education Company
Xerox

Bowker/CIS Congressional Document Series   Facing title page

Verso of title page

Published by R.R. Bowker Co. (A Xerox
  Education Company)
1180 Avenue of the Americas, New York, N.Y. 10036
Copyright © 1973 by Xerox Corporation

American Library Association. <u>Library Standards</u>
   <u>for Microfilm Committee</u>.
   Microfilm norms : recommended standards for
libraries / prepared by the Library Standards for
Microfilm Committee of the Copying Methods Section,
Resources and Technical Services Division, American Library Association ; Peter R. Scott, committee
chairman. -- Chicago : The Division, 1966.
   48 p. : ill. ; 23 cm.

                                                   Figure 11-3. Official
                                                   statements

  I. Scott, Peter R.   II. Title.

                                   Microfilm norms
             Recommended Standards for Libraries prepared by the
                Library Standards for Microfilm Committee
                     of the copying methods section,
Title page   resources and technical services division,
                       American Library Association
                           Peter R. Scott,
                         Committee chairman
          ALA Resources and Technical Services Division
                               Chicago, 1966

Incorporated Association of Assistant Masters in
   Secondary Schools.
   Teaching in comprehensive schools : a second
report / issued by the Incorporated Association
of Assistant Masters in Secondary Schools. --
Cambridge, ₁England₁ : University Press, 1967.   Figure 11-4. Official
   vii, 174 p. : ill. ; 19 cm.   statements—reports

  Includes index.
                         Teaching in Comprehensive Schools
                            a Second Report
                            Issued by the
                        Incorporated Association of
             Assistant Masters in Secondary Schools
  I. Title.   **Cambridge**
                          at the University Press
                              1967

             Title page

Conference on Historical and Bibliographical
  Methods in Library Research (<u>1970 : University
  of Illinois</u>)
Research methods in librarianship : historical
and bibliographical methods in library research :
papers / presented at the Conference on Historical
and Bibliographical Methods in Library Research ;
conducted by the University of Illinois Graduate
School of Library Science, March 1-4, 1970 ; edited
by Rolland E. Stevens. -- Urbana : The School,
c1971.
  140 p. ; 24 cm.
  I. Stevens, Rolland E.   II. University of Illinois.   Graduate School of Library Science.
III. Title.

Figure 11-5. Openly
named conference

Papers Presented at the
Conference on Historical
and Bibliographical Methods
in Library Research
Conducted by the University of Illinois
Graduate School of Library Science
March 1-4, 1970

Research Methods in Librarianship:
Historical and Bibliographical Methods
in Library Research
Edited by Rolland E. Stevens
University of Illinois
Graduate School of Library Science
Urbana, Illinois

Title information on two facing pages

Landscaping with native Arizona plants / Natural
  Vegetation Committee, Arizona Chapter, Soil
  Conservation Society of America. -- Tucson :
  University of Arizona Press, 1973.
  vii, 194 p. : ill. ; 23 cm.

  Spine title: Native Arizona plants.
  Bibliography: p. 183-184.
  Includes index.
  ISBN 0-8165-0385-0

  I. Soil Conservation Society of America.   Arizona
Chapter.   Natural Vegetation Committee.   II. Title:
Native Arizona plants.

Figure 11-6. Work
emanating from a
corporate body not
included in 21.1B2

Landscaping with Native Arizona Plants
Natural Vegetation Committee Arizona Chapter
Soil Conservation Society of America
The University of Arizona Press Tucson, Arizona

Title page

Favorite paintings from the Detroit Institute of
  Arts : fifteen color reproductions / with
  descriptive notes by members of the Detroit
  Institute of Arts staff. -- New York : Archway
  Press, c1948.
  80 p., [8] leaves of plates : 15 col. ill. ;
21 cm. -- (Everybody's gallery)

Figure 11-7. Work
emanating from a
corporate body not
included in 21.1B2

    I. Detroit Institute of Arts.

Title page

Favorite paintings from
The Detroit Institute of Arts
Fifteen color reproductions
with descriptive notes by members of
The Detroit Institute of Arts Staff
Archway Press • New York

Groben, W. Ellis.
  Adobe architecture : its design and construction
/ prepared by W. Ellis Groben. -- [Washington] :
U.S. Dept. of Agriculture, Forest Service, 1941.
  24 leaves, 11 leaves of plates : ill. ; 28 cm.

Figure 11-8. Entry
under personal rather
than corporate author

    I. United States. Forest Service. II. Title.

Title page

United States Department of Agriculture
Forest Service
Adobe Architecture
Its Design and Construction
1941
Prepared by
W. Ellis Groben,
Division of Engineering
T. W. Norcross, Chief

Books of Latin American interest in public libraries
of the United States / prepared for the A.L.A.
Committee on Library Cooperation with Latin
America by William C. Haygood ... [et al.] . --
Chicago : American Library Association, 1942.
26 p. ; 23 cm.

Figure 11-9. Entry
under title (four
personal authors)

I. Haygood, William C.   II. American Library
Association. Committee on Library Cooperation with
Latin America.

Title page

Books of Latin American Interest in
Public Libraries of the United States
Prepared for the
A.L.A. Committee on
Library Cooperation with Latin America by
William C. Haygood
George Finney
Manuel Sanchez
Mary E. Brindley
Chicago
American Library Association
1942

Each of the examples given to illustrate 21.1B3 (figures 11-6 through 11-9) would have been entered under corporate body under provisions of *AACR1*. *AACR2* rules for entry under corporate body are more restrictive than previous codes. Unless a work is clearly one of the types listed under 21.B2, it will not be given main entry under a corporate heading.

21.1B4. Entry under a subordinate unit of a corporate body. If, by terms of 21.1B2, a work would be entered under corporate body, and a subordinate unit of the corporate body is responsible for it, main entry will be under the subordinate unit—if the unit is prominently named (i.e., is listed in the prescribed source for areas 1 and 2). (See discussion under 1.1F1.) See figure 11-1 for an example of a subordinate unit of a corporate body that is prominently named; see also figure 11-2.

21.2C. Serials

See chapter 10 of this text for discussion and examples of proper catalogue entry for a serial with a changed title, specifically figures 10-6 and 10-7.

21.3B. Serials

See chapter 10 of this text for discussion and figures 10-4 and 10-5 for an example of a serial entered under corporate heading with a change in the name of the corporate body.

21.4. WORKS OF SINGLE AUTHORSHIP

Rules 21.1 through 21.3 deal with general principles of authorship responsibility. Rule 21.4 gives guidance for entry of a work that is the responsibility of *one* person or corporate body.

21.4A. Single personal authorship

This simple rule, because it is the foundation of Western cataloguing practice, is probably the most important rule in the entire code. As stated in the Paris Principles (8.1), "The main entry for every edition of a work ascertained to be by a single personal author should be made under the author's name." The Paris Principles deal only briefly with the question of determining the form of the author's name that will appear as a heading in the catalogue. Some authors use full legal name; some use a nickname; some use one or more pseudonyms; and some simply are not at all consistent about the form of name they use to identify their works. *AACR2* chapter 22 gives rules for guidance in these problems. Basically, the rule states that the heading will be the name by which the author is commonly known. Thus, entry for a single work by one author may appear under the person's real name (see figure 1-1), a pseudonym (figure 5-2), or a word or phrase (figure 1-62). See chapter 22 for further discussion and more examples.

A collection or selection of works by one author will also be entered under the name of the author, following guidelines in chapter 22 for the form of the heading; see figure 11-10.

Figure 11-10. Selections from the work of one author

```
Sayers, Frances Clarke.
     Summoned by books : essays and speeches / by
Frances Clarke Sayers ; compiled by Marjeanne Jen-
sen Blinn ; foreword by Lawrence Clark Powell. --
New York : Viking, 1965.
     173 p. ; 22 cm.

     Contents: Summoned by books -- The belligerent
profession -- Of memory and muchness -- Lose not the
nightingale -- Anne Eaton of Lincoln School -- The
later years : Anne Carroll Moore -- "From me to
you" -- The storyteller's art -- Writing for chil-
dren : a responsibility and an art -- The books of

                (Continued on next card)
```

Sayers, Frances Clarke.   Summoned by books.   1965.
  (card 2)

Eleanor Estes -- Eleanor Farjeon's "Room with a
view" -- The flowering dusk of Ella Young --
"Through these sweet fields" -- Books that enchant :
what makes a classic? -- Happy botheration.

  I. Blinn, Marjeanne Jensen.   II. Title.

Title page

Verso of title page

Copyright © 1965 by Frances Clarke Sayers
  and Marjeanne Blinn
First published in 1965 by The Viking Press, Inc.

Summoned by Books
Essays and Speeches by
Frances Clarke Sayers
Compiled by Marjeanne Jensen Blinn
Foreword by Lawrence Clark Powell
The Viking Press / New York

A work known to be by a single author will be entered under the name of
that person even if the name of the person appears nowhere in the work; see
figure 11-11.

Sassoon, Siegfried.
  Memoirs of an infantry officer / by the author
of Memoirs of a fox-hunting man. -- London : Faber
& Faber, 1930.
  334 p. ; 18 cm.

Figure 11-11. Entry
under author—name
not in book.

Memoirs of an Infantry Officer
by the Author of
Memoirs of a Fox-Hunting Man
London
Faber & Faber Limited
24 Russell Square

  I. Title.

Title page

21.4B. Works emanating from a single corporate body

If a single corporate body is responsible for a work under stipulations of 21.1B2, entry will be under it; see figures 11-1, etc., for examples.

21.4D. Works by heads of governments, etc.

This rule is similar to ALA 1949 rule 73B–C and *AACR1* 17C, which called for the entry of official communications of sovereigns, presidents, governors, etc., under the corporate heading for the official. Also included are official communications from high ecclesiastical officials such as popes, bishops, etc. A change from previous rules is the stipulation that a work thus entered under the corporate heading for the official will have an added entry under the personal heading for the person. Under *AACR1* a pair of explanatory references was made leading from the corporate to the personal heading and from the personal to the corporate heading. *AACR2* provides only for one of these references, the one leading from the corporate to the personal heading (21.4D2), and calls for added entries instead to provide access through the personal heading to a corporate heading (21.4D1).

The principle governing 21.4D is basically the same as that of 21.1B2: When the head of a government speaks or writes in an official capacity, he or she represents the office in a fashion that is clearly analogous to 21.1B2c. Therefore, entry is under the corporate heading provided for the office that he or she holds (see 24.20 for form of heading). Such special headings are provided only for *heads* of government, not for subsidiary officials. Typical of officials included in this rule would be the Queen of England, the President of the United States, the governor of Arizona, and the mayor of Tucson. See figures 1-96 and 1-75 for examples.

A collection of official communications of more than one governmental head goes under the general heading for the office. (See figure 11-12.) The rule is unchanged from *AACR1* 17C1c.

21.4D2. Any nonofficial communication from a person covered by provisions of 21.4D1 will be entered under personal heading. The rule is the same as *AACR1* 17C2a. And, as was stipulated under *AACR1* 80, an explanatory reference will be made from the corporate heading to the personal heading; see 26.2D1 for form and figure 11-13 for example.

The book shown in figure 11-13 consists of informal essays on justice, poverty, "the great society," etc. Since these are not official communications, the book is entered under personal heading.

The explanatory reference will be made only once, the first time the personal heading is used for an individual who is the head of a government.

An explanatory reference such as was shown in figure 11-14 is necessary for persons who are heads of governments, because such persons will sometimes be entered under personal name and sometimes under the official heading for their office. Since an added entry will be made under the name of the person as personal author for official communications entered under heading for the office, no reference need be made from the personal heading to the corporate heading.

```
United States. President.
   State of the union : highlights of American his-
tory, momentous events and policies in the polit-
ical, social, and military life of the nation as
revealed in the state-of-the-union and war mes-
sages of the Presidents, George Washington to John
F. Kennedy / selected and edited by Edward Boykin.
-- New York : Funk & Wagnalls, c1963.
   x, 501 p. : ports. ; 22 cm.




   I. Boykin, Edward.  II. Title.
```

Figure 11-12.
Collection of official
communications

Title page

State of the Union
Highlights of American history, momentous events
and policies in the political, social, and
military life of the nation as revealed in the
State-of-the-Union and War Messages of the
Presidents: George Washington to John F. Kennedy.
Selected and edited by Edward Boykin
Funk & Wagnalls Company, Inc.
New York

```
Johnson, Lyndon B.
   My hope for America / by Lyndon B. Johnson. --
New York : Random House, c1964.
   127 p. : ill. ; 21 cm.




   I. Title.
```

Figure 11-13.
Nonofficial
communication from
head of government

My Hope for America
by Lyndon B. Johnson
Random House • New York

Title page

United States. President (1963-1969 : L.B. Johnson)
   Here are entered works of the President acting
in his official capacity. For other works, see
Johnson, Lyndon B.

Figure 11-14.
Explanatory reference

21.4D3. The provisions for entry under personal name holds true when the work is a mixture of official and nonofficial communications. Because part of the work consists of official communications, an added entry will be made under the appropriate heading for the office. The rule is the same as *AACR1* 17C2c. The example shown in figure 11-15 includes speeches made while Lyndon B. Johnson was senator, official speeches to Congress that he made as President, and miscellaneous writings.

Johnson, Lyndon B.
   A time for action : a selection from the speeches
and writings of Lyndon B. Johnson, 1953-64 /
introduction by Adlai E. Stevenson. -- New York :
Atheneum, 1964.
   xv, 183 p. : ill. ; 22 cm.

Figure 11-15. Official
and nonofficial
communications

   I. United States. President (1963-1969 : L.B.
Johnson). II. Title.

Title page

A Time for Action
A Selection from the Speeches
and Writings of
Lyndon B. Johnson
1953–64
Introduction by Adlai E. Stevenson
Atheneum Publishers
New York
1964

A collection containing both official communications and other works by more than one head of a government will be given title main entry under the general rules for collections (21.7). The rule is unchanged from *AACR1* 17C2c (as revised).

21.5. WORKS OF UNKNOWN OR UNCERTAIN AUTHORSHIP OR BY UNNAMED GROUPS

21.5A. This rule is the same as *AACR1* 2A. Enter such works under title, assuming that research has not revealed the name of the author. This rule eliminates cataloguer constructed headings such as "Boston. Citizens," which under ALA 1949 rule 140 would have been given to the second example, "A memorial to Congress . . . ," under 21.5A. It is obvious that such a heading is of no value to the catalogue user; title main entry is appropriate. The example shown in figure 11-16 is a book for which the author is unknown.

See figure 1-51 for an example of title main entry for a work by an unnamed group.

```
Fireside pictures. -- New York : American Tract
   Society, 1863.
   64 p. : ill. ; 16 cm.
```

Figure 11-16.
Unknown author

I. American Tract Society.

Fireside Pictures.
Published by the
American Tract Society,
150 Nassau-Street, New York.

Title page

21.5B. A work that has been attributed to a person will be entered under title, with added entry for the person, unless it is generally assumed that the person is the author. In that case, enter under the heading for the person; see figure 11-17.

21.5C. Entry under word or phrase

If an author, otherwise unknown, is identified in a work by a characterizing word or phrase, enter under the word or phrase, see figure 11-18. Rule 21.5C is a modification of *AACR1* 2C, which likewise stipulated entry under the identifying word or phrase, but only if it was preceded by the definite article ("the," or the equivalent in foreign languages). If the characterizing word or phrase was preceded by the indefinite article (a, an), or if the only clue was a phrase naming another book the author had written, *AACR1* 2C stipulated title main entry for the work. Mercifully, this hair-splitting distinction has been abandoned. See 22.11 for further directions on entry under word or phrase.

Plantin, Christopher.
  Calligraphy & printing in the sixteenth century :
dialogue / attributed to Christopher Plantin ;
edited, with English translation and notes by Ray
Nash ; foreword by Stanley Morison. -- Antwerp :
Plantin-Moretus Museum, 1964.
    77 p., p. 218-255 : ill. ; 19 cm.

  Includes French and Flemish facsimile.

    I. Nash, Ray.   II. Title.

Figure 11-17. Probable author

Title page

Calligraphy & Printing
in the sixteenth century
Dialogue attributed to
Christopher Plantin
in French and Flemish facsimile
Edited, with English translation and notes
by Ray Nash
Foreword by Stanley Morison
Antwerp
The Plantin-Moretus Museum
MCMLXIV

Old author.
  Anecdotes illustrative of the power of the Holy
Scriptures, &c. ; to which is annexed, The Bible /
from an old author. -- Aberdeen : G. and R. King,
1847.
    72 p. ; 15 cm.

Figure 11-18. Author
not known—entry
under word or phrase

    I. Title.   II. Title: The Bible.

Title page

Anecdotes
Illustrative of the
Power of the Holy Scriptures, &c.;
To Which Is Annexed,
"The Bible,"
from an Old Author.
Aberdeen: George and Robert King,
28, St. Nicholas Street,
1847.

The only type of device, under *AACR2*, which cannot be used as a pseudonym, and thus as an entry word, is a nonalphabetic and nonnumeric device that cannot be filed. An author who identifies himself or herself in such fashion will be entered under real name if this is known; if real name is not known, the works of such an author will be entered under title.

21.6. WORKS OF SHARED RESPONSIBILITY

This rule is roughly equivalent to *AACR1* rule 3, "Works of shared authorship." The substitution of the word "responsibility" for "authorship" in the new rule was deliberate, since this rule covers not only personal authors but also corporate bodies, which by the terms of *AACR2* cannot be authors in the same sense that persons can. (See previous discussion of 21.1B2.)

Rule 21.6 gives direction about main entry for works produced by two or more personal authors, whether these authors worked as collaborators in a work of joint authorship or as contributors to a composite work (a work in which each author's contribution is separate and distinct) as long as such a work has a title applicable to the entire work. Paris Principle 10 (Multiple authorship) governs the rule insofar as personal authors are involved: Main entry will be under the name of the person primarily responsible for the intellectual or artistic creation of the work, if this primary responsibility can be determined. If primary responsibility cannot be determined, main entry will be under the heading for the author named first in the prescribed source of information or, if such source lists four or more authors, under title.

In addition to works of personal authorship, rule 21.6 covers entry of works emanating from more than one corporate body if such works are covered by the categories listed under 21.1B2. Also covered are "works resulting from a collaboration or exchange between a person and a corporate body."

21.6B. Principal responsibility indicated

This rule is the same as *AACR1* 3A. It is a fairly obvious rule, closely related to 21.6C; the only instance in which the stipulations of this rule would result in an entry different from that called for under 21.6C is if the layout (type, etc.) of the chief source indicates that a person other than the one named first is principally responsible for the work. Only rarely is a chief source set up in such a fashion. A straightforward and obvious example of the rule is shown in figure 11-19.

21.6C. Principal responsibility not indicated

This rule is the same as *AACR1* 3B. If the chief source of information does not indicate which author has principal responsibility for the work, give main entry to the first author named if the chief source lists either two or three authors. Give added entries to the author or authors not receiving main entry. Figure 1-33 is an example of this rule.

21.6C2. If the chief source of information lists four or more persons or corporate bodies, none of which has the principal responsibility for the work, make title main entry. The rationale for this rule is that the user of the catalogue in thinking of a book with four or more authors is more likely to remember it by title than by author; i.e., authorship is diffuse. The choice of cutoff point for main entry under author at three authors follows Paris Principle 10.22.

Figure 1-31 is an example of this rule, as is figure 1-32. The latter shows entry for a work for which four corporate bodies had responsibility.

```
Asheim, Lester.
  The humanities and the library : problems in the
interpretation, evaluation, and use of library
materials / by Lester Asheim and associates. --
Chicago : American Library Association, 1957.
  xix, 278 p. ; 24 cm.



  I. Title.
```

Figure 11-19. Principal responsibility indicated

Title page

The Humanities and the Library
Problems in the Interpretation,
Evaluation and Use of Library Materials
by Lester Asheim and associates
American Library Association
Chicago • 1957

21.6D. Shared pseudonyms

This rule is the same as *AACR1* 3C. See 26.2D1 for format of explanatory references that need to be made from the pseudonym to the heading for the person(s).

21.7. COLLECTIONS AND WORKS PRODUCED UNDER EDITORIAL DIRECTION

This rule subsumes works covered by *AACR1* rules 4 and 5. Under the stipulations of these rules, the editor or compiler would be given main entry, providing certain conditions were met. This practice was at variance with Paris Principle 10.3, which stipulated title main entry for a collection (and, by extension, an editorially produced work) that had a collective title. *AACR1* rules 4 and 5 were completely rewritten; the resulting rule 4 as it appeared in *Cataloging Service Bulletin* 112 (Winter 1975) was virtually the same as *AACR2* rule 21.7. Notice that although papers and proceedings of named conferences are usually composite works produced under editorial direction, these are specifically exempted from the provisions of 21.7. See 21.1B2 for treatment of named conferences.

21.7B. Item with collective title

A collection of independent works by different persons or bodies having a collective title will be entered under its title; see figure 11-20. Added entries will be made for compilers if not more than three are named prominently; i.e., in the prescribed sources for transcription of the statement of responsibility.

Books, libraries, librarians : contributions to
  library literature / selected by John David
  Marshall, Wayne Shirley, Louis Shores. -- Hamden,
  Conn. : Shoe String Press, 1955.
  xv, 432 p. ; 23 cm.

Includes bibliographies.

Figure 11-20.
Collection entered
under title

  I. Marshall, John David.   II. Shirley, Wayne.
III. Shores, Louis.

Title page

Books Libraries Librarians
Contributions to Library Literature
Selected by
John David Marshall
Wayne Shirley
Louis Shores
Hamden, Connecticut
The Shoe String Press
1955

A work produced under editorial direction is one conceived and planned by one or more editors who select writers for the various sections of the work. If such a work has a collective title, it will be entered under its title (see figure 11-21). An encyclopaedia is one familiar type of editorially produced work.

If more than three editors or compilers are named prominently in a work with a collective title, only the first named (or the principal) editor/compiler's name is transcribed in the statement of responsibility; added entry will be given to that person only. (See figure 11-22.)

Encyclopaedia of librarianship / edited by Thomas
  Landau. -- 3rd rev. ed. -- London : Bowes &
  Bowes, 1966.
  x, 484 p. ; 26 cm.

Figure 11-21.
Editorially produced
work entered under
title

Encyclopaedia of Librarianship
Edited by
Thomas Landau A.L.A., A.I.Inf.Sc.
Third Revised Edition
Bowes & Bowes
London

I. Landau, Thomas.

Title page

Outside readings in American government / the
  editors, H. Malcolm Macdonald ... ɾet al.ɉ. --
  2nd ed. -- New York : Crowell, 1955, c1952.
  x, 884 p. ; 22 cm.

Includes index.

Figure 11-22. More
than three compilers
named prominently

I. Macdonald, H. Malcolm.

Title page

Outside Readings in American Government
Second Edition
Thomas Y. Crowell Company
New York   1955

The Editors
H. Malcolm Macdonald
Wilfred D. Webb   Facing title page
Edward G. Lewis
William L. Strauss

A "collection" may have as few as two works by different authors and still be a collection under the terms of 21.7. If a collection or editorially produced work has two or three items in it, make name-title added entries for each. See figure 2-4 for an example of such a collection.

Sometimes a collection includes more than three separate items but these items are by either two or three contributors. No more than three added entries should be made for items and/or contributors. If a contributor is responsible for only one of the items, make a name-title added entry for that item. For other contributors who are responsible for more than one item, make added entries under the headings for their names. On page 301 of *AACR2*, see the example *A Cornish quintette*.

Ordinarily, if there are more than three contributors, no added entry is given to any of the names. But if the names of the contributors are listed prominently, the first contributor's name will be transcribed as part of the statement of responsibility; this person will be given an added entry. See figure 11-23.

```
Space exploration / Robert M. L. Baker, Jr. ... [et
   al.] ; edited by Donald P. Le Galley, John W.
   McKee. -- New York : McGraw-Hill, 1964.
   xii, 467 p. : ill., maps ; 23 cm. -- (University
of California engineering and sciences extension
series)


   Includes bibliographies.



   I. Baker, Robert M.L.   II. Le Galley, Donald P.
III. McKee, John W.   IV. Series.
```

Figure 11-23. More than three contributors named in chief source

Space Exploration

Title page

Robert M. L. Baker, Jr.
Herbert C. Corben
Paul Dergarabedian
Manfred Eimer
Louis B. C. Fong
A. Donald Goedeke
McGraw-Hill Book Company
New York, San Francisco, Toronto, London

Edited by
Donald P. LeGalley
John W. McKee

University of California
Engineering and Sciences Extension Series

Facing title page

21.7C. Item without a collective title

For an example of main entry and added entry for an item without a collective title, see figure 1-55. A name-title added entry is to be made for the second work in the item; entry is under the author of the first item.

Works of Mixed Responsibility

21.8. SCOPE

Rules 21.1 through 21.7 cover works for which one or more persons or corporate bodies are responsible for the intellectual or artistic content of the item and have performed the same function, either as collaborators or as individuals working on separate parts of the item. Rules 21.8 through 21.27 deal with works in which different persons or corporate bodies have performed different kinds of functions on the same work: e.g. one person has written a work; another has revised, adapted, illustrated, or translated it, or has acted in some other capacity that might lead library users to think of the latter person as being primarily responsible for the work's existence. The Paris Principles do not address themselves specifically to the problem of determining which of these several individuals or corporate bodies is actually principally responsible for the intellectual or artistic content of the work. Rules 21.1 through 21.7 give guidance so that the principle of authorship responsibility may be maintained even when responsibility is mixed.

Rules are divided into two types of mixed responsibility: (1) Modifications of previously existing works and (2) new works to which different types of contributions have been made.

Modifications of Existing Works

21.9. GENERAL RULE

If a work has been rewritten or if the medium has been changed (i.e., a book made into a motion picture), in most cases the resulting product is regarded as a new work although the original author's ideas and even some of his or her words may have been kept. As such, it will be entered under the heading appropriate for the new work, with name-title added entry for the original work. Figure 2-16 is one example of a literary adaptation in which a story, retold by the adapter, is entered under the name of the adapter. The motion picture adaptation of *Alice in Wonderland* (figure 6-3) is a fairly obvious example of a motion picture made from a book, with the resultant motion picture definitely a new work.

However, a sound recording made from a book—as long as the original author's words are retained—will be entered under the heading appropriate to the original work. See figure 5-2. Likewise, "an updating, abridgement, revision, rearrangement, etc." will be entered in the same fashion as the original work as long as the words (etc.) of the original author (creator, etc.) have not been altered. For example, see figure 1-39.

Modifications of Texts

21.10. ADAPTATIONS OF TEXTS

This rule is the same as *AACR1* rule 7A. Covered by this rule are works that have been rewritten in a different literary style. Examples of an adaptation would be a paraphrase in which the original author's ideas were kept but put into different words, a simplified, rewritten version of a work for children, or a novel rewritten as a play. Such works are to be entered under the name of the adapter if it is known. If the name of the adapter is not known, enter under title. In all cases, make a name-title added entry for the original work. See figures 11-24 and 11-25.

Compare and contrast rule 21.10 with rule 21.12, revision of texts.

```
Godolphin, Mary.
  Pilgrim's progress / by John Bunyan ; retold and
shortened for modern readers by Mary Godolphin,
1884 ; drawings by Robert Lawson. -- Philadelphia :
Lippincott, c1939.
  vi, 119 p. : ill. ; 26 cm.
```

Figure 11-24.
Adaptation entered under name of adapter —version rewritten for children

```
  I. Bunyan, John.  Pilgrim's progress.  II. Lawson,
Robert.  III. Title.
```

Title information
on two facing pages

Pilgrim's Progress
by John Bunyan
Retold and Shortened for Modern Readers
by Mary Godolphin   1884
Drawings by Robert Lawson
Published by J. B. Lippincott Company
Philadelphia · New York

```
Howard, Sidney.
  Paths of glory : a play / adapted by Sidney
Howard from the novel by Humphrey Cobb ; with a
foreword for college theatres by Sidney Howard.
-- New York : S. French, 1936, c1935.
  xvii, 174 p. ; 19 cm.
```

Figure 11-25.
Adaptation entered under name of adapter —different literary medium

```
  I. Cobb, Humphrey.  Paths of glory.  II. Title.
```

Title page

Paths of Glory
A Play Adapted by
Sidney Howard
from the novel by
Humphrey Cobb
With a Foreword for College Theatres
By Sidney Howard
Samuel French
New York   Los Angeles
Samuel French Ltd. London
1936

21.11. ILLUSTRATED TEXTS

This rule is the same as *AACR1* rule 8B. An illustrated work is one in which the text was written first and illustrated later. The author of the text is primarily responsible for the work; entry will be under name of the author. See 21.30K2 for guidance in the matter of added entry under the name of the illustrator. In the example shown in figure 11-26, added entry will be made for illustrator because, as is the case with many books for children, illustrations occupy about half of the book and are an important feature of the work.

```
Schiller, Barbara.
  The white rat's tale / by Barbara Schiller ;
illustrated by Adrienne Adams. -- 1st ed. -- New
York : Holt, Rinehart and Winston, c1967.
  [32] p. : col. ill. ; 22 cm.




  I. Adams, Adrienne.  II. Title.
```

Figure 11-26.
Illustrated work entered
under author of text

Title page

The White Rat's Tale
by Barbara Schiller
Illustrated by Adrienne Adams
Holt, Rinehart and Winston
New York   Chicago   San Francisco

See also figure 2-10. And compare this rule with *AACR2* 21.24, works of collaboration between a writer and an artist (photographer, etc.).

21.11B. Illustrations published separately

This rule is the same as *AACR1* rule 8C. Obviously, the artist is chiefly responsible for the content of a work consisting solely of illustrations. Under the principle of author (creator, artist, etc.) responsibility as defined in 21.1A1, main entry will be under the name of the artist. (See figure 1-25.) Note the reappearance of the rule of three for added entries: If not more than three works or three authors are represented by the illustrations, appropriate added entries will be made. If more than three, no added entries will be made.

21.12. REVISION OF TEXTS

Rule 21.12A is a clarification and rewording of *AACR1* 14A. The intent of the rule is unchanged from that of the original. Rule 21.12 deals with works that have been revised, enlarged, abridged, condensed, etc., but for which the text remains substantially in the words of the original author. The cataloguer is not obliged to compare editions to determine whether or not that is the case. As long as the original author's name remains on the title page, that name will be used as the main entry.[8] In all cases, make an added entry for the reviser. (See figures 1-57 and 1-58 for examples.)

21.12B. This rule is a rewording of *AACR1* rule 14B. See figure 1-88 for an example.

21.13. TEXTS PUBLISHED WITH COMMENTARY

ALA 1949 rule 29A in all cases called for entry under the author of the original text for works containing text and commentary. The present rule is virtually the same as *AACR1* rule 11 as modified by LC *Cataloging Service Bulletin*, 111, February 1974. It applies only to publications consisting of a work or a group of works by a single author (personal or corporate) together with commentary on it by someone else. In order for 21.13 to be applied, both text and commentary must be present. No longer is there a separate rule for publications of laws with commentaries; they are subsumed with other materials under this rule.

21.13B. Commentary emphasized

If title page wording indicates that the publication is a commentary, enter it under appropriate heading for the commentary according to 21.1A or 21.1B.

---

[8] That choice was made clear by *Cataloging Service Bulletin* 96 (Nov. 1970): "The choice of entry depends entirely on whatever statement of authorship is prominently presented. For example, if the title page says the work has been 'adapted' or 'rewritten,' enter under the adapter without comparing texts in order to compare literary style or form . . . . Similarly . . . the rule does not operate on the principle of the degree of change in the text as determined from statements in the prefatory material and/or the judgment of the cataloger but rather on the wording of the title page [in regard to textual revisions]. Which person is represented as author of the particular edition, the original author or the person who prepared the edition? This is the only question the cataloger need ask himself."

In the example shown in figure 11-27, the commentary emanates from a corporate body. The publication is not one of the types listed under 21.1B2. Therefore, title main entry is appropriate, with an added entry for the corporate body as well as an added entry for the text of the law included as part of the publication. (Commentary accompanying law was formerly covered by a special rule for legal materials, *AACR1* 24B.) See also figure 1-78 for a further example of text with commentary emphasized.

```
Civil Rights Act of 1964 with explanation :
   Public law 88-352, as approved by the President
   on July 2, 1964. -- Chicago : Commerce Clearing
   House, c1964.
   108 p. ; 23 cm.



   I. Commerce Clearing House.   II. United States.
Civil Rights Act (1964).
```

Figure 11-27.
Commentary with text

Title page

**Civil Rights Act of 1964
With Explanation**
Public Law 88-352, as approved by the
President on July 2, 1964

21.13C. Edition of the work emphasized

This rule is the same as *AACR1* rule 11B, as modified by LC *Cataloging Service Bulletin* 111, Fall 1974. Catalogue such a work as an edition of the work with added entry for commentator. Figure 2-17 is an example. Note that for both 21.13B and 21.13C title page information and format will determine the main entry. If title page information is ambiguous, 21.13D gives some practical guidelines to aid in the decision. If these guidelines do not help, the work should be entered as an edition of the work, with added entry for commentator.

21.14. TRANSLATIONS

This rule is the same as *AACR1* rule 15. The work will be entered under the same heading as the original. Added entry will be made for the translator under much the same provisions as those governing such an added entry in *AACR1* rule 33E: If the translation is in verse, if the translation is important in its own right, if it has been translated into the same language more than once, or if a library user might have reason to think from the wording of the title page that the translator was the author of the work (see 21.30K1).

In the example shown in figure 11-28, both the original and the translation are in verse; the translation by a well-known American poet is important in its own right; and La Fontaine's fables have been translated into English more than once.

La Fontaine, Jean de.
  [Fables choisies. English]
  The fables of La Fontaine / translated by Marianne Moore. -- New York : Viking, 1954.
    x, 342 p. : port. ; 24 cm.

  Includes index.

  I. Moore, Marianne. II. Title.

Figure 11-28.
Translation

Title page

The Fables of La Fontaine
Translated by Marianne Moore
New York
The Viking Press • MCMLIV

In the example shown in figure 11-29, Goethe's *Faust* has been translated into English by more than one translator; thus an added entry will be given to the translator.

Goethe, Johann Wolfgang von.
  [Faust. English]
  Faust : a tragedy / by Johann Wolfgang von Goethe ; translated by Alice Raphael ; with an introduction for the modern reader by Mark Van Doren and woodcuts by Lynd Ward. -- New York : J. Cape, 1930.
    xxi, 262 p. : ill. ; 23 cm.

  I. Raphael, Alice. II. Title.

Figure 11-29.
Translation

```
                        Faust
                      A Tragedy
           By Johann Wolfgang von Goethe
 Title page       Translated by Alice Raphael
        With an Introduction for the Modern Reader
    By Mark Van Doren and Woodcuts by Lynd Ward
                      New York
            Jonathan Cape & Harrison Smith
```

A "free" translation or an adaptation, not a literal translation, should be treated according to the provisions of 21.10 and entered under the name of the translator-adaptor, the translator being regarded in this instance as the author of an adaptation. (See figure 11-30.)

```
Phillips, Stephen.
  Faust / freely adapted from Goethe's dramatic
poem by Stephen Phillips and J. Comyns Carr. --
New York : Macmillan, 1908.
  xix, 208 p. ; 19 cm.
```

Figure 11-30.
Translation-adaptation

```
  I. Carr, J. Comyns.   II. Goethe, Johann Wolfgang
von.  Faust.  III. Title.
```

```
                        Faust
         Freely Adapted from Goethe's Dramatic Poem
 Title page    By Stephen Phillips and J. Comyns Carr
                      New York
                The Macmillan Company
                        1908
                  All rights reserved
```

21.14B. A collection of translations of works by different authors will be entered as a collection under the provisions of 21.7, with added entry under the name of the translator. (See figure 11–31.)

```
An Anthology of Old English poetry / translated
   into alliterative verse by Charles W. Kennedy. --
   New York : Oxford University Press, 1960.
   xvi, 174 p. ; 21 cm.

   Includes index.
```

Figure 11-31.
Collection of
translations

```
   I. Kennedy, Charles W.
```

Title page

An Anthology of Old English Poetry
Translated into Alliterative Verse by
Charles W. Kennedy
New York
Oxford University Press
1960

21.15. TEXTS PUBLISHED WITH BIOGRAPHICAL/CRITICAL MATERIAL

This rule is the same as *AACR1* rule 9. It applies to publications consisting of a group of works, letters, etc., of an author together with biographical or critical material about this author by another person. Main entry for such works, in essence, depends upon the wording of the title page.

21.15A. If the title page refers to the critic-biographer as author, main entry is under his or her name, with added entry for the other person. The example shown in figure 11-32 consists of a thirty-six page section of biography-commentary by Dreiser, followed by selections from Thoreau's works.

```
Dreiser, Theodore.
   Theodore Dreiser presents the living thoughts of
Thoreau / cover photo, Bettman Archive. -- New
premier ed. -- Greenwich, Conn. : Fawcett World
Library, 1958, c1939.
   176 p. ; 18 cm. -- (The Living thoughts series)
(A Premier book ; d63)
```

Figure 11-32.
Biographer as author

```
   I. Thoreau, Henry David, 1817-1862.  II. Title.
III. Title: The living thoughts of Thoreau.
```

Title page

Theodore Dreiser
presents the
Living Thoughts of Thoreau
A Premier Book
The Living Thoughts Series
Cover Photo: Bettmann Archive
Fawcett Publications, Inc.
Fawcett Bldg., Fawcett Place, Greenwich, Conn.

Copyright MCMXXXIX, by David McKay Co., Inc.
The Living Thoughts of Thoreau was originally
published by David McKay Co., Inc., and this new
Premier edition is reissued through arrangement with
that company.
First Premier printing, February 1958
Premier Books are published by
Fawcett World Library

Verso of title page

21.15B. If the author of the biographical material is represented as an editor
or compiler, main entry is under the name of the author of the text. Give an
added entry to the editor, compiler, etc. The example shown in figure 11-33
consists of forty pages of biographical material about the diarist, followed by
the diary, annotated by Mark A. Strang. Guided by the wording of the title
page, main entry will be under the name of the diarist, James J. Strang.

```
Strang, James J.
   The diary of James J. Strang / deciphered, tran-
scribed, introduced, and annotated by Mark A.
Strang ; with a foreword by Russel B. Nye. --
[East Lansing] : Michigan State University Press,
c1961.
   xlv, 78 p. : port. ; 22 cm.




   I. Strang, Mark A.   II. Title.
```

Figure 11-33. Author
of text as author

The Diary of James J. Strang
Deciphered, Transcribed, Introduced
and Annotated
By Mark A. Strang
With a Foreword by
Russel B. Nye
Michigan State University Press

Title page

Modifications of Art Works

21.16. ADAPTATIONS OF ART WORKS

See in this text chapter 7, Graphic Materials, for discussion and examples of this rule, which applies to a single art work.

21.17. REPRODUCTIONS OF TWO OR MORE ART WORKS

This rule is closely related to 21.11B. It is a modification and clarification of *AACR1* rule 8D2, which called for entry of a work consisting of reproductions of the works of an artist under the artist "if the writer of the text is represented as editor or if the textual matter is clearly the minor element of the publication." According to the judgment of individual cataloguers, such art works were liable to be entered under either author of text or artist, depending on what the cataloguer considered to be "minor." Fortunately, this tricky distinction has been eliminated in the present rule. A work without text will be entered under name of artist.

21.17B. Art reproductions with text

If the person who wrote the text is represented as the author (not editor), entry will be under the name of the author of the text, no matter how brief its extent. Fourteen pages of text is a small portion of the total extent of the example shown in figure 11-34. Nonetheless, entry will be under the name of the author of the text. (See also 21.24.)

```
Gaunt, William.
   Turner / William Gaunt. -- London : Phaidon, 1971.
   14 p., 48 p. of plates : col. ill. ; 32 cm.




   I. Turner, Joseph Mallard William.
```

Figure 11-34. Art reproductions with text

Title page

William Gaunt
Turner
Phaidon

If, on the other hand, the person who wrote the text is *not* represented as the author, but is, instead, listed as being an editor, entry will be under the name of the artist. Give added entry to the writer of the text; see figure 11-35.

Walcott, Mary Vaux.
    Wild flowers of America : 400 flowers in full
color / based on paintings of Mary Vaux Walcott
as published by the Smithsonian Institution of
Washington ; with additional paintings by Dorothy
Falcon Platt ; edited with an introduction and
detailed descriptions by H.W. Rickett. -- New York :
Crown, c1953.
    71 p., 400 p. of plates : col. ill. ; 31 cm.
    Walcott's ill. reproduced from: North American
wild flowers / by Mary Vaux Walcott. Washington :
Smithsonian, 1925.
    Includes index.
    I. Platt, Dorothy Falcon.   II. Rickett, H. W.
III. Title.

Figure 11-35. Writer of
text as editor

400 flowers
in full color based on paintings by
Mary Vaux Walcott
as published by the
Smithsonian Institution of Washington
with additional paintings by
Dorothy Falcon Platt
edited with an introduction
and detailed descriptions by
H. W. Rickett

Wild Flowers of America
Crown Publishers, Inc.
New York

Title information
on two facing pages

21.18–21.22. MUSICAL WORKS

See chapter 4 in this text for discussion and examples of rules for choice of
access point for musical works.

21.23. SOUND RECORDINGS

In this text see chapter 5, Sound Recordings, for discussion and examples
of this rule.

Mixed Responsibility in New Works

Rules 21.1 through 21.8 give definitions, general principles, and rules for determining choice of main and added entry first for a work involving a single author and next for a work involving the collaboration of more than one author. Rules 21.9 through 21.23 deal with works that are modifications of other works —texts, art works, musical works, and sound recordings. Rules 21.24 through 21.28 address themselves to new works in which more than one person or corporate body has performed different functions, and in which no one is clearly principally responsible for the intellectual or artistic content of the work.

21.24. COLLABORATION BETWEEN ARTIST AND WRITER

This rule is almost identical to *AACR1* rule 8A. The rule was clarified by LC *Cataloging Service Bulletin* 96 (November 1970), which stated that "the word 'collaboration' as used in this rule means that the author and artist have worked *jointly* to produce the work . . . . If there is an indication, or a reasonable assumption, that the text has been illustrated after its completion, collaboration is not involved."

This rule should be compared with 21.11, illustrated texts, as well as 21.17, reproductions of two or more art works. The distinction between this rule and the previous rules mentioned is the matter of collaboration. Does the work in question seem to have been a joint effort, or was one part done independently of the other? The example shown in figure 11-36 is clearly a collaborative effort. Entry is under the name of the person listed first on the title page; an added entry is made for the other.

Molinard, Patrice.
    Paris / photographies originales de Patrice
Molinard ; texte d'Yvan Christ. -- Paris : Éditions
mondiales, [1953?]
    [59] p. : chiefly ill. (some col.) ; 31 cm. --
(Couleurs du monde ; [3])

French and English.

Figure 11-36.
Collaboration between
artist and author

I. Christ, Yvan. II. Title. III. Series.

Title page

Les Editions Mondiales
2, Rue des Italiens, 2 Paris
présentent
Paris
Photographies Originales
De Patrice Molinard
Texte d'Yvan Christ
"Couleurs Du Monde"
collection dirigée par J.-E. Imbert

21.25. REPORTS OF INTERVIEWS OR EXCHANGES

21.25A. This rule is the same as *AACR1* rule 13B. If the reporter simply records the words of the person(s) being interviewed without participating in the discussion, follow 21.6 (works of shared responsibility) to determine main entry. For an interview involving two participants, as shown in figure 11-37, entry will be under the first named. An added entry is to be made for the other participant, and also for an "openly named" (i.e., listed in the chief source) reporter.

```
Twain, Mark.
   Abroad with Mark Twain and Eugene Field : tales
they told to a fellow correspondent / by Henry W.
Fisher. -- New York : N.L. Brown, 1922.
   xxi, 246 p. ; 21 cm.
```

Figure 11-37. Interview

```
   I. Field, Eugene.   II. Fisher, Henry W.
III. Title.
```

Title page

Abroad with Mark Twain
and Eugene Field
Tales They Told to a Fellow Correspondent
by Henry W. Fisher
New York   Nicholas L. Brown   MCMXXII

21.25B. This rule is the same as *AACR1* rule 13A, with some rewording. The rule is related to 21.10, adaptations. If the reporter has restated the conversation rather than simply making a verbatim report or transcript, then he or she is considered to be responsible for the intellectual content of the interview. The *AACR1* rule was a change from ALA 1949 rule 4B1, which called for entry of a conversation under the participant whose name appeared first on the title page. (See figure 11–38.)

```
Henderson, Archibald.
  Table-talk of G.B.S. : conversations on things
in general between George Bernard Shaw and his
biographer / by Archibald Henderson. -- New York :
Harper, 1925.
  162 p. : ill. ; 20 cm.
```

Figure 11-38. Interview

```
  I. Shaw, George Bernard.   II. Title.
```

Title page

Table-Talk of G.B.S.
Conversations on Things in General between
George Bernard Shaw
and his biographer
By Archibald Henderson, Ph.D., D.C.L., LL.D.
New York and London
Harper & Brothers Publishers
1925

21.26. SPIRIT COMMUNICATIONS

The predecessor of this rule was *AACR1* rule 13C, which like its predecessor, ALA 1949 rule 11, called for main entry under the medium or "person reporting the communication" for communications "purporting to have been received from a spirit." Whether the editors of *AACR2* have joined the society of true believers is not known; it is more likely that they decided that this rule, like all others, should be based on information presented in the work, which is ordinarily to be accepted at its face value, and that the catalogue entry is simply to describe the work rather than to serve as a pejorative judgment of its truth or fiction. At any rate, under *AACR2* the earlier rule is reversed. Main entry will be under the name of the spirit, with added entry for the medium, as shown in figure 11–39.

```
Wilde, Oscar (Spirit)
   Oscar Wilde from purgatory : psychic messages /
edited by Hester Travers Smith ; with a preface by
Sir William F. Barrett. -- New York : Holt, 1926.
   xii, 179 p. : port. ; 22 cm.

   London ed. published as: Psychic messages from
Oscar Wilde.


   I. Smith, Hester Travers.   II. Title.
```

Figure 11-39. Spirit communication

Title page

Oscar Wilde
From Purgatory
Psychic Messages edited by
Hester Travers Smith
With a Preface by
Sir William F. Barrett, F.R.S.
New York
Henry Holt and Company

21.27. ACADEMIC DISPUTATIONS

This rarely used rule is mainly of historical interest, particularly in American libraries, since it applies to dissertations prepared in European universities before 1801. The rule is the same as *AACR1* rule 12, which was identical to ALA 1949 rule 17B. The respondent is the candidate for a degree who defends his thesis against objections proposed by the *praeses*, or faculty moderator.

Related Works

21.28. RELATED WORKS

This rule represents a simplification of *AACR1* rule 19, which as originally stated dealt with two types of related material—works with dependent titles (to be entered by "dashed-on" entry as part of the catalogue card for the main work) and "other related works" (to be entered independently). Under *AACR2* all such works, both "dependent" and "other," which were subsumed under the provisions of *AACR1* rule 19, will be entered independently as separate works, with added entry for the parent work. (See figure 11-40.)

The decision to describe a related work as an independent work is sometimes obvious. Although a concordance could not exist had not the "parent" work been written, the person who puts such a work together is clearly an author, under terms of the definition given in 21.1A1. Under both ALA 1949 and *AACR1* rules such works were entered as independent entries, with added entry for the related work.

```
Hudson, Gladys W.
   Paradise lost : a concordance / compiled by
Gladys W. Hudson. -- Detroit : Gale Research Co.,
c1970.
   viii, 361 p. ; 29 cm.




   I. Milton, John.  Paradise lost.  II. Title.
```

Figure 11-40. Related work—concordance

Paradise Lost | A Concordance
Compiled by Gladys W. Hudson, Baylor University
Gale Research Company
Book Tower, Detroit, Michigan 48226

Title page

A Bible concordance under *AACR1* rule 19B, footnote 19, was an exception to the general rule inasmuch as a subject entry "Bible—Concordances" substituted for the added entry for the related work. This exception has been eliminated under *AACR2*. Make added entry under the appropriate uniform heading for the Bible (see *AACR2* chapter 25); see figure 11-41.

```
Walker, J.B.R. (James Bradford Richmond)
   The comprehensive concordance to the Holy
Scriptures : a practical, convenient, accurate
text-finder ... based on the Authorized Version /
by J.B.R. Walker. -- New York : Macmillan, 1936,
c1929.
   vi, 957 p. ; 23 cm.




   I. Bible. English. Authorized.  II. Title.
```

Figure 11-41. Related work—concordance

The Comprehensive Concordance
to the
Holy Scriptures
By Rev. J. B. R. Walker
A practical, convenient, accurate text-finder.
Title page   Unessential words omitted; all serviceable
words retained. Only one alphabet for all
words, including proper names. Proper names
accented. Fifty thousand more references
than in Cruden.
Based on the Authorized Version
New York
The Macmillan Company
1936

Excerpts from periodicals are to be catalogued as independent works. In many cases these works will fall under the provisions of 21.7, collections, and will be given entry under title. Added entry will be made under a prominently named compiler or editor, under the provisions of 21.7B, as well as under the name of the periodical to which the work is related. (See figure 11-42.)

```
Youth's companion / edited by Lovell Thompson
   with three former Companion editors, M.A. De
   Wolfe Howe, Arthur Stanwood Pier, and Harford
   Powel. -- Boston : Houghton Mifflin, 1954.
   xii, 1140 p. : ill. ; 22 cm.




   I. Thompson, Lovell.   II. Youth's companion.
```

Figure 11-42. Related work—excerpts from periodical

Youth's Companion
Edited by Lovell Thompson
with three former *Companion* editors,
Title page   M. A. DeWolfe Howe,
Arthur Stanwood Pier, and
Harford Powel
with illustrations
Houghton Mifflin Company Boston
The Riverside Press Cambridge
1954

Under *AACR1* rule 19B a libretto was specifically exempted from entry as an independent work under the author of the libretto, even if music was not included in the work. Even in *AACR2* an alternative rule allows entry for a libretto under the heading appropriate to the musical work. Preferred treatment under 21.28, however, is entry under the individual responsible for the intellectual content of the work in hand, the librettist. An added entry is made for the musical work; see figure 11-43.

```
Hammerstein, Oscar.
   Show boat : complete libretto / music by Jerome
Kern ; book and lyrics by Oscar Hammerstein 2nd.
-- New York : T.B. Harms, c1927.
   99 p. ; 27 cm.

"Based on the novel by Edna Ferber."
```

Figure 11-43. Related work—libretto

```
   I. Kern, Jerome.  Show boat.  II. Ferber, Edna.
Show boat.  III. Title.
```

Title page

Show Boat
Music by Jerome Kern
Book and Lyrics by Oscar Hammerstein 2nd
Based on the novel by Edna Ferber
complete libretto
T. B. Harms Company
609 Fifth Avenue
New York 17, N.Y.

Not quite as obvious as the examples shown in figures 11-40–11-43 is entry for a supplement, a teacher's manual, etc., particularly when, except for the generic term "supplement," "teacher's guide," etc., the work has the same title, and often the same author, as the parent volume. If, in the cataloguer's judgment, such a work is of minor importance, it may be entered as accompanying material, the fourth element of the physical description area (1.5E), or as a note (1.7B11). (See figure 11-44a.)

```
The Norton anthology of short fiction /  [compiled
   by]  R.V. Cassill. -- 1st ed. -- New York :
   Norton, c1978.
   xxxiv, 1437 p. ; 21 cm. + instructor's handbook.

   Also available in shorter ed.
   Includes index.
```

Figure 11-44a.
Independent work with
accompanying material

```
   I. Cassill, R. V.
```

**The Norton Anthology of
Short Fiction
R. V. Cassill
W · W · Norton & Company · Inc ·
New York**

Title page

If the cataloguer feels that such a supplement, handbook, etc., warrants separate description, the fourth element will be omitted from the physical description area, and the work will be catalogued separately as a related work, with added entry for the parent work, as shown in figure 11-44b. For another example of separate description of a supplement, see figure 2-3b.

```
Cassill, R. V.
   The Norton anthology of short fiction.  Instruc-
tor's handbook for the complete and shorter edi-
tions / R.V. Cassill. -- 1st ed. -- New York :
Norton, c1977.
   xxiii, 215 p. ; 21 cm.

   ISBN 0-393-09050-7



   I. The Norton anthology of short fiction.
```

Figure 11-44b. Related
work—instructor's
handbook (alternate
practice)

Title page

**The Norton Anthology of Short Fiction
Instructor's Handbook
For the complete and shorter editions
R. V. Cassill
W · W · Norton & Company · Inc.
New York**

Added Entries

Rules 21.29 and 21.30 gather in one place all of the specific rules for added entry set forth in previous sections of chapter 21, sorting them into categories according to function. These rules also make useful generalizations about the purpose of added entries as added points of access to the works included in a library catalogue.

21.29. GENERAL RULE

An added entry should be made if the cataloguer believes that catalogue users might reasonably consider a person or corporate body not listed as main entry responsible for the work. *AACR2* goes farther than previous cataloguing codes in allowing added entries beyond those specifically prescribed in individual rules. For example, under 21.29D added entries may be made in addition to those suggested by 21.30, according to a library's policy.

21.30D. Editors and compilers

This rule, which calls for an added entry for a "prominently named" editor or compiler of a monographic work, is far more liberal than *AACR1* 33D, the corresponding rule in the earlier code. Except for added entries for editors or compilers of collections or editorially produced works, added entry for editor under *AACR1* was to be made only under rather strictly circumscribed conditions. The example shown in figure 11-45 is a catalogue entry that, according to *AACR1* rule 33D, would not have included an added entry for the editor. Since the editor is "prominently named" (i.e., formally listed in the prescribed source), 21.30D calls for an added entry.

```
Holmes, Oliver Wendell.
   Holmes-Pollock letters : the correspondence of
Mr. Justice Holmes and Sir Frederick Pollock,
1874-1932 / edited by Mark De Wolfe Howe ; with
an introduction by John Gorham Palfrey. -- Cam-
bridge, Mass. : Harvard University Press, 1942
-1946.
   2 v. : ill., ports. ; 25 cm.




   I. Pollock, Frederick, Sir.   II. Howe, Mark
De Wolfe.   III. Title.
```

Figure 11-45. Added entry for editor

> Holmes-Pollock Letters
> The Correspondence of Mr. Justice Holmes
> and Sir Frederick Pollock 1874–1932
> edited by
> Mark DeWolfe Howe
> with an introduction by
> John Gorham Palfrey
> Cambridge • Massachusetts
> Harvard University Press   1942

Title page

21.30E. Corporate body

With the tightening of rules for entry under corporate body, an added entry will sometimes be given for the corporate body that would have received main entry under *AACR1*. See, for example, figures 11-7, 11-8, and 11-9. In addition, an added entry will be made for a prominently named corporate body that sponsors a meeting. See figure 11-5.

21.30F. Other related persons or bodies

This rule is almost identical to *AACR1* rule 33H. It specifies, but is not limited to, three examples for which an added entry would be appropriate. One of these is for the person honored by a Festschrift.

A Festschrift is a publication consisting of a number of essays or short articles, generally on the honoree's subject interest, brought together to honor a person or to celebrate an anniversary. Since the selections are written specifically for the publication, under the direction of editors, a Festschrift is an example of a work covered by 21.7. It will be given title main entry; see figure 11-46.

**Figure 11-46.
Festschrift**

> Voices from the Southwest : a gathering in honor
>   of Lawrence Clark Powell / gathered by Donald C.
> Dickinson, W. David Laird, Margaret F. Maxwell.
> -- 1st ed. -- Flagstaff, [Ariz.] : Northland
> Press, 1976.
>   xv, 159 p. : ill., port. ; 25 cm.
>
>   Contents: Seventy suns : to L.C.P. / by William
> Everson -- History of the Spanish Southwest /
> Eleanor B. Adams -- Authors and books in colonial
> New Mexico / Marc Simmons -- Voices from the
> Southwest / Sarah Bouquet -- The faces and forces
> of Pimeria Alta / Bernard Fontana -- The fifth
> world : the ninth planet / Frank Waters -- An
>
>   (continued on next card)

Voices from the Southwest. 1976. (card 2)

amateur librarian / Paul Horgan -- Give this place
a little class / Ward Ritchie -- Richard J. Hinton
and the American Southwest / Harwood Hinton -- J.
Ross Browne and Arizona / Richard Dillon -- Re-
flections on the Powell-Harrison correspondence /
Jake Zeitlin -- The making of a novel / L.D. Clark
-- A chronology of LCP keepsakes / Al Lowman· -- A
checklist of recently published works of LCP /
Robert Mitchell.
   ISBN 0-87358-157-1

   I. Powell, Lawrence Clark.   II. Dickinson, Donald
C.   III. Laird, W. David.   IV. Maxwell, Margaret F.

Title page

Voices from the Southwest
A Gathering in Honor of Lawrence Clark Powell
Gathered by Donald C. Dickinson,
W. David Laird, Margaret F. Maxwell
Northland Press • Flagstaff
MCMLXVI

The addressee of a collection of letters would, under normal provisions of the
rules, not be given an added entry; that person in no way contributed to the
intellectual or artist content of the work being catalogued. Ordinarily, a subject
entry for the addressee would be inappropriate. But, obviously, the name of the
addressee can serve as an important access point to the catalogue entry for the
work. An added entry for such an individual is stipulated by 21.30F, see figure
11-47.

Wise, Thomas J.
   Letters of Thomas J. Wise to John Henry Wrenn :
a further inquiry into the guilt of certain nineteenth-century forgers / edited by Fannie E. Ratchford. -- 1st ed. -- New York : Knopf, 1944.
   xiv, 591, xvi p., [19] leaves of plates : ill.,
ports. ; 25 cm.

   "List of nineteenth-century forgeries in the
Wrenn library, with the dates they were acquired and
the prices Wrenn paid Wise:" p. 578-583.
   Includes index.

   I. Wrenn, John Henry.   II. Ratchford, Fannie E.
III. Title.

Figure 11-47.
Addressee of a
collection of letters

	Letters of Thomas J. Wise to John Henry Wrenn
Title page	A Further Inquiry into the Guilt of Certain
	Nineteenth-Century Forgers
	Edited by
	Fannie E. Ratchford
	Alfred A. Knopf New York 1944

Special Rules

Certain Legal Publications

Rules 21.31 through 21.36 include laws, administrative regulations, constitutions and charters, court rules, and treaties. This section is considerably changed from *AACR1*, parallel rules in which were 20–26. *AACR1* rules 20–26 were criticized from the moment they appeared because, unlike most other sections of *AACR1*, they were based on form rather than authorship. Materials included were to be entered under governmental jurisdiction, followed by a form subheading appropriate to the type of publication. A federal law of the United States would, under *AACR1* rule 20A, have taken the heading "United States. *Laws, statutes, etc.*" Critics of the rules, led by Seymour Lubetzky, argued that these form subheadings were nothing but a kind of subject heading that served to gather material under the name of the governmental jurisdiction. The critics also said that the function could just as well be taken care of by true subject headings. Calling them "bastardized author entries,"[9] Lubetzky called for the elimination of these quasi-author, quasi-subject headings from rules that otherwise dealt with conditions of author responsibility.

But the form subheadings, though they may have lacked consistency with principle, had custom on their side, going back at least as far as the 1908 Anglo-American code.[10] Those in favor of them argued that legal publications offered problems of authorship so complex that it was difficult to arrive at a valid statement of authorship. A law is an act of a particular political jurisdiction, which comes into being by the agency of many different people acting as individuals, committees, etc. A law may be passed by Congress, but it is not valid until it is signed by the President. Who, then, is responsible for bringing it into being? In legal terms Congress and the President merely act as agents, not as authors. The United States is responsible for the law, and therefore the United States is author of the law.

[9] Seymour Lubetzky, *Code of Cataloging Rules: Author and Title Entry, an Unfinished Draft* . . . (Chicago: ALA, 1960), p. 56.

[10] American Library Association, *Catalog Rules: Author and Title Entries*, compiled by committees of the American Library Association and the (British) Library Association. American ed. (Chicago: ALA, 1908), rule 62, p. 18.

Thus reasoned Seymour Lubetzky, as long ago as 1960, in his *Code of Cataloging Rules*. And yet in 1967, when the *AACR1* appeared, the traditional form headings were still a part of the code. Paul Dunkin, though speaking in a slightly different frame of reference, summed the problem up when he said, "The plain fact is that we have here an entry which we accept because it seems to be the practical thing to do . . . . Apparently we have grown so accustomed to the idea that we cannot change."[11]

In a victory for Seymour Lubetzky, and in a return to the stipulations of Paris Principle 9.5,[12] form subdivisions have been eliminated from *AACR2*. Laws, constitutions, court rules, and treaties formerly entered under the name of the governmental jurisdiction, followed by a form subheading, are now entered under the name of the appropriate state or other territorial authority, with a uniform title interposed between the heading and the transcription of the title to aid in organizing the material.

21.31B1. Laws of modern jurisdictions governing one jurisdiction. Such laws will be entered under the heading for the jurisdiction governed. No subheading will be added. A uniform title will be interposed between the heading and the title transcription.

Uniform titles will be discussed more fully in chapter 15 of this text. Briefly, a uniform title serves to bring all the varying issues, editions, translations, etc., of a work together in one place in the catalogue. Uniform titles for laws are to be constructed following 25.15, a rule closely related to *AACR1* 101D.

The descriptive information for a legal publication is transcribed below the uniform title following appropriate rules in *AACR2* Part I, chapter 1, etc. Added entries are to be made for persons or bodies responsible for compiling or issuing the law, but not for the legislative body that actually passed it. That is, as shown in figure 11-48, no added entry will be made for "United States. *Congress*." Nor will an added entry be made for "California. Legislature," the body responsible for the code illustrated in figure 11–49.

```
United States.
   [Employee Retirement Income Security Act of 1974]
   Pension reform act : (Employee Retirement Income
Security Act of 1974) : with official legislative
history : approved September 2, 1974. -- St. Paul,
Minn. : West, 1974.
   xi, 833 p. ; 24 cm. -- (United States Code
congressional and administrative news, 93rd
Congress, second session ; no. 8A)

   Includes index.

   I. West Publishing Co.   II. Title.   III. Series.
```

Figure 11-48. Federal law

[11] Lubetzky, *op. cit.*, p. 15.

[12] "Constitutions, laws and treaties . . . should be entered under the name of the appropriate state or other territorial authority, with formal or conventional titles indicating the nature of the material."

No. 8A   September 20, 1974
United States Code
Congressional and Administrative News
93rd Congress—Second Session
Title page   Pension Reform Act
[Employee Retirement Income Security Act of 1974]
with Official Legislative History
Approved September 2, 1974
West Publishing Co.
50 West Kellogg Blvd.
St. Paul, Minn.   55102
Copyright © 1974 West Publishing Co.

California.
 ⌊ Penal code ⌋
 The penal code of the State of California : with
amendments up to the end of the 1963 regular session
of the legislature. -- Complete peace officers ed.,
with appendix of other penal laws, including rules
of evidence, narcotic laws, juvenile court law,
selected section from the alcoholic beverage control
law, and titles 8, 18, 26 of the United States code.
-- Los Angeles : Legal Book Store, c1963.
   vii, 828 p. ; 23 cm.   Figure 11-49. State laws

 I. Legal Book Store.   II. Title.

The Penal Code of the State of California
With amendments up to the end of the
1963 regular session of the legislature
The Complete Peace Officers Edition
With Appendix of other
Penal Laws
Title page   including
Rules of Evidence
Narcotic Laws
Juvenile Court Law
Selected Section from the Alcoholic
Beverage Control Law, and Titles 8, 18, 26
of the United States Code
Legal Book Store
Law Book Seller and Publisher
122 South Broadway
Los Angeles 12, California

The example shown in figure 11-50 is a work that includes both the code (laws) of a city and the charter. Heading and uniform title will be made for the material listed first on the title page. Name-title added entry is made for the charter.

Tucson (Ariz.)
  ₍Laws, etc.₎
  The code of the city of Tucson, Arizona, 1953 ;
The charter and the general ordinances of the city,
enacted as a whole, January 13, 1953, effective,
February 15, 1953. -- Charlottesville, Va. :
Michie City Publications Co., 1953.
  567 p. ; 24 cm.

Figure 11-50.
Collection

  I. Tucson (Ariz.). Charter. II. Title.

Title page

The Code of the City of Tucson, Arizona 1953
The Charter and the
General Ordinances of the City
Enacted as a Whole, January 13, 1953
Effective, February 15, 1953
Michie City Publications Company
Charlottesville, Virginia
1953

21.33. CONSTITUTIONS, CHARTERS, AND OTHER FUNDAMENTAL LAWS

A constitution or charter will be entered under the heading for the jurisdiction with no further subdivision. Contrast this rule with *AACR1* rule 22A, which stipulated entry under jurisdiction plus the form subheading "Constitution" or "Charter," as appropriate. When a constitution or charter is a law of a jurisdiction other than the one the constitution or charter governs, make an added entry for the one that promulgated the law and in this added entry use a uniform title if appropriate according to 25.15A. The general rule for uniform titles (25.1) may also need to be applied to the question of a uniform title in the main entry.

If there is more than one constitution for the same jurisdiction, add in parentheses the year of adoption to the uniform title for each. Figure 11-51 shows an amended constitution for the State of Louisiana.

```
Louisiana.
  [Constitution (1954)]
  Constitution of the State of Louisiana : as
amended through the election of November 2, 1954 :
adopted in convention at the city of Baton Rouge.
-- Baton Rouge : [s.n.], 1955.
  xiv, 691 p. ; 24 cm.
```

Figure 11-51. Amended constitution

> Constitution of the State of Louisiana
> As amended through the election of
> November 2, 1954
> Adopted in Convention
> at the City of Baton Rouge
> Wade O. Martin, Jr.
> Secretary of State

```
  I. Title.
```

Title page

21.34. COURT RULES

This rule is a return to ALA 1949 rule 89I, which called for entry of court rules under the name of the court. *AACR1* rule 23 stipulated entry under the name of the jurisdiction followed by the form subheading "Court rules." This, in turn, was to be followed by the name of the court governed by the rules. For example in figure 11-52 the heading would have been: Arizona. *Court rules.*

```
Arizona.  Supreme Court.
  Rules of the Supreme Court of the State of
Arizona. -- Phoenix : Arizona State Press, 1912.
  15 p. ; 26 cm.
```

Figure 11-52. Court rules

> Rules of the
> Supreme Court
> of the State of Arizona
> 1912
> Alfred Franklin - - - - - Chief Justice
> D. L. Cunningham - - - - - - Judge
> H. D. Ross - - - - - - - - - Judge
> J. P. Dillon
> clerk
> The Arizona State Press

```
  I. Title.
```

Title page

Supreme Court. The 1967 rule was instituted under recommendation of the American Association of Law Libraries. It was sharply criticized as being no more than a subject heading in a distorted form.[13] According to *AACR2* 21.1B2, court rules should be entered under the heading for the court governed by them. Rule 21.34 reinforces that practice.

21.35. TREATIES, INTERGOVERNMENTAL AGREEMENTS, ETC.

21.35A1. Treaties are agreements between two or more governments. They pose special problems for cataloguers because of their nature and because of the way in which they are drawn up. After representatives of the various governments at a treaty conference have met, they draw up an agreement, which is signed. Then the representatives return to their own countries, where the treaty is ratified by the government. Then the treaty is published by the government under a title that it creates, naming itself, of course, in first place on the title page. Each governing body involved does this, resulting in a number of different versions of the document. Although the text of the document should be the same, the title pages will vary. Under which name should a treaty be entered? ALA 1949 rule 88A called for entry under the party named first on the title page, with form subheading "Treaties, etc." *AACR1* rule 25A1 preferred entry under the country of the cataloguing agency if it was a signatory; otherwise entry would be under the party on one side of a bilateral treaty if it is the only party on that side and there are two or more parties on the other side; or, under the party whose catalogue heading is first in alphabetical order.

AACR2 rule 21.35A1 has dropped the first provision of *AACR1* rule 25A1, and mandates entry for a treaty between two or three national governments according to the second and third preference of the 1967 code. Thus, the example shown in figure 11-53, which under 1967 rules was entered under "United States" (as the country of the cataloguing agency), will now be entered under the country coming first in alphabetical order: Mexico. In addition, the *AACR1* form subheading "Treaties, etc." is dropped to uniform title position below the heading for the jurisdiction. See 25.16B1 for rules for form. Uniform title must be used. Added entry is made for the other government(s) involved; the form is name-uniform title entry. Entry for the example shown in figure 11-54 is under the name of the country that comes first in alphabetical order, regardless of title page order.

21.35A2. Treaties involving four or more parties. In essence, this rule is the same as *AACR1* rule 25A2, Peace treaties and multilateral (other than trilateral) treaties. It is based on the general rule governing diffuse authorship (21.6C2), which states that main entry will be under title if responsibility is shared between more than three corporate bodies (in this case, governments).

If the treaty has been issued under varying titles, do not use the title proper of the work for title main entry. Make main entry under a uniform title. See 25.16B2 for guidance on the proper construction of a uniform title for a treaty.

---

[13] Sumner Spalding, "Main Entry: Principles and Counter Principles," *LRTS* 11 (Fall 1967): 394.

Mexico.
  ₍Treaties, etc. United States, 1933 Feb. 1₎
  Convención entre los Estados Unidos Mexicanos y
los Estados Unidos de América para la rectificación del Rio Bravo del Norte (Grande) en el valle
de Juarez-El Paso ... -- México : Impr. de la
Secretaría de Relaciones Exteriores, 1934.
  63 p., ₍2₎ folded leaves of plates : ill., maps ;
24 cm.

  Spanish and English in parallel columns.

  I. United States. Treaties, etc. Mexico,
1933 Feb. 1.

Figure 11-53. Bilateral treaty

Title page

Convención entre los Estados Unidos Mexicanos y los
Estados Unidos de America para la rectificación del
Río Bravo del Norte (Grande)
en el valle de Juarez–El Paso
[8 lines of text describing the ratification]
México
Imprenta de la Secretaría de Relaciones Exteriores, 1934

Spain.
  ₍Treaties, etc. United States, 1898 Dec. 10₎
  A treaty of peace between the United States and
Spain : message from the President of the United
States, transmitting a treaty of peace between the
United States and Spain : signed at the city of
Paris on December 10, 1898 ... -- Washington :
G.P.O., 1899.
  3 v. in 2 ; 24 cm. -- (Doc. / 55th Congress,
3d session, Senate ; no. 62)

  I. United States. Treaties, etc. Spain, 1898
Dec. 10. II. United States. President (1897–1901 :
McKinley). III. Title.

Figure 11-54. Bilateral treaty

Title page

55th Congress, 3d Session. Senate. Doc. No. 62, Part 1.
A Treaty of Peace between the United States and Spain.
Message from the President of the United States,
Transmitting a Treaty of Peace between the
United States and Spain, signed at the city of Paris,
on December 10, 1898.
[6 lines of text describe the ratification]
Washington: Government Printing Office. 1899.

Note an important change from *AACRI* rules for treaties. The distinction between entry under one or the other of the governments involved in a treaty versus entry under title proper or a uniform title is based solely on the number of parties concerned. If two or three governments are involved, follow 21.35A1 and enter under one of the governments, according to instructions. If four or more governments are involved, follow 21.35A2 and enter under either title proper or uniform title. The subject of the conference, in contrast to treatment under *AACRI* rule 25A2, has nothing to do with choice of entry. Note that under *AACRI* rule 25A2 the example shown in figure 11-54 would have been entered under uniform title, "Treaty of Paris, 1893," simply because it is a peace treaty. This will no longer be done.

Certain Religious Publications

21.37. SACRED SCRIPTURES

This rule is basically the same as *AACRI* rule 27, except that an added entry is substituted for the "see also" reference required by rule 27 for persons or bodies associated with such a work. Although 21.37 now simply states that sacred scripture will be entered under title, problems of varying titles for different issues, editions, etc., will mean in almost every case that entry under *uniform title* rather than title proper will be made. See rules 25.17–25.18 for guidance in the formulation of a proper uniform title and for further examples of this rule. The example shown in figure 11-55 is of sacred scripture entered under uniform title.

```
Doctrine and covenants.
   Book of doctrine and covenants / carefully
selected from the revelations of God and given in
the order of their dates by the Reorganized Church
of Jesus Christ of Latter Day Saints. -- Indepen-
dence, Mo. : Printed by the Board of Publications
of the Church, 1949.
   99 p. ; 19 cm.

   Revelations given to Joseph Smith.


   I. Reorganized Church of Jesus Christ of Latter
Day Saints.  II. Smith, Joseph.  III. Title.
```

Figure 11-55. Sacred scripture

Title page

> Book of
> Doctrine and Covenants
> Carefully selected from the revelations
> of God, and given in the order
> of their dates
> by
> The Reorganized Church of Jesus Christ
> of Latter Day Saints
> Independence, Missouri
> Printed by the Board of Publication of the
> Reorganized Church of Jesus Christ
> of Latter Day Saints
> 1949

21.39. LITURGICAL WORKS

Under *AACR1* rule 29 and ALA 1949 rule 116F, liturgical works were to be entered under the name of the denomination followed by the form subheading "Liturgy and ritual." As previously noted in connection with rules for laws, treaties, etc. (21.31–21.35) *AACR2* has eliminated all use of form subheadings. Thus, a liturgical work will be entered under the heading for the denomination, without further subdivision. A uniform title will be used to organize the file. See rules 25.20–25.23 for guidance. See figure 2-12 for an example of catalogue entry for a liturgical work.

12

Headings for Persons

(*AACR2* Chapter 22)

AACR2, like *AACR1*, is structured so that choice of entry and the form of the heading thus chosen are treated as separate problems. After the cataloguer has determined the correct main entry according to *AACR2* chapter 21, he or she still must determine the correct form if main entry is a personal or corporate name. This consideration is important because once the decision has been made, the same form of name will be used, in most cases, for every work by or about that author. This library practice is of long standing; a consistent heading brings together in one place in the library catalogue all of the works by the author that the library holds, and, in a library which has a dictionary catalogue, all the books about the author.

In many cases, deciding on form for a personal author heading presents no problem. According to library custom, the entry element for most personal authors is the surname. It is a simple matter to take the name as it appears on the title page of the first book by a new author and to transcribe it as the main entry heading; surname first, followed by forenames and/or initials. But things are not always that easy. Personal names as they appear in library items present numerous problems. Most of these may be subsumed into three categories:

1. An author may not use the same name in all of his or her works. What name should be chosen when the author sometimes uses real name and sometimes pseudonym? And what about an author who seems unable to make up her or his mind about the fullness of name which she or he prefers? What is the cataloguer to do when a woman who has written under her maiden name begins to use her married name in her works?
2. Some authors have compound surnames; others have a surname with a prefix; still others have no surname. Which part of the name will be used as the entry element?
3. How is one author to be distinguished from another of identical or similar name?

The rules included in *AACR2* chapter 22 give guidance on these and other problems.

Choice of Name

22.1. GENERAL RULE

Although cataloguers who are familiar with *AACR1* chapter 2 will find many of the rules for form of entry for personal names unchanged from the earlier code, they should be warned that *AACR2* chapter 22 is organized rather differently from its predecessor. Cataloguers should be aware that *AACR2* distinguishes between choice and form of name even in the examples. General rule 22.1, which superficially appears to resemble *AACR1* rule 40 rather closely, addresses itself only to choice, not form of name. Examples illustrating rules 22.1–22.3 are not in catalogue entry format; they only indicate which of several names that a person may use should be chosen for the basis of the heading. For example, "Jimmy Carter" as listed under 22.1A would be entered in the catalogue as "Carter, Jimmy." The example shows how the name would appear in a work by or about President Carter. Not until rule 22.4 do the rules address themselves to the form that personal names should take in the catalogue. Rule 22.1A considers the name only as the raw material from which the heading will be constituted.

As in the preceding code, the rules of chapter 22 are based on Paris Principle 7, which calls for entry under "the most frequently used name . . . appearing in editions of the work catalogued. . . ." The rule differs from ALA 1949 rule 36, which called for the use of the author's full legal name in many instances. Now, the cataloguer will use the author's name as it appears on title pages of works issued in the language in which they were written during the author's lifetime—as long as the form of name is consistent.

If the person is commonly known by a nickname, this form will be chosen; see figure 12-1.

```
Hope, Bob.
   Five women I love : Bob Hope's Vietnam story /
by Bob Hope. -- 1st ed. -- Garden City, N.Y. :
Doubleday, 1966.
   255 p. : ill. ; 22 cm.



   I. Title.
```

Figure 12-1. Nickname

Five Women I Love
Bob Hope's Vietnam Story
by Bob Hope
Doubleday & Company, Inc.
Garden City, New York
1966

Title page

If the person is commonly known by initials, this form will be used (see 22.10); see figure 12-2. This instruction is a change from *AACR1* rule 40, which specifically exempted initials from the general principle of entry under the form of name by which the author is commonly known.

```
H. D.
   Helen in Egypt / by H.D. ; introduction by
Horace Gregory. -- New York : Grove Press, c1961.
   xi, 315 p. ; 21 cm.




   I. Title.
```

Title page

Figure 12-2. Initials

Helen in Egypt
by H. D.
Introduction by Horace Gregory
Grove Press, Inc.   New York

22.1B. The "commonly known" form of an author's name is determined very pragmatically. In almost all cases the name to be chosen will be that form appearing in the chief source (for a book, the title page) for the first item by that author catalogued by the library. No research need be done. If later works by the same author vary in form or fullness from the heading established by the cataloguer, it may be necessary to change the heading. This will not happen very often, however. Virtually the only time it is necessary to go beyond the title page or other chief source of information is in establishing the "commonly known" name of a person who is not an author. In this case, the form listed in reference sources in the language and country of the person being established will be used.

The rule explicitly includes "books and articles about a person" as part of the definition of "reference sources" to be used in determining the commonly known name. The title page of the book used in the example shown in figure 12-3 was the primary source for the name of the colorful Johnny Appleseed. His name may also be found in such sources as Hart's *Oxford Companion to American Literature* (1965). Note that Johnny Appleseed is the *subject* of the book. A title added entry will be made only if the library has a divided catalogue, one in which name-title and subject entries are not interfiled (see 21.30J3).

```
Price, Robert.
   Johnny Appleseed : man and myth / by Robert
Price. -- Gloucester, Mass. : P. Smith, 1967, c1954.
   xv, 320 p. : ill. ; 21 cm.

   Bibliography: p. 299-303.
   Includes index.




     I. Appleseed, Johnny.
```

Figure 12-3. Commonly known name—of a person who is not the author

Johnny Appleseed
Man and Myth
by Robert Price
Gloucester, Mass.
Peter Smith
1967

Title page

22.1C. If the name by which an author is commonly known includes a title of nobility (prince, etc.) or honour (sir, etc.) include it as part of the heading. See, for example, figures 1-34 and 1-35; note that the authors use their titles as part of their names in the chief source of information.

22.1D1. It would seem almost obvious that if an author's name includes accents and other diacritical marks, that they will be retained. (See figure 1-25.) A problem arises only in the few instances when a title page transcription of an author's name—all in capital letters, for example—omits accents. If the cataloguer knows that the author's name ordinarily includes accents, they should be supplied. No research needs to be done to determine this.

22.1D2. Hyphens. Again, it would seem obvious that if an author chooses to spell his or her name with a hyphen joining either given names or parts of a compound surname, this choice ought to be respected by the cataloguer. And so it is, under *AACR2* (see figure 12-4). Previous to this, *AACR1* rule 45C

```
Sartre, Jean-Paul.
   L'imaginaire : psychologie phénoménologique de
l'imagination / Jean-Paul Sartre. -- Paris :
Gallimard, c1940.
   246 p. : ill. ; 23 cm. -- (Bibliothèque des
idées)




     I. Title.  II. Series.
```

Figure 12-4. Hyphen with given name

Title page

Jean-Paul Sartre
L'imaginaire
Psychologie phénoménologique de l'imagination
Gallimard

excepted French names from the general rule that called for the retention of hyphens between given names. In all cases under 22.1D2, the preference of the author will now be followed. This instruction is a change from ALA 1949 rule 40D(2), which called for the omission of hyphens between given names in all languages except Chinese.

22.2. CHOICE AMONG DIFFERENT NAMES

This rule is nearly the same as *AACR1* rule 41. It deals with problems resulting when authors are not consistent about the way their names appear in the chief source of information in their works or when persons are known by more than one name. If there is doubt about the name by which the person is "clearly" most commonly known, the cataloguer makes a choice based on the following guidelines given in order of preference:

1. Choose the name most frequently used by the author in his or her works. In a large library that included a complete collection of the author's works, a survey could be made. However, a mechanical count of the number of times each variant form appears, with the idea of determining by percentages the author's preference, certainly seems to be contrary to the spirit of the rules as well as to common sense.
2. Choose the form of name by which the author is generally identified in reference sources. This check could produce different answers, of course, depending on the reference sources available in a particular library.
3. Choose the latest name the author has used in his or her works.

The guidelines are the same as those given under *AACR1* rule 41, except that the order of the first two has been reversed, indicating the consistent preference of *AACR2* for taking the information given on the chief source at its face value without further research.

22.2B. Change of name

Members of nobility sometimes change their names as they acquire new titles. If one begins to use his or her new title on title pages, headings for earlier works should be changed to reflect the changed usage. The entries should be changed for married women who have written before their marriage and who use their changed name in their later works. The rule is based on general rule 22.1, inasmuch as the later form will usually become more "commonly known."

Clare Boothe Luce, American author and former American ambassador to Italy, wrote a number of works under her maiden name, Clare Boothe. She wrote at least one under an earlier married name, Clare Boothe Brokaw. Since her marriage to Henry Luce, she has used her married name, Clare Boothe Luce. She is clearly "commonly known" by her latest married name, both in reference sources such as *Current Biography* (1953) and in later books and articles by and about her. The heading for all of her works should be the latest form of her name; see figures 12-5 and 12-6.

Luce, Clare Boothe.
   Europe in the spring / Clare Boothe. -- New
York : Knopf, 1940.
    xi, 324 p. ; 21 cm.

Figure 12-5. Changed
name

Europe in the Spring
Clare Boothe
Alfred · A · Knopf
New York 1940

I. Title.

Title page

Luce, Clare Boothe.
   Stuffed shirts / by Clare Boothe Brokaw ; illustrations by Shermund. -- New York : Liveright,
1931.
    326 p. : ill. ; 21 cm.

Figure 12-6. Changed
name

Stuffed Shirts
By Clare Boothe Brokaw
Illustrations by Shermund
Horace Liveright · Inc., New York

I. Title.

Title page

At this point, the reader may wonder what is to become of the library user
who, not knowing the cataloguer's decision to accept the latest form of Luce's
name as the uniform heading for all of her works, may look in the library
catalogue under Boothe or Brokaw. To meet this need, references are made
from forms of the name not used in the catalogue to the form which has been
adopted. Two references will be made for Luce:

      Boothe, Clare
        see
     Luce, Clare Boothe.

      Brokaw, Clare Boothe
        see
     Luce, Clare Boothe.

This sort of reference is variously known as a cross reference or a see reference. It is traced on the authority record for the heading thus:

> Luce, Clare Boothe.
>   x Boothe, Clare
>   x Brokaw, Clare Boothe

AACR2 chapter 26 (References) addresses itself to general principles and guidelines for making references. Rule 26.0 stipulates that a see reference guides the user of the catalogue "from a form of the name . . . that might *reasonably* [italics added] be sought to the form that has been chosen . . . ." In all instances in which the rules do not prescribe a reference, the matter of making one is left up to the cataloguer's judgement. Clearly, a reference should be made from "Boothe" and "Brokaw" to "Luce," since the author has used these names in her works. But how many library users looking for something by Bob Hope would think of looking under his real name so that they would need a reference such as the following:

> Hope, Leslie Townes
>   *see*
> Hope, Bob.

It is doubtful that such a reference would be helpful. As for Johnny Appleseed (figure 12-3), if the cataloguer feels that library users know that his real name is John Chapman and that they might look under that name in the catalogue, a reference may be made:

> Chapman, John
>   *see*
> Appleseed, Johnny.

Reference from the author's real name to initials used in a publication will be made on the same basis. Might the work represented by figure 12-2 reasonably be sought under H.D.'s real name, Hilda Doolittle? If so, the reference should be made. See 22.16 for more information about initials and references to them.

22.2C. Pseudonyms

22.2C1. One pseudonym. The rule for an author who writes consistently under a single name other than his or her real name is simply a reiteration of the basic rule. Since the author chooses to be identified by this name, the cataloguer should use it as any other name would be used, according to provisions of 22.1A. As a matter of fact, since cataloguers are not required to search names of authors that do not present an obvious problem of identification and for which there is not a "conflict" (i.e., another author with an identical or very similar name) in the catalogue, a pseudonym will not be recognized as such in most cases. The book or other material will simply be entered under the name as it appears in the chief source of information. This is a perfectly satisfactory way to catalogue most material. As Jolley put it, "It is as impossible to count undiscovered pseudonyms as undiscovered murders."[1]

---

[1] *The Principles of Cataloging* (London: Lockwood, 1960), p. 52.

The example shown in figure 12-7 is that of a well-established author who consistently uses the same pseudonym on the title pages of her books. Her real name is known to be Mary Dolling Sanders O'Malley, Lady O'Malley. Using ALA 1949 rule 30A, which called for entry of "works published under pseudonym under the author's real name when known," the Library of Congress entered her books under "O'Malley." Had she begun publishing after *AACR1* came out, rule 42A (which is the same as *AACR2* 22.2C1) would have called for entry under the name she uses in her books. The new rule is logical; it provides entry under a sought heading, and it is also consistent with the general principle governing form of heading.

```
Bridge, Ann.
   Julia in Ireland / by Ann Bridge. -- New York :
McGraw-Hill, c1973.
   254 p. ; 22 cm.

   ISBN 0-07-007736-3




   I. Title.
```
Title page

Julia in Ireland
by Ann Bridge
McGraw-Hill Book Company
New York   St. Louis   San Francisco

Figure 12-7. Entry under pseudonym

The reader will notice that the catalogue entry does not indicate that the name used is not the author's real name when main entry is under pseudonym. However, to aid library users who may know the author's real name, 22.2C1 calls for a reference from the real name when it is known.

O'Malley, Mary Dolling Sanders, *Lady*
    see
Bridge, Ann.

As already mentioned, ALA 1949 rule 30 called for entry under the author's real name, when known, rather than under pseudonym. Cataloguers and library users until 1981 will find Library of Congress cards in the catalogue for the works of Ann Bridge entered under "O'Malley, Mary Dolling Sanders, *Lady*." The reason for this is that Ann Bridge—Lady O'Malley—began writing before 1967, when *AACR1* came into force. The Library of Congress established her name in its catalogues under ALA 1949 rules. Except to a limited extent, the Library of Congress was not willing to reprint any old cards done under the 1949 rules to bring them into line with the *AACR1* rules. Books that an author (such as Ann Bridge) wrote after 1967 were entered under the ALA 1949 form of name. The Library of Congress's policy in this regard was called *superimposition*.

This means that the rules for choice of entry will be applied only to works that are new to the Library and that the [*AACR1*] rules for headings will be applied only to persons and corporate bodies that are being established for the first time. New editions, etc., of works previously catalogued will be entered in the same way as the earlier editions. . . . New works by previously established authors will appear under the same heading.[2]

AACR2 rule 22.2C1 applies not only to a single author who consistently uses one pseudonym. It is closely related to 21.6D, shared pseudonyms, which deals with two or more authors who collaborate and who consistently use a joint pseudonym. Since this is the form of name by which these authors wish to be identified, use the name as it appears in the chief source of information. (See figure 12-8.) Make explanatory references from each of the real names to the name chosen for entry.

```
Masterson, Whit.
   Evil come, evil go / Whit Masterson. -- New York :
Dodd, Mead, c1961.
   185 p. ; 22 cm. -- (Red badge detective)


                                                    Figure 12-8. Joint
                                                    pseudonym



                              Evil Come, Evil Go
                                Whit Masterson
   I. Title.               Dodd, Mead & Company
                                   New York
                                  Red Badge
                                   Detective

             Title page
```

See 26.2D1, explanatory references, for form of reference from each real name to the name chosen for entry.

> Wade, Bob
>   For works of this author written in collaboration
>   with Bill Miller *see*
> Masterson, Whit.

> Miller, Bill.
>   For works of this author written in collaboration
>   with Bob Wade *see*
> Masterson, Whit.

[2] Library of Congress, *Cataloging Service Bulletin* 79 (Jan. 1967).

The jacket for the above book tells the identity of the two authors responsible for the work: "Whit Masterson . . . is actually Bob Wade and Bill Miller." Since jacket information is sometimes deliberately erroneous in order to preserve the anonymity of a pseudonymous author, the cataloguer will be well advised to check an appropriate reference source. *Who Done It? A Guide to Detective, Mystery, and Suspense Fiction* by Ordean A. Hagen (Bowker, 1969) lists Whit Masterson as the pseudonym for Bill Miller and Bob Wade. With this corroborating evidence, entry should be under the name as it appears on the title page, and references should be given.

Never investigate a typical name without conflict in the catalogue. But if evidence points to something not quite usual about the name of the author, do a little sleuthing.

22.2C2. Predominant name. This rule is basically the same as *AACR1* rule 42B, but with a couple of critical changes. If an author does not always use the same name in editions of his or her works, choose the name by which the author has come to be "identified predominantly." Thus, all works, both mathematics and children's fantasy, of that split personality Charles Lutwidge Dodgson–Lewis Carroll will be entered under "Lewis Carroll"—not under the author's real name (Dodgson) as was done under ALA 1949 rule 30. See figure 5-2.

Another such author is Dr. Seuss. Theodor Seuss Geisel has written many books under the pseudonym Dr. Seuss and a few under the pseudonym Theo LeSieg. Dr. Seuss is clearly the predominant name and should be used for all of Geisel's output, no matter what name appears on the title page (see figure 12-9). References will be made thus:

> Geisel, Theodor Seuss
> *see*
> Seuss, *Dr.*
>
> LeSieg, Theo
> *see*
> Seuss, *Dr.*

```
Seuss, Dr.
   One fish, two fish, red fish, blue fish / by
Dr. Seuss. -- Book club ed. -- New York : Beginner
Books, c1960.
   62 p. : ill. ; 24 cm.




   I. Title.
```

Figure 12-9.
Predominant name

One fish two fish
red fish blue fish
by Dr. Seuss

Beginner Books
A Division of Random House, Inc.
© Copyright, 1960, by Dr. Seuss.
Book Club Edition

Title on
two facing pages

22.2C3. No predominant name. If there is no clearly predominant name by which a person who uses one or more pseudonyms is identified, enter each work under the name as it appears in the work. This rule is the same as *AACR1* alternate rule 42B. In case of doubt, prefer rule 22.2C3 to 22.2C2.

Evan Hunter, a writer of mystery novels, sometimes uses his real name and sometimes the pseudonym Ed McBain. His novel *Every Little Crook and Nanny*, written under the name Evan Hunter, gives a clue that the alert cataloguer will follow up when he or she reads that "the jacket photo of Evan Hunter was graciously posed for by Ed McBain . . . " (from the book, p. 228). Checking Hagen's *Who Done It?*, the cataloguer will discover that Evan Hunter is the real name of an author who writes under a number of pseudonyms, including the name Ed McBain. Each of Hunter's books will be entered under the name appearing on the title page, as shown in figures 12-10 and 12-11.

```
Hunter, Evan.
   Every little crook and nanny : a novel / by Evan
Hunter. -- 1st ed. -- Garden City, N.Y. : Double-
day, 1972.
   229 p. ; 22 cm.


   I. Title.
```

Figure 12-10. No predominant name

Every Little Crook and Nanny
A novel by Evan Hunter
1972
Doubleday & Company, Inc., Garden City, New York

Title page

```
McBain, Ed.
   Eighty million eyes : an 87th precinct mystery
novel / by Ed McBain. -- New York : Delacorte
Press, c1966.
   190 p. ; 22 cm.


   I. Title.
```

Figure 12-11. No predominant name

Eighty Million Eyes
                    An 87th precinct mystery novel by
                                            Ed McBain
Delacorte Press —— New York

Title page

As previously mentioned, one of the objectives of a library catalogue is to enable the library user to locate all of the works of an author that are in the library, no matter what form of name the author has used in identifying himself or herself. When the cataloguer, applying 22.2C3, decides to use title page (or other chief source of information) form for entry of works of an author who uses more than one name, this author's works will be scattered in the catalogue. They may be connected by means of references (see 26.2D1), such as:

> Hunter, Evan
> > For works of this author written under pseudonym, *see*
> McBain, Ed.
> [and any other of Hunter's pseudonyms represented in the
> library's catalogue]

> McBain, Ed.
> > For works of this author written under his real name, *see*
> Hunter, Evan.

22.3. CHOICE AMONG DIFFERENT FORMS OF THE SAME NAME

22.3A. Fullness

This rule is essentially the same in its intention as *AACR1* rule 43A. An author may consistently use the same name in works published during his or her lifetime, and yet may not be consistent in the form (fullness) of name as it appears on title pages or other chief sources. George Bernard Shaw is an example of this kind of inconsistency. His name has variously been listed on title pages of his works published during his lifetime as Bernard Shaw, G. Bernard Shaw, and George Bernard Shaw. Rule 22.3A solves the question of which of these varying forms should be chosen for entry; the rule is consistent with general rule 22.1A in requiring the cataloguer to choose "the form most commonly found." It is contrary to the spirit of the rules to expect the cataloguer to count titles in a particular library to make this determination; choose the name by which the author is "commonly known" following guidelines given in 22.1B. Shaw will be listed as shown in figures 12-12 to 12-14. Following provisions of 26.2A2, a reference may be made:

> Shaw, Bernard
> *see*
> Shaw, George Bernard.

Another author who has not been entirely consistent about the fullness of name used in her works is Margaret F. Maxwell. Her works have appeared variously under Margaret Nadine Finlayson Maxwell (figure 1-104), Margaret Maxwell (figure 1-105) and Margaret F. Maxwell (figure 11-46). The Library of Congress has established her as Maxwell, Margaret. Since this author's later books have appeared under the name Margaret F. Maxwell, and her preference is for the name including the middle initial, it is the form that should be used.

22.3B. Language

This rule is related to *AACR1* rule 44. It deals with the problem presented by an author whose works appear in more than one language and whose name appears in more than one form, due to translation or transliteration.

```
Shaw, George Bernard.
   You never can tell : a comedy in four acts / by
Bernard Shaw. -- London : Constable, 1906.
   320 p. ; 18 cm.
```

Figure 12-12. Most common form of name

I. Title.

You Never Can Tell:
A Comedy in Four Acts.   by Bernard Shaw
Archibald Constable & Co.
Ltd. London: 1906.

Title page

```
Shaw, George Bernard.
   An unsocial socialist / by G. Bernard Shaw. --
New York : Brentano, 1917.
   378 p. ; 17 cm.
```

Figure 12-13. Most common form of name

I. Title.

An Unsocial Socialist
by
G. Bernard Shaw
New York
Brentano's
1917

Title page

```
Shaw, George Bernard.
   Love among the artists / by George Bernard
Shaw. -- New York : Brentano, 1910, c1900.
   viii, 443 p. ; 19 cm.
```

Figure 12-14. Most common form of name

I. Title.

Love Among the Artists
by George Bernard Shaw
Brentano's New York
MCMX

Title page

22.3B1. This rule covers persons who write in more than one language and whose name therefore appears in different forms. Again, the principle of choice of the "most commonly known" form governs the rule, which states that the form corresponding to the "language of most of the works" should be used. The rule is almost identical to *AACR1* rule 44A2. In case of doubt, choose the form found in reference sources of the person's country of residence or activity.

22.3B2. This rule is based on *AACR1* rule 44A1. It refers chiefly to medieval Latin and Greek authors, not to persons of the classical period (see 22.3B3).

22.3B3. Names written in the roman alphabet established in an English form. This rule is the same as *AACR1* rule 44A3a. It pertains to persons who have no surname and who are to be entered under given name (Horace) or byname (a word or phrase denoting place of origin, occupation, or other characteristic commonly associated with the person's given name in reference sources, e.g. John the Baptist, Saint Francis of Assisi, etc.). The names of many such persons have become firmly established through common usage in English-speaking countries in an English form. Both *AACR1* rule 44A3 and *AACR2* rule 22.3B3 call for entry under the English form of the name as it is found in English-language reference sources.

This instruction is a change from ALA 1949 rule 60, which called for entry of all Latin authors under the Latin form, and ALA 1949 rule 55, which specified entry for sovereigns under their forenames in the vernacular. The rationale for the change is that in the case of a Roman of the classical period, it is difficult to establish his or her preference for form of name from "works by that person issued in his or her language" (22.1B). Establishing the preferred form of name for a classical non-author usually presents similar difficulties; reference sources in classical Greek and Latin are few and far between (22.1B). Rule 22.3B3 is a practical solution for librarians in most English-speaking countries; its retention from *AACR1* indicates its acceptance among library users despite the fact that in theory, at least, it would seem to be a stumbling block in the way of international exchange of cataloguing information.

Cataloguers can best determine common usage in English-speaking countries by checking English-language reference sources and by noting the spelling of the person's name in books written in English. At least a minimal amount of research is required on the part of the cataloguer to establish the name heading, even though the name may not present a "conflict" in the catalogue.

The decision about the form of heading to be used for figure 12-15 was fairly straightforward. The title page of the work being catalogued is one factor to be considered. In addition, the cataloguer will find entry for the classical Roman author Virgil in *Encyclopaedia Britannica* (1971) and *Encyclopedia Americana* (1970) under the form Virgil, with references to the variant form Publius Vergilius Maro. The form Virgil will be used in the heading. Since dates were found in the course of research done for other reasons, they will be used under provisions of 22.18 (option). Reference will be made according to 26.2A2 from the different language form not chosen for the heading:

Vergilius Maro, Publius
see
Virgil, 70–19 B.C.

```
Virgil, 70-19 B.C.
  The Georgics of Virgil / translated by C. Day
Lewis ; with an introduction by Louis Bromfield.
-- 1st American ed. -- New York : Oxford University
Press, 1947.
  xvii, 83 p. ; 22 cm.
```

Figure 12-15. Roman
of classical times

```
  I. Day-Lewis, C.  II. Title.
```

Title page

The Georgics of Virgil
Translated by C. Day Lewis
With an Introduction by Louis Bromfield
New York • Oxford University Press • 1947

22.3C. Names written in a nonroman script
 22.3C1. Persons entered under given name or byname. This rule closely parallels 22.3B3; it is the same as *AACR1* rule 44B1e. A person entered under given name or byname, whose name is written in a nonroman script, will be entered according to form found in English-language reference sources. The Greek poet Homer is such an individual (see figure 12-16).

```
Homer.
  The Odyssey of Homer / translated by William
Cowper. -- London : Dent ; New York : Dutton, 1910.
  368 p. ; 18 cm. -- (Everyman's library ; 454.
Classical)
```

Figure 12-16. Greek of
classical times

```
  I. Cowper, William.  II. Title.
```

Title page

The Odyssey of Homer
Translated by William Cowper
London & Toronto
Published by J. M. Dent
& Sons Ltd & in New York
by E. P. Dutton & Co.

Entry Element

Rules 22.2–22.3 give guidance for the establishment of a personal name that appears in publications in more than one form. Once the form of the name has been determined, rules 22.4–22.11 tell the cataloguer which part of the name will constitute the entry element (the first part of the name in the catalogue entry). The overriding factor governing the rules is the preference of the person when it is known. Lacking that knowledge, the cataloguer will choose the entry element according to linguistic usage: i.e., "that part of the name under which the person would be listed in authoritative alphabetic lists in his or her language or country" (22.4A).

The rules included in this section are basically the same as *AACR1* rules 46–51. They differ slightly from Paris Principle 12, under which entry element is to be based, first, on citizenship and, second, on the language in which the author writes. The editors of *AACR2* believed that principle 12 presented too many problems, particularly when dealing with the names of French origin in a country such as Belgium, where practices seem to be variable. *AACR2* practice, therefore, is based on the language, not the citizenship, of the author.

A. H. Chaplin's *Names of Persons*[3] was drawn up at the behest of the International Conference on Cataloguing Principles (1961) to expedite uniform entry of names internationally. Chaplin's book is an indispensable guide to national usage; it should be referred to in cases in which the rules fail to give specific instructions.

22.4. GENERAL RULE

This rule parallels the introductory section preceding *AACR1* rule 46. It stresses that when a person's name consists of more than one part, the part chosen as the entry element by the cataloguer will be determined by the way that person's name is given in alphabetical lists that show the custom of his or her country. See examples in *AACR2* and further examples in this text.

22.5. ENTRY UNDER SURNAME

This rule is basically the same as *AACR1* rule 46. It is to be applied only to names that contain given name(s) and surname. For names consisting of a surname only, see 22.15A; for names consisting of a forename only, see 22.11B.

22.5C. Compound surnames

This rule is the equivalent of *AACR1* rule 46B. It encompasses the entry of surnames that include "two or more proper names" (e.g. C. Day-Lewis). It does not pertain to single surnames that consist of two or more words (e.g. Antoine de Saint Exupéry). The rule is divided into eight parts, which are to be applied in the order in which they are listed.

[3] *Names of Persons: National Usages for Entry in Catalogues* (Sevenoaks, Kent, Eng.: IFLA, 1967).

22.5C2. Preferred or established form known. Enter a person with a compound surname under the element of the surname which he or she prefers. Only rarely will the cataloguer have information about the author's preference. The second part of the rule is more useful; in fact, it is the only way in most cases that the cataloguer can be positive that he or she is dealing with a compound name rather than with a simple surname and one or more forenames that resemble surnames. The second part of the rule instructs the cataloguer to check reference sources in the person's language and to list the person in the form found there. Footnote 9 on page 359 gives a note of caution: Some reference sources, such as the *Dictionary of National Biography*, enter all persons in a uniform style (in this case, under the last element of the name) regardless of personal preference.

22.5C3. Hyphenated surnames. Such names are to be entered under the first part of the name, with reference made from the second part. (See figure 12-17.)

According to 26.2A3, the following reference will be made:

> Phillipps, James Orchard Halliwell-
> *see*
> Halliwell-Phillipps, James Orchard.

```
Halliwell-Phillipps, James Orchard.
   Popular rhymes and nursery tales : a sequel to
The nursery rhymes of England / by James Orchard
Halliwell-Phillipps. -- Detroit : Singing Tree
Press, 1968.
   xi, 276 p. ; 20 cm.

   Reprint of: London : J.R. Smith, 1849.
```

Figure 12-17.
Compound surname

```
        I. Title.
```

Title page

Popular Rhymes and Nursery Tales:
A sequel to the
Nursery Rhymes of England.
by
James Orchard Halliwell-Phillipps
London:
John Russell Smith,
4, Old Compton Street, Soho Square.
1849
Now Reissued by
Singing Tree Press
Book Tower, Detroit, Michigan 1968

22.5C4. Other compound surnames. Check reference sources in the language of the person when you have reason to suspect that a name not hyphenated may be compound. Enter the person the way he or she is listed in such sources; make references from parts of the surname not used as entry element. Persons other than married women who use their maiden name followed by husband's name are to be entered under the first element of the compound name, whether hyphenated or not.

Many Spanish surnames are compounds consisting of the father's surname followed by the mother's maiden name. Those are to be entered under the first part of the compound, after checking references to be certain that the name is indeed compound. For more detailed information see Chaplin, *Names of Persons* and Charles F. Gosnell, *Spanish Personal Names*.[4]

See figure 1-44 for an example of a compound Spanish name. Entry for Cotarelo y Mori is based on information from *Enciclopedia Universal Ilustrada* (Barcelona: Espasa, 1907–30), familiarly known as *Espasa*. Make reference, following 26.2A3:

> Mori, Emilio Cotarelo y
>   *see*
> Cotarelo y Mori, Emilio.

In the example shown in figure 12-18, the entry for Serafín and Joaquín Álvarez Quintero under the first part of their compound name is based on information from the Spanish-language encyclopedia *Enciclopedia Barsa* (1964). Reference for the two authors will be made following 26.2A3:

```
Álvarez Quintero, Serafín.
   Tambor y cascabel : comedia en cuatro actos /
Serafín y Joaquín Álvarez Quintero. -- Madrid :
Impr. Clásica Española, 1927.
   100 p. ; 19 cm.




   I. Álvarez Quintero, Joaquín.  II. Title.
```

Figure 12-18.
Compound name—
Spanish

Title page

Serafín y Joaquín Álvarez Quintero
Tambor y Cascabel
Comedia En Cuatro Actos
Madrid
1927

[4] New York: Wilson, 1938; reprint, Detroit: Blaine-Ethridge, 1971.

Quintero, Serafín Álvarez
see
Álvarez Quintero, Serafín.

Quintero, Joaquín Álvarez
see
Álvarez Quintero, Joaquín.

Compound Portuguese surnames are formed differently from Spanish. Generally speaking, the mother's name is the first part of the compound, the father's the last. For this reason, 22.5C4 (like its predecessor, *AACR1* rule 46B3a) specifies that such names are to be entered under the last element in the compound. (See figure 12-19.) Reference will be made according to 26.2A3:

Costa Lima, Luiz
see
Lima, Luiz Costa.

```
Lima, Luiz Costa.
   Lira e antilira : (Mário, Drummond, Cabral) /
Luiz Costa Lima. -- Rio de Janeiro : Civilização
Brasileira, 1968.
   413 p. ; 21 cm. -- (Coleção Vera Cruz. Literatu-
ra brasileira ; v. 127)

   Bibliographical footnotes.
   Contents: Introdução -- Permanência e mudança na
poesia de Mário de Andrade -- O princípio : corrosão
na poesia de Carlos Drummond -- A traição con-
seqüente, ou, A poesia de Cabral.

   I. Title.  II. Series.
```

Figure 12-19.
Compound name—
Portuguese

Title page

Luiz Costa Lima
Lira e Antilira
(Mário, Drummond, Cabral)
Civilização
Brasileira

Be wary of names consisting of two or more words not themselves surnames. Do not separate the parts of names such as Castelo Branco, Camilo or Espirito Santo, Vicente Antonio de. It is not necessary to give references from parts of name not used for entry in such cases; see figure 12-20.

Saint Exupéry, Antoine de.
  ₍Le petit prince. English₎
  The little prince / written and illustrated by
Antoine de Saint Exupéry ; translated from the
French by Katherine Woods. -- New York : Harcourt,
Brace & World, c1943.
  113 p. : ill. ; 18 cm. -- (Harbrace paperbound
library ; HPL 30)

  Translation of: Le petit prince.

  I. Title.

Figure 12-20. Not a
compound name

Title page

The Little Prince
Written and Illustrated by
Antoine de Saint Exupéry
Translated from the French
by Katherine Woods
Harbrace Paperbound Library
Harcourt, Brace & World, Inc.
New York

22.5C5. Other compound surnames: married women. Follow general rule 22.1A in establishing the name of a married woman; use the name, either married or maiden name, by which the woman chooses to be known and by which she is most commonly identified. If she chooses to use, in addition to forenames, both her maiden name and her husband's surname, entry will be under the husband's surname, unless her language is Czech, French, Hungarian, Italian, or Spanish. See figures 12-5 and 12-6 for an example of the entry of a married woman writing and best known by her married name.

22.5C6. Nature of surname uncertain. Some English- and Scandinavian-language names have the appearance of compound names when, actually, the author simply has a family name or other surnames as his or her middle name. Such names should be checked in reference sources. If the name cannot be found after reasonable search, or, obviously, if the cataloguer discovers that the name is not a compound surname, enter under the last part of the name. If there is a reasonable possibility that catalogue users will think of the name as a compound name, make appropriate references.

The American author Ernest Thompson Seton has such a name; he is sometimes referred to as Thompson Seton. Information about Seton is to be found in Hart, *Oxford Companion to American Literature* (1965), which enters him as "Seton, Ernest [Evan] Thompson," with the further information that "his name was originally Ernest Seton Thompson," and his dates of birth and death.

Entry will be as shown in figure 12-21. Reference is made according to terms of 26.2A3:

> Thompson, Ernest Seton
> *see*
> Seton, Ernest Thompson, 1860–1946.

```
Seton, Ernest Thompson, 1860-1946.
  The biography of a grizzly and 75 drawings / by
Ernest Thompson Seton. -- New York : Schocken
Books, 1967.
  157 p. : ill. ; 21 cm. -- (Schocken paperbacks ;
SB 152)


  I. Title: The biography of a grizzly.
```

Figure 12-21. Nature of surname uncertain

Title page	The Biography of a Grizzly and 75 Drawings by Ernest Thompson Seton Schocken Books • New York

22.5C8. This rule is the same as *AACR1* rule 46D. The word "junior" and any other word showing relationship is not to be included in the heading for English-speaking persons, even when such a term is used regularly by the person as a part of the name. (It is, however, included in transcribing the name in the body of the card; see figure 1-40.) Portuguese and Brazilian surnames are exceptions to this rule. Such a name will have entry as shown in figure 12-22. Reference is made under terms of 26.2A3:

> Filho, Antônio Martins
> *see*
> Martins Filho, Antônio.

```
Martins Filho, Antônio.
  O universal pelo regional : definição de uma
política universitária / Antônio Martins Filho.
-- 2.a ed. -- Fortaleza : Universitária do Ceará,
1966.
  329 p. : port. ; 24 cm.


  I. Title.
```

Figure 12-22. Word indicating relationship

Title page

Prof. Antônio Martins Filho
O Universal Pelo Regional
Definição de Uma Política Universitária
(2.ª Edição)
Fortaleza • Imprensa Universitária do Ceará • 1966

22.5D. Surnames with separately written prefixes

The guiding principle governing this part of the rule is the same as that for 22.5C, compound surnames: Enter a name with a separately written prefix under the element most commonly used as an entry element in alphabetical listings in the person's language.

22.5D1. Articles and prepositions. This rule is the same as *AACR1* rule 46E1. Specific rules for various languages and countries have been set down to give guidance to cataloguers who are unsure of national customs governing entry in reference sources in the various languages. They are applied to surnames that include a separately written prefix consisting of an article, a preposition, or a combination of the two. This section of *AACR2* has drawn extensively on information contained in Chaplin, *Names of Persons*. For languages not covered under rule 22.5D1, see Chaplin.

English. Enter under the prefix; see figures 12-23 and 12-24. *AACR1* rule 121A3 stated that references were rarely necessary for English names with prefixes since library users expected to find the name in the catalogue under the prefix. This exception is no longer made under terms of 26.2A3. In all cases, no matter what the nationality of the person bearing a name with a prefix, a reference *may* be made if the alternate entry might "reasonably" be sought by library users. In case of doubt, make the reference; it will be made only once, when the author's name is first established. In general, 26.2A3 suggests reference under parts of the surname following a prefix for a name entered under prefix, as are English names. Thus, for Van der Post, suggested references are:

```
Van der Post, Laurens.
   The dark eye in Africa / Laurens Van der Post.
-- New York : Morrow, 1955.
   224 p. ; 21 cm.



   I. Title.
```

Figure 12-24. English
—enter under prefix

Laurens Van der Post
The Dark Eye in Africa
William Morrow & Company, Inc.
New York   1955

Title page

Der Post, Laurens Van
see
Van der Post, Laurens.

Post, Laurens Van der
see
Van der Post, Laurens.

```
Dos Passos, John.
  Airways, inc. / by John Dos Passos. -- New York :
Macaulay Co., c1928.
  148 p. ; 20 cm. -- (A New playwrights' theatre
production)
```

Figure 12-23. English
—enter under prefix

Airways, Inc.
by
John Dos Passos
A New Playwrights' Theatre Production
New York
The Macaulay Company

```
I. Title.
```

Title page

Suggested reference for Dos Passos according to 26.2A3 is:

Passos, John Dos
see
Dos Passos, John.

French. Enter under prefix if the prefix consists of an article (le, la) or of a contraction of an article and a preposition (du, des). (See figure 12-25.) Suggested reference for Des Cars is:

Cars, Guy Des
see
Des Cars, Guy.

```
Des Cars, Guy.
  De cape et de plume : roman vécu / Guy Des Cars.
-- Paris : Flammarion, c1965.
  511 p. ; 20 cm.
```

Figure 12-25. French
—enter under prefix
(contraction)

```
  I. Title.
```

Title page

> Guy Des Cars
> De Cape et de plume
> roman vécu
> Flammarion, Editeur
> 26, rue Racine, Paris

A French name that includes an article (la, le) is to be entered under the part of the name following the preposition. (See figure 12-26.) The article in French, as well as a contraction of an article and preposition (des, du), is always capitalized in a proper name (*AACR2* A.39C). References to be made for La Boétie according to 26.2A3 are:

> Boétie, Estienne de La
> > *see*
> La Boétie, Estienne de.
>
> De La Boétie, Estienne
> > *see*
> La Boétie, Estienne de.

```
La Boétie, Estienne de.
   Oeuvres complètes d'Estienne de La Boétie /
publiées avec notice biographique, variantes, notes,
et index par Paul Bonnefon. -- Genève : Slatkine
Reprints, 1967.
   lxxxv, 444 p. : ill. ; 24 cm.


   I. Bonnefon, Paul.   II. Title.
```

Figure 12-26. French —enter under prefix (article)

Title page

> Oeuvres complètes d'Estienne
> de La Boétie
> Publiées avec Notice biographique, Variantes,
> Notes et Index
> par Paul Bonnefon
> Slatkine Reprints
> Genève
> 1967

If the French surname includes the preposition (de), enter the surname under the part of the name following the preposition. (See figure 12-27.) Reference for Balzac will be:

De Balzac, Honoré
see
Balzac, Honoré de.

Balzac, Honoré de.
  Eugénie Grandet / Honoré de Balzac. -- Paris :
Flammarion, [19--]
  285 p. ; 18 cm.

Figure 12-27. French
—enter under part of
surname following
preposition

I. Title.

Title page

Honoré de Balzac
Eugénie Grandet
Paris
Ernest Flammarion, Editeur

German. Entry of German surnames with prefix follows almost the same pattern as that for French. Enter under prefix if the prefix is an article (der, die, das) or a contraction of a preposition and an article (am, aus'm, vom, zum, zur); see figure 12-28. Reference for Vom Brocke will be made according to 26.2A3:

Brocke, Bernhard vom
see
Vom Brocke, Bernhard.

Vom Brocke, Bernhard.
  Kurt Breysig : Geschichtswissenschaft zwischen
Historismus und Soziologie / von Bernhard vom
Brocke. -- Lübeck : Matthiesen, 1971.
  351 p. ; 24 cm. -- (Historische Studien ; Heft
417)

  Bibliography: p. 317-343.

Figure 12-28. German
—enter under
contraction

I. Title. II. Series.

Historische Studien
Heft 417
Kurt Breysig
Title page   Geschichtswissenschaft zwischen Historismus
und Soziologie
von
Bernhard vom Brocke
1971
Matthiesen Verlag • Lübeck und Hamburg

If a German surname includes a preposition (von) or a preposition followed by an article, enter the name under the part following the prefix. (See figure 12-29.) Reference for Hentig will be made according to 26.2A3:

> Von Hentig, Werner-Otto
> *see*
> Hentig, Werner-Otto von.

```
Hentig, Werner-Otto von.
   Der Nahe Osten rückt näher / Werner-Otto von
Hentig. -- Leipzig : P. List, c1940.
   117 p. : map ; 22 cm.




   I. Title.
```

Figure 12-29. German —enter under part of surname following prefix

Werner-Otto von Hentig
Der Nahe Osten rückt näher
Paul List Verlag Leipzig

Title page

Italian. Enter modern names under prefix. Consult reference sources for medieval or early modern names, which ordinarily did not include an actual surname; the prefix was often part of a byname (e.g. Leonardo da Vinci). See 22.8A for treatment.

The rule for entry of modern Italian names under prefix is the same as *AACR1* rule 46E1. It was a change from ALA 1949 rule 39B1c, which called for entry under prefix only when the prefix was an article (la, li, lo). Otherwise, under ALA 1949, the name was to be entered under the part of the name following the prefix.

Figure 1-68 is an example of an Italian name entered under prefix. Reference will be made by terms of 26.2A3:

> Annunzio, Gabriele d'
> *see*
> D'Annunzio, Gabriele.

It is, by the way, particularly important to make references from part of surname following the prefix to the name as established for cataloguing purposes when, under older rules, the name would have been entered differently in the catalogue. Such is the case with D'Annunzio, which under ALA 1949 rules was entered as "Annunzio, Gabriele d'."

Portuguese. The part of the surname following the prefix is used for entry; see figure 12-30. Reference will be made, following 26.2A3:

> Dos Santos, Francisco Marques
> *see*
> Santos, Francisco Marques dos.

```
Santos, Francisco Marques dos.
  Louça e porcelana / Francisco Marques dos San-
tos ; direção e introdução, Rodrigo M. F. de
Andrade. -- Rio de Janeiro : Edições de Ouro, 1968.
  114 p. : ill. ; 17 cm. -- (As Artes plásticas
no Brasil) (Coleção brasileira de ouro ; 1047)




  I. Title.  II. Series.  III. Series: Coleção
brasileira de ouro.
```

Figure 12-30.
Portuguese—enter under part of surname following prefix

Title page

Francisco Marques dos Santos
As Artes Plásticas No Brasil
Louça e Porcelana
Direção e introdução
Rodrigo M. F. de Andrade
Rio de Janeiro
Brasil

Spanish. In almost all cases, entry will be under the part of the name following the prefix. Note that the rule states that if the prefix consists of an article *only*, the cataloguer is to enter under the article. This means that if the name includes an article (el, la, lo, los, las) and a preposition (de), entry will be under the part of the name following prefixes. (See figure 12-31.) Make references for Casas as follows:

De las Casas, Bartolomé
see
Casas, Bartolomé de las.

Las Casas, Bartolomé de
see
Casas, Bartolomé de las.

```
Casas, Bartolomé de las.
   Doctrina / Bartolomé de las Casas ; prólogo y
selección de Agustín Yáñez. -- 2º ed. -- México :
Universidad Nacional Autónoma, 1951.
   xxxvi, 178 p. : ill. ; 19 cm. -- (Biblioteca del
estudiante universitario ; 22)




I. Yáñez, Agustín.  II. Title.  III. Series.
```

Figure 12-31. Spanish
—enter under part of
name following prefix

Title page

Biblioteca del Estudiante Universitario
22
Fray Bartolomé de Las Casas
Doctrina
Prólogo y selección
de
Agustín Yáñez
Segunda Edición
Ediciones de la Universidad Nacional Autónoma
México   1951

Another example of a Spanish surname with a prefix consisting of an article and a preposition is shown in figure 12-32. It is rare to find a name with *only* the article as a prefix. Make references as follows:

De la Maza, Francisco
see
Maza, Francisco de la.

La Maza, Francisco de
see
Maza, Francisco de la.

```
Maza, Francisco de la.
   El Palacio de la Inquisición (Escuela Nacional
de Medicina) / Francisco de la Maza. -- ₍Mexico₎ :
Instituto de Investigaciones Estéticas, 1951.
   81 p. : ill. ; 24 cm. -- (Ediciones del IV
centenario de la Universidad de México ; v. 9)



I. Title.  II. Series.
```

Figure 12-32. Spanish
—enter under part of
name following prefix

Francisco de la Maza
El Palacio de la Inquisición
(Escuela Nacional de Medicina)
Instituto de Investigaciones Estéticas
1951

Title page

22.6. ENTRY UNDER TITLE OF NOBILITY

This rule, which should be compared with 22.12, is basically the same as *AACR1* rule 47. It is based on *AACR2* rule 22.1A; that is, entry should be made under the form of the name by which the person is commonly known. If a nobleman or woman uses title rather than family name in his or her works, or if such an individual who is not an author is known primarily by his or her title and is so listed in appropriate reference sources, such an individual should be listed under the proper name in the title of nobility rather than under family name. Check reference sources to identify the individual's rank and personal name accurately.

Two noblemen better known by title than by family name are the Duke of Wellington and the Earl of Lauderdale. The *Encyclopedia Americana* lists each of them under his title, followed by his family name, and dates.[5] Entry should be under title; see figure 12-33.

Rule 22.6A stipulates that a reference will be made from the family name for a person entered under name in nobility. References for the example shown in figure 12-33 will be:

> Maitland, James, *Earl of Lauderdale*
> *see*
> Lauderdale, James Maitland, *Earl of*, 1759–1839.

[5] *The Dictionary of National Biography* lists all individuals under family name. Therefore it is not a good source for determining the preferred entry of a British nobleman. *Encyclopedia Americana* and *Encyclopaedia Britannica* list members of the British nobility under title when they are best known by title, under family name when they are best known by it. *Who's Who* is another source of information for living British noblemen.

Wellesley, Arthur, *Duke of Wellington*
   see
Wellington, Arthur Wellesley, *Duke of*, 1769–1852.

```
Lauderdale, James Maitland, Earl of, 1759-1839.
   Three letters to the Duke of Wellington / by the
Earl of Lauderdale (1829). -- New York : A.M.
Kelley, 1965.
   138 p. ; 21 cm. -- (Reprints of economic classics)

   Reprint of: London : J. Murray, 1829.



   I. Wellington, Arthur Wellesley, Duke of,
1769-1852. II. Title. III. Series.
```

Figure 12-33.
Nobleman

Title page

Three Letters to the Duke of Wellington
by
The Earl of Lauderdale
[1829]
Reprints of Economic Classics
Augustus M. Kelley, Bookseller
New York 1965

Proper entry and references for certain members of other ranks of the British peerage will be:

Queensberry, John Sholto Douglas, *Marquess of*, 1844–1900.
   x Douglas, John Sholto, *Marquess of Queensberry*

Grey of Fallodon, Edward Grey, *Viscount*, 1862–1933.
   x Grey, Edward, *Viscount of Fallodon*

Lytton, Edward George Earle Lytton Bulwer-Lytton, *Baron*, 1803–1873.
   x Bulwer-Lytton, Edward George Earle Lytton, *Baron Lytton*

The wife of a peer takes the title corresponding to that of her husband, e.g. duchess, marchioness, countess, viscountess, baroness:

Devonshire, Georgiana Spencer Cavendish, *Duchess of*, 1757–1806.
   x Cavendish, Georgiana Spencer, *Duchess of Devonshire*

Entry under title of nobility for persons of other countries follows the same pattern as that used for British nobility:

Cavour, Camillo Benso, *conte di*, 1810–1861.
   x Benso, Camillo, *conte di Cavour*

Alba, Fernando Alvarez de Toledo, *duque de*, 1508–1582.
   x Alvarez de Toledo, Fernando, *duque de Alba*

The cataloguer should be aware that certain British titles below the rank of baron and certain other titles for persons of other countries are simply terms of honor. These persons are entered under family name, with the title of honor added. See 22.12.

The cataloguer should also be aware of two changes from *AACR1* rule 47. The provisions of rules 47B and 47C have been eliminated. Under no circumstance will sequential numbers be used with a title of nobility; in case two or more of the bearers of such a title have the same personal name, they should be distinguished in the same fashion as other persons with identical names, by adding dates of birth and death (22.18).

Also, mercifully, the nit-picking distinction between entry for a nobleman whose proper name in his title is the same as his surname, and one whose name is not, is eliminated. No matter what the components of the name may be, if a nobleman uses his title, title name should be the entry word. And regardless of what the family name may be, family name in direct order comes next, followed by the title. In the example shown in figure 12-34, no reference is needed from family name to surname in nobility, since they are the same.

```
Tennyson, Alfred Tennyson, Baron, 1809-1892.
   Tiresias and other poems / by Alfred, Lord
Tennyson. -- London : Macmillan, 1885.
   viii, 203 p. ; 18 cm.




I. Title.
```

Figure 12-34.
Nobleman

Title page

Tiresias and other poems
by
Alfred Lord Tennyson
London
Macmillan and Co.
1885

In contrast to previous rules, in almost every instance entry for an author will be under the form of name that the author chooses to use, whether it be a single forename, initials, a pseudonym, a phrase, or a surname. The proper name in a title of nobility is not a surname (which by definition is a name shared by all members of a family). However, the general rule for entry still holds. If a person chooses to use his or her proper name in a title of nobility alone and is commonly known by that name, it should be used in the library catalogue. Baroness Orczy, an entry for whom is shown in figure 12-35, consistently uses only her proper name plus her title of nobility in her works.

```
Orczy, Baroness.
    The Scarlet Pimpernel / by Baroness Orczy ; with
photographs of the author and her environment as
well as illustrations from early editions ; together
with an introduction by Howard Breslin. -- New
York : Dodd, Mead, c1964.
    xii, 267 p. : ill., ports. ; 22 cm.



                                    I. Title.
```

Figure 12-35. Nobility

The Scarlet Pimpernel
by Baroness Orczy
With photographs of the author and her
environment as well as illustrations
from early editions, together with an introduction by
Howard Breslin
New York • Dodd, Mead & Company

Title page

22.7. ENTRY UNDER ROMANIAN PATRONYMIC

A patronymic is a name derived from that of the person's father, usually by addition of a suffix. The rule is of limited application except in libraries having large Romanian collections.

22.8. ENTRY UNDER GIVEN NAME, ETC.

This rule is equivalent to *AACR1* rule 49A. A person who is not commonly identified by a surname (or a name that appears to be a surname) and who is not identified by a title of nobility should be checked in a reference source and entered accordingly.

The black militant Malcolm X is such an individual. *Encyclopedia Americana* (1970) lists him as Malcolm X and reveals his original name: Malcolm Little. Catalogue entry will be as shown in figure 12-36. References will be:

X, Malcolm
see
Malcolm X, 1925–1965.

Little, Malcolm
see
Malcolm X, 1925–1965.

Malcolm X's name did not include words or phrases denoting place of origin, etc. A name that includes such information will be entered in direct order, with the given name separated from the descriptive phrase by a comma. Henry of Huntingdon's name and dates are to be found in the *Dictionary of National Biography* and *Chambers' Encyclopedia* (1973) under "Henry of Huntingdon." The prescribed use of the comma is new to this rule, which is otherwise the same as *AACR1* rule 49A. (See figure 12-37.)

```
Malcolm X, 1925-1965.
  The autobiography of Malcolm X / with the
assistance of Alex Haley ; introduction by M.S.
Handler ; epilogue by Alex Haley. -- 1st pbk.
ed. -- New York : Grove Press, 1966, c1965.
  xiv, 460 p. : ill., ports. ; 24 cm.



  I. Haley, Alex.   II. Title.
```

Figure 12-36. Entry under given name

Title page

The Autobiography of Malcolm X
With the assistance of Alex Haley
Introduction by M. S. Handler
Epilogue by Alex Haley
Grove Press, Inc.   New York

```
Henry, of Huntingdon, 1084?-1155.
  The chronicle of Henry of Huntingdon / translated
and edited by Thomas Forester. -- New York :
AMS Press, 1968.
  xxviii, 442 p. : ill. ; 22 cm.

  Reprint of: London : H.G. Bohn, 1853.
  Originally issued in the series: Bohn's antiqua-
rian library.
  Contents: The history of England from the invasion
of Julius Caesar to the accession of Henry II -- The
acts of Stephen, King of England and Duke of Nor-
mandy.
  I. Forester, Thomas.   II. Title.
```

Figure 12-37. Entry under given name

                    The Chronicle of
                Henry of Huntingdon.
                    comprising
        The history of England, from the invasion of
Title page   Julius Caesar to the accession of Henry II.
                      also,
                The Acts of Stephen,
        King of England and Duke of Normandy.
                translated and edited
                by Thomas Forester, A.M.
                    London:
        Henry G. Bohn, York Street, Covent Garden.
                  MDCCCLIII.
                  AMS Press
                  New York

22.9. ENTRY OF ROMAN NAMES

This rule is the same as *AACR1* rule 50. It should be correlated with 22.3B3; as indicated under that rule, a Roman of classical times "whose name has become well established in an English form" will be searched in English-language reference sources. Entry will be under the part of the name "most commonly used" in such sources.

Cicero is to be found entered under the word "Cicero" in the form established for entry in the *Encyclopaedia Britannica* (1971), the *Encyclopedia Americana* (1970), and the *Oxford Companion to Classical Literature* (1962). Each of these sources also gave his dates. (See figure 12-38.)

```
Cicero, Marcus Tullius, 106-43 B.C.
   Selected letters of Cicero / edited with an
introduction and notes by Frank Frost Abbott. --
New ed. -- Norman : University of Oklahoma Press,
1964.
   lxxvi, 315 p. ; 20 cm.


Latin text with English notes.
Bibliographical footnotes.



   I. Abbott, Frank Frost.   II. Title.
```

Figure 12-38. Roman name

Selected Letters of Cicero
Edited,
with an Introduction and Notes,
by Frank Frost Abbott
University of Oklahoma Press
Norman

Title page

22.10. ENTRY UNDER INITIALS, LETTERS, OR NUMERALS

In a new provision of this rule, if an author consistently uses initials for identification in his or her works, the initials, in direct order, will be used as main entry. If the initials have been used by more than one author, see 22.16 for an addition to resolve a conflict.

Some attempt should be made, by looking in dictionaries of pseudonyms, anonyms, etc. to find the identity of the author. In the example shown in figure 12-39, Cushing[6] gives the information that "A.L.O.E." stands for "A Lady of England," and that the initials are the pseudonym of Charlotte Maria Tucker. Make references from those forms (26.2A2):

> A lady of England
> *see*
> A.L.O.E.
>
> Tucker, Charlotte Maria
> *see*
> A.L.O.E.

```
A. L. O. E.
   The giant-killers, or, The battle which all
must fight / by A.L.O.E. ; with 40 engravings. --
London ; New York : Nelson, 1896.
   201 p. : ill. ; 19 cm.




I. Title.
```

Figure 12-39. Initials

> The Giant-Killer;
> or,
> The Battle Which All Must Fight.
> by
> A. L. O. E.
> with 40 engravings.
> London:
> T. Nelson and Sons, Paternoster Row.
> Edinburgh; and New York.
> 1896

Title page

In addition, make name-title reference from an inverted form of the initials, as directed under 22.10:

> E., A. L. O.
>   The giant-killers
> *see*
> A. L. O. E.

[6] William Cushing, *Initials and Pseudonyms: A Dictionary of Revealed Disguises* (2 vols; New York: Crowell, 1885–88).

Note the format for the reference needed for H.D., who wrote the book catalogued as figure 12-2. See also 22.16 for further discussion and explanation.

22.11. ENTRY UNDER PHRASE

A phrase *that does not contain a real name* is to be entered in direct order. Omit the initial article, if there is one, in transcription of the heading. Note figures 11-18 and 1-6.

22.11B. If a person uses a forename plus another word or phrase in his or her works, enter under forename, followed by the word or phrase. This instruction is the reverse of former procedure. See figure 1-63; *The boy's book of sports and games* was previously entered under "Uncle John." Now the forename is the entry element: John, *Uncle*. A reference is made from the direct form of name:

>　　　Uncle John
>　　　　　*see*
>　　　John, *Uncle*.

22.11D. Correlate this rule with 21.5C. As mentioned before, 21.5C no longer maintains the distinction between entry under a characterizing word or phrase beginning with the definite article and one beginning with an indefinite article. See figure 1-60 for an example. Note omission of the article from the heading.

Rule 21.14A calls for entry under the heading for personal author when one can be determined, whether the person is named in the work or not. In the example shown in figure 11-11, it is a simple matter to look up the title, *Memoirs of a fox-hunting man*, to find out that the author is Siegfried Sassoon. References will be made, following directions in 21.11D:

>　　　Author of Memoirs of a fox-hunting man
>　　　　　*see*
>　　　Sassoon, Siegfried.
>
>　　　Memoirs of a fox-hunting man, Author of
>　　　　　*see*
>　　　Sassoon, Siegfried.

If the identity of the author cannot be ascertained after reasonable search,[7] enter under the phrase heading. (See figure 12-40.) Reference for such an entry will be:

>　　　"Evening amusement," Author of
>　　　　　*see*
>　　　Author of "Evening amusement."

The rules thus far have dealt with general principles governing the choice of names when a name appears in different formats in various places, and to the problem of determining which part of the name chosen (according to rules

---

[7] Harold S. Sharp, *Handbook of Pseudonyms and Personal Nicknames* (Metuchen, N.J.: Scarecrow Pr., 1972) would be useful. *Cushing* is useful for nineteenth-century authors.

22.1–22.3) to use as the entry element. Certain additions to personal names should be made under some circumstances. Rules 22.12 through 22.20 address themselves to these matters.

```
Author of "Evening amusement."
    My young days / by the author of "Evening amuse-
ment," "Letters everywhere," etc. etc. ; with
twenty illustrations by Paul Konewka. -- New York :
Dutton, 1871.
    151 p. : ill. ; 18 cm.
```

Figure 12-40. Entry under phrase

I. Title.

Title page

> My Young Days.
> by the
> Author of "Evening Amusement,"
> "Letters Everywhere," etc. etc.
> with twenty illustrations by
> Paul Konewka.
> New York:
> E. P. Dutton & Co., 713 Broadway.
> London: Seeley, Jackson, & Halliday.
> 1871.

Additions to Names

General

22.12. TITLES OF NOBILITY AND TERMS OF HONOUR AND ADDRESS, ETC.

If a nobleman or noblewoman chooses to write using his or her family name instead of proper name in the title, the person's preference is followed. Thus, although Dorothy Wellesley is the Duchess of Wellington, she chooses to use her family name (Wellesley). Under *AACR1* rule 46G1, her title in nobility was to be added: Wellesley, Dorothy, *Duchess of Wellington*. But under 22.12 the title of nobility will be added only if it is used along with the family name by the individual; see figure 12-41. Reference will be made from Wellesley's name in nobility:

> Wellington, Dorothy Wellesley, *Duchess of*
>   *see*
> Wellesley, Dorothy.

Wellesley, Dorothy.
  Desert wells / Dorothy Wellesley. -- London :
M. Joseph, 1946.
   55 p. ; 21 cm.

Figure 12-41. Name in
nobility not used

I. Title.

Dorothy Wellesley
Desert Wells
Michael Joseph Ltd.
26 Bloomsbury Street, London, W.C.1

Title page

The German title "Fürst," meaning "prince," is a title of honour given the
German statesman Bismarck in 1871. Since Bismarck was known by the title,
it is used as part of the heading; see figure 12-42.

Bismarck, Otto, Fürst von.
  Fürst Bismarcks Briefe an seine Braut und
Gattin / herausgegeben vom Fürsten Herbert Bis-
marck. -- 4. Aufl., mit Erläuterungen und Register
(Ergänzungsband) / von Horst Kohl ; Titelbild nach
Franz von Lenbach und zehn weitere Porträt-Beila-
gen. -- Stuttgart : J.G. Cotta, 1914.
   xvi, 596 p. : ports. ; 24 cm.

Figure 12-42. Term of
honour added

  I. Bismarck, Johanna von Puttkammer, Fürstin
von. II. Title.

Fürst Bismarcks Briefe
an seine Braut und Gattin
Herausgegeben vom Fürsten Herbert Bismarck
Vierte Auflage
Title page Mit Erläuterungen und Register (Ergänzungsband)
von Horst Kohl
Titelbild nach Franz von Lenbach
und zehn weitere Porträt-Beilagen
Stuttgart und Berlin 1914
J. G. Cotta'sche Buchhandlung Nachfolger

22.12B. British titles of honour

This rule is slightly changed from *AACR1* rule 46G2. The cataloguer will no longer add "bart." (baronet) following the name of a baronet. Since this term rarely, if ever, appeared with the name of an author in the chief source of information, it seems sensible to omit it. Use the name by which the author is commonly known; see figure 12-43.

```
Scott, Walter, Sir.
  The fortunes of Nigel / Sir Walter Scott ; edited
with an introduction by Frederick M. Link. --
Lincoln : University of Nebraska Press, c1965.
  xli, 488 p. ; 21 cm. -- (A Bison book ; ₍BB 321₎)



  I. Link, Frederick M.   II. Title.
```

Figure 12-43. British title of honour

	The Fortunes of Nigel
Title page	**Sir Walter Scott**
	Edited with an introduction
	by Frederick M. Link
	A Bison Book
	University of Nebraska Press • Lincoln

22.13. SAINTS

22.13A. The name of a saint will be established according to appropriate rules 22.1–22.11. The word "saint" is added to the name as it is thus established, unless the person was a pope, emperor, empress, king or queen, in which case, see 22.17A–B.

John of the Cross's name, as shown in figure 12-44, is established according to 22.8. English-language form is preferred; English-language reference sources are used (in this case the *National Catholic Encyclopedia*, 1967). (See also figure 1-87.)

```
John, of the Cross, Saint, 1542-1591.
  The poems of St. John of the Cross : original
Spanish texts and English versions / newly revised
and rewritten by John Frederick Nims ; with an
essay, A lo divino, by Robert Graves. -- Rev. ed.
-- New York : Grove Press, c1968.
  151 p. ; 21 cm.


  I. Nims, John Frederick.   II. Title.
```

Figure 12-44. Saint

Title page

> The Poems of St. John of the Cross
> Original Spanish texts and
> English versions newly revised and rewritten by
> John Frederick Nims
> With an essay *A Lo Divino* by Robert Graves
> Grove Press, Inc.   New York

22.13B. This rule is identical to *AACR1* rule 49C2. A suitable word or phrase will be added following the word "saint" and preceding dates (if any) to distinguish between two saints with identical names. The rule seems to be a curious exception to the general rules for distinguishing between identical names by the addition of dates (22.18) or, lacking dates, a distinguishing term in parentheses (22.19A).

A distinguishing phrase was added to the example shown in figure 12-45 because "Cyril, Saint, Patriarch of Alexandria, ca. 370–444" has also been established in the catalogue. The form of Cyril's name is established according to 22.3B3, from English-language reference sources (*Encyclopaedia Britannica*, 1971; *New Catholic Encyclopedia*, 1967). A reference may be made from the Latin form of the author's name:

> Cyrillus, *Saint, Bishop of Jerusalem*
>   *see*
> Cyril, *Saint, Bishop of Jerusalem, ca.* 315–386.

For another example of saint see figure 1-37.

```
Cyril, Saint, Bishop of Jerusalem, ca. 315-386.
   The works of Saint Cyril of Jerusalem / trans-
lated by Leo P. McCauley and Anthony A. Stephenson.
-- Washington : Catholic University of America
Press, c1969.
   2 v. ; 22 cm. -- (The Fathers of the Church ;
v. 61, 64)
```

Figure 12-45. Saint with identical name

```
I. Title.  II. Series.
```

Title page

> The Works of Saint Cyril of Jerusalem
> Translated by Leo P. McCauley, S.J.
> and Anthony A. Stephenson
> The Catholic University of America Press
> Washington, D.C. 20017

22.14. SPIRITS

Purported communications from spirits will now be entered under the name of the spirit, according to 21.26. To distinguish the works of the spirit from those of the flesh, the word "spirit" will be added following the name. See figure 11-39.

22.15. ADDITIONS TO NAMES ENTERED UNDER SURNAME

Under *AACR1* rule 46, entry of a person who chose to identify himself or herself only by a surname, or a surname and a term of address, was a curious contradiction to the general rule (40), which stipulated entry under the name by which the person was commonly identified. If an author chose to use only a forename (e.g. Hildegarde), it was to be used for entry. However, if an author used surname, or surname with a term of address, *AACR1* rule 46 stipulated that the name must be completed from reference sources. The rationale for this apparent inconsistency was that "a writer does not normally identify himself in his works by his forename only, except to conceal his identity. The forename is therefore used as a pseudonym, and is so treated. But the use of one's surname only is one way—an informal way—to identify a person who is bound to be identified also by his full name."[8]

AACR2 rule 22.15 has happily eliminated what had seemed to many a contradiction to the principles behind the rules for form of entry. If an author is "commonly known" by a surname, with or without a term of address, enter the author under the surname, followed by the term of address. See figures 1-52 and 2-5 for examples of an author who is commonly known by surname and a term of address. This author will be entered as: Molesworth, *Mrs.* Reference will be:

> Mrs. Molesworth
>   *see*
> Molesworth, *Mrs.*

22.15B. Terms of address of a married woman

A married woman who chooses to identify herself in her works by her husband's name plus the term of address "Mrs." will be entered in that way. The rule is identical to *AACR1* rule 46G3. See figure 1-39 for an example.

22.16. ADDITIONS TO NAMES CONSISTING OF OR CONTAINING INITIALS

This rule and rule 22.18 (dates) must be applied when necessary to distinguish between two or more persons whose names are identical. If no conflict exists in the catalogue, use the author's name in the form in which it is "commonly known." See H.D., for example (figure 12-2). The name of an author who is commonly known by initials or by a surname and one or more forenames represented by initials does not in itself present a problem. Such a name is governed by 22.1A, and will be entered according to that rule.

---

[8] Seymour Lubetzky, Correspondence, February 8, 1974, with author.

One of the objects of the catalogue is to provide a distinctive and uniform heading for each author represented in the library's collection. In the example shown in figure 12-46, no author has a name identical to Konigsburg's. If that had not been the case, a "conflict" in the catalogue would have existed that would have had to be resolved.

```
Konigsburg, E. L.
   From the mixed-up files of Mrs. Basil E. Frank-
weiler / written and illustrated by E.L. Konigsburg.
-- 1st ed. -- New York : Atheneum, 1967.
   162 p. : ill. ; 22 cm.




I. Title.
```

Figure 12-46. Name including initials

Title page

From the Mixed-up Files of
Mrs. Basil E. Frankweiler
written and illustrated by
E. L. Konigsburg
Atheneum   1967   New York

The problem of "conflicts" in the catalogue has been solved in different ways by the older cataloguing codes. A conflict under ALA 1949 rule 36 would have occurred relatively less frequently since ALA 1949 stipulated the use of the author's name in full, with a search made for forenames represented only by initials. Dates were added when available. Thus, regardless of whether the catalogue included another author of the same name or not, Konigsburg would have been searched and established as:

Konigsburg, Elaine Lobl, 1930–

Few library users know E. L. Konigsburg's forenames; the addition of such information often served to complicate rather than to solve problems of catalogue use. The next code, *AACR1*, brought a distinct improvement with rule 40 being almost the same as *AACR2* rule 22.1A. Under *AACR1* rules Konigsburg's name was established as:

Konigsburg, E   L

The space was left between the first and the second initials of the forenames so that if a future conflict should occur, the cataloguer could then fill in the unused forename(s) to resolve the conflict.

The provision seemed sensible. However, *AACR1* rule 43B directed the cataloguer "always [to] spell out a first forename represented by an initial if the surname is a common one." It seemed to critics of *AACR1* that this violated the spirit of the code, since it disregarded the author's preference and usage.

The rationale behind the provision was that although the catalogue may not now contain another A. S. Jones or T. J. Smith (or other author with common surname), eventually a confict may arise. Better to resolve it now than recatalogue later. Against such a spirit of "borrowing trouble," Michael Gorman said that the rule "represents a failure of nerve, a failure to carry through the logical consequence of the general rule."[9]

The problem of constructing an entry under the commonly known form of the author's name when more than one person has the same name has been solved in a highly satisfactory manner under 22.16. *If necessary to distinguish between identical names in the library's catalogue*, the cataloguer *may* add full forenames following initials. Thus, in the example shown in figure 12-46, if the library's catalogue included another E. L. Konigsburg, the heading for this author would be:

> Konigsburg, E. L. (Elaine Lobl)

In searching for the forenames, the date of birth would have been found as well (*Contemporary authors*, 21/22). At the option of the cataloguer, it may be added:

> Konigsburg, E. L. (Elaine Lobl), 1930–

Reference would be made from the full form of the name:

> Konigsburg, Elaine Lobl
>   *see*
> Konigsburg, E. L. (Elaine Lobl), 1930–

The example given in *AACR2* rule 22.16 for the treatment of H.D. (Hilda Doolittle) is appropriate if more than one author in the library catalogue uses the initials "H.D."

Optionally, a library may make additions according to provisions of 22.16 to all names containing initials, whether a conflict exists or not. The Library of Congress's position on this option is the same as is its practice in the matter of adding dates of birth, death, etc., to an author's name. Except to resolve a conflict, the cataloguer should not search reference sources to try to find information about an author's forenames (etc.) represented by initials. Use the information as it appears in the chief source of information. But if further information is "readily available"—on the dust jacket of the book, in prefatory material, or, for the Library of Congress, included in documentary information from the Copyright Office that is generally with the book as it reaches the cataloguer's desk, it seems only sensible to add it, and the Library of Congress will.[10] In the spirit of this ruling, some of the examples in this text show the application of 22.16; others do not.

---

[9] "A-A 1967: the New Cataloguing Rules," *Library Association Record* 70 (Feb. 1968):29.

[10] Library of Congress, Memorandum, April 13, 1978.

22.17. ADDITIONS TO NAMES ENTERED UNDER GIVEN NAME OR BYNAME

22.17A. Royalty

This rule is the same as *AACR1* rule 49B. See 22.8A for rules for form for the name of a monarch. The name will be given as it appears in English-language reference sources (see figure 12-47). The title will be in English if there is an English equivalent.

Henry VIII, King of England, 1491-1547.
    The letters of King Henry VIII : a selection, with a few other documents / edited by M. St. Clare Byrne. -- New ed., reprinted. -- New York : Funk & Wagnalls, c1968.
    xxiii, 455 p. : port. ; 22 cm.

    Bibliography: p. 430-441.
    ISBN 304-93969-1

Figure 12-47. Royalty

    I. Byrne, M. St. Clare.   II. Title.

Title page

The Letters of King
Henry VIII
A Selection, with a few other Documents
Edited by
M. St. Clare Byrne
Funk & Wagnalls
New York

Given in the appendixes is a list of headings formulated according to *AACR2* rules for personal entry for British sovereigns. If a library chooses to follow *AACR2*, the headings should be used. However, by Library of Congress policy decision (*LC Information Bulletin*, November 17, 1978), LC will continue to use "*King* (or *Queen*) *of England*" for monarchs through Elizabeth I. Beginning with James I and continuing to the present, LC will use "*King* (or *Queen*) *of Great Britain*" for all British monarchs.

As previously stated, examples in this text follow LC policy decision.

In addition, see Appendix II for a chart giving official *AACR2* format for British sovereigns acting in an official capacity.

To sum up provisions of 22.17A1–22.17.A3: Use English-language reference sources to determine the name of the monarch. Use a roman numeral if the name of the monarch has such associated with it. Do not include epithets or the word "saint." Royalty takes precedence over all other titles.

The form for the Prussian king Frederick the Great illustrates provisions of the rule. Despite the fact that German-language reference sources such as *Der grosse Brockhaus* (1953) list him as "Friedrich II, der Grosse," his name is to be established according to the form found in English-language sources. *Encyclopaedia Britannica* (1974) gives his name, with dates, as "Frederick II, the Great, of Prussia." Give references from the name by which he is commonly known in his home country:

> Friedrich II, *der Grosse*
> > *see*
> Frederick II, *King of Prussia*, 1712–1786.

A second reference is made from the epithet in English:

> Frederick, *the Great*
> > *see*
> Frederick II, *King of Prussia*, 1712–1786.

Catalogue entry will be as shown in figure 12-48.

```
Frederick II, King of Prussia, 1712-1786.
   Frederick the Great on the art of war / edited
and translated by Jay Luvaas. -- New York : Free
Press, c1966.
   xvi, 391 p. : ill., maps ; 22 cm.

   Bibliography: p. 375-378.
   Includes index.


   I. Luvaas, Jay.   II. Title.
```

Figure 12-48. Royalty

Title page

Edited and Translated by
Jay Luvaas
Frederick the Great on the Art of War
New York   The Free Press
London   Collier-Macmillan Limited

22.17A4. This rule is the same as *AACR1* rule 49B2. Appropriate title, as well as the phrase "consort of" and the name of the ruler, will be given for consorts of rulers. Prince Philip, Duke of Edinburgh and consort of Queen Elizabeth II of the United Kingdom, is an example of such a name. The *Encyclopedia Americana* lists him as "Philip, Prince, Duke of Edinburgh and consort of Queen Elizabeth II of England." Thus, he has two titles, Prince and Duke of

Edinburgh. The cataloguer should list him by his higher title, Prince. See figure 1-35 for an example, with Philip as author.

In the example shown in figure 12-49, added entry is made for the consort, under the terms of 21.30F.

```
Charles I, King of Great Britain, 1600-1649.
    Charles I in 1646 : letters of King Charles the
First to Queen Henrietta Maria / edited by John
Bruce. -- London : Printed for the Camden Society,
1856.
    xxi, 104 p. ; 22 cm. -- (Publications / Camden
Society ; no. 63)


    I. Henrietta Maria, Queen, consort of Charles I,
King of Great Britain, 1609-1669.  II. Title.
III. Series.
```

Figure 12-49. Consort of a ruler

Title page	Charles I. in 1646. Letters of King Charles the First to Queen Henrietta Maria. Edited by John Bruce, Esq. F.S.A. Printed for the Camden Society M.DCCC.LVI.

22.17B. Popes

A pope assumes a new name when he is elevated to the papacy. This name should be used, rather than his secular name, since it is the name by which he is commonly known. By the terms of 22.3B3, a person entered under given name whose name has become well established in an English form will be entered under the English form, as found in English-language reference sources. The rule is the same as *AACR1* rule 49D, but differs from ALA 1949 rule 48, which specified entry for a pope under his Latin pontifical name.

Pope John XXIII is listed in the *New Catholic Encyclopedia* (1967) as "John XXIII, Pope," with dates of birth and death and his secular name. By terms of 26.2A1 and 26.2A2, references should be made:

> Roncalli, Angelo Giuseppe
> *see*
> John XXIII, *Pope*, 1881-1968.

> Johannes XXIII, *Pope*
> *see*
> John XXIII, *Pope*, 1881-1968.

Catalogue entry will be as shown in figure 12-50.

John XXIII, Pope, 1881-1968.
  Mission to France, 1944-1953 / Angelo Giuseppe
Roncalli, Pope John XXIII ; edited by Loris Capo-
villa ; translated by Dorothy White. -- New York :
McGraw-Hill, c1966.
  xiv, 216 p. : ill., ports. ; 24 cm.

Figure 12-50. Pope

I. Capovilla, Loris. II. Title.

Title page

Angelo Giuseppe Roncalli
Pope John XXIII
Mission to France
1944–1953
Edited by Don Loris Capovilla
Translated by Dorothy White
McGraw-Hill Book Company
New York

22.17C. Bishops, etc.

Add the title, in English if possible, after the name of a high ecclesiastical official *who is entered under given name or byname*. The rule is the same as *AACR1* rule 49E; it differs from ALA 1949 rules 49, 50, 51, and 52 in that it applies *only* to persons entered under given name. No longer does the cataloguer add the designation after the name of a cardinal, bishop, etc., who is entered under surname. See for an example figure 1-42. Although Cardinal Newman consistently used his ecclesiastical title in his later writings, and although he is commonly known as Cardinal Newman, the fact that he is entered under surname means that his ecclesiastical title will not be retained in the heading.

22.17D. Other persons of religious vocation

This rule is the same as *AACR1* rule 49F. Like the previous rule, it applies *only* to persons of religious vocation who are commonly known by given name and who are thus entered. Add to such a name in the vernacular terms of honor, address, or title as customarily used by the person. Do *not* add a religious title to the name of a person of religious vocation who is entered under surname. This rule differs from ALA 1949 rule 53 in this respect.

The author represented in the example given in figure 12-51 occasionally writes under his secular name, William Everson. He is best known as Brother Antoninus; under the stipulations of 22.2C2 the cataloguer will choose that name as the predominant name, to be used for all of this author's works. Reference will be made from his secular name to his name in religion (26.2A1):

> Everson, William
> *see*
> Antoninus, *Brother*.

Antoninus, <u>Brother</u>.
   The crooked lines of God : poems, 1949–1954 / by Brother Antoninus. -- 2nd ed. -- ₍Detroit₎ : University of Detroit Press, 1960, c1959.
   88 p. ; 22 x 23 cm. -- (Contemporary poets series)

I. Title. II. Series.

Figure 12-51. Person of religious vocation

Title page

The Crooked Lines of God

Poems 1949–1954
by Brother Antoninus
Contemporary Poets Series
The University of Detroit Press / 1960

Likewise, for the example shown in figure 12-52, the cataloguer will make a reference from Father Cuthbert's secular name to the name by which he is commonly known:

> Hess, Lawrence Anthony
> *see*
> Cuthbert, *Father*, O.S.F.C.

Cuthbert, <u>Father</u>, O.S.F.C.
   The Capuchins : a contribution to the history
of the counter-reformation / Father Cuthbert,
O.S.F.C. -- New York : Longmans, Green, 1929.
   2 v. : ports. ; 22 cm.

Includes bibliographical references.

Figure 12-52. Person of
religious vocation

I. Title.

Title page

Father Cuthbert, O.S.F.C.
The Capuchins
A Contribution to the History of the
Counter-reformation
Longmans, Green and Co.
55 Fifth Avenue, New York
210 Victoria St., Toronto
1929

Additions to Distinguish Identical Names

22.18. DATES

This rule is slightly changed in its intent from the corresponding *AACR1* rule 52, which stipulated that dates would be added as the last element of the heading "if they are readily ascertainable at the time the heading is established." The Library of Congress interpreted "readily ascertainable" to mean that "a cataloger should search for a birthdate when the likelihood is great that it can be found in a work in the cataloger's reference collection."[11] *AACR2* states that dates will be added to distinguish between two or more authors "if the headings are otherwise identical."

According to an option in 22.18, dates may be added to personal names even when there is no need to distinguish between headings. The Library of Congress has determined to apply this option "where the necessary information is readily available."[12] Presumably it will continue to interpret "readily avail-

[11] Library of Congress, *Cataloging Service Bulletin* 99 (April 1971).
[12] Library of Congress, Memorandum, April 13, 1978.

able" as was done under *AACR1*. Another interpretation, probably more feasible for most cataloguers, is that dates are to be considered "readily available"—and thus to be recorded—if they are found in the work being catalogued. They are also "readily available" if they are found in the course of otherwise necessary searching, as when checking reference sources to determine the proper form of a name of a person to be entered under 22.3B3, 22.3C1, etc. Dates have been added to headings in this text in the spirit of the optional rule, which seems a sensible provision for cataloguers to follow.

22.19. DISTINGUISHING TERMS

Obviously, if a person's name is the same as another name in the catalogue, the cataloguer will need to make every reasonable effort to provide dates, preferably for both headings. But if the cataloguer cannot find dates to resolve a conflict, a suitable brief descriptive designation may be added. More leeway about terminology is given in the case of names entered under given name; when distinguishing between two names entered under surname, the rule stipulates that the cataloguer is to confine distinguishing terms to statements appearing on the title page of the work catalogued or taken from reference sources. This instruction is the same as that in *AACR1* rule 53; it differs from ALA 1949 rule 42, which allowed the cataloguer to create "descriptive designations denoting profession, occupation, residence, etc." as each case warranted and as the cataloguer's fancy dictated. The designations were often more a source of confusion to library users than a help. The provisions of the present rule are more useful in the few cases in which a conflict cannot otherwise be resolved.

13

Geographic Names

(*AACR2* Chapter 23)

The rules for geographic names, formerly buried in the middle of *AACR1* chapter 3, Headings for Corporate Bodies, are now properly placed as a brief introductory chapter covering a very important aspect pertinent to many headings for corporate names. Geographic names are needed to represent governments as headings (24.3E); in addition, many government bodies are entered subordinately to such geographic names (24.17–24.26). Other geographic names are used to differentiate between identical corporate names (24.4C). Chapter 23 gives guidance about the form of name that should be used.

23.2A. Language

This rule is the same as *AACR1* rule 72. The English form of geographic name is to be used, rather than the form used by residents of the place, if there is a common English form. In some cases this instruction may prove to be a barrier to international exchange of cataloguing information, but it is an easy and satisfactory rule for English-language libraries. It will certainly lead to a "sought" heading in such libraries.

23.4. ADDITIONS TO PLACE NAMES

This rule is the same in its intent as was *AACR1* rule 73 as modified by LC *Cataloging Service Bulletin* 88 (January 1970). The original intent of rule 73 was to eliminate the addition of the name of a larger geographic entity (such as a state) to the name of a place (such as a city or town) unless the cataloguer knew that there were two or more places with the same name. The intent was in keeping with the philosophy of the authors of the rules, that the catalogue was not, after all, a reference tool. It was not the business of the catalogue in the illustrations given in *AACR1* rule 65A1, for example, to inform the user that Decorah was in Iowa, New Ulm was in Minnesota, and Wahoo was in Nebraska, when the three cities were added to three institutions having identical names: Luther College. It was sufficient for purposes of differentiating between the three

Luther Colleges to add the name of the city without distinguishing it by state. This rule put a burden on the cataloguer who accepted the directive at its face value. In order to be sure, the cataloguer had to look up every town or city in a gazetteer to see if, indeed, there might be another Decorah somewhere, or another Wahoo, in which case the state would be added. Perhaps this practice entered into the thinking of the committee in revising the rule. The revision given in the *Cataloging Service Bulletin* pretty much returned to practices prescribed under earlier ALA 1949 rule 153. It called for the addition of state or province to the name of cities or towns in the United States and Canada, in accepted abbreviated form (153A), and the name of country or other entity to cities outside of the United States and Canada, in abbreviated form (153B), except for "largest or best-known city of its name, in America or elsewhere." Cities on this list (153C) were to be entered without further designation.

AACR2 rule 23.4B no longer makes the distinction between "largest or best-known" cities and others. Officially, the rule is much like the original version of *AACR1* rule 73: The larger place is to be added to distinguish between two or more places of the same name. However, the option allows addition of the larger place even if there is no need to distinguish between identical names. LC has stipulated that it means to adopt this option. Probably other libraries will do likewise. Notice that whenever the larger place is added, it is added in parentheses.

14

Headings for Corporate Bodies

(AACR2 Chapter 24)

Once the cataloguer has determined, according to *AACR2* chapter 21, that a corporate body is to serve as either main or added entry in a catalogue, the problem of proper form of name remains to be decided. In many respects the chapter giving rules for corporate names parallels that for personal headings. Each chapter starts with a general rule (22.1 for personal headings, 24.1 for corporate headings); the principle behind each rule is the same: Enter either the person or the corporate body under the name most likely to be known by the library user, i.e., the sought heading.

24.1. BASIC RULE

With certain exceptions, which are necessary because of the complexity of corporate structure and which are treated later in the rules, the cataloguer is to enter a corporate body directly under its name. This rule is basically the same as *AACR1* rule 60; it differs from comparable rules in ALA 1949, which made a distinction between entry of a society (to be entered directly under its name, rule 91) and an institution (to be entered under place, rule 92). These two ALA rules, with their subtle distinctions and exceptions that puzzled cataloguers and library users alike, were subsumed by *AACR1* rule 60 under the general principle governing all of the *AACR* rules for form of names: the name by which the corporate body identifies itself will be the preferred form for the heading.

As with a personal heading (22.1B), the "predominant" form of name will be determined by works issued by the body in its language; see figure 14-1.

The name of a corporate body that consists of or contains initials will be recorded following stipulations of *AACR2* rule 1.1B6. Do not leave a space between initials, or between full stop and a following initial. Include or omit full stops between initials according to the body's usage; see figures 14-2 and 14-3.

```
Das Verlagswesen in der Bundesrepublik Deutschland
   / dargestellt vom Deutschen Bucharchiv München.
   -- Rastatt : Verlag für Zeitgeschichtliche
   Dokumentation, 1971.
   71 p. : ill. ; 20 cm. -- (Deutschland Report ;
4)
```

Figure 14-1. Form of name in language of body

```
I. Deutsches Bucharchiv München.   II. Series.
```

Title page

Das Verlagswesen
in der Bundesrepublik Deutschland
Dargestellt vom Deutschen Bucharchiv München
Verlag für Zeitgeschichtliche Dokumentation

```
The Teachers' library : how to organize it and
   what to include / AASL-TEPS Coordinating Com-
   mittee for the Teachers' Library Project ;
   Margaret Nicholsen, chairman ... [et al.]. --
   1968 ed. -- Washington : American Association of
   School Librarians : National Education Association,
   1968.
   208 p. ; 23 cm.
```

Figure 14-2. Initials as part of name

```
   I. AASL-TEPS Coordinating Committee for the
Teachers' Library Project.
```

AASL-TEPS Coordinating Committee
for the Teachers'
Library Project
Margaret Nicholsen, Chairman
Ruth Bauner
Don Davies
Lawrence A. Lemons

The Teachers' Library
How to Organize It and What to Include
1968 Edition
American Association of School Librarians
National Commission for Teacher Education
and Professional Standards
National Education Association

Facing title page

Title page

```
Du Pont : the autobiography of an American enter-
   prise : the story of E.I. Du Pont de Nemours &
   Company : published in commemoration of the 150th
   anniversary of the founding of the company on
   July 19, 1802. -- Wilmington, Del. : The Company ;
   New York : Distributed by Scribner, c1952.
   138 p. : ill. (some col.), ports. (some col.) ;
32 cm.
```

Figure 14-3. Initials as part of name

```
I. E. I. Du Pont de Nemours & Company.
```

Title page

Du Pont
The Autobiography of an American Enterprise
The Story of E. I. Du Pont de Nemours & Company
published in commemoration of the 150th anniversary
of the founding of the company on July 19, 1802.
E. I. Du Pont de Nemours & Company
Wilmington, Delaware
Distributed by Charles Scribner's Sons, New York

24.1B. Changes of name

This rule is the same as *AACR1* rule 68. The *AACR1* rule was an important change from ALA 1949 rules 91 and 92, which called for entry of societies and institutions under the latest form of name. The ALA rules, which are similar to *AACR2* 22.2B for personal names, served, as does 22.2B for personal authors, to bring together in one place in the catalogue all of the publications of a corporate body, no matter how many names it had used during the course of its history. However, it remained for Seymour Lubetzky, in his *Cataloging Rules and Principles*, to point out that corporate bodies as authors are not at all like personal authors. A person, even though he or she may change names, remains the same person. On the other hand, said Lubetzky,

> The life of a corporate body may be considerably longer than that of a personal author and it is always subject to various organizational and constitutional changes. These changes are normally reflected in changes in its name. The question arises, therefore, whether a body whose name has been changed should be regarded, for purposes of entry, as the same body or as a different body.[1]

[1] Washington: Library of Congress, 1953; p. 50.

The present rules take the position that a corporate body that has changed its name is, indeed, a different entity. Entry will be made under successive names used by the body. References will be made between the various names. For examples, see figures 10-4 and 10-5. A reader seeking all of the publications of the Center under its various names would be aided by explanatory references from both names:

> Midwest Inter-library Center
> > For works by this body see also the later heading:
> Center for Research Libraries.

> Center for Research Libraries
> > For works by this body see also the earlier heading:
> Midwest Inter-library Center.

24.2. VARIANT NAMES. GENERAL RULES

As long as the name of a corporate body appears in a consistent form in its publications, the name is to be used as it appears. But sometimes a corporate body, although it has not changed its name, lists it in different forms in its publications. Rule 24.2, which is the equivalent, somewhat modified, of *AACR1* rule 62, gives guidance about which of the varying forms to choose as heading.

24.2B. This rule is the same as the introductory paragraph in *AACR1* rule 62, with a slight modification in wording. Prefer the form of a corporate name that is found in the chief source of information (the title page of a book) rather than forms found elsewhere in the item (in the text, in running titles, or elsewhere in the book).

24.2D. If the chief source of information gives the name in more than one form, prefer a "formal" presentation (i.e., at the head of the title, in the imprint, in the statement of responsibility) rather than another form, such as might be presented in the title of the work. If this instruction does not solve the problem, the suggestion that the cataloguer use the "predominant" form seems to involve a combination of counting and cataloguer's judgment.

In case of doubt, prefer a brief form over the spelled-out form of the body's name. The tenuous distinction made in *AACR1* between a brief form that has been written in capital and lowercase letters as a word (62A1) and one formed of syllables of the name (62A2), in contrast to an acronym such as AFL-CIO, as an acceptable entry is no longer made. If a brief form is the predominant form, it will be used; see figure 14-4.

Following 26.3A3, reference will be made:

> Educational Resources Information Center
> > *see*
> ERIC.

Aslib is another example of a corporate body that uses a brief form of name on its publications. Note that the cataloguer will transcribe the name with capitalization according to the body's preferences, e.g. "ERIC" consistently appears in all capital letters; "Aslib," in contrast, is written as a word, with an initial capital and the rest lowercase letters (see figure 14-5).

ERIC.
　How to use ERIC / U.S. Department of Health,
Education, and Welfare, National Institute of Education, Educational Resources Information Center.
-- Rev. -- Washington : ERIC, 1972.
　14 p. : ill. ; 20 x 26 cm. -- (DHEW publication
no. (OE) 72-129)

Figure 14-4. Brief form
of name

I. Title. II. Series.

Title page
　　　　How to Use ERIC
U.S. Department of Health, Education, and Welfare
National Institute of Education
Educational Resources Information Center

As with ERIC, reference will be made for Aslib:

Association of Special Libraries and Information Bureaux
　　　see
Aslib.

Robertson, S. E.
　Five specialised information centres : a report /
by Aslib to the Office for Scientific and Technical
Information ; S.E. Robertson and R. Reynolds,
[authors]. -- London : Aslib, 1969.
　ix, 48 p. : ill. ; 30 cm. -- (OSTI report ; no.
5050)

Figure 14-5. Brief form
of name

I. Reynolds, R. II. Aslib. III. Great Britain.
Office for Scientific and Technical Information.
IV. Title.

Title page

OSTI Report No 5050

October 1969

Five Specialised Information Centres

A report by Aslib to the

Office for Scientific and Technical Information

S. E. Robertson and R. Reynolds

Aslib,

3 Belgrave Square,

London, S.W.1.

The name American Philosophical Society appears on the title page (chief source) for figure 1-77. The half title lists the society's full name, American Philosophical Society held at Philadelphia for Promoting Useful Knowledge. The cataloguer will choose the briefer, title-page form for entry.

Sometimes the brief form of the name used by a corporate body in some of its publications is the same as the name of another organization, or it does not provide adequate identification for cataloguing. If this is the case, the last paragraph of 24.2D directs the cataloguer to use the form found in reference sources or "the official form." This instruction is the same as *AACR1* rule 62B.

The National Research Council of Canada sometimes is so listed in its publications; sometimes it appears as National Research Council. The brief form is not sufficient to identify the body, since there is another organization of the same name based in Washington, D.C. *World of Learning* (1973–74) gives the official form of name for the Canadian body as National Research Council of Canada. This is the form, rather than the brief form, that will be used for entry. See figure 1-88.

24.3. VARIANT NAMES. SPECIAL RULES

24.3A. Language

This rule is the same as *AACR1* rule 64. When the name of a corporate body appears in its publications in different languages, the official language of the body is to be used for the heading. In countries, such as Canada, where there is more than one official language, if one of the languages is English, use the English-language form. The Canadian School Library Association is an example of such a corporate body; see figure 14-6.

24.3B. Language. International bodies

Use the English form, if one exists, for works issued by an international body. See, for example, added entry II under figure 2-17. This rule is the same as *AACR1* rule 64A.

24.3C. Conventional name

This rule is the same as *AACR1* rule 63A. It has no parallel in ALA 1949. The cataloguer is directed to make entry under conventional name in preference to official name or the name as it appears on publications when such a conventional name appears in reference sources in the language of the publications. LC *Cataloging Service Bulletin* 96 (November 1970) amplified the rule, stating:

> It is important that catalogers be alert to recognize that, at a given point in a corporate body's history, it may become "frequently identified by a conventional form of name" . . . . When that point is reached, headings under the official form of name should be changed to the conventional form . . . .

```
Canadian School Library Association.
  Standards of library service for Canadian
schools / recommended by the Canadian School Li-
brary Association. -- Toronto : Ryerson Press,
c1967.
  xii, 68 p. ; 23 cm.

Bibliography: p. 65-68.



  I. Title.
```

Figure 14-6. One of official languages is English

Title page

Standards of Library Service
For Canadian Schools

Recommended by the
Canadian School Library Association
Association Canadienne des Bibliotheques Scolaires

The Ryerson Press

One of the headings that the Library of Congress changed in accordance with the provisions of this rule is that for the report of the President's Commission on the Assassination of President John F. Kennedy. This commission has become better known as the Warren Commission; it is so listed in the *Encyclopedia Americana* (1970) under Warren Commission report, with the following information:

> The published findings of the investigation of the U.S. President's Commission on the Assassination of President John F. Kennedy. The Warren Commission was established November 29, 1963.

The heading should appear as shown in figure 14-7. According to 26.3A3, reference will be made:

> President's Commission on the Assassination of President
>   John F. Kennedy
>   *see*
> Warren Commission.

```
Warren Commission.
  The Warren report : report of the President's
Commission on the Assassination of President John
F. Kennedy. -- [New York] : Associated Press,
[1964?]
  xiii, 366 p. : ill., maps, ports. ; 26 cm.
```

Figure 14-7.
Conventional name

```
I. Title.
```

Title page

The Warren Report
Report of
the President's Commission on the
Assassination of
President John F. Kennedy

24.3C2. Ancient and international bodies. This rule is identical to *AACR1* rule 63B. It is limited to bodies of ancient origin or those international in character with names that have become established in an English form in English-language usage. With a directive that is analogous to that given in 22.3B3 for a similar situation, the cataloguer is told to enter such a body in the English-language form of its name. Check English-language reference sources to determine the name when in doubt.

The Orthodox Eastern Church is a body of ancient origin and one that is international in character. It is listed in *Encyclopaedia Britannica* (1971) as the Orthodox Eastern Church, with information that it is also known as the Orthodox Church and the Greek Orthodox Church. The heading for this body will be the one found in the *Encyclopaedia;* see figure 14-8. References will be made:

> Orthodox Church
>> *see*
> Orthodox Eastern Church
>
> Greek Orthodox Church
>> *see*
> Orthodox Eastern Church.
>
> L'Église orthodoxe
>> *see*
> Orthodox Eastern Church.

```
Meyendorff, John.
  [L'Église orthodoxe.  English]
  The Orthodox Church : its past and its role in
the world today / by John Meyendorff ; translated
from the French by John Chapin. -- New York :
Pantheon Books, c1962.
  xii, 244 p. ; 21 cm.

  Translation of: L'Église orthodoxe.
  Includes bibliographies and indexes.


  1. Orthodox Eastern Church.  I. Title.
```

Figure 14-8.
Conventional name

Title page

The Orthodox Church
Its Past and Its Role in the World Today
by
John Meyendorff
Translated from the French by John Chapin
Pantheon Books
A Division of Random House
New York

24.3D. Religious orders and societies

This rule is the same as *AACR1* rule 96A. As with other ancient and international bodies, the English-language form should be chosen for entry. In figure 2-12 the religious body (added entry I) should be entered in conventional English form rather than in the language of the country of its origin. Reference will be made:

> Benedictines. Congrégation de France (Solesmes)
>   *see*
> Benedictines of Solesmes.

24.3E. Governments

This rule is the same as *AACR1* rule 75. If the name of a government appears in varying forms, use the conventional name rather than the official name. Thus, the cataloguer will use "France" rather than "République Française." However, do not forget that a change has been made from *AACR1* rule 77 A2. Use the name Union of Soviet Socialist Republics rather than Russia. (See 23.2A.)

Another word of caution: If the name of the government changes, the cataloguer will use the heading appropriate to the date of the original issue of a publication. Cataloguers who choose to follow *AACR2* without regard for LC policy will use the heading "England" for publications issued before 1536; *AACR2* calls for "England and Wales" as the heading for official publications issued during 1536–1706. "Great Britain" will be used for official publications issued during 1707–1800. For official publications issued 1801 to present, "United Kingdom" is the official *AACR2* heading (see 26.3C1b).

However, the Library of Congress, in a statement issued in the *LC Information Bulletin* November 17, 1978 (p. 710) plans to continue to use the heading "Great Britain" as it has done in the past. This decision, referred to in this text as "LC policy decision" will be reflected in examples in this text, since this text attempts to follow LC practice.

24.3F. Conferences, congresses, meetings, etc.
This rule is directed to choice among varying names of conferences. For conferences, see the discussion in this text, under 24.7.

24.3G. Local churches, etc.
This rule is the same as *AACR1* rule 98 as modified by LC *Cataloging Service Bulletin* 109 (May 1974). Use the name of the church as it appears in its publications in the chief source of information. If the name varies, use the predominant form. If there is no predominant form, choose a name according to order of preference as given under 24.3G. For examples and discussion of the entire rule, see under 24.10 in this text.

Additions, Omissions, and Modifications

The foregoing rules have dealt with basic problems of entry. The basic rule is constructed on the same principle as that governing personal names: Use the name by which the body is predominantly identified. If this name changes, see 24.1B for guidance. If, without actually changing its name, the body uses varying forms of the same name in its publications, 24.2–24.3 give directions for choosing among varying forms. But sometimes the name of the body as it appears in its publications is the same as that of another corporate body. Sometimes the name as it appears does not clearly give the idea that it belongs to a corporate body. Other problems also enter into the formation of corporate headings that necessitate additions, omissions, and modifications of the name in some instances. The following rules give guidance in such cases.

24.4. ADDITIONS
All additions to corporate names will be enclosed in parentheses.

24.4B. Names not conveying the idea of a corporate body
For such bodies, in a ruling analogous to that for the addition of distinguishing terms to personal names (22.19A), a suitable general designation or qualification will be added, simply for clarification. The example given in figure 14-9

has as its subject the yacht named Britannia. The word "Britannia," its commonly known name, has many possible meanings aside from the intended one. Therefore a general designation (*Ship*) should be added.

```
Philip, Prince, consort of Elizabeth II, Queen of
   Great Britain, 1921-
   Seabirds in southern waters / His Royal Highness
the Prince Philip, Duke of Edinburgh. -- 1st ed. --
New York : Harper & Row, c1962.
   62 p. : ill. ; 25 cm.



   1. Britannia (Ship).   I. Title.
```

Figure 14-9. Addition
to name

Title page

Seabirds in Southern Waters
His Royal Highness
The Prince Philip
Duke of Edinburgh
Harper & Row, Publishers
New York

Note the example given under 24.4B: Friedrich Witte (*Firm*). Except for the addition of the qualifying word, it would appear to be a personal name. Use this form for subjects or for main or added entry headings only, not for the name of such a firm appearing in the publisher statement.

24.4C. Two or more bodies with the same or similar names

24.4C1. When two persons have the same name or names so similar that they are likely to be confused, the names are distinguished by spelling out forenames in parentheses (22.16), by adding dates of birth and death (22.18), or by adding a distinguishing term (22.19). To distinguish between corporate bodies with an identical or similar name, a word or phrase may be added to the name. Optionally, the name of a place may be added, even where there is no need to distinguish between bodies. The Library of Congress will apply this option on a limited, case-by-case basis.[2]

24.4C2. Names of countries, states, provinces, etc. This rule is the same as *AACR1* rule 65B. For organizations of national, state, provincial, etc., character that need to be distinguished from other organizations with the same name, add in parentheses the name of the country, state, etc. as appropriate, using abbreviations from *AACR2* Appendix B.

[2] Library of Congress, Memorandum, April 13, 1978.

The British organization called Social Science Research Council has the same name as a similar organization in the United States. Since it is a national organization, the name of the country (Great Britain) will be added in parentheses after the name of the body. See figure 1-64 for this example.

24.4C3. Local place names. This rule is basically the same as *AACR1* rule 65A, except for the fact that the name of the local place is added in parentheses instead of the format prescribed by rule 65A. In adding a local place name, omit the name of the larger geographic entity if that entity is part of the name of the body. In figure 14-10 added entry III illustrates the provisions of this rule.

```
Computers and education : a workshop conference at
    University of California, Irvine / edited by R.W.
    Gerard with the assistance of J.G. Miller. --
    New York : McGraw-Hill, c1967.
    xxi, 307 p. : ill. ; 24 cm.

    "Organized by University of California, Irvine,
with support of U.S. Office of Education ... project
no. 5-0997, contract no. OE-5-16-022."

    I. Gerard, R.W.  II. Miller, J.G.  III. University
of California (Irvine).  IV. United States.  Office
of Education.
```

Figure 14-10. Local place name

Title page

Computers and Education
A Workshop Conference at
University of California, Irvine
Edited by R. W. Gerard
With the Assistance of J. G. Miller
McGraw-Hill Book Company
New York   St. Louis   San Francisco
Toronto   London   Sydney

24.4C4. The name of the town or city in which the body is located will be added to distinguish between bodies having similar or identical names, or, optionally, such a place name may be added to other bodies. If the option is applied, the place name, despite the examples shown under 24.4C4, should include the name of the larger place, e.g. state, for a city in the United States; province, for a city in Canada; county, for a place in the British Isles; or country for other places (cf. 23.4). Note that if the option is applied, state will be added following city for *all* cities in the United States; there is no longer a list of "best known" cities for which state need not be added.

In the example shown in figure 14-11, place was added following the name of this corporate body because there is another association of the same name in Detroit.

```
Players (New York, N.Y.)
  Catalogue of the paintings and the art treasures
of the Players. -- New York : Players, 1925.
  112 p. ; 21 cm.
```

Figure 14-11. Addition
of place

```
I. Title.
```

Title page

Catalogue of the Paintings and the
Art Treasures of The Players
MCMXXV
16 Gramercy Park
New York

24.5. OMISSIONS

24.5A. Initial articles

This rule is virtually the same as *AACR1* rule 66A, with one important difference. No longer will the initial article ("the" or its equivalent in foreign languages) be included when the cataloguer thinks it is needed "for reasons of clarity." It will be included only if it is required for grammatical reasons. See examples under 24.5A for instances in which grammatically the initial article must be kept. According to *AACR1* rule 66A, the heading for figure 14-11 would have been "The Players." The initial article will now be dropped.

24.5C. Terms indicating incorporation, etc.

This rule is the same as *AACR1* rule 66E. Terms indicating incorporation, etc., may be omitted, in most instances, from the name of a corporate body. See added entry I in example shown in figure 14-12. Note, by the way, that "Inc." is now capitalized wherever it appears in the entry.

```
Carr, William H.
  The desert speaks : the story of the Arizona-
Sonora Desert Museum, Inc., 1951-1973 / by William
H. Carr. -- 4th rev. ed. -- Tucson : The Museum,
1973.
  44 p. : ill. ; 23 cm.
```

Figure 14-12. "Inc."
omitted

```
I. Arizona-Sonora Desert Museum.  II. Title.
```

Title page

The Desert Speaks
The Story of the
Arizona-Sonora Desert Museum, Inc.
1951–1973
by William H. Carr
Founder and Director Emeritus,
Arizona-Sonora Desert Museum
Fourth Revised Edition, 1973
Arizona-Sonora Desert Museum, Inc.
Tucson, Arizona

If such a term is necessary to make it clear that the name is that of a corporate body, include the term; see figure 14-13. If the term indicating incorporation cannot be omitted, follow the punctuation customarily used by the corporate body, either including or omitting the comma preceding the term, as appropriate.[3] (See figure 14-14.)

```
Flavor research and food acceptance : a survey of
   the scope of flavor and associated research /
   compiled from papers presented in a series of
   symposia given in 1956-1957 ; sponsored by
   Arthur D. Little, Inc. -- New York : Reinhold,
   c1958.
   vi, 391 p. : ill. ; 24 cm.

Includes bibliographies and index.


I. Arthur D. Little, Inc.
```

Figure 14-13. "Inc." included

Title page

Flavor Research and Food Acceptance
Sponsored by
Arthur D. Little, Inc.
A survey of the scope of flavor
and associated research, compiled
from papers presented in a series
of symposia given in 1956–1957.
Reinhold Publishing Corporation
New York
Chapman & Hall, Ltd., London

[3] *Cataloging Service Bulletin* 96 (Nov. 1970).

```
Elson, Robert T.
  Time Inc. : the intimate history of a publishing
enterprise, 1923-1941 / by Robert T. Elson ;
edited by Duncan Norton-Taylor. -- 1st ed. -- New
York : Atheneum, 1968.
  x, 500 p. : ill., ports. ; 24 cm.


  Includes bibliographical footnotes and index.




  1. Time Inc.  I. Norton-Taylor, Duncan.
```

Figure 14-14. "Inc." included

Title page

Time Inc.
The Intimate History of a Publishing Enterprise
1923-1941
By Robert T. Elson
Edited by Duncan Norton-Taylor
New York   Atheneum   1968

24.6. GOVERNMENTS

This rule is the equivalent of *AACR1* rule 77. The headings are used, with or without subdivision, as appropriate, for official publications of a government. For examples and further discussion see under 24.17 in this text. See also *AACR2* 21.31–21.36.

24.7. CONFERENCES, CONGRESSES, MEETINGS, ETC.

This rule is the equivalent of *AACR1* rules 37–91. A conference, workshop, institute, etc., is a meeting convened "for the purpose of discussing and acting on topics of common interest."[4] By terms of 21.1.B2d, a conference heading may be the main entry for works that record the collective activity of the conference, e.g., its proceedings or collected papers. To be used as the main entry heading, however, the conference name must appear prominently in the item being catalogued.

Before making main entry under the name of a conference, the cataloguer must first determine whether the conference actually is a named conference according to 21.1B1 or whether the phrase referring to it is only a general

[4] *AACR2* Appendix D, Glossary, p. 565, s.v. "Conference."

description. Very often a meeting is called simply by a generic term such as "conference," "meeting," or "convention." Do not consider these terms alone as names. Many meetings referred to in this way are meetings of organizations. As long as the meeting itself is considered unnamed and the item being catalogued deals with the internal policies, procedures, and/or operations of the body (21.1B2), the work may be entered under the name of the organization holding the meeting. See figure 14-15.

```
Society of American Foresters.
  Proceedings / Society of American Foresters
meeting, September 28-October 2, 1958, Hotel Utah,
Salt Lake City, Utah. -- Washington : The Society,
c1959.
  215 p. : ill., ports. ; 23 cm.




  I. Title.
```

Figure 14-15. Meeting of an organization

Title page

Proceedings
Society of American Foresters
Meeting
September 28-October 2, 1958
Hotel Utah
Salt Lake City, Utah
Published by
Society of American Foresters
Mills Building
Washington 6, D.C.
Copyright 1959, by Society of American Foresters

Many conferences do not include the word "conference" as part of their name. In addition, a smaller seminar, symposium, conference, etc., held in conjunction with a larger meeting may be treated as a corporate body if it is a "named" meeting, according to *AACR2* 21.1B1. See figure 14-16. For another example of a conference publication, see figure 11-5.

```
Graduate Record Examinations Board Research
   Seminar (1972 : New Orleans, La.)
   Papers / presented at the Graduate Record Exami-
nations Board Research Seminar at the 12th annual
meeting of the Council of Graduate Schools. --
Princeton, N.J. : Educational Testing Service,
1973.
   38 p. : graphs ; 28 cm.

   Contents: Background, purpose, and scope of the
GRE Board research program / Bryce Crawford, Jr. --
Predicting success in graduate education / Warren
W. Willingham -- Research on testing and the
minority student / Ronald L. Flaugher.

   I. Council of Graduate Schools.  II. Title.
```

Figure 14-16. Named conference

Title page

Papers Presented at the
Graduate Record Examinations Board
Research Seminar
at the
12th Annual Meeting of the
Council of Graduate Schools
Educational Testing Service
Princeton, N.J. 08540
May, 1973

24.7A. Omissions

This rule is the same as *AACR1* rule 88C. The number of the conference, if it appears as the first word of the name, is omitted and given in parentheses as the first addition to the name of the conference (24.7B2). See figure 14-17.

```
Lunar Science Conference (5th : 1974 : Houston,
   Tex.)
   Lunar science V : abstracts of papers submitted
to the Fifth Lunar Science Conference ; sponsored
by NASA through the Lunar Science Institute and
the Johnson Space Center, March 18-22, 1974 ;
compiled by the Lunar Science Institute. --
Houston : The Institute, 1974.
   xxv, 900 p. : ill. ; 28 cm.


   I. United States.  National Aeronautics and
Space Administration.  II. Lunar Science Institute.
III. Johnson Space Center.  IV. Title.
```

Figure 14-17. Named conference (omit number from the name)

Lunar Science V
Abstracts of Papers Submitted to the
Fifth Lunar Science Conference
Sponsored by NASA through
The Lunar Science Institute
and
The Johnson Space Center
March 18-22, 1974
Compiled by The Lunar Science Institute
3303 NASA Road 1, Houston, Texas　77058

Title page

24.7B. Additions

24.7B1. The order in which additions to the conference name will be recorded is different from that given in *AACR1* rule 87. Additions will now be in the following order: number of conference, year, and place.

24.7B2. Number. If a conference has a number, it is the first of the additions that follow the name of the conference. (See figure 14-17.) Not all conferences are numbered. Simply omit this element if the conference has no number (cf. figure 14-16). Note, however, that a number may be inferred when information available to the cataloguer clearly indicates the position of the meeting within a series of meetings of the same name.

24.7B3. Date. In almost all cases, the date to be added is the *year only;* see figure 14-18. Add specific dates as shown in the last example under 24.7B3 in *AACR2* only if more than one conference of the same name was held in the same year. Such a coincidence will occur only rarely.

LARC Institute on Automated Serials Systems (1973 :
　St. Louis, Mo.)
　Proceedings of the LARC Institute on Automated
Serials Systems held May 24-25, 1973 at the Chase
Park Plaza, St. Louis, Missouri / coordinated by
Estelle Brodman ; edited by H. William Axford. --
Tempe, Ariz. : LARC Association, c1973.
　128 p. ; 23 cm.

　Contents: State of the art review / Glyn T. Evans
-- The National Serials Data Program / Paul Vassallo
-- Management problems of the network manager /
Jacqueline Felter -- Serline : on-line serials
bibliographic and locator system / Cecile C. Quintal

　　(continued on next card)

Figure 14-18. Named conference (add year)

LARC Institute on Automated Serials Systems (<u>1973</u> :
    <u>St. Louis, Mo.</u>).   Proceedings ... c1973.   (card 2)

The problems of entering a computerized serials network / Priscilla Mayden -- The PHILSOM network /
Virginia Feagler -- The PHILSOM network / Neil
Falvey -- The PHILSOM network / Millard Johnson --
The PHILSOM network / Dean Schmidt -- Case study of
the computer assisted serials system at the University of California, San Diego / Don Bosseau.
    ISBN 0-88257-097-8 hdbd

    I. Brodman, Estelle.   II. Axford, H. William.
III. LARC Association.   IV. Title.

Title page

Proceedings of The LARC Institute
on Automated Serials Systems
Held May 24-25, 1973
at the Chase Park Plaza
St. Louis, Missouri
Coordinated by Dr. Estelle Brodman
Edited by H. William Axford
Copyright © 1973 — The LARC Association
P.O. Box 27235
Tempe, Arizona 85282
Hardbound — ISBN 0-88257 — 097-8

24.7B4. Location. The last element added to the name of the conference, etc., is the name of the location. The name of the institution at which the conference was held may be used (see figure 11-5). If the conference is simply held at a hotel, civic meeting place, etc., prefer the name of the city. See figures 2-17, 14-16, 14-17, and 14-18.

A final word of caution regarding conferences: If a conference does not have a name, treat the publication as though no conference were involved. The example shown in figure 14-19 is an unnamed conference sponsored by the Graduate Library School, University of Chicago. The nature of the contents of the publication excludes it from consideration as a work to be entered under the heading for the Graduate Library School (see 21.1B2). Instead, it should be regarded as a work produced under editorial direction (21.7B) to be entered under title.

Library catalogs : changing dimensions : the
    twenty-eighth annual conference of the Graduate
    Library School, August 5-7, 1963 / edited by
    Ruth French Strout. -- Chicago : University of
    Chicago Press, 1964.
    127 p. ; 25 cm.

   Figure 14-19. Unnamed
   conference

   "Published originally in the Library quarterly,
January 1964."
   Contents: Introduction / Ruth French Strout --
The information needs of current scientific research / Herbert Menzel -- The changing character
of the catalog in America / David C. Weber -- The
catalog in European libraries / Felix Reichmann --
      (continued on next card)

Library catalogs. 1964. (card 2)

Duplicate catalogs in university libraries / George
Piternick -- The National Union and Library of
Congress catalogs / John W. Cronin -- Studies
related to catalog problems / Henry J. Dubester --
The relation of library catalogs to abstracting and
indexing services / Frank B. Rogers -- Dialogues
with a catalog / Don R. Swanson.
   ISBN 0-226-77731-6

   I. Strout, Ruth French. II. University of
Chicago. Graduate Library School.

Library Catalogs
Changing Dimensions
The Twenty-eighth Annual Conference
of the Graduate Library School
August 5-7, 1963
Edited by Ruth French Strout
The University of Chicago Press
Chicago and London

Title page

24.8. EXHIBITIONS, FAIRS, FESTIVALS, ETC.

A named exhibition, like a named conference, is regarded as the author of its publications that fall within the scope of 21.1B2d. Rules for exhibitions are new to *AACR2;* they parallel those for conferences in elements to be added to the name of the exhibition, etc.

24.9. CHAPTERS, BRANCHES, ETC.

This rule is the same as *AACR1* rule 69C2. See figure 11-6, added entry I, for for an example of a chapter as an addition to the name of a corporate body.

24.10. LOCAL CHURCHES, ETC.

See 24.3G for rules on variant forms of the name of a local church.

Rule 24.10 is based on *AACR1* rule 98 as modified by *Cataloging Service Bulletin* 109 (May 1974). Originally, rule 98, like its ALA 1949 predecessor, called for entry of a local church under the place where it was located. The change in 1974 brought names of local churches into line with names for other corporate bodies: Entry is to be made under the name by which the church is predominantly identified.

24.10A. Add a general designation if the name of the local church does not convey the idea of a church, as was done to indicate the nature of other corporate bodies. (See figure 14-20.)

24.10B. Add the name of the place unless it is part of the name of the church; see figure 14-21.

St. Mary at Hill (Church : London, England)
   The medieval records of a London city church
(St. Mary at Hill), A.D. 1420-1559 / transcribed
and edited with facsimiles and an introduction by
Henry Littlehales. -- London : Published for the
Early English Text Society by K. Paul, Trench,
Trübner, 1904-1905.
   2 v. : ill. ; 23 cm. -- (Early English Text
Society : ₁publications₁ ; original series, no.
125, 128)

   Includes glossarial index.

   I. Littlehales, Henry. II. Title. III. Series.

Figure 14-20. Local church

The Medieval Records of a
London City Church
(St. Mary at Hill)
A.D. 1420–1559.
Transcribed and Edited
With facsimiles and an Introduction
by
Henry Littlehales.
London:
Published for the Early English Text Society
by Kegan Paul, Trench, Trübner & Co., Limited,
Dryden House, 43, Gerrard Street, Soho, W.
1904.

Title page

St. Bartholomew's Church (<u>London, England</u>)
    The book of the foundation of St. Bartholomew's
Church in London, the church belonging to the
priory of the same in West Smithfield / edited
from the original manuscript in the British Museum,
Cotton Vespasian B ix, by Sir Norman Moore. --
London : Published for the Early English Text
Society by H. Milford, 1923.
    xii, 72 p. : ill. ; 23 cm. -- (Early English Text
Society : [publications] ; original series, no. 163) '

I. Moore, Norman, Sir.   II. Title.   III. Series.

Figure 14-21. Local
church

The Book of the Foundation of
St. Bartholomew's Church in London,
The Church belonging to the Priory
of the Same in West Smithfield.
Edited from the Original Manuscript in the
British Museum,
Cotton Vespasian B ix.
by
Sir Norman Moore, Bart., M.D.,
London:
Published for the Early English Text Society
By Humphrey Milford, Oxford University Press,
1923.

Title page

Because *ACCR1* rule 98 originally called for entry of local churches under place, the cataloguer should make a reference from this form of name for each church in the library catalogue (see 26.3A7). Thus, for the two examples given, shown in figures 14-20 and 14-21, references would be made:

> London (*England*). *St. Mary at Hill* (*Church*)
> *see*
> St. Mary at Hill (*Church : London, England*)
> London (*England*). *St. Bartholomew's Church*
> *see*
> St. Bartholomew's Church (*London, England*)

24.11. RADIO AND TELEVISION STATIONS

This rule is substantially the same as *AACR1* rule 97.

Subordinate and Related Bodies

In many respects the rules governing corporate bodies are analogous to those for personal authors. But in one important respect corporate bodies are unlike personal authors: Corporate bodies may have subdivisions, units subordinate or related in some way to the parent body. When dealing with a subordinate body, one of two options are open to the cataloguer:

1. If the name of the subordinate body includes a term that implies subordination, the subordinate body will be entered as a subheading under the name of the higher body to which it is related (24.13).
2. If the subordinate body has a distinctive name that is sufficient to identify it in the catalogue, it will be entered as an independent unit under its own name (24.12).

24.12. GENERAL RULE

This rule is the same, in effect, as *AACR1* rules 70 and 71. It is actually only a restatement of the general rule governing headings for corporate bodies (24.1). If a subordinate body has a distinctive, self-sufficient name that it consistently uses in its publications, enter it directly under that name. This is a change from ALA 1949 rule 102, which called for entry of all institutions forming an integral part of a larger organization as a subheading under the name of the larger organization, no matter what the character of the name of the smaller body might be. Thus, under ALA 1949 rules the Chapin Library of Williams College was entered as: Williams College. *Chapin Library*. After the rule was changed (*AACR1* 70), the heading was the same as it is under *AACR2;* see figure 14-22.

AACR2 rule 24.12 calls for a reference from the name of the body as a subheading under the parent organization:

Williams College. *Chapin Library*
    see
Chapin Library.

```
Chapin Library.
  A short-title list / the Chapin Library,
Williams College ; compiled by Lucy Eugenia
Osborne. -- Portland, Me. : Southworth-Anthoensen
Press, 1939.
  viii, 595 p. : port. ; 27 cm.




  I. Osborne, Lucy Eugenia.    II. Title.
```

Figure 14-22.
Subordinate body
entered under its own
name

Title page

The Chapin Library
Williams College
A Short-Title List
Compiled by
Lucy Eugenia Osborne
Portland, Maine
The Southworth-Anthoensen Press
London; Bernard Quaritch, Ltd.
1939

24.13. SUBORDINATE AND RELATED BODIES ENTERED SUBORDINATELY

This rule is in effect the same as *AACR1* rule 69. It enumerates five types of subordinate bodies that are to be entered as subheadings under the name of a higher body. These five types have their origin in Paris Principle 9.61, which calls for entry of a corporate body under a higher body "if this name itself implies subordination or subordinate function, or is insufficient to identify the subordinate body."

Type 1. A subordinate body whose name includes a word such as "department," "division," etc., or some other word implying that the body is a component part of something else will be entered as a subheading under the higher body. Do not repeat the name of the higher body or any words that link the lower to the higher body. (See figure 14-23.)

Annotated list of graduate theses and dissertations
  : the Department of Education, the University of
  Chicago, 1900-1931. -- Chicago : The University,
  [1932?]
  iv, 119 p. ; 24 cm.

Figure 14-23.
Subordinate body—
type 1

I. University of Chicago. Dept. of Education.

Title page

Annotated List of
Graduate Theses and Dissertations
The Department of Education
The University of Chicago
1900–1931
The University of Chicago • Chicago, Illinois

Type 2. If the name of a committee, etc., is worded in such a fashion that it implies subordination to a higher body, it will be entered as a subheading under the name of the higher body. For an example, see added entry II in figure 14-24.

Adventuring with books : a book list for elementary
  schools / prepared by Elizabeth Guilfoile, editorial chairman, and the Committee on the Elementary School Book List of the National Council of
  Teachers of English. -- New York : New American
  Library, c1966.
  256 p. : ill. ; 18 cm. -- (A Signet book ; T2914)

  Bibliography: p. 222.

Figure 14-24.
Subordinate body—
type 2

  I. Guilfoile, Elizabeth. II. National Council
of Teachers of English. Committee on the Elementary
School Book List.

Title page

Adventuring With Books
A Book List for Elementary Schools
Prepared by
Elizabeth Guilfoile
Editorial Chairman and
The Committee on the Elementary School Book List
of the
National Council of Teachers of English
A Signet Book
Published by The New American Library
P.O. Box 2310, Grand Central Station,
New York, N.Y. 10017

Type 3. Some subordinate or related bodies have names so general that the name of a higher body is needed for identification. Enter such a body as a subheading under the name of the higher body. See figure 14-25.

```
Coranto : journal of the Friends of the Libraries.
   -- Vol. 1, no. 1 (fall 1963)-    . -- Los
Angeles : University of Southern California,
1963-
      v. ; 24 cm.

Biannual.




   I. University of Southern California.  Friends
of the Libraries.
```

Figure 14-25.
Subordinate body—
type 3

Coranto
Journal of the Friends of the Libraries

University of Southern California : Fall 1963

Cover

Coranto
Volume 1 • Los Angeles, Fall 1963 • Number 1
Ruth Pryor, Editor
Published twice a year

Contents

Type 4. As with the headings covered by type 3, those covered by type 4 would be incomplete, ambiguous, and insufficient to provide proper identification for the subordinate unit if they were entered independently. Type 4 is limited to names of university schools or colleges that simply are descriptive of the field of study; see figure 14-26.

```
Sample catalog cards for use in connection with
   courses in technical services in libraries and
   organization of materials / Columbia University,
   School of Library Service. -- 3rd ed. -- New
   York : The School, 1958.
   [70] p. : chiefly ill. ; 28 cm.



   I. Columbia University.  School of Library
Service.
```

Figure 14-26.
Subordinate body—
type 4

Title page

Columbia University
School of Library Service
Sample Catalog Cards
For use in connection with courses in
Technical Services in Libraries and
Organization of Materials
Third Edition
School of Library Service
Columbia University
New York
1958

Type 5. If the subordinate body uses in its publication a name that includes the *entire* name of the higher body, it will be entered as a subheading under the name of the higher body. The name of the higher body is not repeated as part of the subheading; see figure 14-27.

```
University of New Mexico.  Library.
   Manuscripts and records in the University of
New Mexico Library / by Albert James Diaz. --
Albuquerque : The Library, 1957.
   57 p. ; 24 cm.



   I. Diaz, Albert James.  II. Title.
```

Figure 14-27.
Subordinate body—
type 5

Title page

Manuscripts and Records
in the University of New Mexico Library
by
Albert James Diaz
University of New Mexico Library • Albuquerque
1957

Notice two of the examples in *AACR2*. Under 24.13 type 5, "BBC Symphony Orchestra" is not a name that includes the *entire* name of the body (British Broadcasting Company). See also the example "Harvard Law School" in 24.12. As with BBC, the name of the institution does not include the entire name of the higher body (Harvard University).

24.14. DIRECT OR INDIRECT SUBHEADING

This rule is the same, in intent, as *AACR1* rule 69A. Sometimes a corporate body that is to be entered as a subdivision is part of a whole chain or hierarchy of agencies, each dependent upon the one above it. Entry of the lowest link of the chain, the most subordinate of the subordinate units, can present problems. Sometimes it is necessary to give the entire hierarchy, as in the third example under 24.14 in *AACR2*. In the example, each of the elements in the hierarchy depends directly on the one above it: Board of Directors is a type 3 name; Resources and Technical Services Division is a type 1 name; the board's name is meaningless without the name of the division to which it is attached; the division has a name that implies subordination and so it must be attached to that of the parent organization, American Library Association.

But as the above example demonstrates, such a practice often results in a very long heading. More important, over the years the intervening bodies between the first and last link of the hierarchy may change, or control of the subordinate agency may be shifted from one higher body to another. When this happens, if all of the links of the hierarchy have been displayed in the heading, the heading must be changed. Such a change often means extensive recataloguing. Rule 24.14 offers a good solution to the problem. Enter the subdivision at hand directly under the first larger body that can stand independently. Leave out the intermediate units as long as they are not needed to clarify the function of the smaller body. Figure 11-3 is a good example of this practice. The hierarchy for this body, as shown on the title page of the book, is

American Library Association
Resources and Technical Services Division
Copying Methods Section
Library Standards for Microfilm Committee.

The lowest element of the hierarchy that can be entered independently is American Library Association. The name Library Standards for Microfilm Committee is not likely to be used by any other body that is a subordinate unit of the American Library Association. In addition, the intermediate links of the hierarchy are not needed to identify or clarify the function of the committee. Therefore, the heading will be: American Library Association. *Library Standards for Microfilm Committee.*

Added entry I in figure 14-28 is another illustration of 24.14. The hierarchy for this heading is

American Library Association
Division of Cataloging and Classification
Board on Cataloging Policy and Research.

```
Lubetzky, Seymour.
  Cataloging rules and principles : a critique of
the A.L.A. rules for entry and a proposed design
for their revision / prepared for the Board on
Cataloging Policy and Research of the A.L.A. Divi-
sion of Cataloging and Classification by Seymour
Lubetzky. -- Washington : Processing Dept., Library
of Congress, 1953.
  xi, 65 p. ; 24 cm.

  Bibliographical references.

  I. American Library Association.  Board on Cata-
loging Policy and Research.  II. Library of Congress.
Processing Dept.  III. Title.
```

Figure 14-28. Direct subheading

Title page

Cataloging Rules and Principles
A Critique of the A.L.A. Rules for Entry
and a Proposed Design for Their Revision
Prepared for the Board on Cataloging Policy and
Research of the A.L.A. Division of
Cataloging and Classification
by Seymour Lubetzky
Consultant on Bibliographic and Cataloging Policy
Processing Department, Library of Congress
Washington : 1953

The heading is: American Library Association. *Board on Cataloging Policy and Research.* The intermediate link was dropped because the function of the committee and its identity are clear without it. Also, no other division of ALA is likely to have a Board on Cataloging Policy and Research.

Notice the difference between the subheading Board on *Cataloging* Policy and Research and the subheading that is the lowest element in the hierarchy of the second example given under 24.14 in *AACR2:* Policy and Research Committee. Any of the sections or divisions, etc., of the American Library Association might have a Policy and Research Committee. Its function and identity are not clear without the addition of the next higher unit: the Cataloging and Classification Section. However, no other ALA division is likely to have a section called Cataloging and Classification Section; the name of the division may be omitted.

As just shown, the cataloguer cannot always drop all of the intervening links of a hierarchy. If the bottom link is of a type that is dependent on the next link according to the stipulations of 24.13 types 1–5, that link must be included. For example, referring once more to added entry I of figure 14-28, suppose the cataloguer has a publication of the Program Committee of ALA's Board on Cataloging Policy and Research. If all of the intervening links between Program Committee and American Library Association were dropped, the entry would be: American Library Association. *Program Committee.* It would give the impression that this body was a Program Committee for the entire Association, not just for the Board on Cataloging Policy and Research. Therefore, the cataloguer would need to include the name of the subdivision that identifies which Program Committee this one is. The heading would be: American Library Association. *Board on Cataloging Policy and Research. Program Committee.*

If the cataloguer has omitted some of the connecting links in a hierarchy in setting up a heading, a reference must be made that includes at least the immediately superior body. The reference to the heading in figure 11-3 discussed earlier will be

> American Library Association. *Copying Methods Section.*
> *Library Standards for Microfilm Committee*
> see
> American Library Association. *Library Standards for Microfilm Committee.*

The reference to added entry I in figure 14-28 will be:

> American Library Association. *Division of Cataloging and Classification. Board on Cataloging Policy and Research*
> see
> American Library Association. *Board on Cataloging Policy and Research.*

Particular Applications

24.15A. Joint committees, commissions, etc.

This rule is the same as *AACR1* rule 71B, which was unchanged from ALA 1949 rule 139C. A joint committee will be entered under its own name if it is made up of representatives of two or more *separate, independent* corporate bodies. A joint committee sponsored the conference in the example shown in figure 14-29.

```
Conference on Total Community Library Service
  (1972 : Washington, D.C.)
  Total community library service : report of a
conference / sponsored by the Joint Committee of
the American Library Association and the National
Education Association ; edited by Guy Garrison. --
Chicago : ALA, 1973.
  x, 138 p. ; 23 cm.

  Bibliography: p. 116-121.
  ISBN 0-8389-0149-2


  I. Garrison, Guy.  II. Joint Committee of the
American Library Association and the National
Education Association.  III. Title.
```

Figure 14-29. Joint committee entered under its own name

Title page

Total Community Library Service
Report of a Conference Sponsored
by the Joint Committee of the
American Library Association and the
National Education Association
Edited by
Guy Garrison
American Library Association
Chicago 1973

Make reference from each of the corporate bodies involved in the joint committee, with the name of the joint committee as subdivision:

> American Library Association. *Joint Committee of the*
> *American Library Association and the National Education*
> *Association*
> *see*
> Joint Committee of the American Library Association and the
> National Education Association.

Make a similar reference under the heading for the National Education Association.

24.15B. If the two bodies making up a joint committee are themselves subordinate to a single larger body, the joint committee will be entered as a subordinate heading under the name of the larger body. The many joint committees of the United States Congress are entered as subdivisions under "United States. *Congress.*" See also example in *AACR2* under 24.15B.

24.16. CONVENTIONALIZED SUBHEADINGS FOR STATE AND LOCAL ELEMENTS OF AMERICAN POLITICAL PARTIES

This rule is in essence the same as *AACR1* rule 71C2.

Government Bodies and Officials

Under the 1949 ALA rules, governments and their agencies, with certain specified exceptions, were regarded as authors of publications for which they were responsible. Such publications were to be entered under the name of the government, with the agency as a subheading (ALA 1949 rules 71–72). Cataloguers were required to determine whether there was any administrative or financial link between the name of a corporate body and a government jurisdiction in order to be certain that this rule was followed. All such headings had to be looked up in official manuals such as (for the United States government) the *United States Government Organization Manual* or another appropriate reference source. The rule caused cataloguers much grief; it was difficult to apply consistently.

In an attempt to solve the difficulties and inconsistencies of the 1949 rules, the editors of *AACR1* arrived at a general rule for government headings, which, in its own way, was even more complex than the ALA 1949 rules which it replaced. The rule was based on the function of the agency rather than type of name; an agency that exercised legislative, judicial, or executive functions was to be entered as a subheading under the name of the government. All other agencies were to be entered under their own names. To aid cataloguers in determining agencies that were not regarded as legislative, judicial, or executive, the editors drew up an elaborate list of seven types of agencies with numerous examples, all to be entered under their own names. But almost immediately the cumbersome rule fell into difficulties; exceptions were made for government agencies whose names included terms suggesting subordination, such as "bureau," "administration," etc., regardless of the function of the body. The rule proved too complex to be satisfactory.

The present rule adheres to the same principles governing nongovernment bodies, as set forth in 24.12 and 24.13; in fact, these two rules very closely parallel 24.17 and 24.18 and should be compared. As with the rule for nongovernment bodies, the general rule for choice of entry either subordinately or independently may be summarized: If the government agency has a unique name not likely to be duplicated elsewhere and one that does not include terms that suggest dependent status, it should be entered under its own name. If the name of the agency includes terms that suggest dependent status or that need the name of the government to identify the agency, the agency should be entered as a subordinate unit under the name of the government.

24.17. GENERAL RULE

Enter a government agency under its own name if its name is unique and if it does not contain terms that suggest dependent status.

The Library of Congress has a name that is unique. See figure 11-1 for one example of a heading for one of the subordinate units of the Library of Congress. Rule 24.17 stipulates that a reference will be made from the name of the agency entered as a subheading:

> United States. *Library of Congress*
>   *see*
> Library of Congress.

This reference is particularly important since under 1949 rules most of these agencies were entered as subheadings under the name of the government; many library users may seek them under government heading.

Likewise, the National Gallery of Art has a name that sounds independent; see figure 14-30. Reference will be made:

> United States. *National Gallery of Art*
>   *see*
> National Gallery of Art.

The British government-controlled Bank of England also has a name that sounds independent; see figure 14-31. Reference will be made:

> Great Britain. *Bank of England*
>   *see*
> Bank of England.

```
National Gallery of Art.
  American paintings and sculpture : an illustrated
catalogue / National Gallery of Art. -- Washington :
The Gallery, 1970.
  192 p. : ill. ; 23 cm.

  Includes index.




  I. Title.
```

Figure 14-30.
Government body
entered under its own
name

Title page

National Gallery of Art
American Paintings and Sculpture:
an Illustrated Catalogue
Washington   1970

United Kingdom overseas investments, 1938 to
    1948. -- London : Bank of England, 1950.
    33 p. ; 26 cm.

Figure 14-31.
Government body
entered under its own
name

I. Bank of England.

United Kingdom Overseas Investments
1938 to 1948
Title page   **Bank of England, 1950**

The Arts Council of Great Britain, controlled by the British government, has
a distinctive name that sounds independent; see figure 14-32. Reference will be
made:

> Great Britain. *Arts Council of Great Britain*
> *see*
> Arts Council of Great Britain.

Daumier : paintings and drawings : an exhibition /
    organized by the Arts Council of Great Britain
    at the Tate Gallery. -- [London] : The Council,
    1961.
    70 p., 36 p. of plates : ill., port. ; 25 cm.

Figure 14-32.
Government body
entered under its own
name

I. Daumier, Honoré.   II. Tate Gallery (London,
England).   III. Arts Council of Great Britain.

Title page

Daumier
Paintings and Drawings
An exhibition organized by
the Arts Council of Great Britain
at the Tate Gallery
The Arts Council of Great Britain 1961

24.18. GOVERNMENT AGENCIES ENTERED SUBORDINATELY

This rule is the equivalent of *AACR1* rule 78B. It parallels 24.13; the types of corporate bodies that will be entered as subheadings under the name of a higher body as given in 24.13 are closely correlated, and in some cases identical, to the types of government agencies that will be entered under the name of the government. In both instances, the principle is the same: If the name of the subordinate unit contains terms that imply subordination, or that are incomplete or not clearly identified without the name of the governmental jurisdiction, the agencies will be entered as subordinate bodies under the name of the government. The rule is based strictly on the way the agency's name is formulated.

Type 1. If an agency's name includes a word such as "department," "section," "service," "bureau," etc. (or foreign equivalents), which implies that the agency is subordinate to a higher body, enter the agency subordinately. Figure 1-28, a publication of the State of Arizona's Department of Education includes an example of such a heading.

Type 2. Notice the exact parallel between this rule and 24.13 type 2. A good rule of thumb for a decision about whether "the name of the government is required for the identification of the agency" or not is if the commission or committee's name is made up simply of generic words signifying its function or if (as with government agencies covered by 24.17) it has a distinctive name. Thus, the Warren Commission (figure 14-7) is entered as an independent body. In contrast, the Commission on Obscenity and Pornography (figure 14-33) needs the name of the government for identification.

```
United States.  Commission on Obscenity and
   Pornography.
The report of the Commission on Obscenity and
Pornography / special introduction by Clive Barnes.
-- Toronto ; New York : Bantam Books, 1970.
   xvii, 698 p. ; 18 cm.

At head of title: A New York Times book.
Includes bibliographies.



I. Title.
```

Figure 14-33.
Subordinate agency—
type 2

A New York Times Book
The Report of the Commission on
Obscenity and Pornography
Special Introduction by Clive Barnes of
The New York Times
Bantam Books
Toronto • New York • London

Title page

Type 3. An agency with a name that has been used by other governments, or so commonplace that it is likely to be so used, will be entered as a subordinate body under the name of the government. The Bibliothèque Nationale, the French national library (figure 14-34), is such an institution. Following 26.3A7, make reference:

> Bibliothèque nationale (*France*)
> > *see*
> France. Bibliothèque nationale.

Le dessin d'humour du XVe siècle à nos jours / Bibliothèque nationale. -- Paris : La Bibliothèque, 1971.
164 p. : ill. ; 22 cm.

Bibliography: p. 161-164.

I. France.   Bibliothèque nationale.

Figure 14-34.
Subordinate agency—
type 3

Title page

Bibliothèque Nationale
Le Dessin d'humour
du XVe siècle à nos jours
Paris
1971

Type 4. A top-level *executive agency* in a government will be entered as a subordinate heading under the name of the government, regardless of whether its name includes words such as "department," "ministry" "administration," or not. However, names of most such agencies do include such terms; in most cases, these agencies are also examples of 24.18 type 1, having names that imply that the body is a part of another.

In the example shown in figure 14-35 added entry I is a type 4 government agency. Note that according to stipulations of 23.2A, the cataloguer will use the English form of name for the government: Austria, rather than Österreich. But the name of the government agency (translated as "Federal Ministry of Agriculture and Forestry") is always to be given in the vernacular. Make reference from the vernacular form of the name of the government, according to the provisions of 26.3A1.

> Öesterreich
> > *see*
> Austria.

Österreichische Waldstandsaufnahme, 1952/56 :
Gesamtergebnis / herausgegeben vom Bundesministerium für Land- und Forstwirtschaft und von der
Forstlichen Bundes-Versuchanstalt Mariabrunn in
Schönbrunn. -- Wien : Der Bundes-Versuchanstalt,
1960.
323 p. : ill., maps ; 27 cm.

Final summary report for: Erbegnisse der öster-
reichischen Waldstandsaufnahme, 1952/56 / herausgegeben vom Bundesministerium für Land- und Forstwirtschaft.

I. Austria. Bundesministerium für Land- und
Forstwirtschaft. II. Forstliche Bundes-Versuchanstalt Mariabrunn in Schönbrunn. III. Title.

Figure 14-35.
Subordinate agency—
type 4

Title page

Österreichische
Waldstandsaufnahme
1952/56
Gesamtergebnis
Herausgegeben
vom
Bundesministerium für Land- und Forstwirtschaft
und von der
Forstlichen Bundes-Versuchanstalt Mariabrunn
in Schönbrunn
1960

24.19. DIRECT OR INDIRECT SUBHEADING

This rule is parallel to 24.14. Its *AACR1* counterpart is rule 79. It applies only to agencies entered as subheading of the government according to 24.18. As with nongovernment corporate bodies, sometimes a government agency is a part of a chain or hierarchy of agencies, each dependent upon the one above it. As with nongovernment corporate bodies, sometimes one or more of the links in the chain may be omitted in the heading. See discussion in this text under 24.14 for full explanation.

Figures 14-36 and 14-37 show government agencies that may be entered directly under the name of the government. The United States Office of Education is an agency under the control of the Department of Health, Education, and Welfare. The name of the department is not needed to identify or clarify the function of the Office of Education. Therefore, the heading will be: United States. *Office of Education.*

Criteria for technical education : a suggested
  guide. -- Washington : U.S. Dept. of Health,
  Education, and Welfare, Office of Education :
  For sale by the Supt. of Docs., U.S.G.P.O., 1968.
  vi, 84 p. ; 24 cm.

  Bibliography: p. 77-78.
  OE-80056; Supt. of Docs. catalog no.
FS 5.280:80056.

  I. United States. Office of Education.

Figure 14-36. Direct
subheading

Criteria for Technician Education   OE–80056
A Suggested Guide

U.S. Department of Health, Education, and Welfare
Wilbur J. Cohen, Secretary
Office of Education
Harold Howe II, Commissioner

Title page

November 1968   Superintendent of Documents
Catalog No. FS 5.280:80056
United States Government Printing Office
Washington: 1968
For sale by the Superintendent of Documents,
U.S. Government Printing Office
Washington, D.C. 20402

Verso of title page

United States Geological Survey.
  Suggestions to authors of the reports of the
United States Geological Survey. -- 5th ed. --
Washington : U.S.G.P.O., 1958.
  xii, 255 p. ; 24 cm.

  Fourth ed. has title: Suggestions to authors of
papers submitted for publication by the United
States Geological Survey.
  Includes bibliographies.

  I. Title.

Figure 14-37. Direct
subheading

Title page

Suggestions to Authors of the Reports
of the United States Geological Survey
Fifth Edition
United States Government Printing Office,
Washington 1958

For similar reasons, the United States Geological Survey may be entered as a direct subheading under the name of the government. The survey is controlled by the Department of the Interior; however, the department's name is not needed to identify or clarify the function of the subordinate agency.

Following stipulations of 26.3A7, make reference from the full hierarchy:

> United States. *Dept. of Health, Education, and Welfare. Office of Education*
> see
> United States. *Office of Education.*

> United States. *Dept. of the Interior. Geological Survey*
> see
> United States. *Geological Survey.*

Special Rules

24.20. GOVERNMENT OFFICIALS

Except for minor revisions in wording and some revision in style of heading, this rule is the same as *AACR1* rule 80. The rule covers form of heading for official messages, proclamations, etc., that will be entered under the heading for a head of a government according to 21.4D.

24.20B. Heads of state, etc.

This rule includes governors as well as sovereigns and presidents. Headings for such individuals include the inclusive years of reign or incumbency and the name of the individual; see figure 14-38.

```
California.   Governor (1967-1975 : Reagan)
   Environmental goals and policy / Ronald Reagan,
governor ; John S. Tooker, director, Office of
Planning and Research, Governor's Office. --
Sacramento : State of California, Governor's
Office, 1972.
   86 p. : ill., maps (some col.) ; 28 cm.

   Transmitted to the California Legislature,
Apr. 26, 1972.

   I. Reagan, Ronald.  II. Tooker, John S.  III.
California. Legislature.  IV. Title.
```

Figure 14-38. Governor

State of California
Environmental Goals and Policy
Ronald Reagan
Title page   Governor
John S. Tooker
Director, Office of Planning and Research
Governor's Office
March 1, 1972

Ronald Reagan
Governor   First preliminary page
State of California
Governor's Office
Sacramento 95814

For official heading for the United States President, see figure 1-75. Note that if more than one incumbent of the same office has the same surname, the cataloguer will add initials of forenames. Otherwise, surname alone is sufficient.

See figure 11-12 for an example of the collective heading used for more than one United States President. See Appendix II for a list of headings for Presidents acting in an official capacity.

24.20C. Heads of governments aside from heads of state and governors

This rule is the same as *AACR1* rule 80B. Official statements from heads of governments aside from those covered by 24.20B are entered under a heading similar in form to that given heads of state, except that dates and names of incumbents are not included in the subheading. As will be done for heads of state entered under official title, an added entry will be made for the incumbent. See figure 1-96 for an example.

By policy decision, headings for *all* corporate entries dealing with the United Kingdom at any point in its history will be "Great Britain." The Library of Congress will use this conventional heading rather than, for example: United Kingdom. *Sovereign (1952– : Elizabeth II)*. Examples in this text follow LC policy. A library that chooses to follow *AACR2* format without regard to LC policy decision (see discussion in this text, under 22.17A) will use the headings for British sovereigns acting in an official capacity given in Appendix II.

24.20E. Other officials

This rule is the same as *AACR1* rule 80D. Official statements from a government official who is not a head of a government will be entered under the heading for the agency he or she represents; see figures 14-39 and 14-40. Added entry will be made for the name of the person if the person is prominently named in the publication. An added entry is also to be made, when appropriate, for the name of the body to which an official report, statement, etc., is transmitted. Reference is made from the title of the official:

> Librarian of Congress
> *see*
> Library of Congress.

> United States. *Comptroller General*
> *see*
> United States. *General Accounting Office.*

Library of Congress.
  Report of the Librarian of Congress on the Bryant
memorandum / submitted to the Joint Committee on
the Library. -- Washington : The Library, 1962.
  54 leaves ; 27 cm.

  Signed: L. Quincy Mumford, Librarian of Congress.

Figure 14-39. Head of
an agency

  I. Mumford, L. Quincy.   II. United States.
Congress.   Joint Committee on the Library.   III.
Title.

Title page

> **Report of the Librarian of Congress**
> **on the Bryant Memorandum**
> **Submitted to**
> **The Joint Committee on the Library**
> **September 1962**
> **Washington, D.C.**

United States.   General Accounting Office.
  Report to the Congress of the United States :
need to reexamine planned replacement and augmen-
tation of high-endurance vessels, western area,
United States Coast Guard, Treasury Department / by
the Comptroller General of the United States. --
Washington : U.S. General Accounting Office, 1966.
  28 p. ; 27 cm.

  Cover title.

Figure 14-40. Head of
an agency

  I. United States.   Congress.   II. Title.

Title page

> Report to
> The Congress of the United States
> Need to Reexamine
> Planned Replacement and Augmentation of
> High-Endurance Vessels
> Western Area
> United States Coast Guard
> Treasury Department
> by the Comptroller General
> of the United States
> February 1966

24.21. LEGISLATIVE BODIES

This rule is basically the same as *AACR1* rule 81, with a few minor changes.

24.21A. Notice the change from *AACR1* rule 81A. It and earlier rules called for "United States. *Congress. House of Representatives*" to be shortened to "U. S. *Congress. House*." This practice will be discontinued by a library following *AACR2*. However, LC policy decision retains the old form. Examples in this text follow LC policy. See figure 14-41.

24.21B. This rule is the same as *AACR1* rule 81B. A committee will be entered as a subheading under the chamber of the legislature to which it is related or under the whole legislature, as appropriate. See figures 14-39 and 14-41.

```
United States.  Congress.  House.  Committee on
   Un-American Activities.
   Thirty years of treason : excerpts from hearings
before the House Committee on Un-American Activities,
1938-1968 / edited by Eric Bentley. -- New York :
Viking, c1971.
   xxviii, 991 p. ; 24 cm.

Includes index.



I. Bentley, Eric.  II. Title.
```

Figure 14-41.
Legislative committee

Title page

> Thirty Years of Treason
> Excerpts from Hearings
> before the House Committee
> on Un-American Activities,
> 1938–1968
> Edited by Eric Bentley
> New York / The Viking Press

24.21C. This rule is the same as *AACR1* rule 81B as revised by the 1970 supplement. Legislative subcommittees of the *U.S. Congress only* are an exception to provisions of 24.19 that otherwise calls for entry directly under either Congress or the appropriate chamber. Such subcommittees are to be entered under the name of the committee to which each is subordinate. See figure 11-2 as well as 14-42.

United States. Congress. Senate. Committee on
  the Judiciary. Subcommittee on Patents, Trademarks, and Copyrights.
  Copyright law revision : hearings before the
Subcommittee on Patents, Trademarks, and Copyrights
of the Committee on the Judiciary, United States
Senate, Ninety-third Congress, first session, pursuant to S. Res. 56 on S. 1361, July 31 and August
1, 1973. -- Washington : U.S.G.P.O., 1973.
  v, 675 p. ; 23 cm.

  I. Title.

Figure 14-42.
Legislative
subcommittee

Title page

Copyright Law Revision
Hearings before the Subcommittee on
Patents, Trademarks, and Copyrights
of the
Committee on the Judiciary
United States Senate
Ninety-third Congress
First Session
Pursuant to S. Res. 56
on
S. 1361
July 31 and August 1, 1973
U.S. Government Printing Office
Washington : 1973

24.21D.

This rule is basically the same as *AACR1* rule 81C, with some variations in the format of the heading. The new pattern is as given in added entry II of figure 14-43.

Memorial addresses and other tributes in the
   Congress of the United States on the life and
   contributions of Carl T. Hayden, Ninety-second
   Congress, second session. -- Washington :
   U.S.G.P.O., 1972.
     vii, 174 p. : port. ; 24 cm. -- (92d Congress,
2d session, Senate document ; no. 92-68)

   I. Hayden, Carl T.   II. United States.
Congress (92nd, 2nd session : 1972).

Figure 14-43.
Numbered session of
Congress

92d Congress, 2d Session   Senate Document No. 92–68
Memorial Addresses and Other Tributes in the
Congress of the United States
on the Life and Contributions of
Carl T. Hayden
Ninety-second Congress
Second Session
U.S. Government Printing Office
Washington : 1972

Title page

24.22. CONSTITUTIONAL CONVENTIONS

This rule is a clarification and rewording of *AACR1* rule 82.

24.23. COURTS

This rule is basically the same as *AACR1* rule 83. The name of the court is entered as a subheading under the name of the governmental jurisdiction whose authority it exercises. In the example shown in figure 14-44, added entry is made for the United States Supreme Court under the provisions of 21.30F. Make references from the titles of the officials to the name of the Justice Department:

      United States. *Attorney General*
        see
     United States. *Dept. of Justice.*

      United States. *Solicitor General*
        see
     United States. *Dept. of Justice.*

24.23B. Ad hoc military courts

Headings are slightly changed from those called for under *AACR1* rule 83D.

```
United States.  Dept. of Justice.
   Prejudice and property : an historic brief
against racial covenants / submitted to the Supreme
Court by Tom C. Clark, Attorney General of the
U.S., and Philip B. Perlman, Solicitor General of
the U.S. -- Washington : Public Affairs Press, 1948.
   104 p. ; 21 cm.

   Bibliography: p. 86-104.
```

Figure 14-44. Court

```
   I. Clark, Tom C.   II. Perlman, Philip B.   III.
United States.  Supreme Court.   IV. Title.
```

Title page

Prejudice and Property
An Historic Brief against Racial Covenants
Submitted to the Supreme Court
by Tom C. Clark
Attorney General of the U.S.
and
Philip B. Perlman
Solicitor General of the U.S.
Public Affairs Press
Washington, D.C.

24.24. ARMED FORCES

This rule is the same as *AACR1* rule 84.

24.25. EMBASSIES, CONSULATES, ETC.

This rule is the same as *AACR1* rule 85.

24.26. DELEGATIONS TO INTERNATIONAL AND INTERGOVERNMENTAL BODIES

This rule is the same as *AACR1* rule 86. It differs from ALA 1949 rule 79, which formulated a conference heading with the name of the delegation as a subheading following the name of the conference for such a group. Under ALA 1949 rule 79, the example shown in figure 14-45 would have received the heading:

Inter-American Conference for the Maintenance of Peace, *Buenos Aires, 1936. Delegation of the United States of America.*

Rule 24.26, as well as its predecessor *AACR1* rule 86, represents a return to 1908 rules.

United States. Delegation to the Inter-American
  Conference for the Maintenance of Peace, Buenos
  Aires, 1936.
  Report of the Delegation of the United States of
America to the Inter-American Conference for the
Maintenance of Peace, Buenos Aires, Argentina,
December 1-23, 1936. -- Washington : U.S.G.P.O. :
For sale by the Supt. of Docs., 1937.
    vi, 280 p. ; 24 cm. -- (Conference series ; 33)
(Department of State publication ; 1088)

I. Title.

Figure 14-45.
Delegation to
international conference

Report of the Delegation of the
United States of America to the
Inter-American Conference for the
Maintenance of Peace
Buenos Aires, Argentina
December 1–23, 1936
United States
Government Printing Office
Washington : 1937

Title page

The Mexican delegation to the Inter-American Conference also made a report
to its home country. According to ALA 1949 rule 79 the heading, like the previous one, would have been the name of the conference followed by the name
of the delegation in the vernacular: Inter-American Conference for the Maintenance of Peace, *Buenos Aires, 1936. Delegación de México.* As can be seen, such
a heading served to gather all of the various reports together in one place in
the catalogue.

Rule 24.26 calls for main entry under the name of the government of the
delegation, with the subheading in the vernacular; see figure 14-46.

A general explanatory reference serves to bring together in the catalogue all
of the names of the various delegations to the conference. Under the stipulations
of 24.3B, the name of the conference will be given in English. Reference from
the Spanish form of the name will be made under provisions of 26.3A3:

> Conferencia Internacional de Consolidación de
>   la Paz (*1936 : Buenos Aires*)
>   *see*
> Inter-American Conference for the Maintenance of Peace
>   (*1936 : Buenos Aires*)

Mexico. Delegación a la Conferencia Interamericana
   de Consolidación de la Paz, Buenos Aires, 1936.
     Informe de la Delegación de México a la Conferen-
   cia Interamericana de Consolidación de la Paz,
   reunida en Buenos Aires, Republica Argentina, del
   1º al 23 de diciembre de 1936. -- México : D.A.P.P.,
   1938.
     xiv, 308 p. ; 23 cm.

   At head of title: Conferencia Internacional de
Consolidación de la Paz.

   I. Title.

Figure 14-46.
Delegation to
international conference

Title page

Conferencia Internacional
de Consolidación de la Paz
Informe de la Delegación de Mexico
a la
Conferencia Interamericana
de Consolidación de la Paz
Reunida en Buenos Aires, Republica Argentina
del 1° al 23 de diciembre de 1936
D·A·P·P
México, 1938

   The general explanatory reference will be:

   Inter-American Conference for the Maintenance of Peace
      (*1936 : Buenos Aires*). *Delegations*
   Delegations to the Inter-American Conference for the
   Maintenance of Peace are entered under the name of the
   nation followed by the name of the delegation, e.g.
   United States. *Delegation to the Inter-American Conference
   for the Maintenance of Peace, Buenos Aires, 1936.*
   Mexico. *Delegación a la Conferencia Interamericana de
   Consolidación de la Paz, Buenos Aires, 1936.*

15

Uniform Titles

(*AACR2* Chapter 25)

25.1. USE OF UNIFORM TITLES

Many works appearing in library catalogues are published in varying issues, translations, etc., with different titles. Since one of the objects of the library catalogue is to show what works the library has by a given author,[1] some method must be devised to bring these works issued with varying titles together in the catalogue. Probably the best way to do it is for the cataloguer to choose one title and to gather all of the manifestations of the work together under this one title. Such a title is known as a uniform title.

The use of uniform titles in library catalogues is not new. Such works as sacred scriptures (the Bible, etc.) have long been entered under uniform title. So-called anonymous classics (epics, folk tales, etc., whose authors are unknown) are likewise by longstanding custom entered under uniform title. *AACR2*

---

[1] Charles Ammi Cutter's objectives of the library catalogue are still the basis of cataloguing theory. As he saw it, the library catalogue had three objectives:

1. To enable a person to find a book of which either
   A. the author
   B. the title   } is known.
   C. the subject

2. To show what the library has
   D. by a given author
   E. on a given subject
   F. in a given kind of literature

3. To assist in the choice of a book
   G. as to its edition (bibliographically)
   H. as to its character (literary or topical)

(*Rules for a Dictionary Catalog*, 4th ed. [Washington: GPO, 1904], p. 12).

chapter 25 in a similar fashion to that of its predecessor *AACR1* chapter 4 brings together not only these long-established and familiar uses of uniform titles but also utilizes uniform titles to bring together varying titles for modern works (those published after 1501).

Most libraries use uniform titles for sacred scriptures and anonymous classics. The use of uniform title for modern works aside from music has not had similar widespread acceptance. This practice is recognized by the editors of *AACR2* with their statement under 25.1, "The need to use uniform titles varies from one catalogue to another and varies within one catalogue." The Library of Congress has always used in its internal card catalogues any appropriate uniform titles for all types of materials. (Those uniform titles not printed on cards have been typewritten on cards intended for the Library's card catalogues.) Until recent years the Library of Congress has limited the display of these uniform titles on printed catalogue cards to a few categories only (sacred scriptures, anonymous classics, music, etc.). Following *AACR2*, the Library will continue to formulate all uniform titles and will display them without exception in all published records.[2] Illustrations and discussion in this chapter are based on the policy that all uniform titles are displayed as part of the catalogue entry.

AACR2 chapter 25 is organized in a similar fashion to that of previous chapters. It begins with a basic rule (25.2), which is followed by some general rules for choice and form of title. They are followed by special rules for particular types of works that may be arranged using uniform titles.

25.2. BASIC RULE

25.2A. If a work appears under various titles, select one of the titles as the uniform title under which all manifestations of the work will be catalogued. This rule is simply a restatement of the first sentence of Paris Principle 7:

> The uniform heading should normally be the most frequently
> used name (or form of name) or title appearing in editions of
> the work catalogued or in references to them by accepted authorities.[3]

It goes without saying that a work for which a uniform title may be provided will be entered, like any other work, in the catalogue according to the rules in *AACR2* chapter 21, Choice of Access Points. According to it, if a work should be entered under author, the uniform title will be interposed in brackets between the author heading and the transcription of the title page (see figure 15-1). Reference will be made, according to 25.2D2 and 26.2B:

> Dickens, Charles.
>   The adventures of Oliver Twist
>   *see*
> Dickens, Charles.
>   Oliver Twist.

---

[2] Library of Congress, *Cataloging Service Bulletin* 2 (Fall 1978).
[3] International Conference on Cataloguing Principles, 1961, *Statement of Principles* (London: IFLA Committee on Cataloguing, 1971), p. 23.

```
Dickens, Charles.
  [Oliver Twist]
  The adventures of Oliver Twist / by Charles
Dickens ; illustrated by Barnett Freedman. -- New
York : Heritage Illustrated Bookshelf, c1939.
  431 p. : ill. (some col.) ; 22 cm.
```

Figure 15-1. Uniform
title

```
  I. Title.
```

Title page

The Adventures of Oliver Twist
By Charles Dickens
Illustrated by Barnett Freedman
New York
The Heritage Illustrated Bookshelf

According to provisions of chapter 21, if a work would be entered under title as main entry and the title varies in different versions, such a work may also be given a uniform title. Rule 25.2A suggests that such a title be enclosed in brackets. Optionally, the brackets may be omitted. Library of Congress has never used brackets for such uniform titles; LC will apply this option.[4]

25.2B. Uniform title is *not* to be used to connect different revised editions of a work that appear under different titles. See figure 1-91 for one example.

25.2D. Added entries and references

25.2D1. Works entered under title. Figure 15-2 is a work entered under a uniform title. Such a work will have an added entry under the title as it appears in the chief source of information of the item being catalogued. A general reference to the uniform title (*Mother Goose*) will also be made the first time this "variant" title (i.e., title other than the uniform title) appears in the catalogue.

> A Book of nursery songs and rhymes
> *see*
> Mother Goose.

[4] Library of Congress, Memorandum, April 13, 1978.

```
Mother Goose.
  A book of nursery songs and rhymes / edited by
S. Baring-Gould ; with illustrations by members of
the Birmingham Art School under the direction of
A. J. Gaskin. -- Detroit : Singing Tree Press, 1969.
  xvi, 159 p. : ill. ; 23 cm.

  Reprint of: London : Methuen, 1895.
```

Figure 15-2. Uniform
title as main entry

```
  I. Baring-Gould, S.   II. Birmingham Art School.
III. Title.
```

Title page

A Book of Nursery Songs and Rhymes
Edited by S. Baring-Gould: with illustrations by
Members of the Birmingham Art School under the
Direction of A. J. Gaskin
London: Methuen & Company
Essex St. Strand: MDCCCXCV
Detroit: Reissued by Singing
Tree Press, Book Tower, 1969

Like other references, this reference is made one time only; it does not refer to a specific issue of *Mother Goose* but simply to the work in all of its variant manifestations. A similar reference will be made from any other variant of the uniform title in the library's collection. For the example shown in figure 15-3, make reference:

> Mother Goose nursery rhymes
> *see*
> Mother Goose.

```
Mother Goose.
  Mother Goose nursery rhymes / illustrations by
Esmé Eve. -- New York : Grosset & Dunlap, c1958.
  200 p. : col. ill. ; 27 cm.
```

Figure 15-3. Uniform
title as main entry

```
  I. Eve, Esmé.  II. Title.
```

Illustrations by Esmé Eve	Mother Goose Nursery Rhymes Grosset & Dunlap • New York	Title on two facing pages

25.2D2. Works entered under personal or corporate heading. Figure 15-1 is an example of a work entered under personal heading. Also given above is the format for the reference that will be made the *first time* the work known as *Oliver Twist* appears with the variant title *The Adventures of Oliver Twist*. The reference refers not to the Heritage Illustrated Bookshelf edition of Dickens' tale, but simply to the work *Oliver Twist* generally. In contrast, the title added entry, an added entry for the *title proper* (*The Adventures of Oliver Twist*) of this edition, refers specifically to this edition and to no other. The rule stipulates that a title added entry will be made for each new edition of such a work; a reference will be made *once* for each varying title.

Individual Titles

25.3. WORKS CREATED AFTER 1500

25.3A. This rule has its counterpart in *AACR1* rule 101B, but it is somewhat revised. When editions of a modern work (i.e., one published since 1500) have appeared under varying titles, use the best-known title in the original language of the work. "Best-known title" should be determined either through checking reference sources to see how they refer to the work or through examining issues and editions of the work to see which title is most frequently used. Obviously, for an author such as William Shakespeare, examination of citations to his individual plays, etc., in reference sources would be appropriate.

The first time an edition of *Macbeth* with the title *The Tragedy of Macbeth* is received in the library, a reference will be made:

> Shakespeare, William.
> >The tragedy of Macbeth
> >*see*
> Shakespeare, William
> >Macbeth.

This reference simply refers to the work *Macbeth* in general, not to a specific edition. The title added entry given for figure 15-4 refers specifically to the Folio Society's 1951 edition.

25.3B. If no title is clearly best known, choose the title proper of the original edition of a work as the uniform title.

Shakespeare, William.
 ₍Macbeth₎
 The tragedy of Macbeth / by William Shakespeare ;
introduction by Sir Lewis Casson ; designs by
Michael Ayrton and John Minton. -- 2nd ed. --
London : Folio Society, 1951.
  96 p. : col. ill. ; 23 cm.

Figure 15-4.
Best-known title

 I. Title.

Title page

The Tragedy of Macbeth
By William Shakespeare
Introduction by Sir Lewis Casson
Designs by Michael Ayrton and John Minton
The Folio Society : London : 1951

If a statement of responsibility has been transcribed as part of the title proper
(particularly if this statement of responsibility obscures the actual title proper),
a uniform title may be used to properly identify the work. See figure 1-59. An
optional choice of cataloguing is shown in figure 15-5.

Bright, James W.
 ₍Anglo-Saxon reader₎
 Bright's Anglo-Saxon reader / revised and
enlarged by James R. Hulbert. -- New York : Holt,
c1935.
  cxxxii, 395 p. ; 20 cm.

Figure 15-5. Statement
of responsibility
omitted from
uniform title

 I. Hulbert, James R.   II. Title.

25.4. WORKS CREATED BEFORE 1501

25.4A. General rule

This rule is essentially a composite of *AACR1* rules 102A and 102C1. Most works created before 1501 exist in many varying versions, editions, etc., with almost as many variant titles. The cataloguer is to identify the best-known title, using modern reference works in the language of the original work (or a modern language derived from the language of the original work).

Some of these works are known to be the responsibility of a particular author. Entry for such works is governed by general rule 21.1A2; uniform title is added, following 25.2A, between the name of the author and transcription of the title proper from the chief source of information. (See figure 15-6.)

```
Dante Alighieri, 1265-1321.
   [Inferno.  English & Italian]
   Inferno : the Italian text / Dante Alighieri ;
with translation and notes by Allan Gilbert. --
Durham, N.C. : Duke University Press, 1969.
   xlvi, 373 p. ; 24 cm.

   Bibliographical references included in "Notes":
p. 297-347.



   I. Gilbert, Allan.   II. Title.
```

Figure 15-6. Entry under known author

Title page

Dante Alighieri
Inferno
The Italian text
with translation and notes by
Allan Gilbert
1 9 6 9
Duke University Press
Durham, N.C.

Many works created before 1501 have no known author. Of these, many epics, poems, romances, tales, plays, chronicles, etc., have been retold, reprinted, published, translated, etc., many times in many versions over the centuries. Cataloguers have given the name "anonymous classic" to the genre. Because anonymous classics find a place, often in translation, even in small general libraries, the cataloguer should have some familiarity with some of the better-known anonymous classics and should know the rules for entry of such works.

As for anonymous works, title main entry is appropriate (21.5A). Because the title varies from one edition to the next, the cataloguer will identify the best-known title, according to general prescriptions in 25.4A, and will give main entry to this title for all editions of the work. *Mother Goose* (figures 15-2 and 15-3) is an example of an anonymous classic. No one knows the author of most of the traditional rhymes usually included in such collections; titles vary with the ingenuity of the compiler or editor. The best-known title, *Mother Goose*, will serve as the uniform title for all manifestations of this work.

A list of a few of the common anonymous classics with uniform headings used by the Library of Congress, which may be helpful to the beginning cataloguer, is given in Appendix II.

A uniform heading given in the appendix or another appropriate heading will be used alone for an edition of the work in the language of the original. If the edition being catalogued is a translation, the name of the language of the translation is to be added after the uniform title (25.5D). See figures 25-7 and 25-8. References will be made:

> Song of Roland
> *see*
> Chanson de Roland. *English.*

```
Chanson de Roland.  English.
   The song of Roland / newly translated into
English with an introduction by Jessie Crosland.
-- New York : Cooper Square Publishers, 1967.
   xxiii, 143 p. : ill. ; 17 cm. -- (The Medieval
library)

   Includes index.



   I. Crosland, Jessie.  II. Title.
```

Figure 15-7.
Anonymous classic

Title page

The Song of Roland
Newly Translated into English
with an Introduction by
Jessie Crosland
Cooper Square Publishers, Inc.
New York
1967

The poem of the Cid
>*see*

El Cid Campeador. *English*.

El poema del mio Cid
>*see*

El Cid Campeador.

```
El Cid Campeador.  English.
   The poem of the Cid : a verse translation / by
W.S. Merwin. -- London : Dent, c1959.
   xiii, 240 p. ; 20 cm.


   Spanish title: El poema del mio Cid.


   I. Merwin, W.S.   II. Title.   III. Title: El
poema del mio Cid.
```

Figure 15-8.
Anonymous classic

Title page

The Poem of the Cid
(El Poema del Mio Cid)
A Verse Translation by
W. S. Merwin
London
J. M. Dent & Sons Ltd.

In cataloguing anonymous classics, the cataloguer should be wary of publications presented as adaptations. These are to be entered under the name of the adapter, following provisions of 21.10. Give added entry to the uniform title for the original work as shown in figure 15-9.

```
Hull, Eleanor.
   The boys' Cuchulain : heroic legends of Ireland /
by Eleanor Hull ; with sixteen illustrations in
colour by Stephen Reid. -- New York : Crowell,
[19--]
   279 p., [16] leaves of plates : col. ill. ; 22 cm.




   I. Cuchulain.   II. Title.
```

Figure 15-9.
Adaptation
of anonymous
classic

The Boys' Cuchulain
Heroic Legends of Ireland
by Eleanor Hull
with sixteen illustrations in colour by
Stephen Reid
Thomas Y. Crowell & Company New York
Publishers

Title page

25.4B. Classical and Byzantine Greek works

The rule for uniform title for a work in classical or Byzantine Greek is an exception to the general rule of using a uniform title in the original language of the work. Rule 25.4B, which is the same as *AACR1* rule 102B, is analogous to 22.3C1, which directs the cataloguer to make entry for persons whose names were written in a nonroman script in the form in which they are found in English-language reference sources. As with anonymous classics, if the edition being catalogued is a translation, the cataloguer will add the name of the language of the translation to the uniform title. See figure 15-10.

```
Homer.                                              Figure 15-10.
  ₁Odyssey.  English₁                               Greek work
  The Odyssey / Homer ; a new verse translation by
Albert Cook. -- 1st ed. -- New York : Norton, c1967.
  xi, 340 p. ; 22 cm.


                                                   Title page

                    Homer        The Odyssey
                  A New Verse Translation by Albert Cook
  I. Cook, Albert.    II. Title. W. W. Norton & Company • Inc. • New York
```

25.4C. Anonymous works not written in Greek nor in the roman script

With the addition of the word "Greek," this rule is virtually the same as *AACR1* rule 102C2. It is closely related to 25.4B, which directs the use of an English-language title for classical and Byzantine Greek works. Likewise, the cataloguer is to prefer a title in English for an anonymous work created before 1501 whose original language is not written in the Greek or roman script. See figure 15-11.

```
Book of the dead.  English & Egyptian.
  The book of the dead : the papyrus of Ani in the
British Museum : the Egyptian text / with inter-
linear transliteration and translation, a running
translation, introduction, etc., by E.A. Wallis
Budge. -- New York : Dover, 1967.
  clv, 377 p. : ill. ; 24 cm.

  Cover title: The Egyptian book of the dead.     Figure 15-11.
  Reprint of: London : British Museum, 1895.      Anonymous work not
  Bibliography: p. ₁371₁-377.                     in roman or Greek
                                                  script
  I. Budge, E. A. Wallis. II. Papyrus Ani.  III.
British Museum.  IV. Title.  V. Title: The Egyptian
book of the dead.
```

Title page

The Book of the Dead
The Papyrus of Ani
in the British Museum.
The Egyptian Text with Interlinear
Transliteration and Translation,
a Running Translation, Introduction, etc.
by
E. A. Wallis Budge
Dover Publications, Inc., New York

The Arabian Nights is an anonymous work originally written in Arabic script. The cataloguer is directed to prefer an established title in English as uniform title. See figure 2-14 for an English translation of *The Arabian Nights*. Reference will be made from the variant title:

> Book of the thousand nights and a night
> *see*
> Arabian nights. *English.*

In contrast to entry shown in figure 2-14, an adaptation of *The Arabian Nights* will be entered under the name of the adapter, with added entry for the uniform title of the original work (21.10). See figure 15-12.

```
Williams-Ellis, Amabel.
   The Arabian nights : stories / retold by Amabel
Williams-Ellis ; illustrated by Pauline Diana
Baynes. -- New York : Criterion Books, c1957.
   348 p. : ill (some col.) ; 23 cm.
```

Figure 15-12.
Adaptation

I. Arabian nights.

The Arabian Nights
Stories retold by Amabel Williams-Ellis
Illustrated by Pauline Diana Baynes
Criterion Books   New York

Title page

25.5. ADDITIONS TO UNIFORM TITLES

25.5D. Translations

In essence, this rule is the same as *AACR1* rule 105. For an example of language added to uniform title for an anonymous classic, see figures 15-7 and 15-8.

A translation of a modern work may be brought into the same place in the library catalogue as the original work by means of uniform title made up of the original title of the work plus the language of the translation. See figure 15-13. Reference will be:

> Hürlimann, Bettina.
>> Three centuries of children's books in Europe
>>> *see*
> Hürlimann, Bettina.
>> Europäische Kinderbücher in drei Jahrhunderten. *English.*

```
Hürlimann, Bettina.
  [Europäische Kinderbücher in drei Jahrhunderten.
English]
  Three centuries of children's books in Europe /
Bettina Hürlimann ; translated and edited by Brian
W. Alderson. -- 1st U.S. ed. -- Cleveland : World,
c1969.
  xviii, 297 p. : ill. (some col.), ports. ; 25 cm.

  Translation of: Europäische Kinderbücher in drei
Jahrhunderten.
  Bibliography: p. 272-284.
  Includes index.

  I. Alderson, Brian W.  II. Title.
```

Figure 15-13.
Translation

Title page

Bettina Hürlimann

Three Centuries of
Children's Books in Europe
Translated and edited by Brian W. Alderson
The World Publishing Company
Cleveland and New York

To reiterate: Although libraries customarily use uniform headings for anonymous classics, not all libraries will choose to use uniform titles to collect translations of modern works under a single heading in the catalogue. For a non-research library, which is unlikely to acquire works such as those illustrated in figures 15-13, 1-7, 11-28, and 11-29 in the original language, the addition of a uniform title to the entry may actually be undesirable. For this reason, the use of uniform titles is subject to the policy of the cataloguing agency (25.1).

25.6. PARTS OF A WORK

25.6A. Single parts

This rule is a change from *AACR1* rule 106A. One of the problems that the cataloguer must solve is the question of how to handle separately published parts of a work, particularly if library policy is to relate such parts to the main work from which they have been taken. One way to accomplish this is by the use of uniform title. The title of the part by itself serves as uniform title with a "see" reference from the whole work. C. S. Lewis's *Chronicles of Narnia* is an example of a whole work, each of whose parts may be handled in such a fashion; see figure 15-14. Reference will be:

Lewis, C. S. (Clive Staples)
    The chronicles of Narnia.
        For separately published novels in
           this series see
Lewis, C. S. (Clive Staples)
    The lion, the witch and the wardrobe
    Prince Caspian
    The voyage of the Dawn Treader
    The silver chair
    The horse and his boy
    The magician's nephew
    The last battle.

```
Lewis, C. S. (Clive Staples)
   The last battle / by C.S. Lewis ; with illustra-
tions by Pauline Baynes. -- New York : Macmillan,
c1956.
   174 p. : ill. ; 21 cm. -- (The Chronicles of
Narnia)




     I. Title.
```

Title page

The Last Battle
By C. S. Lewis
With illustrations
by Pauline Baynes
New York
The Macmillan Company

Figure 15-14. Parts of a work

It goes without saying that such a reference should list only titles held in the library for which the reference is being made. An alternate method of gathering separate parts of a series into one place in the catalogue would be to make an added entry for the series in each case.

25.7. TWO WORKS ISSUED TOGETHER

This rule is the same as *AACR1* rule 107F. Not too infrequently two works by an author will be issued together in one physical volume, with or without a collective title. This is the case with the example of the two Horatio Alger novels, which most libraries would catalogue as shown in figure 15-15a. An alternate method of cataloguing this item would be to use a uniform title, thus arranging the work under the author's name by the title of the first item. Name-title added entry will be given for the uniform title of the second work. See figure 15-15b.

```
Alger, Horatio.
  Strive and succeed : two novels / by Horatio
Alger ; introduction by S.N. Behrman. -- 1st ed. --
New York : Holt, Rinehart and Winston, c1967.
  xii, 173 p. : ill. ; 22 cm.

  Contents: Julius, or, The street boy out West --
The store boy, or, The fortunes of Ben Barclay.

  I. Title.  II. Title: Julius, or, The street boy
out West.  III. Title: The store boy, or, The
fortunes of Ben Barclay.
```

Figure 15-15a. Two works by same author

```
Alger, Horatio.
  [Julius]
  Strive and succeed : two novels / by Horatio
Alger ; introduction by S.N. Behrman. -- 1st ed. --
New York : Holt, Rinehart and Winston, c1967.
  xii, 173 p. : ill. ; 22 cm.

  Contents: Julius, or, The street boy out West --
The store boy, or, The fortunes of Ben Barclay.

  I. Alger, Horatio. The store boy.  II. Title.
III. Title: Julius, or, The street boy out West.
IV. Title: The store boy, or, The fortunes of Ben
Barclay.
```

Figure 15-15b. Two works by the same author—alternative

Title page
Strive and Succeed
Julius or The Street Boy Out West
The Store Boy or The Fortunes of Ben Barclay
Two Novels by Horatio Alger
Introduction by S. N. Behrman
Holt, Rinehart and Winston
New York   Chicago   San Francisco

Collective Titles

25.8. COMPLETE WORKS

This rule is the same as *AACR1* rule 107A. In a library in which it seems advantageous to gather all editions of an author's complete works together in the catalogue, regardless of the title proper appearing on the various chief sources of information, a conventional uniform title in English, "Works," may be used. See figure 15-16.

```
Persius, 34–62.
  [Works]
  A. Persi Flacci Satvrarvm liber / accedit vita ;
edidit W.V. Clavsen. -- Oxford : Clarendon Press,
1956.
  xxviii, 43 p. ; 22 cm.

  Bibliographical footnotes.




  I. Clavsen, W. V.
```

Figure 15-16. Complete works

Title page

A. Persi Flacci
Satvrarvm Liber
Accedit Vita
Edidit
W. V. Clavsen
Oxford
At The Clarendon Press
1956

25.9. SELECTIONS

This rule combines *AACR1* rule 107B and C. As with the conventional uniform title "Works," the conventional uniform title in English "Selections" may be used if it seems advantageous to gather various editions of a voluminous author's work in one place in the library's catalogue. See figure 15-17.

```
Horace.
  ₁Selections.  English & Latin₁
  Satires ; Epistles ; and, Ars poetica / Horace ;
with an English translation by H. Rushton Fair-
clough. -- Cambridge : Harvard University Press,
1936.
  xxx, 508 p.  ; 17 cm.  -- (The Loeb classical
library)

  Latin and English on opposite pages.
  Bibliography: p. xxvii-xxx.
  Includes index.

  I. Fairclough, H. Rushton.  II. Title.
```

Figure 15-17. Selections

Title page

Horace
Satires, Epistles and Ars Poetica
With an English Translation by
H. Rushton Fairclough
Cambridge, Massachusetts
Harvard University Press
London
William Heinemann Ltd.
MCMXXXVI

25.11. TRANSLATIONS, ETC.

This rule is the same as *AACR1* rule 107E. It refers to works entered under uniform title according to rules 25.8 through 25.10. See figure 15-14 for an example of name of language added to the uniform title "Selections."

Special Rules for Certain Materials

25.13. COMPOSITE MANUSCRIPTS AND MANUSCRIPT GROUPS

This rule is in essence about the same as *AACR1* rule 103. It pertains to a manuscript that contains more than one work and that lacks a title, or a manuscript group that lacks a title. Many such manuscript groups have acquired titles subsequent to their writing; if this is so, use the title that has been assigned to the manuscript or that title by which the manuscript is commonly known. If the manuscript has no "commonly known" title, create one according to directions under 25.13c.

The Dead Sea scrolls qualify as an example of a manuscript group that has come to be identified in reference sources by a familiar name. Use this name as the uniform title. Add the name of the language of the translation, if any, following the uniform title. See figure 15-18.

```
Dead Sea scrolls.  English.
   The Dead Sea scriptures in English translation /
with introduction and notes by Theodor H. Gaster.
-- Garden City, N.Y. : Doubleday, c1956.
   x, 350 p. ; 18 cm. -- (Doubleday anchor books ;
A92)

   Bibliography: p. [323]-326.
   Includes index.


   I. Gaster, Theodor H.  II. Title.
```

Figure 15-18.
Manuscript group

Title page

The Dead Sea Scriptures
In English Translation
With Introduction and Notes by
Theodor H. Gaster
Doubleday Anchor Books
Doubleday & Company, Inc.
Garden City, New York

Legal Materials

25.15. LAWS, ETC.

This rule is an enlargement of *AACR1* rule 101D. For examples of uniform title as applied to laws, see 21.31; see also discussion in this text under 21.31 and figures 11-48 through 11-50.

25.16. TREATIES, ETC.

This application of uniform titles has no antecedent in *AACR1*. See 21.35 for rules governing entry of treaties and other intergovernmental agreements. See discussion in this text under 21.35 and figures 11-53 and 11-54 for examples of use of uniform headings for treaties.

Sacred Scriptures

25.17. GENERAL RULE

This rule should be correlated with rule 21.37, which stipulates that sacred scriptures will be entered under title. However, because of the nature of sacred scripture, such works have, in almost all cases, been issued many times, with varying titles, over a long period of time. Main entry under a uniform title is thus appropriate; see figure 15-19. Uniform title will be the title by which the scripture is most commonly known in English-language reference sources—if possible, official sources authorized by the religious group involved. As with other uniform titles, add the language of the translation to a translated work. See figure 15-20; see also figure 11-55.

```
Book of Mormon.
   The Book of Mormon : an account / written by the
hand of Mormon upon plates taken from the plates
of Nephi ; translated by Joseph Smith, Jun. --
Salt Lake City, Utah : Church of Jesus Christ of
Latter-day Saints, 1961, c1963.
   558 p. : ill. ; 18 cm.



   I. Smith, Joseph.   II. Church of Jesus Christ
of Latter-day Saints.
```

Figure 15-19. Sacred scripture—original language

Title page

The Book of Mormon
An Account Written by
The Hand of Mormon
Upon Plates
Taken from the Plates of Nephi
Translated by Joseph Smith, Jun.
Published by
The Church of Jesus Christ of Latter-day Saints
Salt Lake City, Utah, U.S.A.
1961

```
Book of Mormon.  French.
   Le Livre de Mormon : récit / écrit de la main de
Mormon sur des plaques prises des plaques de
Néphi ; traduit en anglais par Joseph Smith, Junior ;
traduit de l'anglais par John Taylor et Curtis E.
Bolton. -- 2e éd. / divisé en chapitres et en
versets, et pourvu de renvois, d'après l'édition
anglaise, par James L. Barker et Joseph E. Evans.
-- Zurich : S.F. Ballif, 1907.
   623 p. ; 17 cm.


   I. Smith, Joseph.
```

Figure 15-20. Sacred
scripture in translation

Title page

Le Livre de Mormon
Récit écrit de
la main de Mormon
sur des plaques prises des plaques de Néphi
Traduit en anglais par Joseph Smith, Junior
Traduit de l'Anglais par John Taylor
et Curtis E. Bolton
Deuxième édition
Divisé en chapitres et en versets,
et pourvu de renvois,
d'après l'édition anglaise,
par James L. Barker et Joseph E. Evans
Publié par
Serge F. Ballif, Zurich
1907

25.18. PARTS OF SACRED SCRIPTURES AND ADDITIONS

It is indicative of the broader frame of reference on which *AACR2* is based that special rules for the Bible are no longer emphasized virtually to the exclusion of the sacred scriptures of other religions as they were in previous codes. Rules for uniform heading for special parts, versions, etc., of the Koran, Talmud, etc., are worked out in a parallel fashion to those for the Bible and subsumed as parts of the same rule governing headings for the Bible.

25.18A. Bible

This rule subsumes *AACR1* rules 108 through 114. The uniform title for the Bible will be the word "Bible." To this the cataloguer will add (in this order) language, name of version, and year of publication:

Bible. *English. Authorized. 1969.*

The prescribed order of elements is the same as that called for under *AACR1* rule 108. The order of elements differs from ALA 1949 rule 34, which prescribed Bible, language, year, and version. *AACR* order brings editions of the Bible together in the catalogue by version rather than by year of publication, a more useful arrangement, particularly since the date of publication is often a fugitive element in Bibles.

25.18A2. Testaments. Entry for parts of the Bible is treated as a subheading following the uniform title "Bible." "O.T." stands for Old Testament; "N.T." stands for New Testament. These designations will be used when cataloguing a separate edition of the Old Testament or the New Testament; see figure 15-21. Make reference:

> Old Testament
> *see*
> Bible. *O.T.*

```
Bible.  O.T.  English.  Smith.  1927.
   The Old Testament : an American translation / by
Alexander R. Gordon ... [et al.] ; edited by J.M.
Powis Smith. -- Chicago : University of Chicago
Press, c1927.
   xii, 1712 p. ; 23 cm.



   I. Gordon, Alexander R.  II. Smith, J. M. Powis
(John Merlin Powis).
```

Figure 15-21. Old Testament

Title page

> The Old Testament
> An American Translation
> by
> Alexander R. Gordon • Theophile J. Meek
> J. M. Powis Smith • Leroy Waterman
> Edited by
> J. M. Powis Smith
> The University of Chicago Press
> Chicago, Illinois

25.18A3. Books. A separate book of the Bible will be entered, as appropriate, as a subheading to "Bible. *O.T.*" or "Bible *N.T.*" See figure 15-22. Make reference:

> Mark (*Book of the New Testament*)
> *see*
> Bible. *N.T. Mark.*

Bible. *Mark*
   see
Bible. *N.T. Mark.*

```
Bible.  N.T.  Mark.  English.  New English.  1965.
   The Gospel according to Mark / commentary by
C.F.D. Moule. -- Cambridge, ₁England₁ : University
Press, 1965.
   x, 133 p. : map ; 21 cm. -- (The Cambridge Bible
commentary : New English Bible)



I. Moule, C. F. D.   II. Title.   III. Series.
```

Figure 15-22. Book of
the Bible

Title page

The Gospel According to Mark
Commentary by
C.F.D. Moule
Cambridge
At The University Press
1965

25.18A4. Groups of books. The list of groups of books of the Bible commonly identified by a group name given under 25.18A4 includes all of the groups that can be gathered in this manner.

25.18A9. Selections. The word "selections" will be inserted as a subheading between the version and the date for combinations of three or more books that cannot be encompassed by any of the groupings given in 25.18A4. The word is also used for condensations, abridgments, etc., of the Bible; see figure 15-23.

25.18A10. Language. This rule is the same as *AACR1* rule 110. Add the name of the language of the text after the word "Bible" or the part being catalogued. See figures 15-21, 15-22, and 15-23.

25.18A11. Version. This rule is the same as *AACR1* rule 111A. The following list gives some of the commonly used versions as cited by the Library of Congress. See figures 15-24–15-26 for examples.

Rheims—Rheims New Testament, originally translated in 1582

Douai—Douai Old Testament and the Rheims New Testament

Authorized—King James Version of 1611

Revised—Revised Version (N.T. 1881, O.T. 1885)

American Revised—American Revised Version (1901)

Revised Standard—Revised Standard Version (N.T. 1946; O.T. 1962; Apocrypha 1957)

New English—New English Bible (N.T. 1961; O.T. 1966)

Today's English—Today's English Version, 1966.

```
Bible.  English.  Revised Standard.  Selections.
  1964.
  A shortened arrangement of the Holy Bible,
Revised Standard Version / edited by Robert O.
Ballou. -- 1st ed. -- Philadelphia : A.J. Holman
Co. for Lippincott, c1964.
  xxxii, 773 p. ; 22 cm.



  I. Ballou, Robert O.   II. Title.
```

Figure 15-23. Bible—selections

Title page

A Shortened Arrangement of
The Holy Bible
Revised Standard Version
Edited by Robert O. Ballou
Published by A. J. Holman Company
for J. B. Lippincott Company
Philadelphia

```
Bible.  English.  Authorized.  1948.
  The Holy Bible : containing the Old and New
Testaments and the Apocrypha / translated out of
the original tongues ; and with the former trans-
lations diligently compared and revised by His
Majesty's special command ; appointed to be read
in churches. -- Cambridge, [England] : University
Press ; New York : Distributed by Dryden Press,
1948.
  xxii, 662, 870 p. : maps ; 20 cm.



  I. Title.
```

Figure 15-24. Bible—version

The Holy Bible
Containing the Old and New Testaments
and the Apocrypha
Translated out of the original
tongues: and with the former translations
diligently compared and revised, by
his Majesty's Special Command
Appointed to be read in Churches
Cambridge
At The University Press
Distributed in
American Colleges and Universities by
The Dryden Press, Publishers, New York

Title page

Bible. <u>English. American Revised. 1929.</u>
   The Holy Bible : containing the Old and New
Testaments / translated out of the original tongues ;
being the version set forth A.D. 1611 compared
with the most ancient authorities and revised
A.D. 1881-1885 ; newly edited by the American
Revision Committee, A.D. 1901. -- Standard ed. --
Philadelphia : Made specially for Publication
Dept., Presbyterian Board of Christian Education
by T. Nelson, c1929.
   x, 996, v, 288 p. ; 18 cm.

   I. American Revision Committee.   II. Title.

Figure 15-25. Bible—
version

The Holy Bible
Containing the Old and New Testaments
Translated Out of the Original Tongues
Being the version set forth A.D. 1611
Compared with the most ancient authorities and revised
A.D. 1881–1885
Newly Edited by the American Revision Committee
A.D. 1901
Standard Edition made specially for
Publication Department
Presbyterian Board of Christian Education
Philadelphia, Pa.
By the Publishers Thomas Nelson & Sons

Title page

```
Bible.  N.T.  English.  Today's English.  1966.
  Good news for modern man : the New Testament
in Today's English Version. -- New York : American
Bible Society, c1966.
  iv, 599 p. ; 18 cm.
```

Figure 15-26. Bible—version

```
I. American Bible Society.  II. Title.
```

Title page

Good News
for Modern Man
The New Testament
in Today's English Version
American Bible Society
New York

Some versions are identified by the name of the translator. Use the translator's name in place of version if identification is by translator; see figure 15-21. Some names thus used in Library of Congress headings for the Bible are:

Kleist-Lilly—New Testament by James A. Kleist and Joseph Lilly

Knox—translation by Ronald Knox

Moffatt—translation by James Moffatt

Montgomery—translation of the New Testament by Helen Barrett Montgomery

Lamsa—translation by George M. Lamsa

Phillips—J. B. Phillips translation

Schonfield—New Testament translation by Hugh Schonfield

Smith-Goodspeed—O.T. translation by J. M. Powis Smith; N.T. translation by Edgar Goodspeed.

For further information about versions of the English Bible, see a Bible encyclopaedia or dictionary, such as *Harper's Bible Dictionary*.

25.18A12. Alternatives to version. This rule is essentially the same as *AACRI* rule 112. Another term can be substituted for the name of the version when the text is in the original language, when the version is unknown, when it has been altered, when it cannot be identified by translator's name, or when more than two versions are involved. The use of the surname of the person who has altered the text as an alternative to use of name of version is analogous to using the name of a translator in place of version. See figure 15-27.

```
Bible.  English.  Smith.  1970.
   Joseph Smith's "New translation" of the Bible :
a complete parallel column comparison of the
Inspired Version of the Holy Scriptures and the
King James Authorized Version / introduction by F.
Henry Edwards. -- Independence, Mo. : Herald Pub.
House, 1970.
   523 p. ; 23 cm.

   ISBN 0-8309-0032-2

   I. Smith, Joseph.  II. Bible.  English.
Authorized.  1970.  III. Title.
```

Figure 15-27.
Alternative to version

Title page

Joseph Smith's
"New Translation"
Of The Bible
A complete parallel column comparison of the
Inspired Version of the Holy Scriptures and the
King James Authorized Version
Introduction by F. Henry Edwards
1970
Herald Publishing House, Independence, Missouri

24.18A13. Year. The year of publication is the last element of the uniform heading for the Bible. The rule is the same as *AACR1* rule 113.

Liturgical Works

Compare rules 25.19–25.23 with *AACR1* rule 119. They should also be correlated with 21.39, the rule for entry. Liturgical works were formerly entered under the name of the denomination followed, by the form subheading "Liturgy and ritual." Entry is now to be under the name of the denomination, with a uniform title for the work interposed between the heading and the transcription of the title proper. See figure 2-12 for an example of catalogue entry for a liturgical work.

Music

Rules 25.25–25.36 are devoted to music. For examples of uniform titles for musical works, see chapter 4, Music, in this text. See also chapter 5, Sound Recordings, especially figures 5-1, 5-4, 5-8, 5-11, 5-12, 5-13.

APPENDIX I

Comments on Practice Shown in Figures

CHAPTER 1

1-1. Main entry: Form of heading, 22.1A. Choice of form is the name by which the person is commonly known. No longer will the cataloguer fill out forenames represented by initials, even if two authors have the same name. See 22.16A on procedure to be followed to distinguish between two authors having identical names. In all cases, under *AACR2* practice, initials in the heading will be closed with a full stop.

Title area: 1.1B6. Initials with a full stop between them are to be recorded without any internal spaces.

1-2a–c. "Proper names" including those of allegorical characters are to be capitalized. If the ampersand appears on the title page, it is transcribed thus.

Publication area: 1.4B8

Subseries: 1.6H1

1-3. Punctuation: 1.1B1. In general, the title is to be transcribed as it appears on the title page. However, punctuation on the title page that is the same as punctuation prescribed for some particular cataloguing function cannot be used. A dash (—) should replace ellipses (. . .). No confusion will result from the use of the dash in this manner as the dash is not separated from the preceding word by a space.

Edition area: Colophon gives "Erste Auflage 1973"

Publication area: Verso of title page: ©1973, Insel Verlag, Frankfurt am Main.

1-4. Contrast the format of this entry with that of figure 1-1. In contrast to the paragraphed entry used when main entry is under the name of an author, this entry has main entry with hanging indention. This is always used when main entry is under title (21.7B, work produced under the direction of an editor).

1-6. Main entry: Entry will be made under any name, nickname, or other appellation the person chooses to use, whether it is a real name or not: 22.1A. See 22.11 for examples and discussion of entry under phrase. Rule for entry under phrase is much more liberal than *AACR1* 2C. Virtually the only appellation ruled out as a possible heading is a nonalphabetic or nonnumeric device, and this exclusion is only because of filing problems. (See 21.5C.)

Added entries: The word "title" as an added entry indicates that the cataloguer wants the entire title proper to appear as an added entry in the catalogue. According to *AACR2*, the alternative title is now a part of the title proper. If the cataloguer does not want the entire title proper to appear as the title added entry, this must be specified in the tracing, shown in figure 1-6 (see also figure 1-7). In most instances, the entire title proper should appear as the title added entry, in which case it is not necessary to write out, the title when indicating a title added entry.

1-7. Publisher: Shorten name, but do not leave out names of any members of a partnership: when the title page shows an ampersand (&), transcribe it thus. Likewise transcribe "and" if it is given on the title page.

Note: In all cases, when the cataloguer knows the original title of a translated work, this title should be given, usually as a formal note (see 1.7A3), 1.7B4. In addition, original title may be given as a uniform title preceding the title proper (25.5D).

1-8. Main entry: 21.23C
GMD: 1.1C1; see also *AACR2* chapter 7
Publication area: 1.4E1
Physical description area: 6.5
Notes:
   1. 6.7B18
   2. 6.7B19
   3. 6.7B19

1-9. Main entry: 21.1B2d; form 24.7
Title: Discussed in text; see also 1.1F12
Notes:
   1. 2.7B6
   2. 2.7B18
Added entries:
   I. 21.30D
   II. 21.30E

1-10. Main entry: 21.1B2c. Fewer works will be entered under corporate body under *AACR2* rules than were allowed by *AACR1* rules. The cataloguer should read 21.1B2 with care to determine whether a work is of such a nature that it will be given main entry under corporate body. The work catalogued in figure 1-10 is an official statement of position on external policies,

recording the collective thought of ALA's Subcommittee on the ALA Rules for Filing Catalog Cards. Therefore, it is given entry under the name of the body.

Publication area: 1.4D4. If the publisher's name appears in "recognizable form" in the title–statement of responsibility area, it may be abbreviated to initials. However, the initials which appear in the statement of responsibility in this entry do not constitute enough information to identify the body clearly. In case of doubt, do not abbreviate.

Added entry: 21.30D. A "prominently named" editor will be given an added entry.

1-11. Title created by the cataloguer: 1.1B7. Descriptive cataloguing of microscope slides is governed by *AACR2* chapter 10. It falls under the category of realia since such slides generally include a naturally occurring object mounted for viewing.

GMD: 1.1C. The general material designation is a useful addition to catalogue entries for nonbook materials. Note that capitalization is different from that shown in *AACR Chapter 12* (1975).

Publication area: For handmade, one of a kind items, conventional format of place, publisher, and date would be inappropriate. 10.4F2 stipulates date only.

Physical description area: 10.5D1
Notes:
   1. 10.7B3
   2. 10.7B6
   3. 10.7B10

1-13. Main entry: Initials are closed with a full stop and recorded without any internal spaces.

Title–statement of responsibility area: GMD selected from 1.1C1. Initials recorded with full stop and without internal spaces. See *AACR2* chapter 10 for rules for games.

Publication area: Publisher name shortened, 1.4D2.

Physical description area: 10.5B1, 10.5D2

Note: 10.7B10

1-14. See *AACR2* chapter 8 for rules for slides.

Publication area: Date, 1.4F7

Physical description area: 8.5D5, 8.5E1

1-15. See *AACR2* chapter 8 for rules for filmstrips.

Physical description area: 8.5B1, 8.5B2, 8.5C4, 8.5D2

1-16. Main entry: 21B2a; form, 24.1, 24.13

Publication area: Place of publication bracketed because it was not found in the book.

Note: 1.7B2

1-17. Main entry: 25.4, 25.5D

Title–statement of responsibility area: 1.1F7. Include titles of nobility (sir) in transcription. However, "Shri" is a title of address, not part of the name, and not a title of nobility. Thus, this title is omitted from transcription.

1.1F12. "The Sanskrit text" is a noun phrase indicative of the role of the translator; give it as part of the statement of responsibility.

Physical description area: Leaves of plates, 2.5B10

1-19. Note: 1.7B17. A summary, which may be given at the discretion of the cataloguer, is often given as part of the catalogue entry for books for children and young people.

1-20. Added entry for illustrators: 21.30K2c. Illustrations are an important feature of many books for children and young people. For such books, give an added entry for illustrator unless the illustrations are clearly of slight importance and extent (as happens to be the case in the example shown in figure 19).

1-21. Note: 1.7A4, 1.7B7

1-22. "With numerous engravings": 1.1F15. See discussion of rationale in this text under 1.1F15.

1-23. See *AACR2* chapter 8 for specific rules on slides.

Chief source is the slide itself (8.0B1); title was transcribed from the first slide of the set.

Publication area: From accompanying material. Date is certain because of dates of exhibits and date of acquisition of slide set.

Physical description area: 8.5B1, 8.5C12, 8.5D5, 8.5E

Note: 8.7B6

Added entry: 21.30E

1-24. Series: Choice among variants, 1.6B2

Physical description area: Paging, 2.5B7. For a book totalling more than 100 pages, but unpaged, pagination may be estimated rather than counted. Illustrations, 2.5C6

Note: Punctuation, 1.1G2; form, 2.7B5

1-25. Publication area: Place of publication was found on the book jacket. The jacket is not one of the prescribed sources of information. Therefore, place is bracketed.

Physical description area: Illustrations, 2.5C6

Added entry I: 21.30D

1-26. Physical description area: 2.5B10. The plates are printed on both sides, but not numbered. Count them as pages, not as leaves, and record number of "p. of plates" in brackets.

1-27. Main entry: 21.17B. Reproductions of the works of an artist with text about the artist are to be entered generally under the author of the text. Contrast with *AACR1* 8D.

Edition area: 1.2B3. Although we disregard a statement that is simply a publication statement, "First Schocken edition 1968" is a true edition statement and should be transcribed as such. Note that when the edition statement includes the date of publication, the date is not transcribed as part of the edition statement; the information is transferred to the publication area.

Physical description area: 2.5B1. Plates in this book are printed on both sides and numbered.

1-28. Main entry under corporate author: 21.1B2c.

Title–statement of responsibility area: Transcription of initials in title, 1.1B6.

Publication area: See discussion under 1.4C3 for addition of state to place for identification. Not necessary here because the name of the publisher includes name of state. The date is from the page following the title page.

Physical description area: 2.5B7. Count the pages for an unpaged work and record in brackets.

Note: 2.7B3

Added entry I: 21.30E; form, LC policy decision to abbreviate "Department" in headings. According to *AACR2*, heading will be: Arizona. Department of Education.

1-29. Main entry: 21.7B. Note capitalization for title main entry; if the first word of the title main entry is an article, capitalize also the second word (A.4D).

1-30. Physical description area: 10.5B2, 10.5D2

Note: 10.7B17

Added entry: 24.5C1. Include "Inc." as part of the corporate heading to make it clear that the name is that of a corporate body. Note that the word "Inc." is now capitalized (A.18E).

1-31. Statement of responsibility area: Notice that brackets do not take the place of the full stop, which must close each area. Full stop precedes and follows bracket.

Note: 2.7B18

1-32. Title–statement of responsibility area: Discussed in text. Editor's name is taken from the verso of the title page, i.e., a "prominent" position. The name is transcribed within the same set of square brackets needed for "et al." See discussion in *AACR2* under 1.1F1. The mark of omission (. . .) is not used when transcribing

information from sources other than the chief source of information.

Edition: 1.2B3. An edition statement need not include the word "edition."

Publication area: 1.4D4. Name of publisher shortened to initials.

Added entries:

I. 21.30E

II. 21.30D

1-34. Main entry: Form of heading, 22.12B. By LC policy decision, British titles of honour will always be transcribed at the end of the name. According to *AACR2* rule, this heading should be Sitwell, *Sir* Osbert.

Note: 2.7B9

1-35. Main entry: Form of heading, 22.17A4. Philip has two titles, Prince and Duke of Edinburgh. The cataloguer should choose the higher title, Prince.

Series: Taken from cover, which reads "The fourteenth Fawley Foundation lecture, 1967." If series title begins with a date or number that varies from issue to issue, omit it from the title. Transcribe the omitted data as a series number.

Note: 2.7B6

Added entry for series: 20.30L

1-36. Added entry: Form of name, 22.5D1, Spanish

1-37. Main entry: Form of name, 22.13B

1-38. Main entry: Form of name, 22.15A

1-39. Main entry: Form of name, 22.15B. Please note that although 22.15B calls for the title "Mrs." to precede forenames, LC policy requires that this title follow the name. *AACR2* order would be: Dana, *Mrs.* William Starr.

Edition area: Statement of responsibility, 1.2C1

1-40. Notes:

1. 2.7B9

2. 2.7B18

Standard number: 1.8, 2.8B

1-41. Main entry: 21.12A

Series: Taken from cover

Added entry I: 21.12A

1-42. Main entry: Form of name, 22.17C. Note that the rule applies only to persons entered under given name. Do *not* add "Cardinal" to the name of an individual entered under surname.

Publication area: 1.4B8

1-43. Main entry under title: 21.6C2

Contents note: 2.7B18

Added entry: For Danielou: 21.6C2; for La Mothe, 21.30K1

1-44. Main entry: Form of name, 22.5C4

Title–statement of responsibility area: Note in chief source of information the items not transcribed as part of this area. For a discussion of omissions pertinent to this figure, see chapter 1 of this text under 1.1F15.

Publication area: Inclusion of "Tip." as part of name: 1.4D3; date, 1.4F8.

Physical description area: 2.5B17

1–45. Main entry under title: 21.7B

Physical description area: Size, 2.5D2

1-46. Main entry under title: 21.7B

Note: 2.7B18

Added entries:
  I. 21.7B
  II. 21.7B
  III. 21.30F

1-47. Physical description area: Leaves of plates, 2.5B10

1-48. Main entry: Form of name, 22.5D1, French

1-49. Physical description area: 2.5B10

1-51. Main entry under title: 21.6C2

Statement of responsibility: Omissions, 1.1F5

Added entries:
  I. 21.6C2; form of name, 24.1, paragraph 2
  II. 21.30B

1-52. Main entry: Form, 22.15A

Publication area: 1.4B8, 1.4F7

Added entry I: 21.30K2c

1-53. Main entry under title: 21.B3. Note capitalization of title main entry which begins with an article (A.4D).

Note 1: 2.7B10

Added entry: 21.30E; form, 24.19

1-54. Title–statement of responsibility area: The heroine of this story is a young girl named Carol Bird; thus, all words should be capitalized.

Series: 1.6E

Contents: 1.7B18

Added entries: II–V. 21.30M

1-55. Publication area: 1.4B8

Subseries: 1.6H1

Added entry II: 21.30M

1-56. Main entry: 21.7C

Added entries:
  I. 21.7B
  II. 21.30J
  III. 21.30L

1-57. Main entry: 21.6B2

Title–statement of responsibility area: 1.1F6

Edition area: 1.2B1. Note that "second" is now transcribed as "2nd" rather than "2d," the previously prescribed abbreviation (C.7).

1-58. Main entry: 21.12A

Added entry I: 21.12A

1-59. Main entry: 21.12A

Added entry I: 21.12A

1-60. Main entry: 21.5C; form, 22.11D. Notice that *AACR2* does not maintain the tenuous distinction between phrases beginning with "a" and those beginning with "the" made in *AACR1* 2C.

1-61. Main entry under title: 21.7

Added entry: 21.7

1-62. Title–statement of responsibility area: 1.1F13

Added entry I: 21.30D

1-63. Main entry: 21.4A; form of heading, 21.11B

1-64. Main entry under title: 21.7

Publication area: 1.4B8

Added entries:
  I. 21.7. Give added entry for personal author before added entry for corporate body.
  II. 21.30E; form: 24.4C2. LC policy determines the use of Great Britain rather than United Kingdom as a qualifier.

1-65. Games are covered by *AACR2* chapter 10.

Physical description area: 10.5B1, 10.5B2, 10.5D2

Note: 10.7B1, 10.7B14

Added entry: 21.30E

1-66. Videorecordings are covered by *AACR2* chapter 7.

GMD: 1.1C2. If GMD is to be used, it is added immediately following the title proper.

Physical description area: 7.5B2, 7.5C3, 7.5C4, 7.5D3.

Notes:
  1. 7.7B7
  2. 7.7B17

Added entries:
  I. 21.30E; form, 24.2D
  II. 21.30E

1-67. Main entry under title: 21.5A. Note capitalization of title main entry when first word is an article (A.4D).

Physical description area: 2.5C3. Some of the maps are folded. Folded leaves of plates are so indicated (2.5B11). Contrast with 141D3 in *AACR Chapter 6* (1974).

1-68. Main entry: Form of name, 22.5D1, Italian

1-69. Main entry: 21.6B2; form, 22.5C3

Note 1: 2.7B6

Added entry II: 21.30E; form, 24.1 (Note change from *AACR1* 66B.)

1-71. Main entry: 21.9 (adaptation)

Filmstrips are covered in *AACR2* chapter 8.

Title–statement of responsibility area: "Prairie" is not capitalized in this context. Capitalize soil names only when they are part of a scientific classification (*AACR2* A.28).

Physical description area: 8.5B2, 8.5C4, 8.5D2, 8.5E1

Notes:
  1. 8.7B3
  2. 8.7B6
  3. 8.7B7
  4. 8.7B10
  5. 8.7B17

Added entries:
  I. 21.10. Name-title added entry is not appropriate since this filmstrip is an adaptation of all of Wilder's books.
  II. 21.30E

1-72. Main entry: 21.1B3

Added entry: 21.1B3

1-73. Main entry: 21.23C. Sound recordings are covered in *AACR2* chapter 6.

Notes:
  1. 6.7B18
  2. 6.7B19

1-74. Notes: 2.7B5

1-75. Main entry: 21.4D; form, 24.20

Added entries:
  I. 21.30F; form, 24.21
  II. 21.4D1

1-76. Main entry: 21.1B2; form, 24.17, 24.19. By LC policy, "Department" in the heading is abbreviated to "Dept." *AACR2* calls for: Library of Congress. *Processing Department.*

Added entry I: 21.30E

1-77. Main entry: 21.1B2; form, 24.17, 24.19

Physical description area: 2.5B10

Series: 1.6

1-78. Main entry: 21.13B

Publication area: 1.4D3, 1.4D7

Physical description area: 1.5B5

Added entry II: 21.13B

1-79. Notes:
  1. 2.7B10
  2. 2.7B20

1-80. Main entry: 21.1B2; form, 24.1

1-81. When initials occur in the inverted part of the name in the main entry (forenames), they are to be closed with a full stop and recorded without any internal spaces. Likewise they will be recorded with full stops but without any internal spaces in the statement of responsibility.

Edition area: Note the spelling "2nd," which (along with "3rd") is different from previous cataloguing practice (C.7A).

Publication area: 1.4B4. Omit accompanying preposition from name of publisher. For discussion of the date, see this text under 1.4F2.

Physical description area: The rule for recording leaves of plates (2.5B10) is basically the same as 141B1d in *AACR Chapter 6* (1974) except that if illustrations are on both sides of the plate, the cataloguer may now record "pages of plates" and count the plates accordingly. See figure 1-26 for an example. In figure 1-17 illustrations are only on one side of the leaves; thus, leaves of plates.

Standard number: 1.8B1. Number will be recorded as found, with or without hyphens.

1-82. Note: 2.7B8

1-83. Main entry under title: 21.5A. Note capitalization when first word is an initial article (A.4D).

Added entry: 21.30E; form, 24.12

1-84. Main entry: 21.33A
Uniform title: 25.3A
Title–statement of responsibility area: 1.1G1
Notes:
1. 2.7B3
2. 2.7B5
Added entries:
I. 21.30E, 24.17
II. 21.30M
III. 21.30L

1-85. Main entry: Form, 22.18. Dates should be added to distinguish between otherwise identical names. They may optionally be added to other names.

1-86. For a full discussion of reprint publications, see 1.11. Cataloguing is done for the *reprint*, i.e., the publication in hand. Only information pertaining to the reprint will appear in the body of the entry. All pertinent information about the original edition is combined in one note arranged according to 1.7A3. See 1.11B5.

1-87. Main entry: Form, 22.8A, 22.13
Added entry: 21.30D

1-88. Main entry: 21.1B2d; form, 24.7
Publication area: 1.4D4
Series: 1.6E
Added entries:
I. 21.30E
II. 21.30E

1-89. Main entry: 21.7
Publication area: Place of publication is bracketed because it is not given in the book. Also see 1.4D3.
Note: 2.7B6
Added entry: I. 21.30E

1-90. Games are covered by *AACR2* chapter 10.
Physical description area: 10.5B2, 10.5D2
Note: 10.7B14
Added entry: 21.30E

1-91. Main entry under title: 21.7
Other title information: 1.1E
Edition area: 1.2C1
Note: 2.7B6
Added entries:
I. 21.7
II. 21.7
III. 21.30E

1-92. Main entry: 21.12B
Edition area: 1.2C1
Note 1: 1.7B7, 1.7A4
Added entries:
I. 21.12B
II. 21.30B
III. 21.30B

1-93. Main entry: Form, 22.16A (optional addition)
Notes:
1. 1.7B2
2. 1.7B18

1-95. Publication area: Place of publication is bracketed because it is not in the book.
Notes:
1. 1.7B2, 1.7B7. Two notes combined in accordance with 1.7A5.
2. 1.7B18
3. 1.7B18
Added entry I: 21.3K1a

1-96. Main entry: 21.4D; form of heading, 24.20C; addition, 23.4B.
Publication area: Place and date are bracketed because they are from sources other than prescribed sources.
Physical description area: 2.5B2
Notes:
1. 2.7B3
2. 2.7B6
Added entry I: 21.4D

1-97. Main entry: 21.28A (libretto)
Added entry I: 21.28B

1-102. Slides are covered by *AACR2* chapter 8.
Physical description area: 8.5C12, 8.5D5, 8.5E1

Notes:
1. 8.7B10
2. 8.7B17

1-103. Main entry: 21.10
Notes:
1. 2.7B9
2. 2.7B11
Added entry I: 21.10

1-104. A typescript of a thesis is regarded as a manuscript and is catalogued according to rules in *AACR2* chapter 4 (Manuscripts). See *Cataloging Service Bulletin* 118 for further discussion of this matter.
Main entry: Form, 22.3A
Date area: 4.4B1
Notes:
1. 4.7B1
2. 4.7B9
3. 4.7B11
4. 2.7B13
5. 2.7B18

1-105. Main entry: Form, 22.3A

1-106. Main entry: 21.12B, 21.6C2
Statement of responsibility: 1.1F5
Notes:
1. 2.7B7
2. 1.7B14
3. 2.7B18
Added entries:
I. 21.6C2
II. 21.12B

1-107. Transparencies are covered in *AACR2* chapter 8.
Entry under title: 21.1C3
Publication area: 1.4D4
Physical description area: 8.5C16, 8.5D4
Note: 8.7B11
Added entries:
I. 21.30E
II. 21.30E

1-108a & b. A kit is covered in *AACR2* 1.10.

1-109. The cataloguing of photographic reprints is covered in *AACR2* 1.11. This reprint is discussed in detail in the text.

1-110. Note omission of information about the original publication from the title–statement of responsibility area.

Do not use ellipses to show omission. Give information about the original publication in the notes area, using conventional punctuation.

1-111. Title–statement of responsibility area: 1.11B.
Notes:
1. 1.7A3
2. 1.7B18

CHAPTER 2

2-1. Main entry: 21.7B
Added entry: 21.7B; form, 22.15A
Physical description area: 2.5B6, 2.5B10
Notes:
1. 2.7B4
2. 2.7B10

2-2. Main entry: 21.7B
Added entries: 21.7B
Note: 2.7B4
Standard number: 2.8

2-3b. Title: Bracketed word "by" is added to clarify the relationship of the title and authorship statement of the main work to the *Teacher's Resource Book* here catalogued. The title proper of the work covered by figure 2-3b consists of title, author statement of main work, and designation "Teacher's resource book." Cf. 2.1B1, 1.1B9.

2-4. Main entry: 21.7B
Publication area: Date from verso of title page
Note: 2.7B18
Added entries:
I. 21.7B
II–IV. 21.7B ("If such a work includes two or three contributions or independent works, make name-title added entries for each of them."); form, 25.3A, 25.5D. In addition, Library of Congress practice is to add date as the last element following language in the uniform heading for a translated work, i.e.: Vega Carpio, Lope de Fuente ovejuna. English. 1963.

2-5. Main entry: Form, 22.15A
Publication area: Date, 1.4F1, 1.4G4. The actual date of publication is speci-

fied on the verso of the title page. The date on the title page, 1910, is a printing date. Rule 1.4G4 provides as an option that the cataloguer "give the ... date of manufacture [printing date] if [such date should] differ from the ... date of publication ... and [is] considered important by the cataloguing agency." LC will apply this option.

Physical description area: 2.5B10

2-6. Main entry: 21.7B

Added entry: 21.7B

Notes: 2.7B18

2-7. Notes:
1. 2.7B7
2. 2.7B17

2-8. Main entry: 21.6C2

Title–statement of responsibility area: 1.1D, 1.1E, 1.1F5

Publication area: 1.4A2

Physical description area: 2.5B1, 2.5D4

2-9. Title–statement of responsibility area: 1.1F12

Publication area: 1.4D3. Information from colophon.

Physical description: 2.5B1, 2.5D4

Notes:
1. 2.7B7
2. 2.7B10, 2.7B20.

Two notes combined in accordance with 1.7A5. Information from colophon.

2-10. Added entry I: 21.30K2a–c

2-11. Title–statement of responsibility area: 1.1B2. (Title means "Cornelius Tacitus's histories.")

Transcription of title: 1.1B1. Note that the instructions in *AACR Chapter 6* (1974) 134B1 that "typographic peculiarities, e.g. the use of v for u and i for j, are disregarded in works printed after 1500" are *no longer* part of the rule for transcribing the title. Transcribe what is in the source, following spelling as it appears.

Publication area: 1.4B4, 1.4C2. Publisher's name is in the dative case and

so the accompanying preposition must be included.

Added entry: 21.30D

2-12. Main entry: 21.39A1

Title–statement of responsibility area: 1.1F14

Publication area: 1.4B8, 1.4D5

Added entry I: 21.39A1; form, 24.3D1

2-13. Main entry: 21.17B

Added entry: 21.17B

Edition area: Edition from verso of title page ("First U.S. edition.")

Physical description area: Number of illustrations is given as in accordance with 2.5C4: 19 numbered "figures" on the 5 scattered pages of plates; 137 numbered "plates," which are included in the pagination of the book.

Note: 2.7B18

Standard number: 2.8

2-14. Main entry: 21.5A modified by 25.4C and 25.5D

Title–statement of responsibility area: 1.1F12

Physical description area: 2.5B18

Added entries:
I. 21.30K1
II. 21.30K2c

2-16. Main entry: 21.10

Added entries:
I. 21.30K2
II. Author-title added entry is always made for the original text from which the adaptation was made.

2-17. Main entry: 21.1B2d; form, 24.7

Edition area: 1.2C1

CHAPTER 3

3-1. Main entry: 21.1C3

Physical description area: 3.5D1

Standard number: 3.8B1, 1.8E1

Added entry: 21.30E

3-2. Main entry: 21.1C3

Edition area: 1.2B5

Publication area: 1.4B5

Added entry I: 21.30E

3-3. Main entry: 21.1A1

Publication area: Date is inferred from "2-71" at bottom of text. Information about place and publisher from verso of map, folded area.

Notes:
  1. 3.7B4
  2. 3.7B18
Added entry I: 21.30E
3-4. Main entry: 21.1B2c
  Mathematical detail area: 3.3B1
  Physical description area: 3.5D1
3-5. Main entry: 21.1C3
  Mathematical detail area: 3.3B2, 3.3C1
  Physical description area: 3.5D1
  Notes:
    1. 3.7B7
    2. 3.7B18
3-6b–c. Main entry: 21.1C3
  Mathematical detail area: 3.3B1
  Physical description area: 3.5B4
  Notes:
    1. 3.7B18
    2. 3.7B21
  Added entries: 21.30E
3-7a. Main entry: 21.1C3
  Note: 3.7B7
3-7b. Main entry: 21.1C3
  Mathematical detail area: 3.3B4
3-8. Main entry: 21.1C3
  Publication area: 3.4D1
  Note: 3.7B12
3-9. Main entry: 21.1C3
  Notes:
    1. 3.7B2
    2. 3.7B9
    3. 3.7B18
  Added entry: 21.30E
3-10. Main entry: 21.1A1, 21.1A2
  Physical description area: 3.5B1
  Note: 3.7B7, 1.11
3-11. Main entry: 21.1C3
  Notes:
    1. 3.7B4
    2. 3.7B18
3-12. Main entry: 21.1C3
  Physical description area: 3.5B3, 3.5C2,
    3.5D2
3-13. Main entry: 21.1A2
  Notes:
    1. 3.7B1
    2. 3.7B9
3-14. Main entry: 21.1A1, 21.1A2
  Statement of responsibility: 1.1F3,
    1.1F6

Notes:
  1. 3.7B10
  2. 3.7B11
  3. 3.7B18
  4. 3.7B19

CHAPTER 4
4-1. Uniform title: 25.27A
  Title–statement of responsibility area:
    1.1D3, 1.1E5
  Physical description area: 5.5B1
  Notes:
    1. 5.7B2
    2. 5.7B7
4-2. Uniform title: 25.31B2, 25.35
  Added entry I: 21.18B
4-3. Uniform title: 25.32
  Series area: 1.6E1
  Notes:
    1. 5.7B11
    2. 5.7B19
  Added entries:
    I. 21.18C
    II. 21.30D
4-4. Uniform title: 25.27A, 25.31B7
  Title–statement of responsibility area:
    1.1D2, 5.1B2
  Note 2: 5.7B19
4-5. Uniform title: 25.27A, 25.31B3
4-6. Notes:
    1. 5.7B8
    2. 2.7B18. A bibliography note is re-
      garded as a partial contents note.
  Standard number: 5.8B1
4-7. Uniform title: 25.31B1
  Publication area: Place from cover;
    date from first page of music (5.4F1)
  Series area: Taken from cover
  Notes:
    1. 5.7B6
    2. 5.7B10
    3. 5.7B19
4-8. Uniform title: 25.27A, 25.31B3
  Publication area: 1.4B8
  Series area: 1.6E1, 1.6J1
  Notes:
    1. 5.7B1
    2. 5.7B7; capitalization, A19C
    3. 5.7B19

4-9. Uniform title: 25.27B, 25.29A3, 25.31A2, 25.31A5
  Publication area: 1.4B8
  Physical description area: 5.5D1

4-10. Uniform title: 25.27B, 25.29A1
  Added entry I: 21.30D

CHAPTER 5

5-1. Main entry: 21.23A. Dates "readily available" on container (22.18 option)
  Uniform title: 25.27A, 25.31A6, 25.31B6, 25.5E
  Publication area: 6.4D2. Place and trade name from disc; date from container
  Physical description area: 6.5B2. Playing time approximated; none given on item
  Notes:
    1. 6.7B6
    2. 6.7B11
    3. 6.7B19

5-2. Main entry: 21.23A; form, 22.2C2
  Title–statement of responsibility area: 6.1E, 6.1F1
  Publication area: Place from container; releaser from label; date estimated from recording date information on container
  Physical description area: 6.5B2. Playing time approximated; none given on item
  Notes:
    1. 6.7B6
    2. 6.7B7
    3. 6.7B11
    4. 6.7B17
    5. 6.7B19

5-3. Physical description area: 6.5B2

5-4. Main entry: 21.23B
  Uniform title: 25.27A, 25.32B2, 25.5E
  Publication area: Place from *The American Music Handbook;* date estimated from date of disc version
  Notes:
    1. 6.7B6
    2. 6.7B16
    3. 6.7B19

5-5. Main entry: 21.23C
  Publication area: Place from container; trade name and date from label

Notes:
  1. 6.7B1
  2. 6.7B11
  3. 6.7B18

5-6. Main entry: 21.23C; form, 24.1, 1.1B6 (no space between initials)
  Publication area: Place from label; date from *National Union Catalog*
  Series area: 6.4D3, 6.6B1
  Notes:
    1. 6.7B2
    2. 6.7B6
    3. 6.7B11
    4. 6.7B18
    5. 6.7B19

5-7. Main entry: 21.23D; form, 24.5C1 exception
  Physical description area: See 6.5C6 on including number of tracks.
  Note: 6.7B18, 6.7B19. Twenty works are listed on the label. At the discretion of the cataloguer, and depending on the importance of the material to the library collection, contents may be omitted from the notes area. Some libraries use fifteen as the arbitrary cut-off point for the number of works to be cited in a contents note. The cataloguer must use her or his professional judgement in this decision.

5-8. Main entry: 21.23A; form, 22.1A, 22.18 option
  Uniform title: 25.27B, 25.29A3, 25.29G, 25.31A4, 25.31A5, 25.5E
  Publication area: Place from *The Music Yearbook*
  Physical description area: 6.5B3
  Notes:
    1. 6.7B6
    2. 6.7B11
    3. 6.7B19
    4. 6.7B21

5-9. All cataloguing information was taken from the label on the cassette with the exception of the date and playing time, which were stated on the container.
  Main entry: 21.5A
  Notes:
    1. 6.7B17
    2. 6.7B18

5-10. Main entry: 21.19A

Title–statement of responsibility area: 6.1F3

Publication area: Place from *Billboard International Buyer's Guide;* date estimated from date of motion picture

Notes:

   1. 6.7B6

   2. 6.7B7

   3. 6.7B11

   4. 6.7B18

   5. 6.7B19

Added entry II: 21.19

5-11. Main entry: 21.23A

Uniform title: 25.36B, 25.36C

Title proper: 1.1G2

Publication area: Place from container; publisher from label; date estimated from recording date given on container

Series area: 1.6B2, 1.6H2. Series—in German, English, and French—from container. German title used as it appears on container cover.

Notes:

   1. 6.7B6

   2. 6.7B7

   3. 6.7B11

   4. 6.7B19

5-12. Main entry: 21.23A; form, 22.1A

Uniform title: 25.27B, 25.29A3, 25.29G, 25.31A4, 25.31A5

Title proper: 1.1G2

Publication area: Place from *The Music Yearbook;* date from container

Notes:

   1. 6.7B6

   2. 6.7B10

   3. 6.7B11

   4. 6.7B19

5-13. Main entry: 21.23A

Uniform title: 25.27B, 25.29G, 25.31A5

Publication area: Place from *The Music Yearbook;* date from container

Physical description area: 6.5B3

Notes:

   1. 6.7B6

   2. 6.7B11

   3. 6.7B19

   4. 6.7B21

5-14. Main entry: 21.23A

Uniform title: 25.9

Publication area: Place from *The American Music Handbook.* Date estimated (1.4F7); date left open since this is the first volume of a set (1.4F8)

Physical description area: Statement of extent left open because set is not complete (1.5B5)

Series area: 6.4D3; information taken from label

Notes:

   1. 6.7B11

   2. 6.7B18; "Vol. 1" on container

   3. 6.7B19

5-15. Main entry: 21.23C. Narrator's name ("Miranda") is given in each of the accompanying booklets and as the opening statement on the recording: "Hi there. You can call me Miranda ...." The relationship between Miranda and Mary Shelton, whose name is listed on the record label, is unknown. Give Shelton as an added entry (21.30F).

Notes:

   1. 6.7B6

   2. 6.7B14; based on statement on container: "Educators and psychologists agree that the child who is influenced to read early in life has a better chance to develop. *Reading records* give the child helpful tools to master reading skills as soon as he is able."

   3. 6.7B17, 6.7B6, 6.7B11. Notes may be combined when appropriate (1.7A5).

   4. 6.7B19. The publisher's number, found on container, seems to be that rather than a "series," which is what it is called. Each container bears "Series: RR 1000." In addition, labels bear a seemingly random control number. Number given in note seems to be the "principle number"; other numbers are omitted.

5-16. Main entry: 21.23C

Publication area: Place from *American Music Handbook;* date from container

Notes

   1. 6.7B4

2. 6.7B11
3. 6.7B18
4. 6.7B19

CHAPTER 6

6-1. Main entry: 21.1C3. Title, producer, releasing agent, and date of release from the film; other cataloguing information taken from the *Doubleday Multimedia Catalog* listing of the film.
Notes:
  1. 7.7B7
  2. 7.7B9
  3. 7.7B17
Added entry I: 21.30E

6-2. Main entry: 21.1B3. Title from film; other cataloguing information taken from *Educators Guide to Free Films* (1973) and from material accompanying the film
Notes:
  1. 7.7B6
  2. 7.7B17

6-3. Statement of responsibility: 7.1F1
Notes:
  1. 7.7B6
  2. 7.7B7
Added entries:
  I. 21.30G
  II. 21.30E
  III–IV. 21.30F

6-4. Main entry: 21.6B1
Statement of responsibility: 7.1F1
Publication area: Place from Texture Films catalog, 1974–75
Notes:
  1. 7.7B6
  2. 7.7B17

6-5. Added entry I: 21.30G

6-6. Physical description area: 7.5B1 (type of cassette from the container), 7.5B2, 7.5C3, 7.5C4, 7.6D3
Publication area: Distributing agent from accompanying material
Notes:
  1. 7.7B6
  2. 7.7B17

6-7. Main entry: 21.1B2a
Publication area: Name and location of the distributing agent and date from *Educators Guide to Free Films* (1973)

CHAPTER 7

7-1. Main entry: 21.1A2; form, 22.1A, 22.1B, 22.2A
Title: 8.1B2
GMD: 1.1C1
Publication area: 8.4A2, 8.4F2
Physical description area: 8.5B1, 8.5C1, 8.5D4
Note: 8.7B10

7-2. Main entry: 21.16B; form, 22.1B, 22.18
Physical description area: 8.5B1, 8.5C3, 8.5D4
Notes:
  1. 8.7B8
  2. 8.7B10
Added entry I: 21.16B

7-3. Main entry: 21.1A2; form, 22.1B, 22.18
Publication area: 8.4A2, 8.4F2
Physical description area: 8.5B1, 8.5C1, 8.5D4

7-4. Main entry: 21.16A
Publication area: 8.4A2, 8.4F2
Physical description area: 8.5B1, 8.5C2, 8.5D4
Note: 8.7B7
Added entry I: 21.16A

7-5. Note: 8.7B17

7-6. Main entry under title: Capitalization, *AACR2* A.4D.
Publication area: Information is bracketed because it is from an advertising blurb, not one of the prescribed sources.
Physical description area: 8.5B1, 8.5D6
Note: 8.7B17
Added entry: 21.30E; form, 24.5C1 exception

7-7. Main entry: 21.9
Title–statement of responsibility area: 1.1F14, 1.1E
Publication area: Date from booklet; other information from container
Physical description area: 1.10C2a
Series area: 1.6C1 (series with parallel title on container), 1.6J1 (second series from booklet). Cataloguer should list the more specific of the two series first.
Notes:
  1. 8.7B6, 8.7B7

2. 8.7B14

3. 8.7B17

Added entry I: 21.10

7-8. Title–statement of responsibility area: Information from container, including parallel titles (8.1D)

Publication area: Date from cassettes and filmstrip containers; other information from container

Physical description area: 1.10C2a

Notes:

   1. 8.7B2

   2. 8.7B14; information taken from teacher's guide

   3. 8.7B16

   4. 8.7B17

   5. 8.7B18

7-9. Main entry: 21.9

Title–statement of responsibility area: Information from title frame on filmstrip

Publication area: Information from guide

Physical description area: 8.5B1, 8.5B5, 8.5C4, 8.5D2, 6.5B1, 8.5E1

Notes:

   1. 8.7B7

   2. 8.7B17

Added entry I: 21.30G

7-10. Main entry: 21.17B

Publication area: 1.4C6

Physical description area: 8.5B1, 8.5C10, 8.5D1

7-11. Publication area: Date estimated according to date of last President included in set (Lyndon B. Johnson)

Physical description area: 8.5B1

Note: 8.7B17

7-12. Main entry: 21.1A

Publication area: 1.4C3

7-13. All cataloguing information was taken from title frame, except for location of Encyclopaedia Britannica Films, which was taken from EB Films catalogue (1.4A2).

Notes:

   1. 8.7B10

   2. 8.7B17

7-14. All information was taken from title frames, except for the location of Encyclopaedia Britannica Films,

which was taken from EB Films catalogue (1.4A2).

Main entry: 21.9

Note: 8.7B17

7-15. Main entry: 21.1A1

Title–statement of responsibility area: Title from container; statement of responsibility from accompanying material ("prominent" source) is enclosed in brackets (1.1F1).

Notes:

   1. 8.7B17; information from guide

   2. 8.7B19; information from container

7-16. Main entry: 21.6B2

Notes:

   1. 8.7B10

   2. 8.7B17

Added entry I: 21.6B2

7-17. Title: 8.1B2

Note: 8.7B18

7-18. Notes:

   1. 8.7B10

   2. 8.7B17

7-20. Main entry: 21.24

7-21. Notes:

   2. 8.7B11

   3. 8.7B14

   4. 8.7B18

   5. 8.7B19

CHAPTER 8

8-1. Main entry: 21.1A1

Title–statement of responsibility area: Title and name of sculptor are incised on work. Transcribe as found.

GMD: See definition in *AACR2* Glossary, Appendix D.

Publication area: Date only given, 10.4F2. Date estimated from time of purchase (1969); decade probable but not certain (1.4F7)

Physical description area: 10.5B1, 10.5C1, 10.5C2

Note: 10.7B1, 10.7B17. Two notes combined, 1.7A5

8-2. Title–statement of responsibility area: Title from label affixed to item

GMD: See definition in *AACR2* Glossary, Appendix D.

Publication area: Name of manufacturer from label. Year of manufacture not certain; decade certain (1.4F7)

Physical description area: 10.5B1, 10.5C1, 10.5C2

Note: 10.7B1

Added entry: 21.30E; form, 24.4B

8-3. Main entry: 21.1A1

Title–statement of responsibility area: Title proper, 1.1A2; GMD, 1.1C1; other title, 1.1E2, 1.1E3; statement of responsibility, 1.1F

Publication area: All information from container, chief source of information

Physical description area: 10.5B1, 10.5B2, 10.5D2

Notes:

1. 10.7B14
2. 10.7B17

8-4. Main entry: 21.1A1

Title: 1.1B7

GMD: See definition in *AACR2* Glossary, Appendix D

Publication area: 10.4F2. Date certain

Physical description area: 10.5B1, 10.5C1, 10.5C2, 10.5D1

Notes:

1. 10.7B6
2. 10.7B10

8-5. Title: 1.1B7

GMD: See definition in *AACR2* Glossary, Appendix D.

Publication area: Not given, 10.4F2

Physical description area: 10.5B1, 10.5C1, 10.5C2, 10.5D2

Note: 10.7B20

8-6. Physical description area: 10.5B1, 10.5B2, 10.5C1, 10.5C2, 10.5D1, 10.5D2

Notes:

1. 10.7B10
2. 10.7B19

Added entry: 21.30E

8-7. Publication area: 1.4F7. Date estimated from date of acquisition; decade likely but not certain

Physical description area: 10.5B1, 10.5D2

Note: 10.7B10

Added entry: 21.30E; form, 24.13

8-8. Main entry: 21.9

Statement of responsibility: 1.1F14

Publication area: 1.4F7. Decade probable but not certain

Physical description area: 10.5B1, 10.5B2, 10.5D1

Notes:

1. 10.7B7
2. 10.7B19

Added entries:

I. 21.30G
II. 21.30K2

8-9. Title: 1.1B7

GMD: See definition in *AACR2* Glossary, Appendix D.

Publication area: 1.4C6, 1.4D6

Physical description area: 10.5B1, 10.5C1

Note: 10.7B10, 10.7B17. Two notes combined, 1.7A5

8-10. Information taken from container and accompanying textual material

Physical description area: 10.5B1, 10.5C1, 10.5D2, 10.5E1

Series area: 10.6

Notes:

1. 10.7B10
2. 10.7B18

Added entry I: 21.30E; form, 24.13

CHAPTER 9

9-1. Main entry: Form, 22.18 option. Date included because it was given on title frame. Dates should be included when readily accessible (LC policy decision).

GMD: 1.1C1

Publication area: Microfilm publication data found on title frames

Physical description area: 11.5B1, 11.5D4

Note: 11.7B ("Combine the notes relating to the original . . . .")

9-2. Main entry: 21.1B2d; form, 24.7

Physical description area: 11.5B1, 11.5C1, 11.5D3

9-3. Main entry: Date included because it was given on the title frame (22.18 option).

Physical description area: 11.5B1, 11.5D5

Notes:

1. 11.7B
2. 11.7B19

9-4. Main entry: 21.6C2

Publication area: Place in brackets because not given in item 10.0B2.

Physical description area: 11.5B1, 11.5C2, 11.5D4

Note: 11.7B7

9-5. Physical description area: 11.5B1, 11.5C3, 11.5D3

CHAPTER 10

10-1. When cataloguing a serial, rules for the type of material should be consulted first. Rules for cataloguing a sound cassette are in *AACR2* chapter 6. Chief source of information for a cassette is the cassette itself (6.0B1). Title is from the cassette.

Physical description area: 6.5B1 option; 6.5B2, 6.5C3, 6.5C6, 6.5C7, 6.5C8, 6.5D5, 6.5E1

Notes: Information taken from "Liner notes."
1. 12.7B1
2. 1.7B1
3. 12.7B11
4. 12.7B11

10-2. Numeric area: 12.3E; see also 12.2B2

Note 2: 12.7B5

10-4. Title: 12.1B2. The Midwest Interlibrary Center refers to this publication as *Newsletter*.

10-5. Title: 12.1B2. The Center for Research Libraries refers to this publication as *Newsletter*. Information taken from various issues of the *Newsletter*.

10-6. Note 2: 12.7B7c

10-7. Note 2: 12.7B7b

10-8. Notes:
2. 12.7B7b
3. 12.7B10
4. 12.7B18

10-9. Numeric area: 12.3C1

Note: 12.7B7h. Frequency note not needed as "Yearbook" infers an annual (12.7B1).

10-10. Numeric area: 12.3C1

10-11. Notes:
2. 12.7B5
3. 12.7B6

10-12. Cataloguing is to be done from first official issue. All information has been taken from this source. Pilot issue is recorded in a note.

Notes:
1. 12.7B1
2. 12.7B3
3. 12.7B8

10-15. Note 2: 12.7B8

10-16. Note: 12.7B6. Frequency note not needed.

10-17. Notes:
1. Despite the fact that the title page of the first issue proclaimed that *Letter* was to be published monthly, it never was. *Letter* was issued about four times a year. The last issue bears only the designation of the year, 1949, and the volume and number. It was the only issue to appear in 1949.
2. 12.7B6

10-18. Title: Taken from cover

Publication area: Taken from caption page and verso

Numeric area: Taken from caption

Note 3: 12.7B7d

10-19. Notes:
2. 12.7B5
3. 12.7B6

10-20. Notes: 2. 12.7B6

10-21. Notes:
1. 12.7B1
2. 12.7B6
3. 12.7B7k

CHAPTER 11

11-1. Main entry: 21.1B2a; form, 24.17, 24.13

11-2. Main entry: 21.1B2b; form, 24.21C. "House" rather than "House of Representatives" is LC policy decision.

11-3. Main entry: 21.1B2c; form, 24.14

Publication area: 1.4D4

11-4. Main entry: 21.1B2c; form, 24.1

Publication area: 1.4C3

11-5. Main entry: 21.1B2d; form, 24.7

Publication area: 1.4D4

11-6. Main entry: 21.5A

Notes:
1. 2.7B4
2. 2.7B18
3. 2.7B18
Standard number: 2.8
Added entry I: Form, 24.13
11-7. Main entry: 21.1B3
 Physical description area: 2.5B10, 2.5C4
11-8. Main entry: 21.4A
 Added entry I: Form, 24.19
11-9: Statement of responsibility: 1.1F5
11-10. Note: 2.7B18
 Added entry I: 21.30D
11-11. Statement of responsibility area: 1.1F1
11-12. Main entry: Form, 24.20B
 Added entry I: 21.30D
11-13. Main entry: 21.4A
11-14. Reference: Form, 26.2D1
11-15. Title–statement of responsibility area: 1.1F12
 Added entry I: Form, 24.20B
11-16. Added entry: 21.30E
11-17. Title–statement of responsibility area: 1.1F12
 Physical description area: 2.5B2, 2.5B6
 Note: 1.7B2
11-18. Main entry: Form, 22.11D
 Title–statement of responsibility area: 1.1G2. "The Bible" is the title of a section of this work that discusses the Bible. Capitalization, A.4A
11-19. Statement of responsibility: 1.1F1
11-20. Statement of responsibility: 1.1F4
 Note: 1.7B18
11-22. Statement of responsibility: 1.1F5
 Publication area: 1.4F5
11-23. Statement of responsibility: 1.1F5
11-25. Statement of responsibility: 1.1F12
 Publication area: 1.4F5
11-26. Physical description area: 2.5B3. Count pages if less than 100 in book; estimate if more than 100.
11-27. Title: Capitalization, A.20
 Statement of responsibility: 1.1F2
 Added entry I: 21.30E
 Publication area: Information from verso of title page (2.0B2)

11-28. Main entry: Form, 22.5D1
11-29. Main entry: Form, 22.5D1
11-31. Note capitalization of title main entry; capitalize second word when first word of title main entry is an article (A.4D).
11-32. Series area: 1.6J1
11-33. Publication area: Place of publication is not to be found in the book; therefore it is bracketed (2.0B2).
11-34. Title–statement of responsibility area: 1.1A2
 Physical description area: 2.5B10. Pages of plates are numbered accurately; therefore the number is not bracketed.
11-35. Statement of responsibility: 1.1F12
 Physical description area: 2.5B10. Pages of plates are numbered accurately; therefore the number is not bracketed.
 Note 1: 1.7B7
11-36. Statement of responsibility: 1.1F12
 Physical description area: 2.5B3, 2.5C6
 Series area: Number of series is from the dust jacket, not one of the prescribed sources of information. Therefore the number is bracketed (2.0B2).
 Note: 1.7B2
11-37. Main entry: Form, 22.1A
11-39. Main entry: Form, 22.14
 Statement of responsibility: 1.1F5
 Note: 1.7B7
11-41. Main entry: Form, 22.16
 Other title information: 1.1E3
 Added entry I: Form, 25.18A
11-43. Title–statement of responsibility area: 1.1A2
 Note: 1.7B7
 Added entries:
  I. 21.28
  II. 21.10
11-44a. Statement of responsibility: 1.1F8
 Note 1: 1.7B16
11-45. Publication area: 1.4F8
11-46. Statement of responsibility: 1.1F4
 Publication area: 1.4C3
 Added entries:
  I. 21.30F
  II–IV. 21.7B

11-47. Physical description area: 2.5B10. The item catalogued includes both leaves and pages of plates, none of which is numbered. There are more leaves than pages; therefore, the extent of the plates is counted as leaves and so recorded.
Note: 1.7B18

11-48. Uniform title: Form, 25.15A2; capitalization, A.20.
Added entry I: 21.30E

11-49. Uniform title: 25.15A1
Title proper: Capitalization, A.18B
Added entry I: 21.30E

11-50. Main entry: Form, 23.4C
Title: 1.1G2

11-51. Statement of responsibility: 1.1F15
Publication area: 1.4D6

11-52. Title–statement of responsibility area: 1.1F15. Names on the title page are not those of persons who should be included in a statement of responsibility. They are to be omitted.

11-53. Physical description area: 2.5B11
Note: 2.7B2

11-54. Statement of responsibility area: 1.1F14
Physical description area: 2.5B19
Series area: 1.6E1

11-55. Note: 2.7B6

CHAPTER 12

12-1. Edition area: Statement from verso of title page (2.0B2)

12-2. Title–statement of responsibility area: Form, 1.1B6

12-3. Publication area: 1.4F5
Subject entry tracing: Form, 22.5A, 22.11A

12-4. Publication area: Place from verso of title page (2.0B2)

12-10. Edition area: Statement on verso of title page (2.0B2)

12-12. Publication area: 1.4D2; see also discussion of 1.4D2 in this text.

12-13. Publication area: 1.4D2; see also discussion of 1.4D2 in this text.

12-14. Publication area: 1.4D2, 1.4F5

12-15. Main entry: 22.18 option; note form for dates B.C.
Edition area: Information from verso of title page (2.0B2)

Added entry I: Form, 22.5C3. Day-Lewis's name is frequently hyphenated; thus, it is established with hyphens, even though on the title page of this work it appears without the hyphens. Use form as "commonly known." This poet consistently writes as "C. Day-Lewis." The example given under *AACR2* 22.5C3 with his forename filled out as Cecil seems to be in error.

12-16. Series area: 1.6H1
Added entry I: 21.30K1c

12-17. The work catalogued is a facsimile. For the cataloguing of facsimiles, see discussion of rule 1.11 in this text.

12-18. Publication area: 1.4D3

12-19. Series area: 1.6H1
Notes:
1. 1.7B18
2. 1.7B18

12-20. Note: 2.7B2
Added entry: None is made for translator as this work has not been translated more than once into the same language; see 21.30K1c.

12-22. Edition area: C.7B (numerals)

12-25. Publication area: 1.4D2; date from verso of title page

12-26. Publication area: 1.4C1
Added entry I: 21.30D

12-27. Publication area: 1.4F7

12-28. Title: Capitalization according to German-language practice: All nouns are capitalized in German.

12-29. Main entry: Form, 22.1D2 (forenames hyphenated)
Title area: Capitalization according to German-language practice

12-30. Series area: 1.6J1

12-31. Edition area: C.7B (numerals)

12-32. Publication area: Place of publication is not given in book; therefore it must be bracketed.

12-33. Statement of responsibility: 1.1F15
Note: 1.7B7

12-36. Edition area: Information from verso of title page
Added entry I: 21.30C

12-37. Main entry: 22.18 option (dates). See 1.11, facsimiles, for rules on transcribing this entry. The entry must represent the work in hand—which is a facsimile—not the original, from which the facsimile has been made.

Notes:
1. 1.7B7
2. 1.7B12. The series is *not* a series for the facsimile reprint. It is the series of which the original publication was a part. As such, the series should be transcribed in a note, not in the body of the entry.
3. 1.7B18

Added entry I: 21.30D

12-38. Main entry: 22.18 option (dates).
Edition area: Information from verso of title page (2.0B2)
Note:
1. 1.7B2
2. 1.7B18
Added entry I: 21.30D

12-39. Statement of responsibility area: 1.1F15

12-42. Title area: 1.1B2
Edition area: 1.2C1, C.7B (numerals)
Added entry I: 21.30H; form, 22.12

12-43. Series area: Numbering bracketed because information is taken from dust jacket, not a prescribed source (2.0B2).
Added entry I: 21.30D

12-44. Added entry I: 21.12

12-45. Series area: 1.6D1
Added entry: None is made for translators (21.30K1).

12-47. See 26.3C1b, Explanatory references, for information on change of heading for the United Kingdom during various periods of its history. These official headings should be represented in the personal heading for the monarch, unless the library is following LC policy decision. This text follows LC policy.
Edition area: Information from verso of title page (2.0B2)
Added entry I: 21.30D

12-48. Added entry I: 21.30D

12-49. See discussion above under 12-47 for form of heading. Dates, etc., checked in *Encyclopaedia Britannica* (1974) and included under 22.18 option.

Other title information: 1.1E4
Publication area: 1.4D3
Series area: 1.6E1

12-50. Statement of responsibility area: "Don" is a title of respect like "Reverend"; it is to be omitted from transcription of the title page (1.1F7).
Added entry I: 21.30D

12-51. Publication area: 1.4F5 (date). Place of publication is not in book; therefore it is bracketed (2.0B2).

CHAPTER 14

14-1. Title main entry: 21.1C3. Capitalization follows rules for transcription of titles in German language; see *AACR2* Appendix A, Capitalization.
Publication area: 1.4D2
Series: Capitalization follows German-language practice
Added entry I: 21.30E

14-2. Title main entry: 21.1C3. In title main entry, capitalize the second word if the first word is an article (A.4D).
Publication area: 1.4D5. NEA is distinguished by typography as being the principal publisher; its name should be added as a second publisher.
Added entry: 21.30E; form, 24.15A

14-3. Title main entry: 21.1C3
Other title information: Initials, 1.1B6
Statement of responsibility area: 1.1F14
Publication area: 1.4B8, 1.4D4
Added entry: According to *AACR1*, an entry for a corporate name that began with initials followed by a surname would have been: Du Pont de Nemours (E.I.) & Company. Because of the rule change, reference should be made:

Du Pont de Nemours (E.I.) & Company
see
E. I. Du Pont de Nemours & Company.

14-4. Main entry: 21.1B2a
Statement of responsibility: The cataloguer must transcribe the statement of responsibility as it appears. Unless abbreviations (e.g. U.S.) appear in the prescribed source for transcribing in-

formation, no abbreviations may be used.

14-5. Main entry: 21.1B3, 21.6C1

Added entries:

    I. 21.6C1

    II. 21.1B3

    III. 21.30F. Added entry will always be made for the agency receiving the report. Form, 24.19 type 3. "Great Britain" is used as geographic heading rather than "United Kingdom" in accordance with LC policy decision.

14-6. Main entry: 21.1B2c

    Statement of responsibility: 1.1F11

14-7. Main entry: 21.1B2c

    Publication area: Place is not given in book; publisher on verso of title page; date in preface.

14-8. Uniform title may be used to gather all editions of a work together (25.3A and 25.5D).

    Notes:

      1. 1.7B7

      2. 1.7B18

14-9. Heading: Form, 22.17A4

    Statement of responsibility: 1.1F7

14-10. Main entry: 21.1B3, 21.7 (work produced under editorial direction); an unnamed conference is not an example of 21.1B2d.

    Note: 1.7B6, 1.7B19. Two notes combined, in accordance with 1.7A5.

    Added entries:

      I. 21.7B

      III. 21.30F (make added entry for sponsor of a conference)

      IV. 21.30F; form, 24.19

14-11. Main entry: 21.1B2a

14-12. Title: The title is to be transcribed "exactly as to wording, order, and spelling" (1.1B1). Follow rules in Appendix A for capitalization. Thus, following A.18E, the name of the corporate body is given as "Arizona-Sonora Desert Museum, Inc." in title transcription.

    Edition statement: 2.2B1. When more than one edition statement appears in a work, transcribe only the statement that applies to the work being cata-logued, e.g. the latest edition statement.

    Publication area: 1.4D4

    Added entry I: 21.30E. Form, 24.5C. Remember that rules in chapter 24, Headings for Corporate Bodies, apply *only* to the form of name as it will be transcribed in *headings*, i.e., main or added entries in the catalogue.

14-13. Main entry: 21.1B3

    Added entry: 21.30E. ALA 1949 rule 144A would have given entry to this body as: Little (Arthur D.), inc. Because of rule change, reference should be made:

      Little (Arthur D.), Inc.

        see

    Arthur D. Little, Inc.

14-14. Added entry I: 21.30D; form, 22.5C

14-15. Main entry: 21.1B2a

    Title–statement of responsibility area: 1.1E4

    Publication area: 1.4D4

14-16. Main entry: 21.1B2d

    Title–statement of responsibility area: 1.1F14

    Note: 1.7B18

    Added entry I: 21.30E

14-17. Main entry: 21.1B2d

    Title–statement of responsibility area: 1.1F14

    Added entries:

      I. 21.30E; form, 24.18 type 4

      II. 21.30E; form, 24.1

      III. 21.30E; form, 24.2D. (Prefer brief form over formal name: Lyndon B. Johnson Space Center.)

14-18. Main entry: 21.1B2d

    Note: 1.7B18

    Added entries:

      I. 21.30D

      II. 21.30D

      III. 21.30E

14-19. Notes:

      1. 1.7B7

      2. 1.7B18

    Added entries:

      I. 21.30D

      II. 21.30E; form, 24.13 type 4

14-20. Main entry: 21.1B2a

Publication area: 1.4B8

Series: 1.1B3, 1.1E6, 1.6D1, 1.6H1

Note: 1.7B18

Added entry I: 21.30D

14-21. This example is governed by same rules as 14.20, discussed above.

14-22. Main entry: 21.1B2a

Added entry I: 21.30D

14-23. Main entry: 21.1B3

Publication area: 1.4B8. Date taken from preface.

Added entry: 21.30E. "Dept." is abbreviated according to LC policy decision.

14-24. Main entry: 21.1B3, 21.7 (work prepared under editorial direction)

Added entries:

I. 21.30D

II. 21.30E

14-25. Main entry: 21.1B3, 21.7. Contents of the journal are general in nature; entry under title as editorially produced work. See serials rules for form of entry, particularly 12.3, numeric, etc., area.

Note: 12.7B1

Added entry: 21.30E

14-26. Main entry: 21.1B3, 21.5. The sample catalogue cards are not for use specifically in Columbia University School of Library Service's courses; they are designed for library school classes generally, according to the foreword. Title main entry is appropriate because of uncertain authorship.

Publication area: 1.4B8

Physical description area: 2.5B7. The volume is almost entirely made up of catalogue card facsimiles; thus "chiefly ill."

Added entry: 21.30E

14-27. Main entry: 21.1B2a

Publication area: 1.4B8

Added entry I: 21.30C

14.28. Main entry: 21.1A1

Publication area: Use appropriate abbreviations from *AACR2* Appendix A, e.g. Dept.

Added entries:

I. 21.30E

II. 21.30E; form, 24.13 type 1

14-29. A conference is considered to have a name if it is named openly—i.e., in one of the prescribed sources. This conference is named on verso of title page.

Main entry: 21.1B2d; form, 24.7

Publication area: 1.4B8

Added entries:

I. 21.30D

II. 21.30E

14-30. Main entry: 21.1B2a

14-31. Main entry: 21.1B3

Added entry: 21.30E

14-32. Main entry: 21.1B3, 21.17B

Publication area: Place is not given in book, but headquarters of the Council are London. Publisher, 1.4B8.

Added entries:

I. 21.17B

II. 21.30E

III. 21.30E

14-33. Main entry: 21.1B2c

Notes:

1. 2.7B6

2. 2.7B18

14-34. Main entry: 21.1B3

Added entry: 21.30E

Publication area: 1.4D4

14-35. Main entry: 21.1B3

Publication area: 1.4B8

Note: 2.7B7

Added entry II: 21.30E; form, 24.17. This government agency is not one that will be entered under heading for government; name sounds distinctive. Reference will be:

Austria. *Forstliche Bundes- Versuchanstalt Mariabrunn in Schönbrunn*

see

Forstliche Bundes- Versuchanstalt Mariabrunn in Schönbrunn.

14-36. Main entry: 21.1B3

Publication area: 2.4D1. "For sale," etc., is on verso of title page (2.0B2).

Notes:

1. 2.7B18

2. 2.7B19

Added entry: 21.30E

14-37. Main entry: 21.1B2a

Notes:
1. 2.7B7
2. 2.7B18

14-38. Main entry: 21.4D1
Added entries:
I. 21.4D1
II. 21.30C
III. 21.30F

14-39. Main entry: 21.4D1; form, 24.17
Note: 2.7B6

14-40. Main entry: 21.1B2b

14-41. Main entry: 21.1B2b. Use of "House" rather than "House of Representatives" follows LC policy decision.
Added entry I: 21.30D

14-42. Main entry: 21.1B2b

14-43. Main entry: 21.1B3, 21.7 (work produced under editorial direction)
Added entry II: 21.30F

14-44. Main entry: 21.1B2b; form, 24.18 type 1
Added entries:
I. 21.30C
II. 21.30C

CHAPTER 15

15-2. Facsimile publication is covered by 1.11. Imprint is that of facsimile.
Note: 1.7B7
Added entries:
I. 21.30D
II. 21.30K2c

15-3. Added entry I: 21.30K2

15-6. Main entry: Form, 22.8C. *Encyclopaedia Britannica* (1974), *Encyclopedia Americana* (1974), and *Chambers' Encyclopedia* (1973) list the author as Dante Alighieri; *Chambers* gives the information that Dante is the son of Alighiero di Bellincioni. Entry according to 22.8C is thus appropriate.
Added entry I: 21.30K1c

15-7. Added entry I: 21.30K1c

15-8. Title transcription: 1.1D3
Note: 1.7B4
Added entry I: 21.30K1

15-10. Main entry: Form, 22.3C1
Added entry I: 21.30K1a

15-11. Main entry: Addition of language, 25.5D (item in 2 languages)

Notes:
1. 1.7B4
2. 1.7B7
3. 1.7B18

Added entries:
I. 21.30D
II. Form, 25.13a
III. 21.30F

15-13. Added entry I: 21.30D

15-14. Main entry: Form, 22.16

15-15a & b. Title transcription: 2.1B2

15-16. Main entry: Form, 22.3B3
Title transcription: 1.1B1, 1.1B2
Added entry: 21.30D

15-17. Main entry: Form, 22.3B3
Title: 1.1G2
Notes:
1. 1.7B2
2. 1.7B18
3. 1.7B18
Added entry I: 21.30K1c

15-18. Added entry I: 21.30K1

15-19. Title–statement of responsibility area: 1.1F12
Added entries:
I. 21.30K1b
II. 21.30E

15-20. Title–statement of responsibility area: 1.1F12
Edition area: 1.2C1; numerals, C.7B
Added entry: 21.30K1b

15-21. Title–statement of responsibility area: 1.1F12, 1.1F5
Added entries:
I. 21.30K1b
II. 21.30D; form, 22.16

15-22. Main entry: 21.13C
Title–statement of responsibility area: 1.1F12
Publication area: 1.4C3, 1.4B3
Series: 1.6D1
Added entry I: 21.13C

15-23. Publication area: 1.4B8
Added entry I: 21.30D

15-24. Publication area: 1.4C3, 1.4B3

15-25. Added entry I: 21.30E

15-26. Added entry I: 21.30E

15-27. Added entries:
I. 21.30K1
II. 25.18A11

Lists

GEOGRAPHIC NAMES

If desired, the cataloguer may omit the designation of country—in the publication area only—for the following cities outside the United States and Canada. This list does not apply to geographic names used in headings.

Aachen	Budapest	Guatemala	Madrid	Pretoria
Adelaide	Buenos Aires	(City)	Mainz	Reykjavik
Amsterdam	Cairo	Hague	Manila	Rio de Janeiro
Ankara	Calcutta	Hamburg	Maracaibo	Rome (City)
Antwerp	Cape Town	Hanover (City)	Marseille	Rotterdam
Athens	Caracas	Havana	Melbourne	San Salvador
Augsburg	Cologne	Istanbul	Mexico (City)	Santiago de
Barcelona	Copenhagen	Jaffa	Milan	Chile
Basel	Damascus	Jerusalem	Monte Carlo	Seville
Beirut	Danzig	Johannesburg	Montevideo	Shanghai
Belfast	Delhi	Kiel	Moscow	Sofia
Belgrad	Dresden	Kiev	Munich	Stalingrad
Berlin	Dublin	Kyoto	Naples	Stockholm
Bern	Düsseldorf	Lahore	Nice	Strassburg
Bogotá	Edinburgh	Leipzig	Nuremberg	Stuttgart
Bologna	Essen	Lima	Oslo	Sydney
Bombay	Florence	Lisbon	Oxford	Tokyo
Bonn	Frankfurt am	Liverpool	Padua	Tunis (City)
Bordeaux	Main	London	Panama (City)	Valparaiso
Bremen	Geneva	Lübeck	Paris	(City)
Breslau	Genoa	Luxemburg	Peking (also	Venice
Brisbane	Ghent	(City)	known as	Vienna
Brussels	Glasgow	Lyons	Peiping)	Warsaw
Bucharest	Graz	Madras	Prague	Wiesbaden
				Zurich

Source: David Haykin, *Subject Headings, a Practical Guide* (Washington, D.C.: Library of Congress, 1951) p. 107.

433

In a similar fashion the cataloguer may omit the designation of state or province—in the publication area only—for the following cities and towns in the United States and Canada. The list does not apply to geographic names used in headings.

Albany	Cleveland	Jersey City	Philadelphia	Scranton
Annapolis	Colorado	Los Angeles	Pittsburgh	Seattle
Ann Arbor	Springs	Memphis	Princeton	Spokane
Atlanta	Dallas	Milwaukee	Providence	Stanford
Atlantic City	Denver	Minneapolis	Quebec	Tacoma
Baltimore	Des Moines	Montreal	Richmond	Tallahassee
Boston	Detroit	Nashville	St. Augustine	Toledo
Brooklyn	Dubuque	New Haven	St. Louis	Toronto
Buffalo	Duluth	New Orleans	St. Paul	Trenton
Cambridge	Fort Wayne	New York	San Antonio	Wheeling
Chattanooga	Grand Rapids	Oklahoma City	Salt Lake City	Washington
Chicago	Hartford	Omaha	San Francisco	
Cincinnati	Indianapolis	Ottawa	Savannah	

Source: *ALA Cataloging Rules for Author and Title Entries* (Chicago: ALA, 1949), p. 217.

HEADINGS FOR PERSONAL ENTRY OF BRITISH SOVEREIGNS

The list below is to be used by cataloguers following *AACR2* rather than LC policy. Cataloguers using LC format will use "King [or Queen] of England" through Elizabeth I. Cataloguers will use "King [or Queen] of Great Britain" beginning with James I; for example, James I, *King of Great Britain*, 1566–1625.

William I, *King of England*, 1027?–1087.
William II, *King of England*, 1056?–1100.
Henry I, *King of England*, 1068–1135.
Stephen, *King of England*, 1097?–1154.
Henry II, *King of England*, 1133–1189.
Richard I, *King of England*, 1157–1199.
John, *King of England*, 1167?–1216.
Henry III, *King of England*, 1207–1272.
Edward I, *King of England*, 1239–1307.
Edward II, *King of England*, 1284–1327.
Edward III, *King of England*, 1312–1377.
Richard II, *King of England*, 1367–1400.
Henry IV, *King of England*, 1367–1413.
Henry V, *King of England*, 1387–1422.
Henry VI, *King of England*, 1421–1471.
Edward IV, *King of England*, 1442–1483.
Edward V, *King of England*, 1470–1483.
Richard III, *King of England*, 1452–1485.
Henry VII, *King of England*, 1457–1509.
Henry VIII, *King of England and Wales*, 1491–1547.
Edward VI, *King of England and Wales*, 1537–1553.
Mary I, *Queen of England and Wales*, 1516–1558.
Elizabeth I, *Queen of England and Wales*, 1533–1603.
James I, *King of England and Wales*, 1566–1625.

Charles I, *King of England and Wales*, 1600–1649.
Cromwell, Oliver, 1599–1658.
Cromwell, Richard, 1626–1712.
Charles II, *King of England and Wales*, 1630–1685.
James II, *King of England and Wales*, 1633–1701.
Mary II, *Queen of England and Wales*, 1662–1694.
William III, *King of England and Wales*, 1650–1702.
Anne, *Queen of Great Britain*, 1665–1714.
George I, *King of Great Britain*, 1660–1727.
George II, *King of Great Britain*, 1683–1760.
George III, *King of the United Kingdom*, 1738–1820.
George IV, *King of the United Kingdom*, 1762–1830.
William IV, *King of the United Kingdom*, 1765–1837.
Victoria, *Queen of the United Kingdom*, 1819–1901.
Edward VII, *King of the United Kingdom*, 1841–1910.
George V, *King of the United Kingdom*, 1865–1936.
Edward VIII, *King of the United Kingdom*, 1894–1972.
George VI, *King of the United Kingdom*, 1895–1952.
Elizabeth II, *Queen of the United Kingdom*, 1926–.

HEADINGS FOR BRITISH SOVEREIGNS ACTING IN AN OFFICIAL CAPACITY

The list below is to be used by cataloguers following *AACR2* rather than LC policy. LC will use the conventional heading "Great Britain" for *all* corporate entries dealing with the United Kingdom at any point in its history; for example, Great Britain. Sovereign (*1952–   : Elizabeth II*).

England. *Sovereign (1066–1087 : William I)*
England. *Sovereign (1087–1100 : William II)*
England. *Sovereign (1100–1135 : Henry I)*
England. *Sovereign (1135–1154 : Stephen)*
England. *Sovereign (1154–1189 : Henry II)*
England. *Sovereign (1189–1199 : Richard I)*
England. *Sovereign (1199–1216 : John)*
England. *Sovereign (1216–1272 : Henry III)*
England. *Sovereign (1272–1307 : Edward I)*
England. *Sovereign (1307–1327 : Edward II)*
England. *Sovereign (1327–1377 : Edward III)*
England. *Sovereign (1377–1399 : Richard II)*
England. *Sovereign (1399–1413 : Henry IV)*
England. *Sovereign (1413–1422 : Henry V)*
England. *Sovereign (1422–1461 : Henry VI)*
England. *Sovereign (1461–1483 : Edward IV)*
England. *Sovereign (1483 : Edward V)*
England. *Sovereign (1483–1485 : Richard III)*
England. *Sovereign (1485–1509 : Henry VII)*
England and Wales. *Sovereign (1509–1547 : Henry VIII)*
England and Wales. *Sovereign (1547–1553 : Edward VI)*
England and Wales. *Sovereign (1553–1558 : Mary I)*
England and Wales. *Sovereign (1558–1603 : Elizabeth I)*

England and Wales. *Sovereign (1603–1625 : James I)*
England and Wales. *Sovereign (1625–1649 : Charles I)*
England and Wales. *Sovereign (1649–1658 : O. Cromwell)*
England and Wales. *Sovereign (1658–1659 : R. Cromwell)*
England and Wales. *Sovereign (1660–1685 : Charles II)*
England and Wales. *Sovereign (1685–1688 : James II)*
England and Wales. *Sovereign (1689–1694 : William III & Mary II)*
England and Wales. *Sovereign (1694–1702 : William III)*
Great Britain. *Sovereign (1702–1714 : Anne)*
Great Britain. *Sovereign (1714–1727 : George I)*
Great Britain. *Sovereign (1727–1760 : George II)*
United Kingdom. *Sovereign (1760–1820 : George III)*
United Kingdom. *Sovereign (1820–1830 : George IV)*
United Kingdom. *Sovereign (1830–1837 : William IV)*
United Kingdom. *Sovereign (1837–1901 : Victoria)*
United Kingdom. *Sovereign (1901–1910 : Edward VII)*
United Kingdom. *Sovereign (1910–1936 : George V)*
United Kingdom. *Sovereign (1936 : Edward VIII)*
United Kingdom. *Sovereign (1936–1952 : George VI)*
United Kingdom. *Sovereign (1952–   : Elizabeth II)*

HEADINGS FOR U.S. PRESIDENTS
ACTING IN AN OFFICIAL CAPACITY

United States. *President (1789–1797 : Washington)*
United States. *President (1797–1801 : Adams)*
United States. *President (1801–1809 : Jefferson)*
United States. *President (1809–1817 : Madison)*
United States. *President (1817–1825 : Monroe)*
United States. *President (1825–1829 : Adams)*
United States. *President (1829–1837 : Jackson)*
United States. *President (1837–1841 : Van Buren)*
United States. *President (1841 : Harrison)*
United States. *President (1841–1845 : Tyler)*
United States. *President (1845–1849 : Polk)*
United States. *President (1849–1850 : Taylor)*
United States. *President (1850–1853 : Fillmore)*
United States. *President (1853–1857 : Pierce)*
United States. *President (1857–1861 : Buchanan)*
United States. *President (1861–1865 : Lincoln)*
United States. *President (1865–1869 : Johnson)*
United States. *President (1869–1877 : Grant)*
United States. *President (1877–1881 : Hayes)*
United States. *President (1881 : Garfield)*
United States. *President (1881–1885 : Arthur)*
United States. *President (1885–1889 : Cleveland)*
United States. *President (1889–1893 : Harrison)*
United States. *President (1893–1897 : Cleveland)*
United States. *President (1897–1901 : McKinley)*
United States. *President (1901–1909 : Roosevelt)*

United States. *President (1909–1913 : Taft)*
United States. *President (1913–1921 : Wilson)*
United States. *President (1921–1923 : Harding)*
United States. *President (1923–1929 : Coolidge)*
United States. *President (1929–1933 : Hoover)*
United States. *President (1933–1945 : Roosevelt)*
United States. *President (1945–1953 : Truman)*
United States. *President (1953–1961 : Eisenhower)*
United States. *President (1961–1963 : Kennedy)*
United States. *President (1963–1969 : Johnson)*
United States. *President (1969–1974 : Nixon)*
United States. *President (1974–1977 : Ford)*
United States. *President (1977–1981 : Carter)*
United States. *President (1981–   : Reagan)*

UNIFORM HEADINGS FOR COMMON ANONYMOUS CLASSICS

AVESTA

The sacred book of the Zoroastrians and Parsees, consisting of writings and oral traditions of Zoroaster before 800 B.C. in five parts: Yasna (Gathas or hymns); Vispered; Vendidad (laws); Yashts (stories of gods); Khordah (private devotions). Sometimes called "Zend-Avesta" (interpretation of the Avesta).

ARABIAN NIGHTS

Collection of ancient Persian-Indian-Arabian tales, originally in Arabic, arranged in present form about 1450 AD. Some of the tales are well known and often are published separately; these are entered under their own names, with general reference as follows:

Arabian nights
For separately published stories from this work see
Aladdin.   Ali Baba.   Sindbad, the sailor.

BEOWULF

Anglo-Saxon epic dating from early eighth century. Concerns a hero-warrior, Beowulf, who rescues Hrothgar, king of the Danes, from Grendel and Grendel's mother, two monsters whom Beowulf wrestles single-handedly and unarmed, in the best heroic tradition.

CHANSON DE ROLAND

French *chanson de geste* (song of deeds) probably written in the middle of the 11th century. Decasyllabic lines (4002 in all), using assonance rather than rhyme, are divided into lays and stanzas of unequal length. Charlemagne's nephew Roland, fighting under Charlemagne in Spain, is betrayed by Ganelon and ambushed by 400,000 Saracens at the pass of Roncesvalles. Roland refuses to

Most of the factual information about the anonymous classics has been taken from William Rose Benét, *Reader's Encyclopedia* (New York: Crowell, 1965). A more extensive list of uniform headings for anonymous classics is contained in International Federation of Library Associations, *Liste internationale de vedettes uniformes pour les classiques anonymes—International List of Uniform Headings for Anonymous Classics*, edited by Roger Pierrot (Paris: IFLA, 1964). The list given here is used by the Library of Congress.

sound his horn and recall the main body of Charlemagne's army; the unequal contest between his small group and the Saracens occupies most of the poem. When he finally does sound his horn, it is too late; Roland and his army are dead when Charlemagne reaches them.

EL CID CAMPEADOR

Epic poem in Spanish, similar in form to *Chanson de Roland*. Concerns the adventures of Rodrigo or Ruy Diaz de Bivar (c.1043–1099), known as *el Cid* (the Lord) and *el Campeador* (the champion), who fought for and against Moorish rulers in control of the Iberian peninsula and was active in the conquest of Valencia (1094). The poem includes much legendary detail. El Cid is presented as the model Castilian warrior.

CUCHULAIN

Legendary Irish warrior and hero, sometimes described as "the Achilles of the Gael." As a child, he was attacked by a ferocious dog and killed it. When he saw the grief of its owner, Culain, he took on the role of watchdog until a replacement could be found; thus his name, which means "the hound of Culain." Stories about his heroic exploits in love and war are favorite subjects for many modern Irish poets, notably William Butler Yeats (see his "On Baile's strand"). The form of the name is also found as Cu Chulainn, Cuculain, Cuchulin, Cu Cullin, Setana.

DOMESDAY BOOK

A Latin record of census and survey of England compliled by order of William the Conqueror in 1086. It served as basis for tax assessments until 1522. Also known as Doomsday Book.

EDDA

The name given to two collections of early Scandinavian mythology. "Edda Saemundar" is the uniform heading used to refer to the Elder (or Poetic) Edda, erroneously attributed to Saemund Sigfusson (1056–1133) and thus called the "Edda of Saemund" (Edda Saemundar), mythological stories of Norse gods and heroes. "Edda Snorra Sturlusonar" is the uniform heading used to refer to the Younger (or Prose) Edda (early 13th century), also called "Snorra Edda." It was written by Snorri Sturluson (1178–1241), an Icelandic historian. The Prose Edda tells of the creation of the world and of pagan poetry; it includes the Skalda (rules of ancient prosody) and Hattatal (technical analysis of meters). Also gives early Scandinavian myths and legends of the gods not included in the Poetic Edda.

GESTA ROMANORUM (Deeds of the Romans)

A Latin collection of tales, many of them of Oriental origin, very popular in the Middle Ages. Printed in England 1473 and frequently thereafter, it included 100–200 tales in different versions. There is little real history, although the episodes are arbitrarily assigned to the reign of a Roman emperor. A "moral" or "application" follows each tale. Chaucer, Shakespeare, and other English writers drew on these tales for plot material, and they were favorite reading for English children until the 18th century.

GRETTIS SAGA

The story of Grettir the Strong, a historical Icelandic hero of the late 10th and early 11th century, set down in the 14th century. Parts bear strong resemblance to *Beowulf*. Translated into English by William Morris.

GUDRUN

A German epic poem written about 1210 by an unknown Austrian, apparently in imitation of the *Nibelungenlied*. There are three sections: Hagen, king of Ireland; Hetel's courtship of Hagen's daughter Hilde and their marriage; the abduction of their daughter Gudrun (also known as Kudrun) by Hartmut of Normandy and her rescue by her betrothed and her brother.

KALEVALA

The Finnish national epic, compiled from popular songs and oral tradition by the Finnish philologist Elias Lonnrott (1802–1884). Written in unrhymed, alliterative, trochaic verse, it includes an account of the origin of the world and of adventures of the three sons of Kaleva. A German translation in the same meter suggested to Longfellow the form and epic style for his Hiawatha (1855).

MABINOGIAN

A collection of Welsh tales, first written down in the 14th century but probably originated much earlier. Concerned with Celtic mythology and folklore, it was first translated into English by Lady Charlotte Guest in 1839; "Mabinogian" is her term for the collection. J. R. R. Tolkien (*Lord of the Rings; The Hobbit*) and Lloyd Alexander (*High King; Black Cauldron*, etc.) draw heavily on these Welsh medieval legends for the spirit and flavor of their works.

MAHABHARATA

One of two great epic poems of ancient India, the other being the *Ramayana*. The story concerns the five Pandavas, or sons of Pandu, and their struggle with the Kauravas (the family of Pandu's brother) who refuse to give up the throne to the Pandavas, the rightful heirs. It also concerns the exploits of two of the brothers, Yudhishthira, the eldest, who finally gains the kingdom, and Arjuna, who wins the hand of the lovely Draupadi in open contest and brings her home as the wife of all five brothers. Evidently they all lived happily ever after; the end of the epic concerns the journey of the five brothers, their wife, and their dog, to seek admission to the heaven of Indra on Mount Meru. The *Mahabharata* has been called "an encyclopaedia of Hindu life, legend, and thought."

MOTHER GOOSE

NIBELUNGENLIED

A medieval German epic poem in four-line stanzas, probably written about 1190 or 1200; author and exact original version are unknown. Based in part on the *Edda Saemundar* (poetic Edda) and the Volsunga saga, it includes much more German legendary material and omits much of the supernatural aspects of the two earlier sources. The story of Siegfried—who killed the Nibelung kings and took their name, their treasure of gold, and their cape of darkness, which makes the wearer invisible—and his exploits in wooing Kriemhild and in duping the fabulously strong Queen Brunhild of Iceland into marrying Kriemhild's brother Gunther make up the first part of the Nibelungenlied. Seigfried—like Achilles, Baldur, and other heroes invulnerable except for one spot on their bodies—is killed by treachery. The story ends in a general blood bath, with none of the main characters left alive. Wagner drew on this material in part for *Der Ring des Nibelungen*.

PANCHATANTRA

A collection of fables in Sanskrit, dating from about the fifth century A.D. Arthur W. Ryder translated them into English (1955).

REYNARD THE FOX

A medieval beast-fable in French, Flemish, and German folklore. Episodes in various versions differ, but all are based on the countless animal fables circulating in Europe in the Middle Ages. Most of the tales concern the cunning fox Reynard and his struggle for power with the physically powerful (but stupid) wolf Isengrim. Other episodes involve Reynard with King Noble the Lion, Sir Bruin the Bear, Tibert the Cat, and Chanticleer the Cock (see Chaucer's "Nun's Priest's Tale").

A number of distinct variants or versions of these tales exist, each with an individuality all its own. The Library of Congress makes a separate uniform title entry for each. An explanatory reference card will be made for "Reynard the Fox":

Reynard the Fox.

The story of Reynard the Fox appears in many versions in varying languages. Versions will be found in this catalog under their own titles. Here are entered critical discussions of the cycle, and miscellaneous editions of which the immediate source or relation to other versions is not known or is uncertain.

For the varying versions see entries under

Ecbasis captivi	(Early Latin version)
Rainaert de Vos	(Flemish version)
Reineke Fuchs	(High German version)
Reinke de Vos	(Low German version)
Renart le contrefait	(French sequel to original French version)
Roman de Renart	(French version)
Reinaerts historie	(Dutch version)

When cataloging any version of *Reynard the Fox*, make an added entry under "Reynard the Fox," with language as subheading. See *AACR2* 25.12.

SECOND SHEPHERD'S PLAY

A medieval English miracle play (also called "Secunda Pagina Pastorum") written about the end of the 14th century, the second in the Towneley cycle of plays (see Towneley Plays below). It deals with the Nativity in terms of Yorkshire life; full of rollicking, farcical fun. The best-known episode deals with Mak the sheep stealer, who pretends that a stolen sheep concealed in a cradle is his wife's new-born baby.

Entry of the *Second Shepherd's Play* (one part of a cycle) is under its own title, (25.6A1). Use the title of the part by itself as the uniform title if it is a unit, with a well-established title of its own, of an anonymous cycle or collection of stories or other works. Make appropriate references from the heading for the larger work to the headings for the parts that have been cataloged as independent works. The complete cycle takes the uniform heading.

TOWNELEY PLAYS

Also known as Towneley Mysteries and Wakefield Mysteries because they were probably acted at the fairs of Widkirk, near Wakefield. All of the plays in this cycle were popular, lively, jocular in tone. Mystery and miracle plays were medieval dramas based on the Old and New Testaments and on the lives of the saints. Other well-known cycles are Chester Plays, Coventry Plays, and York Plays. Form for reference:

Towneley plays

For separately published parts of this cycle *see*

Second Shepherd's play

(etc.—list all parts in your library)

VEDAS

The four sacred books of the Hindus composed about 2500 B.C.: the Rig Veda, the Yajur Veda, the Sama Veda, and the Atharva Veda. Prayers and hymns in verse and prose; formulas for consecration, imprecation, expiation, etc.

VÖLSUNGA SAGA

A Scandinavian prose cycle of legends, the major source of the German epic poem *Der Niebelungenlied* (q.v.) and of Wagner's *Der Ring des Nibelungen*. The saga takes its name from Völsung, grandson of the god Odin and father of Sigmund. The hero Sigurd (Siegfried) is Sigmund's son. William Morris retold the saga in his *Sigurd the Völsung* (1876).

Examples Illustrating AACR2

Bible. *English. American Revised. 1929.* The Holy Bible. Figure 15-25, 407

———. *English. Authorized. 1948.* The Holy Bible. Figure 15-24, 406

———. *English. Revised Standard. Selections. 1964.* A shortened arrangement of the Holy Bible. Figure 15-23, 406

———. *English. Smith. 1970.* Joseph Smith's "New translation" of the Bible. Figure 15-27, 409

———. *N.T. English. Today's English. 1966.* Good news for modern man. Figure 15-26, 408

———. *N.T. Mark. English. New English. 1965.* The Gospel according to Mark. Figure 15-22, 405

———. *O.T. English. Smith. 1927.* Figure 15-21, 404

A biographical directory of librarians in the United States and Canada. Figure 1-91, 83

Birket-Smith, Kaj. The Eyak Indians of the Copper River delta, Alaska. Figure 1-69, 58

Bishop, Dorothy Sword. Leonardo y Ramon (kit), Figure 7-7, 184

Bismarck, Otto. *Fürst von.* Fürst Bismarcks Briefe. Figure 12-42, 323

Bizet, Georges. L'Arlesienne. (sound recording), Figure 5-4, 154

Black box (sound recording), Figure 10-1, 216

Blume, Judy. Tales of a fourth grade nothing. Figure 1-70, 59

Boeing 737 (motion picture), Figure 6-2, 171

Book collecting and scholarship, Figure 1-31, 32

Book of Mormon. Figure 15-19, 402

———. *French.* Le Livre de Mormon. Figure 15-20, 403

Book of the Dead. *English & Egyptian.* The book of the dead. Figure 15-11, 394

Books, libraries, librarians, Figure 11-20, 252

Books of Latin American interest in public libraries of the United States, Figure 11-9, 242

Bridge, Ann. Julia in Ireland. Figure 12-7, 293

Bright, James W. Bright's Anglo-Saxon reader, Figure 1-59, 52; Bright's Anglo-Saxon reader, Figure 15-5, 390

British Columbia, Alberta, and the Yukon Territory, Figure 3-5, 127

Brown, Esther. Parts and wholes (flash card), Figure 7-15, 192

Brueghel, Pieter. Death of the Virgin (art original), Figure 7-3, 181

Cairo, Egypt (slide), Figure 7-19, 196

California. *Governor (1967–1975 : Reagan),* Figure 14-38, 376

———. The penal code of the State of California. Figure 11-49, 279

Canadian School Library Association. Standards of library service, Figure 14-6, 344

Carr, William H. The desert speaks. Figure 14-12, 350

Carroll, John M. American Indian posters (picture), Figure 7-10, 186

Carroll, Lewis. Alice's adventures in Wonderland. (sound recording), Figure 5-2, 152

Casas, Bartolomé de las. Doctrina. Figure 12-31, 313

Cassill, R. V. The Norton anthology of short fiction. Instructor's handbook. Figure 11-44b, 273

Catholic Church. The liber usualis, Figure 2-12, 114

Center for Research Libraries. Newsletter, Figure 10-5, 221

Central United States (map), Figure 3-6c, 130

Chanson de Roland. *English.* The song of Roland. Figure 15-7, 392

Chapin Library. A short-title list. Figure 14-22, 361

Charles I, *King of Great Britain.* Charles I in 1646. Figure 12-49, 331

Child, *Mrs.* The mother's book. Figure 1-38, 36

Children (kit), Figure 7-8, 185

Christmas scene (diorama), Figure 8-6, 203

Moore, Clement C. The night before Christmas, Figure 1-111, 100

Mosley, Shelley. Black cat with yellow flower (art original), Figure 7-1, 180

Mother Goose. A book of nursery songs and rhymes. Figure 15-2, 388; Mother Goose nursery rhymes. Figure 15-3, 388

Mozart, Wolfgang Amadeus. Concerto in C major, K299 (sound recording), Figure 5-8, 159; Concerto in C major (sound recording), Figure 5-12, 163

Myers Demonstration Library Project. The Myers Demonstration Library. Figure 1-28, 29

N.C.R.V. Vocal Ensemble. Renaissance choral music for Christmas (sound recording), Figure 5-6, 156

National Gallery of Art. American paintings and sculpture. Figure 14-30, 370

National Research Council of Canada, Figure 1-88, 343

National Weather Service stations as of March 1975, Figure 3-7a, 130

Navajo (videorecording), Figure 1-66, 56

Nelson, Stan. Typefounding by hand, Figure 2-9, 112

Newman, John Henry. On the scope and nature of university education, Figure 1-42, 38

The Norton anthology of short fiction. Figure 11-44a, 273

Old author. Anecdotes illustrative of the power of the Holy Scriptures, &c., Figure 11-18, 249

Old sleuth. Detective Dale, or, Conflicting testimonies, Figure 1-6, 16

Orczy, Baroness. The Scarlet Pimpernel. Figure 12-35, 317

Orliac, Jehanne d'. Francis I, prince of the Renaissance, Figure 1-48, 42

Osmonds. The Osmonds "live" (sound recording), Figure 1-73, 62

Österreichische Waldszandsaufnahme, 1952/56. Figure 14-35, 374

Outside readings in American government, Figure 11-22, 253

Oxford economic atlas of the world, Figure 3-12, 137

Parish, Peggy. Hermit Dan, Figure 2-7, 110

Patterson, A. J. Flinch (game), Figure 1-13, 20

Perry, James W. Machine literature searching, Figure 1-33, 33

The Perry pictures of our thirty-five Presidents (picture), Figure 7-11, 187

Persius, 34–62. A. Persi Flacci Satvrarvm liber. Figure 15-16, 399

Philip, *Prince, consort of Elizabeth II, Queen of Great Britain.* The evolution of human organisations. Figure 1-35, 34; Seabirds in southern waters. Figure 14-9, 348

Phillips, Stephen. Faust, Figure 11-30, 261

Piano keyboard (model), Figure 8-9, 204

Pictograph-cuneiform unit (model), Figure 8-10, 205

Pictures and stories from forgotten children's books. Figure 1-45, 40

Plantin, Christopher. Calligraphy & printing in the sixteenth century, Figure 11-17, 249

Players (*New York, N.Y.*) Catalogue of the paintings. Figure 14-11, 350

Ploutz, Paul. Evolution (game), Figure 8-3, 200

Poesia = Poetry, Figure 2-8, 111

Policies and procedures, Figure 11-1, 237

Population (game), Figure 1-30, 31

Price, Robert. Johnny Appleseed. Figure 12-3, 289

Pryce-Jones, David. Next generation, Figure 1-82, 72

Quinnam, Barbara. Fables, Figure 1-94, 85

RSR : reference services review. Figure 10-12, 225

Index

Additions to statements of responsibility, Figure 1-45, 40
Addressee of a collection of letters, 276; Figure 11-47, 276
Administrative work (21.1B2a), 236
Alternative titles, 15; Figure 1-6, 16
American Association of Law Libraries, 282
American Library Association. *Cataloging Rules for Author and Title Entries* (1949), *see* ALA 1949
American Library Association. RTSD Catalog Code Revision Committee, 5, 235
American Philosophical Society, Figure 1-77, 343
Ancient and international bodies (24.3C2), 345
Anglo-American cataloging rules (1908), 277
Anonymous classics, 386, 391, 392, 393; Figure 15-7, 392; figure 15-18, 393
Anonymous works (21.5), 248; Figure 11-16, 248; figure 15-11, 394
Aperture card, 208
Arrangements, Figure 4-2, 142
Arrangements, transcriptions, etc. (music) (21.18B), 141
Art original, 180, 188; Figure 7-1, 180; figure 7-3, 181
Art prints, 188; Figure 7-12, 189
Art reproductions, 181, 188, 264; Figure 7-2, 181
Art reproductions with text, Figure 11-34, 264
Artefacts, commercial, Figure 8-2, 200
Artefacts, noncommercial, Figure 8-4, 201
Article in French, 309
Association for Educational Communication and Technology, 123
"At head of title" note, 118; Figure 2-17, 119
Atlases, 136; *see also* Cartographic materials
Atlases, Figure 3-12, 137
Audience of item, notes on (1.7B14), 91; Figure 1-106, 94
"Author of," 321
Author statement, *see* Statement of responsibility

Baronet, 324
Bible, 270, 403, 408
Bible, books of (uniform title), Figure 15-22, 405
Bible, Old Testament, Figure 15-21, 404

Bible, selections (uniform title), Figure 15-23, 406
Bible, versions (uniform title), Figure 15-24, 406; figure 15-25, 407
Biographer as author, Figure 11-32, 262
Biographer as editor, Figure 11-33, 263
Biographical/critical text, 262
Biographical dictionary, Figure 10-2, 217
"Bird's eye view," Figure 3-10, 135
Bishops, etc. (22.17C), 332
Books (definition), 101
Books, pamphlets, and printed sheets (AACR2 chapter 2), 101–20
Brackets, 387
Brief forms of corporate names, Figure 14-4, 342; figure 14-5, 342
British sovereigns, 329
British titles of honour, 315, 316, 324; Figure 1–34, 34; figure 2-8, 111
Broadside, 112; Figure 2-8, 111
Byname, 299, 300, 329

Canadian Library Association, 123
Capitalization, 13, 14
Cardinals, 332
Cartographic materials (AACR2 chapter 3), 121–40
Cartridges, sound, *see* Sound cartridges
Cassettes, sound, *see* Sound cassettes
Catalog Code Revision Committee, *see* American Library Association. RTSD Catalog Code Revision Committee
Change of name, 290, 340
Change of name, personal names, Figure 12-5, 291; figure 12-6, 291
Chapters, branches, etc. (24.9), 358
Characterizing word or phrase, 248
Charters, 280; Figure 11-50, 280
Charts, 189; Figure 7-6, 183
Choice of access points, *see* Access points, choice
Choice of name, *see* Personal names, choice
Churches (24.3G), 347, 358; Figure 14-20, 358; figure 14-21, 359
Collaborators, artists and writers, Figure 11-36, 266
Collation, *see* Physical description area
Collections, 251, 254; Figure 11-20, 252; figure 11-23, 254
Collections of musical settings of songs, Figure 4-6, 145
Collections of official communications, 247; Figure 11-12, 246
Collections of translations, 261; Figure 11-31, 262
Collective titles, 104, 252, 399

Cover and text design of
Anglo-American Cataloging Rules, second edition,
adapted for this work by Vladimir Reichl
Composed in mono/lino Times Roman,
Printed on 50# Glatfelter Antique, a pH neutral stock, and
Bound by the University of Chicago Printing Department